Software Architectures

Manfred Nagl • Bernhard Westfechtel

Software Architectures

Topics Usually Missed in Textbooks

 Springer

Manfred Nagl
Lehrstuhl für Informatik 3 (Software Engineering)
RWTH Aachen
Aachen, Germany

Bernhard Westfechtel
Lehrstuhl für Angewandte Informatik I
Universität Bayreuth
Bayreuth, Germany

ISBN 978-3-031-51334-3   ISBN 978-3-031-51335-0   (eBook)
https://doi.org/10.1007/978-3-031-51335-0

This Springer imprint is published by the registered company Springer Nature Switzerland AG
The registered company address is: Gewerbestrasse 11, 6330 Cham, Switzerland

Paper in this product is recyclable.

Preface

Characterization of the Book

Software Architectures came up in the 80ies to 90ies. The corresponding discipline grew rapidly and is nowadays a standard in software engineering or, more general, in computer science/ informatics study programs.

Architecture modeling is the most influential subprocess of software development or maintenance, and the software architecture is the key to all results of that process. Nevertheless, there are different approaches to software architectures, with respect to how to think, how to denote, and how to interrelate architectures with other results of the development process.

Surprisingly, there are topics, which are important for software architectures or their influence on the development process, which are not or not deeply enough discussed in software architecture textbooks. This statement applies to all software architecture books, irrespective, which approaches they follow. This finding led to this book and, more specifically, also to the title of this book.

Another topic is to relate software architectures to other activities and results in the development or maintenance process. Here we emphasize the central role of architectures and how this role implies strong connections and implications. The book is an architecture-centric book: It concentrates on architectures, but also discusses other activities and results, especially, if they are in a strong relation to the architecture.

The aim of this book is to discuss such topics. As these topics are usually missing in textbooks, the lecturer of a course on software architecture can decide, which chapter of this book he/she will take to the lecture. This can apply to one or more chapters. This applies to any software architecture approach. Especially, this characterizes the value of the book in the context of software architecture literature. The book does not claim to cover all such topics.

The Book Structure and its Medial Form

The chapters are mostly independent, which implies a certain redundancy. The literature is given in each specific chapter, i.e. there is no comprehensive and complete references chapter at the end of the book. The reader should be able to read from one single to all chapters. At the end of the book, we have a summary and its message for any chapter, and also messages across chapters. The same applies to open problems. An index chapter facilitates browsing and searching. The articles are on textbook level, not on the level of technical articles in proceedings or in journals.

Electronic books are dramatically changing the book market. Publishers sell (or will sell in the future) more electronic books than printed ones. One reason for this change are the flat rate agreements between universities and publishers, in Germany or elsewhere. For a flat rate fee, the universities, their students, and also employees can access the publications of a publisher. That implies that a lot of downloads of university members are a consequence of these flat rate agreements. That also implies that less printed and bound books appear.

This is an electronic book, which also exists in printed form. We expect that the majority of readers uses the electronic form. Thus, independence of chapters, combination with lectures (even of a different background), exchange of ideas, and discussions are intended.

Thus, for every chapter, there is a problem it addresses, a question it tries to answer, attention it demands, a message the chapter wants to transport, further questions it raises, thereby showing that still many open questions exist.

History, Focus, and Breadth of the Presented Ideas

First books on Software Architectures, were restricted to the static view of architectures, the abstract view, and to component models. Other aspects were added in the software architecture literature later. Not many of them are included in textbooks, as mentioned. Therefore, the book also gives some *historical sketch* about the development of software architectures.

Not all books on software development approaches see or saw the architectures in the focus of the process. This book does. We concentrate on an architecture-centric approach of software development.

Such ideas are also found in other fields, like mechanical, electrical, and civil engineering. Even outside of engineering disciplines, like architectural design of buildings (even historical ones), or even in book or presentation writing, similar ideas can be used. We follow an approach having the similarities between different disciplines in mind.

We introduce a specific understanding and view of integration: Design or development processes demand for integration, as different artifacts have to be elaborated, have to be in mutually dependent and consistent form. The underlying way of integration is not to put everything into one container database, but to separate artefacts corresponding to their nature, logical, or modeling level on one hand and to integrate them by regarding their mutual relations on the other.

This way of integration is enforced by the architecture-centric view we have in mind. This way of integration – having clear and distinguishable subprocesses with corresponding results on one hand, but also to care about their interaction and also about the integration of their results – is a main topic of the book. In an architecture-centric approach, the design process (modeling architectures) and the architecture results play a significant role.

Every chapter contributes to this integration view. The problem is specified in the abstract, the message in the summary. For example, chapter 2 introduces different aspects of an architecture language, and how they have to be put together. Subprocesses of the architectural design are regarded in chapter 3, and how they interact. To have one language with different and well-defined aspects, striving to demonstrate, how they are integrated, and looking on the interaction of their design subprocesses, are the messages of these chapters.

The book uses specific notations for architectures. These notations, however, do not restrict our way of looking on architectures, see for example the chapter on styles/patterns. Thus, the book can also be taken as supplement for other approaches of software architectures, as the title announces.

Survey of the Book

Part I is the introductory part of this book and deals with 'Relevance of Architectures' and 'The Central Role of the Design Subprocess', in the development or maintenance process, and the importance of the results in the overall result. Another topic is the spectrum of views an architecture language has to offer, or that there are different architectures from abstract and static to detailed, technical, and specific, we have to regard.

Part II is the first main part and discusses 'Important Topics' on architecture level. It deals with adaptability especially for embedded systems, with integrating styles/pattern notations, with different reuse forms and how to find them, with the role of architectures for integrating different existing systems, and with reverse and reengineering of legacy systems. For all these topics architectures are the key.

Part III, the second main part, discusses architecture modeling and its relation to surrounding activities, or architectures to surrounding other results. There are chapters on transformation between requirements and architectures, architectures and programming, architectures and project management and organization, as well as architectures and their relation to quality assurance or documentation.

Part IV, the conclusion part, summarizes, emphasizes the messages, and delivers open problems. We do this chapter for chapter, but also across chapters. There are many activities for the future. To facilitate searching in the book, there is an index.

Thanks

We would like to thank several persons and institutions:
The ideas presented here have some history. There were involved W. Altmann, R. Gall, C. Lewerentz, G. Engels, W, Schäfer, A. Schürr, J. Börstler, and P. Klein. Other members of the group worked on applications, trying to push them forward and, thereby, contributing to the applicability and extension of the concepts, as Th. Janning, M. Lefering, V. Bacvanski, A. Zündorf, Ch. Kohring. C.-A. Krapp, K. Cremer, R. Baumann, A. Behle, A. Winter, A. Radermacher, R. Pritsch, A. Schleicher, D. Jäger, M. Münch, D. Herzberg, A. Marburger, F. Gatzemeier, O. Meyer, M. Kirchhof, O. Meyer, B. Böhlen, B. Kraft, U. Norbisrath, S. Becker, M. Heller, U. Ranger,

Ch. Mosler, Th. Körtgen, I. Armac, D. Retkowitz, R. Wörzberger, E. Weinell, Th. Heer, and C. Mengi.

We also thank colleagues as J. Ebert, G. Engels, J. Börstler, and A. Schürr for viable and deep discussions, which have influenced the presentation given here.

We should also mention the persons involved in supporting the software architecture lecture in the last years, namely Th. Kurpik, M. v. Wenckstern, D. Raco, S. Stüber, and M. Stachon. The support included discussions about topics and also presentation. Thanks go to all of them.

Especially, we would like to thank R. Gerstner from Springer and the Springer - Verlag for the engagement and the good cooperation over a very long time.

Manfred Nagl   Bernhard Westfechtel
RWTH Aachen University   University of Bayreuth

Aachen and Bayreuth, November 2023

Contents

Part 1 Importance of Software Architectures

Part 2 Important Topics on Architecture Level

Part 4 Summaries, Conclusions, Open Problems, Index

1 The Architecture is the Center
of the Software Development Process

Manfred Nagl

Software Engineering, RWTH Aachen University, nagl@cs.rwth-aachen.de

Abstract

The purpose of this chapter is to explain the specific role architecture modeling and the resulting architectures have in software development projects: The processes are only possible by extracting the essentials of the system and denote them separately on architecture level. The architecture is the most important collection of artifacts, as the architecture influences most of the results gained in the process in a more or less substantial way. The architecture not only determines the structure, the quality, and the clearness of the system to be constructed or maintained. It also influences the structure, quality, and clearness of the code, of quality assurance, documentation, and of project organization.

From this central importance of architecture modeling and the resulting architecture, we continue with further aspects as sketches: The architecture determines the adaptability of the system, the architecture is the key for project organization, the architecture determines whether maintenance is possible (also via reverse and reengineering), and it determines the level of reuse. All these further aspects are later explained in more detail and in own chapters.

Keywords: Architecture as essential structure for the realization of a software system and its long term properties, all development artifacts are determined/ influenced, the role in the process/ product w.r.t structure, coding, quality or documentation, changes and adaptability, maintenance, reuse

1.1 Introduction

The *architecture* of a software system /BC 03, BM 96, BR 05, GS 94, Sc 13, SEI 10, SG 96, SS 00/, *unites* different and important *aspects*, as explained in some textbooks on architectures. We just enumerate them and omit explanations, as they are obvious and commonly available /TP 16/.

The *aspects are* the *following*: The architecture exposes the essential structure and hides details. It realizes all use cases and scenarios, and it addresses the requirements of different stakeholders. Together, it both handles functional as well as non-functional requirements (restrictions and demanded quality attributes). It reduces the problems of system ownership and strengthens the organization's market position. It helps to improve the quality and functionality of a system. It improves external confidence in either the organization or the system. Altogether, it reduces the business risks associated with building a technical solution and builds a bridge between business and a technical solution.

Another argument for the importance of architectures is that the *architecture* of a software system must be *known by different members* of the development team -

M. Nagl, B. Westfechtel, *Software Architectures*, https://doi.org/10.1007/978-3-031-51335-0_1

not only by the architect(s) - at least to some extent. It is important for designers of subsystems, for programmers of components, for quality engineers to check whether the requirements are met, or to handle integration tests, for project managers to organize the group work, etc. The architecture also is the basis for discussions between different *stakeholders* of the system: developer, business manager, project manager, owner, end user, etc.

Another introductory remark corresponds to the *role of abstraction*, which is the main reason for the importance of software architectures. Nobody is able to grasp many details. Abstraction eliminates the details and extracts the essentials of a system. There is no chance to design a system and to organize its development process without this step of abstraction. The missing details are delivered afterwards in the development process and at the right time.

A fourth remark corresponds to the *variety* of *concepts* of software architecture modeling: We find a rather *different understanding* of *architectures* /SEI 10/: (a) There is literature, influenced by *practice* and industry /BC 03, BR 05, HK 07, Ru 12/, or (b) by *theory* as /GG 07, Gu 76, LZ 74, PH 12/, or (c) by programming languages having a built-in *module interconnection* language as Ada /Bu 84, Na 03/, Eiffel /Me 91, Me 97/, or (d) by patterns/ styles /BM 96, GH 95, GS 94, SG 96/, (e) *object orientation* /JC 92/, or (f) *model-based* development /BF 10/, (g) domain-driven /Ev 04/ or (h) service-oriented /KM 04/, etc. Introductory and historical papers of the field are /DK 76, HP 80, Pa 72/. Here, we rely on a classical component/ relation approach /Na 90-20, PW 92/. This, however, is not important for the message of this chapter.

The term architecture comes from *house building*. There, the essentials are determined and planned before the physical construction starts. A similar role has the architecture of a software system. Today architects – of whatever domain they belong to – are supported by systems for document writing / retrieval and by tools helping to build up the design or construction. Architectures and their way of thinking have *long tradition*, shown for the design of gothic cathedrals and comparing it to software engineering in /Na 19/.

The *architecture* of a software system *should not be* just nice conceptual pictures, as often found (e.g. in /So 18/), nor a sheer collection of vague building blocks belonging to the environment for software in a car /EN 93/, nor different levels of a DB schema, without its operating application or data concepts /Wi DA/, nor an accumulation of different artifacts with more or less loose connection /BR 05/. On the contrary, it is a *precise build plan* containing all essential design decisions and a structure, by which we can study most of the problems occurring in the later realization, evaluate the main quality characteristics, and estimate the effort of the realization or of changes.

This chapter is mostly on *motivation* or *explanation* level. The reader should be convinced that the architecture is the key point of software development. Technical details, as how to achieve this development, how to support it by a suitable notation or corresponding helpful tools, are not the focus.

The *contents* of this chapter are as *follows*: In sect. 1.2, we introduce a model – different from usual lifecycle models – by which we explain the different tasks and resulting product parts occurring in software engineering, as well as the relations between these different tasks and results. The next two sections explain by qualitative and quantitative arguments that architecture modeling is the most important and the most influential part of the software development or maintenance process. Sect. 1.5 shows the dual result that the architecture is the center of all products. This central role implies the importance of architectures for adaptability (sect. 1.6), for project organization, for maintenance, and for reuse (sect. 1.7). Sects. 1.6 and 1.7 are only sketches, as the arguments are refined in following chapters. We conclude with a summary and with open questions in sect. 1.8.

1.2 The Working Area Model and its Dependencies

The *waterfall model* is well known and often criticized /Wi WM/. It orders activities according to their chronological occurrence from analysis to maintenance. It is an idealization, as no development follows a linear order in time. In practice, we have forward steps (thinking about future realization), backward steps (backtracking, if there was a mistake), and also iterations. The same is true for the *V-model* /Wi VM/, which goes down (detailing) from analysis to implementation and then up (integrating) to the whole system and its operation and maintenance. Despite of their problems, these models are widely used, not as a true mapping of reality but as simplification and idealization.

These models have the disadvantage that modeling on a certain level is done at *different places* of the *time order*. Architecture activities are done in analysis, thinking about the future realization, in design when building up the architecture incrementally, but also in integration, installation and especially in maintenance.

Therefore, we introduce here a different model, which we call *working area model* /Na 90-20/. Its essence is to look on the *logical level* of models, and to give up the *distinction* between development, change, and maintenance, as development is more often to change or iterate than to go straightforward. We clearly distinguish what and where we model, and also what the relations between these levels are, see fig. 1.1.

We distinguish between three technical *working areas*, namely (a) *Requirements Engineering* (RE), where we model the outside requirements and behavior, (b) *Architectural Design* (AR), where we make decisions for the realization on abstract levels, corresponding to structure and also other aspects, and (c) *Programming* in the Small or Implementation (PS), where the program code of components is developed. Furthermore, there are areas as (d) *Quality Assurance* (QA), (e) *Documentation* (DOC) (see /CB 03/ for the various aspects of documentation), and (f) *Project Organization* and Management (PO), which accompany the technical areas.

All edges between working areas of fig. 1.1 define a *dependency relation* in the sense that the second working area has to follow some result of the first, or in other words, its result in some way has to be consistent with the result of the first. Any of these dependency relations means something different as we can see from tab. 1.2 and the following discussion.

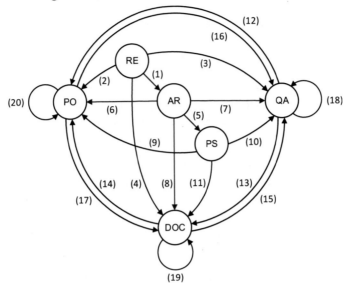

Fig. 1.1: Working area model and relations between working areas, in red relations corresponding to architecture modeling /Na 90-20/

(1) RE - AR: AR results in a *possible structure* to *fulfil* the requirements, AR is not determined by the requirements.

(2) RE - PO: The work packages of RE are fixed and determined, who is working for them, how the group of requirements engineers is built up, the total effort is determined.

(3) RE - QA: The requirements are *checked* for *completeness*, internal *consistency*, for the possibility to approve, whether a *system* can be *built along* these requirements. The corresponding risks are determined. This is done by human inspections.

(4) RE - DOC: The essential functional and nonfunctional requirements are described and explained in the documentation. Specific internal relations within and between these parts are explained. Documentation corresponds to "why" and "why not".

(5) AR - PS: The architecture *determines* the structure of the final program system, *programming* adds the *details* for the bodies of identified components.

(6) AR - PO: During and after AR the organization is built up, the tasks for realizing the system can be planned more precisely: Who is doing what and in which order. The total effort is estimated, as well as the price, to find out later, whether the contract will end with a positive financial result.

(7) AR - QA: The architecture is checked for *completeness*, *validity*, and as a suitable realization structure for the requirements, or able to be *programmed.*

(8) AR - DOC: The design decisions for components and relations between components, for the big parts of the architecture and their internal structure, are given in the documentation. Technical details are given within the architecture.

(9) PS - PO: The programming activities have to be planned, can be estimated w.r.t. their effort, and can be checked for risks, etc.

(10) PS - QA: test by black or white box test for components, integration test in addition using the architecture, formal verification or whatever QA approach is used.

(11) PS - DOC: The realization ideas of the internals of components are sketched as well

as the purpose of a component in the system. Again, only "why".

(12) QA - PO: All QA activities are organized (planned, estimated, checked for risks).

(13) QA - DOC: The QA methods taken have to be explained and documented.

(14) DOC - PO: The documentation activities have to be organized.

(15) DOC - QA: The documentation has to be checked for completeness, expressiveness, and consistency.

(16) PO - QA: The PO activities have to be quality checked.

(17) PO - DOC: The PO activities have to be explained and documented.

(18) QA - QA: The quality assurance activities themselves have to be approved (completeness, coverage, and a suitable relation of effect and price).

(19) DOC - DOC: The specific forms chosen for documentation are documented.

(20) PO - PO: The work in PO has to be organized as well.

Table 1.2: Different consistency relations between working areas

All the above *relations are different* in their *nature,* what we now explain: From RE to AR: Construct something new consistent with the RE result, which usually is not similar. From AR to PS: Construct the bodies to the components of AR and therefore extend them. From RE, AR, and PS to QA: Check corresponding artifacts by using appropriate QA methods. From RE, AR, and PS to DOC: Describe the essential ideas and why they have been taken. From RE, AR, and PS to PO: Estimate, plan, organize, and monitor the corresponding technical work. From QA to PO and DOC: Organize and document the QA activities. From DOC to QA and PO: Assure the quality and organization of documentation. From PO to QA and DOC: Assure the quality of PO and document the PO activities. Finally, the loops at QA, DOC, and PO mean that QA itself has to be quality assured, the different forms of documentation have to be documented, and PO has to be organized as well. We see: Any of the dependency relations means something different w.r.t. consistency.

All the above working areas and relations are important for a software project. Especially *important* in order *to avoid* a complete *breakdown* of the project are: RE in the sense of to build the "right" system, AR to build a system "right" (namely with long-term properties like adaptability, portability and reuse), and PO for determining the costs, avoiding chaos, and evaluating risks. Many of the project failures explained in lectures correspond to the last item.

The graph of fig. 1.1 is completely *symmetric.* It allows to describe and explain *backtracking* steps in a development process. For example to go back to RE, if an error has been detected in PS which forces to correct the requirements, then going forward to architecture modeling, to change according to the changed requirements. After that, we go to PS, to program/ change the corresponding bodies and relations between components. More explanation is given in ch. 10. All steps are accompanied by corresponding QA, DOC, and PO steps.

The working area model can also be used for any *classical lifecycle model.* Even more, it facilitates *modern* life cycle *models,* as for example agile, interactive, incremental, or spiral lifecycle models, as it is clear where and what to do in a working area and what the dependency relations between different working areas mean.

It helps to better understand what to do on which level and what to regard, as it makes activities and dependencies clearer. It also helps, if an activity is taken up again, and where to change and extend.

The working area model is applicable not only to software engineering, but also to *any engineering discipline*. These disciplines usually distinguish between conceptual design (comparable to architecture modeling) and detail design (in software engineering corresponding to implementation, here called PS). However, as these disciplines usually create material products (which by the way contain more and more software), their life cycle in addition regards production preparation, production, and later on hardware maintenance.

Software is *immaterial* and, therefore, easy to *morph*. It can be used for any application, and is often misused to correct mistakes of hardware construction. Software developers are like general engineers, as they may change the application area and often have less knowledge or experience in and of a domain. This also applies to the working area AR 'architectural design', which is the center of this chapter.

1.3 Architecture Modeling is the Most Important Part

We start with a quantitative investigation and later go to the qualitative side.

A Big Part of the Development Depends Directly on the Architecture

We go back to fig. 1.1, there to the technical activities and their relation to the accompanying activities, and consider the *workload* of different *working areas*, see fig. 1.3.a. The thickness of a working area's bubble regards, which amount of work is spent for the corresponding working area in a software development process. Without going into details, we assume that PS and QA take about 25% of the overall amount of work. As QA is split into QA of a developer made by him/ herself and QA made externally by a member of the QA team, we get the rough figure of fig. 1.3.a. The same is done for documentation, which also is a common activity of the technical developers and a documentation group. For simplicity, we assume that all the other remaining working areas need a minor effort.

Furthermore, we look at the dependency *relations* and regard their *degree of determination* for the target working area. Initially, the relation RE - AR is drawn by a thin arrow, as there can be different architectures for a system fulfilling the requirements. Therefore, there is little determination. On the other hand, the relation is intensively looked at in the backward direction, as the architect after essential steps looks, whether the architecture is consistent with the requirements. Putting both arguments together, the arc from RE - AR is made a bit thicker. The relation of AR - PS is very thick, as the coarse structure of the system's code is completely determined by the architecture. PS delivers the bodies of the components defined in AR. The relation AR - QA is thick, as the architecture plays a big role for QA (human inspection whether the system is consistent to RE, fulfills long-term properties as adaptability/ portability, the architecture determines the order of components for an integration test, etc.). This is true for the work done by the architect (internal

QA) as well as that of the external QA engineer. The relation AR - PO is thick, as after a preliminary architecture the PO activities become clear, and after the architecture has been designed, the PO activities (estimating effort and price, workload assignment, risks) have a solid ground. The relation AR - DOC is important, too.

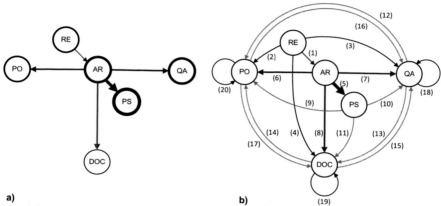

Fig. 1.3: (a) Workload of working areas/ determination of the influence of architectures, (b) indirect influence

If we now put both arguments together, the amount of work in working areas and the degree of determinations of relations, we conclude: *AR* does not represent the biggest workload but it *determines* by its design decisions a *big part of the overall workload*. This was the first part of the quantitative discussion. The second statement, we can derive from fig. 1.3.a, is that architecture modeling is the *central part* of the whole development/ maintenance process.

Also Indirect Dependence of the Architecture

We have learned from the arguments of above that the architecture has a strong and direct influence on PS, and also a direct influence on QA, DOC, and PO. As PS, QA, and DOC also influence PO, we can conclude, that the *indirect influence of AR* on PO even emphasizes and strengthens the importance of PO, see yellow-brown relations in fig. 1.3.b. It even strengthens the dependency of PO on itself (PO has to be organized, which gets more complicated by these indirect dependences). The same arguments can also be applied to get an *indirect dependency of AR on QA,* and in the same way *on DOC*.

In a smaller amount this even applies to RE, as the first step of AR is to sharply look at RE to learn the requirements. Later on, the architect permanently looks on RE in order to find out, whether the requirements are met, when building up the architecture. So, also here, we have some *indirect dependence of RE* via AR.

Summing up we can argue: The architecture has to map the requirements, but there are different ways to find the right architecture. The architecture determines the long-term properties of the program system. A good architecture also makes QA,

DOC, and PO easier. A big part of the development work is more or less determined by the architecture, directly or indirectly. This is true for the technical activities, but also for the activities in QA, DOC, and PO, via transitive relations.

1.4 And also the Most Influential Part

Above we have argued from the viewpoint of quantity. Now, we switch to a *qualitative perspective*. Let us go back to the graph model of fig. 1.1 and come to the question what parts are *determined* by architecture modeling, see tab. 1.4. Thereby, we recognize that the architecture parts are very influential.

(a) Internal Influence on design level

The architecture defines the *essential* structure (a clear abstraction from the code) of the system to be developed or maintained. It reflects all the essential *decisions* made on design level. The structure is complete (all components, relations, and layers).

The architecture *explains* the structure and makes it *understandable*: This part is functional, that part object-oriented, that part reflects layers of data/ detail abstractions. We can see, which parts of the system have been taken from *outside,* e.g. from a library, and which parts are developed in the running project. We also find the architecture of an underlying *old system* (in most cases not well designed), which gets new interfaces to be able to add *new parts* with a clear interface structure to the system.

We immediately detect *micro patterns* (as three components forming a model-view-controller MVC pattern), patterns for data abstraction *layers* (often at the bottom), patterns for *input* or *output* structures, for *coupling* systems, or even *global* patterns for the whole system corresponding to a structure class (as batch systems, interactive systems, or embedded systems) or an application domain (as business administration, automotive).

The architecture can be *evaluated*, e.g. for long-term internal properties, as *adaptability* (by looking on all the places where data/ detail abstraction should have been used), *portability* (looking on all the realization changes which might hinder), reuse (checking whether all potentials have been seen).

Even more, the architecture can be evaluated, whether we have found a good *example for explanation* and *teaching*. We need good examples in a company to get some conformity for the solutions of that company, and we also need it in a lecture. Software architecture modeling does not exhaust the possibilities and potentials of good examples. Architects of houses learn from good examples. Even in software engineering or architecture books you can find examples, from which you cannot learn very much.

(b) Influence on other working areas

The architecture is the build plan for the code of the system. All the above qualitative arguments of (a) therefore also hold for the code, which is programmed according to the architecture. In the working area *programming* and coding (PS) no architecture decisions in the sense of this chapter are made. The decisions made are only on the level how to structure the internals of components. The essential code quality is to a certain extent already determined on architecture level. AR modeling is restricted: If in architecture modeling we use concepts, which are not available in the programming language (e.g. OO: programming by extension, variant programming, and dispatching for an old Fortran version), we would have to extend the programming system, which is not reasonable.

The architecture determines most of the form and quality of *quality assurance*: module tests according to the white or black box approach, covering of test cases, integration tests, order of these tests, evaluating runtime traces or formal verification. The architecture also determines the organization of quality assurance, either of the work done by developers themselves, or quality assurance done by the external quality assurance group.

The *documentation* should contain the explanations, what has been decided, but also where and why these decisions have been made. Therefore, the quality of documentation is already mostly determined on architecture level, as there the main and essential decisions are taken. The design rationale, often commonly written by the designer and a person of the documentation group, often gets its structure 1:1 from the architecture.

Architectures and *project organization* are closely connected. This has the implication that the role of the architect is often not clearly distinguished from the role of the project organizer / manager. A clear architecture facilitates PO, an unclear architecture hinders PO. The reason is that in a good architecture work packages are clearly defined, and the relations between work packages are simple to handle, if the components' relations are loose.

The architecture has to follow the decisions made in *requirements engineering*. This is checked during and after architecture modeling. Thereby, we detect over-specification (unnecessary determination) as well as under-specification (items, which should have been specified). Especially, in the nonfunctional requirements specification we assure aspects of the process (a certain methodology to follow) as well as for the product (a certain software component to be used, the system has to run on certain hardware, etc.). To a big part, this can be verified or falsified on architecture level.

Finally, we have *indirect influences* according to indirect relationships and even loops (both shown in yellow brown in fig. 1.2.b). Thus, we also have corresponding indirect and significant influences from the architecture side to all the target working areas of yellow-brown relationships.

Table 1.4: Influence of the architecture: (a) internal, (b) on other working areas

The arguments of the second part of sect. 1.3 and those of sect. 1.4 *strengthen* the statement of above that architecture modeling is the *center* of the development and maintenance process. However, we also have further conclusions.

A good architecture is the *result* of an *intellectual challenge*, it never comes for free. In rare areas, where everything is clear and where we have advanced reuse mechanisms (extreme case generating the system or parts of it from a specification), the challenge has been solved by several past projects, with many good designs, by corresponding reusable structures, by tools like generators, see ch.7.

We need corresponding *concepts* for the notation of *architectures*, either graphical (for overviews) or textual (module interconnection language for details), which have to offer an *integrated whole* and not a variety of different and unrelated languages. We only touch this briefly here, for more details see next chapter. The variety is spanned by: components for functional and data abstraction, components on object or on type level, components of different granularity (modules and subsystems), relations for different purposes as local, general and object-oriented use, generic (parametrized) components, altogether in a combined language, where relations between artifacts are clear and not only imagination of developers.

Architectures should be able to deal with the problems of *practice*, like maintenance, reverse or reengineering, and extension. Architectures should be independent of the programming language, but we cannot map all architectural concepts to all old programming languages. The notations should be able to cover architectures for different *domains* (BA, automotive systems, etc.), and also different *structure classes* (batch, interactive, and concurrent systems). Furthermore, the architecture goes through different stages, from rather abstract to very concrete and technical. It is the *integrated view* on architectures, which makes the difference.

Software *architectures* had a great importance in our *group*, in *software engineering* and its subdisciplines as architecture modeling /Bö 94, Kl 00, Le 88, Na 90-20/, but also variant/ version control /We 91/, nonstandard data base systems /KS 95/, authoring support, and tool construction /Ga 05, Me 06/. We also made research in different *engineering domains*, as mechanical engineering /NW 03/, process engineering /NM 08/, but also automation, embedded systems, eHome, house construction /KN 07/, telecom systems /Ma 05/.

Patterns play an important *role* in *architecture* modeling. They *range* from micro patterns between few components (the usual meaning of patterns /GH 95/), over basic layers, input/ output parts, integration mechanisms for connecting different systems, to global patterns how to structure a system (multiphase compiler) out of a structure class (batch systems, interactive systems etc.) or a domain (as BA).

1.5 The Architecture and Configurations

Above, we have discussed the central role of architecture modeling in the overall development or maintenance process by arguing with the *working area model* (WAM). This model is on process level. But it does *not determine* and *restrict* the *processes* in a project, as explained in sect. 2. Its purpose is to distinguish different logical levels and to make the relations between these levels clear, see tab. 1.2.

We can show that *different kinds of processes* – coarse and detailed, classical or modern – can be used above of the WAM. This is discussed in ch. 10. We can also show that the level of the architecture evidently corresponds to the level of project organization, as it defines the work to be organized, see ch. 13.

Development Results as the Overall Configuration

In this section, we continue by looking on the *results* of the development or maintenance process. The results consist of different parts with a detailed inner structure and relations between these parts and within these parts. We call the complex result the *overall configuration*.

We go into details of this structure, see fig. 1.5. We see that for any working area there is a complex result, which is again a *configuration* with structures and relations inside the parts and between the parts. There are the *RE* configuration, the *AR* configuration, the *PS* configuration, the *PO* configuration, the *QA*, and the *DOC* configuration. These configurations depend on the languages and methods used in the working areas. Whatever we use, the configurations look differently. However, the following *characterization* remains valid and *stable*.

The RE *configuration* e.g. has documents for four *views*, namely processes (SA model), data (EER model), control of processes (control model), and details (RE dictionary). Any of them can be structured internally in different *documents*. Fig. 1.5 simplifies in giving only one document for each aspect. There are *relations inside* a view, e.g. between a process and an internal part of it (here not shown, see ch. 11). There are relations *between views*, as a data store contains data of a certain entity type. Specifically, there are relations between *parts of RE view documents* and components of the *architecture*, introduced for realizing these parts.

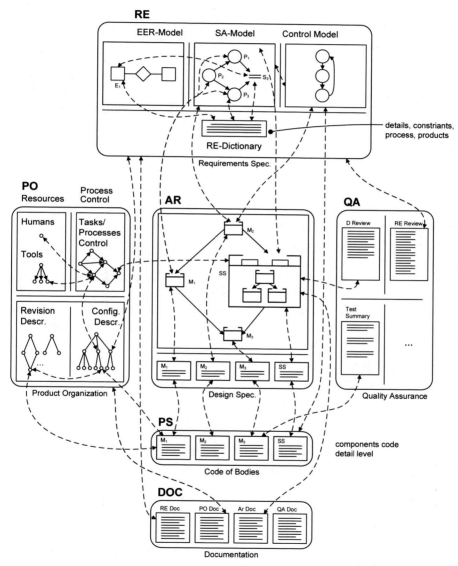

Fig. 1.5: The Architecture as center within the overall configuration

The explanation is continued. We see the *architecture configuration*, having an overview architecture, with parts named modules (not further decomposed) or bigger subsystems (being composed) in a separate document. They form the diagram part. Details are given in the textual parts below, specifying the export interfaces and the detailed relations between components. Again, we have relations between the AR parts, e.g. the relations of diagram parts are detailed in the textual parts.

Also, there are relations between the textual parts of AR and the corresponding components of *Programming* in the Small (PS). The textual parts are "identical", but may be specifically denoted in the corresponding programming language. The bodies of components are developed here.

We continue to explain the configuration for project *organization*, for *quality assurance*, and for *documentation*. We abbreviate this discussion here and postpone the details to later chapters. For any of the above configurations, being a part of the overall configuration, we have the characteristics already explained: They are structured internally, the internal structures have relations inside and between parts. Specifically, there are also relations between the internal parts to internal parts of other configurations. This is true, whatever methods and languages we use for denoting the results.

We end this section with the statement that the *architecture is the center of the overall configuration*. This is the dual statement to the characterization of above that architecture modeling is the center of the process.

The architectural configuration gives the key ideas for mastering all the technical results (*detailed* structures necessary for the code), but also for *integrating* the different parts (system integration). Furthermore, the project *organization* needs the essential decisions of the architecture, the *quality assurance* is mainly driven by the architecture, and also the documentation to *understand* what has happened. Besides of further remarks within this chapter, the more detailed discussion is taken up in chs. 10 to 14.

Different Forms of Processes and Results

The WAM is for processes, the overall configuration and its parts stand for results. *Processes, results and relations are on three levels*. The WAM is on coarsest grained (*lifecycle*) level, even a working area is only a node. The same is true for the overall configuration, if we forget about the inner structure of subconfigurations. The management configuration is on *administration* level (middle-grained), it contains processes and results, but does not show, how individual processes are built up or documents are structured internally, see ch. 13. The documents internals are on fine-grained level, which have no equivalent here on the process side (see /MJ 08/ for an approach regarding processes on a *fine-grained* level, describing how individuals proceed). What we have argued for three-level products also holds for processes and also for relations. We take up this discussion again in ch. 10.

The discussion above and specifically fig. 1.5 with the overall configuration indicate our *understanding of integration*. This understanding is not to put everything of whatever level into one and the same basket. Instead, we distinguish according to the logical level and the semantics first (*separation*). Then, we work out the mutual connections (relations), again on different levels (*integration*). This gives clearness and a more specific support by tools.

The overall *configuration* interpreted as *graph-like structure* is a graph with sub-configurations as graphs (and coarse-grained relations). These subconfigurations have an internal structure consisting of documents: A document is again a graph with internal structure by nodes (increments) and arcs. Arcs also exist between different documents (middle-grained) and, especially, between increments of different documents, of the same subconfiguration or between different subconfigurations. Thus, we have the overall configuration being a graph of subconfigurations, every subconfiguration being again a graph of documents, which again have an internal structure. We have relations over three levels. In the center of this complex structure is the architecture, if we interpret the graph semantically.

1.6 Architectures and Mastering Changes

The term *architecture paradigm* describes an *idealized* situation, which never appears in practice: We build up an architecture, which contains all layers, all components of whatever granularity, all relations between components, and this all before implementation. Then, we program the components.

Mostly there are *changes* of the architecture on the *way* from architectures *to implementation* of components in detail, and also afterwards. However, the *idealization* is *unavoidable*, if we want to be able to divide labor, to check quality in advance (e.g. by human inspections), or to think in reuse before we go to realization. Thus, changes will always come up. Thereby, the architecture is changed as well.

Abstraction

No complex technical system is *correct*. This is not only true for software but for any complex technical system. Incorrectness means that there are errors, but we do not know, where and when they become evident. Traceability to estimate the effort of changes, and also to carry out the changes, are important. So, again, *changes* are unavoidable and necessary. This also applies to assure quality and to keep the architecture in a state that future changes are possible again.

The key to handle changes is abstraction. That means that we define interfaces, above which we forget about changes of *data* representation (data abstraction, e.g. how a complex record is built up, which files are used, which layout, style, or UI system is used, etc.) and also of a different physical, chemical, electrical, or protocol realization of an abstract *functionality* (functional abstraction), mostly in embedded systems. In both cases, we forget about details. So, *detail abstraction* is the key to get clear and flexible architectures.

Abstraction always belongs to *layers*. The underlying form of hierarchy is specific. It might be locality, general usability, or object-orientation. It might belong to a *flat* architecture or to enclosing something by a wall, as the body of a component or a subsystem (*component granularity*).

The *discussion* of *"What can change?"* is very important for making architectures stable w.r.t. changes. There are two discussions: (a) *Changes* of the *requirements*, after having determined these requirements. This opens our mind for more general solutions on architecture level. We do not only design an architecture for the given requirements. We also try to think about slight changes and build the architecture to cover these changes as well. A good architecture never relates 1:1 to the requirements, but it already takes care for some possible and future changes.

The second discussion is about (b) *changes* of the *realization* after having worked out the architecture. That leads to all parts of the architecture, where we should have used detail (data or functional) abstraction. Such abstractions make the architecture stable: Changes are within the body of a component or below of an aggregated interface, and they do not go up in the architecture to client components. Thus, changes stay within a *certain range*.

A Simple Example

We discuss a simple example to clarify both changes (a) and (b) and the importance of an architecture making use of abstractions, see fig. 1.6. We introduce a very *simple batch system* Telegram Counting System. The component Telegram_Input provides the data of different telegrams. Each telegram has a telegram identification (TID) and following words. We count the number of postal *words* (of a certain maximum length, otherwise we split; a punctuation word STOP is not counted). The *price* is determined depending on the number of postal words. Both is done by Comp_Telegram. The computed data of the telegrams are stored in Telegram_Data. The component Prepare_Print produces a paper list of the telegram data ordered by their TID. The component TD_Computation controls the program.

Fig. 1.6 shows the *resulting architecture*. We see functional layers on top and data abstraction layers at the bottom. Although we have data abstraction components and even abstract data types, object-orientation in the strict sense (classes and modeling commonalities and differences of these classes) plays no role here.

We first discuss *changes of the realization*, part (b) of above, to demonstrate the stability against realization changes. The Telegram_Input has two data abstraction interfaces, one for getting the data of a single telegram (get_TID, get_NextWord, was_Last_Word, etc.), and one for the collection of telegrams (get_Next_Telegram, Was_Last Telegram, etc.). Both interfaces prevent that details of how to store a telegram or the collection of telegrams are used by the clients. The same is true for the interface of Telegram_Data. The component Prepare_Print uses the interface of Layout_Indep_Output, which hides all the layout and style details of the print list. All the bottom components make use of devices or files, which is only shown here at the right side of fig. 1.6. We conclude: Any realization change has no effect up of the interface, only below of it.

Let us now discuss *changes of the requirements*, so (a) of above. We assume an extension of the telegram system, such that the input also contains the data of the sender and the receiver of the telegram, a change of the *functionality*. Thus, the interface for single telegrams is extended. We see by the import relation that Comp_Telegram can take these data. If this component does not make use of these new data, nothing further is changed. If it makes use, then the computed data are changed. These data are usually stored in Telegram_Data, which means that the interface has to be changed. If this extended interface is not used in Prepare_Print, we are done. If they are used, the interface of Layout_Indep_Output has to be changed. We see that we can *trace within the architecture* to *discuss* and *control* the *extensions* according to changed requirements. The discussions of above also lead us to *estimate* the changes w.r.t. time, costs, and planning of personnel.

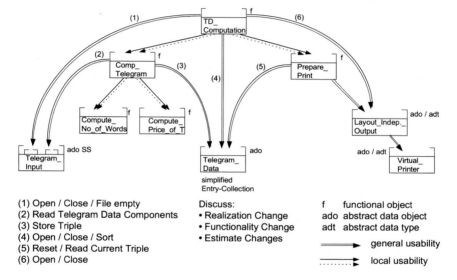

Fig. 1.6: a) data abstraction and stable architectures, b) trace of interface changes

Summing up: The *organization* of the development process and, especially, of *changes* in that process is *facilitated* by a good *architecture* making use of detail abstractions. In other words, a good design has / or errors in the design have a tremendous influence not only in architecture modeling, but also on the whole development process, as already argued above.

The biggest *mistakes* are (i) to construct an architecture, which is a *1:1 mapping* of the requirements. Any change of requirements then induces a change of the architecture. The other big mistake is (ii) to ignore abstractions and *use* many *details* in the architecture. Again, in this case, any change of details implies a nontrivial and often far-reaching change within the architecture.

1.7 The Architecture and Further Aspects

The Architecture and its Role for Project Organization and Dynamic Changes

Building up the architecture of a software system and realizing the corresponding software system is not a linear and steady activity. We see steps, which say how to go further and we face mistakes, which have to be corrected. Altogether, we cannot plan the activities in PO beforehand by a static description. We call this the *dynamics of the development process*, as the corresponding information is only available in the running development process /HH 10, HJ 08/.

The evolving plan depends primarily on the architecture. After we have designed a part of the architecture, we see how many and which components are introduced and how they are connected to each other. We see what has to be implemented, tested, integrated, documented, etc. We call this *evolution dynamics* /HJ 96/. This part of the architecture allows to define a development subprocess, which now can be planned corresponding to time, money, division of labor, etc. This planning should not be done on fine-grained code level. This would be too detailed. We need the essential structure, namely the architecture.

Another situation is that when building up the architecture or realizing the corresponding part of the software system, we detect, that there was a serious error/ mistake done before. Thus, we have to go back in the development history to find the place, where we have to correct. Then, there are different possibilities how to proceed forward, after having corrected: (1) the correction takes place within one component and the rest is untouched. That is the best case. (2) A part of the development process results after the mistake remains valid, other parts have to be changed. (3) The correction was so fundamental that all the results after the change have to be given up (worst case). We call such situations *backtracking dynamics*. We need the architecture level for such cases.

A further case is that in the running development process a decision comes up to use a certain component from outside. This has some implications around this new component (other imports, other form of usage of this component). Let us call this case *replacement dynamics*. The situation is first covered on architecture level.

So, the architecture is the right level to study these different forms of dynamics. We need a description of the tasks, which *corresponds to the management level*: What to do, who is doing it, connection to other tasks, collecting activities for a group of developers. The architecture has the necessary degree of granularity. On requirements (RE) level, we do not know enough for the organization of the realization; on the PS level we have too many details. The *relation* of the architecture to project organization is *deepened* in ch. 13.

Maintenance, Reverse and Reengineering

Maintenance means modifications. Modifications of the system have to be planned, estimated by costs, and checked for risks. This is *not possible without an architecture* for the system to be maintained. In the very good case, the underlying architecture has been carefully developed and is adaptable. In this case, at least some of the changes can easily be performed.

The usual case is that we have an architecture, but this architecture is neither of a suitable structure and, consequently, not adaptable. Thus, we have to modify it before making modifications. We call this modification *reengineering*. In many cases we have to compromise: The way to get a suitable architecture is complicated, the following reimplementation is too costly.

Quite often, the situation is even worse. There is only an old program, but no architecture. So, we start by detecting the "architecture" of this old program. This step is called *reverse engineering*. Then, we proceed by reengineering.

In all cases of above, the *architecture* is again the *center,* for reengineering, or it has to be created by reverse engineering and is the center afterwards, see ch. 9.

Reuse Ideas in Different Projects and Families of Systems

Reuse /Co 98, ICSR, LS 09/ is usually a *bottom-up endeavor* across different projects. Reuse knowledge grows from project to project. The first projects profit from doing a similar task more than once, the experience and the competence is growing. We do it similarly but better /W 95/ and more productive /SZ 19/ (*shallow reuse*). The architecture runs through incremental improvement steps.

Then, we start to think about the process for a solution using our experience, what we have learned, what we can do better, how we can *reorganize the process* or even, where there is room for steps of automation. This is usually done in different projects. Again, experience and competence is growing, but now in major steps. We call this *deep reuse*, see ch. 7. Deep reuse changes the architecture such that after a series of changes the architecture looks completely different and the steps to be "manually" done shrink dramatically.

Another and even more complicated situation is, if we design, plan, and realize *families* of systems or *product lines* /CN 07, Ja 00, PB 05, PK 09/. Here, we do not think about one system, but about a set of systems, where the members share some similarity relation. We try to make *use of this similarity* in the development process. This is another form of deep reuse.

These forms of deep reuse are *rare in industry*. Deep reuse demands for time, intelligent people, money, and the clear insight and commitment of the management that the advantage in the longer run is worth the spent money. The effect can be dramatic, but also the costs.

Again, we only give a sketch for an example here, see ch. 7 for more details. There, the *construction* of a *multi-phase compiler* /AS 06, WG 84/ is studied as running example. It started with shallow reuse, learning and doing better. Then the deep reuse steps followed: The basic layers, the global architecture of the compiler, the framework for the compiler as reusable product, such that only the specific phase components have to be developed. Learning about formalization and automation of these phases followed, and finally ended producing generators, which do the phase's translation automatically (compiler-compiler approach). The different steps and their transition can be described by process interaction diagrams (ch. 6).

As argued above, reuse is improved from project to project. In rare cases, we also have dramatic changes within one project. An example is that we have a core component, planned to be developed internally. As this failed, something from outside had to be used, which demanded a different program structure. This subsequently induced a *dynamic change* of the process *due to reuse* within the development. Another possibility is that this component is delivered by a subcontractor project, which is decided in the development process. This implies a *different form of organization* /Jä 03, He 08, He 11/.

Knowledge about the development method and process usually grows from project to project. The same applies in in the case of *deep reuse*. In both cases, dynamic changes are mid and not short term. In some rare cases it can happen in the running development process (a new and important component or tool is introduced, from an old system we derive a framework for the new). Even the process knowledge may grow. In these cases, we have *dynamic changes* within development /Sc 04/.

1.8 Summary, Importance, and Open Problems

Summary and Lessons Learned

The essential *ideas* and *statements* of this chapter are the following:

- The architecture of a software system unites different *aspects* and it has to be *known* by different members of a development team (not necessarily by the same level of deepness). It is based on the concept of *abstraction* (architecture paradigm). It has to have a clear syntax and semantics (not often formally defined). Thus, it is not a vague "conceptual picture". Its role should be commonly accepted, as it is the case for house building.
- We introduced the WAM, an activity *model*, which is organized along *levels of modeling*, not regarding the time order or a difference of construction and change, and also not the different process steps within a project, see fig. 1.1. This yields clear working areas, and also clear relations between them, see tab. 1.2. The model is symmetric and it can also be used for engineering projects.
- By looking where the main structural decisions are made, regarding the part of work being determined by these decisions, and estimating the amount of work for these parts, we concluded that *architecture modeling* is in the *center* of the development process with respect to *quantity* and also *quality*.
- The dual statement: The architecture is the *center* of all *project results*, the overall configuration, containing processes, data, and relations on three levels.
- Development means permanent *changes* of results. The architecture is the artifact to master the changes. The changes can be determined by brainstorming discussions on two levels, *requirements* and *realization*. A good architecture handles realization changes by having used detail abstraction for corresponding situations. Requirements changes are facilitated on architecture level by looking on changed interfaces and on traceability of use edges.
- A good architecture is never a 1:1 extension of the requirements specification, has hidden all details which can evidently be changed, and is also stable if minor requirements change.
- There are *dynamic changes* within a development process and also from project to project, i.e. in successive processes. The architecture is the key level to study these dynamic changes, as e.g. evolution dynamics or backtracking dynamics.

- In the ideal case, maintenance can use an adaptable architecture. In the usual case, we have to reengineer the architecture. In the bad case, there is no architecture, but only an old program. This has to be reverse engineered to get something like an "architecture", which then has to be reengineered.
- *Reuse* can happen in a *shallow* and in a *deep* form. The base for the latter are transformations of the architecture. Any transformation increases the value of reuse. In the case of the architectures with reuse, we regard variations according to requirements, which sustain the similarity between the systems. We speak of families of systems or product lines if we regard solutions for a set of systems. This makes architecture modeling even harder. For reuse as well as for families/ lines, the architecture is the right level for discussions.

In this chapter, we did *not study* the *transformations* between working areas, not even those, where the *architecture* is directly *involved* as, e.g. the transformation from the RE to AR. These transformations are studied in chs. 10-14.

Open Problems

There is no *standard model for software architectures*. Object-oriented architectures in BA applications and data flow architectures in embedded systems seem to have not very much in common. There are ideas of unifying these different architectural notations/ styles by a component- and relation-oriented approach /PB 16/, or a classical module/ subsystems and use relations approach (ch. 2), which both are not broadly used in industry. We have no standardizations as it is for the architecture of houses, where we find ground plan, floor plans, views and perspectives from different directions, and refinements for installation, plumbing, etc. An initiative for a standard in house building - more than plans - has got attention /ET 08/.

Architectures also have a central role in *all engineering disciplines*. Again, the commonalities of architectures in electrical engineering and subdisciplines as layout plans, in mechanical engineering for machines and also factories, in process engineering for plants together with their automation and control are not worked out. We find some ideas in this direction /NM 08, NW 99, NW 03/. There is much room for initiatives *bridging* the different *disciplines*.

In all the above domains, the architecture has a central role for the development process and even further, as pointed out for software systems in this chapter. There are different opinions about architectures in various domains. A less ambitious question could be: Is there at least some agreement which *questions the architecture* of different engineering domains *should answer* or which problems should be *solved* by using the architecture?

There is a strong link with an even growing importance for all engineering domains, namely the *software* part of *engineered systems*. Could that part be the starting point of thinking in commonalities in a deeper way? A trend of this kind has started in architecture of houses and civil engineering /KN 07, Rü 07/.

In any of the above disciplines, there is furthermore room for *intelligent tools* /Na 96, NM 08/, more than painting or writing tools. We need intelligent tools, which support the work in depth by syntactical and semantical support for specific working areas. Especially we need tools for integrating the different aspect- and domain-specific artifacts. Here again, we have a huge field for future activities.

1.9 References

/AS 06/ Aho, A,V,/ Lam, M.S./ Sethi, R./ Ullman, J.D.: Compilers: Principles, Techniques, and Tools, Addison-Wesley, 2nd ed. (2006)

/BF 10/ Broy, M./ Feilkas, M. et. al.: Seamless Model-based Development: From Isolated Tools to Integrated Model Engineering Environments, Proc. IEEE, 98, 4, 526-545 (2010)

/BC 03/ Bass, L./ Clements, P. et al.: Software Architecture in Practice,, 3rd ed. Pearson (2013)

/BM 96/ Buschmann, F./ Meunier, R. et al.: Pattern-oriented Software Architecture- A System of Patterns, Wiley (1996):

/Bö 94/ Börstler, J.: Programming in the large: Languages, Tools, Reuse (in German), Doct. Diss. RWTH Aachen University, 205 pp. (1994)

/BR 05/ Booch, G./ Rumbaugh, J. et al.: The Unified Modeling Language User Guide, Addison Wesley (2005)

/Bu 84/ Buhr, R.: System Design with Ada, Prentice Hall (1984)

/CB 03/ Clements, P./ Bachmann, F. et al.: Documenting Software Architectures, Views and Beyond, Addison Wesley/ Pearson Education , 485 pp. (2003)

/CN 07/ Clements, P./ Northrop, L.M.: Software Product Lines: Practices and Patterns, 563 pp., 6th ed., Addison Wesley (2007)

/Co 98/ Coulange, B.: Software Reuse, 293 pp., Springer (1998)

/DK 76/ DeRemer, F./ Kron, H.H.: Programming in the Large versus Programming in the Small, IEEE Transactions on Software Engineering, SE-2, 2, 80-86 (1976)

/EN 93/ ECMA/NIST: Reference model for frameworks of softw. engg. environments, http://www.ecma-international.org/publications/files/ECMA-TR/TR-055.pdf

/ET 08/ Eastman, C./ Teicholz, P. et al.: BIM Handbook. Wiley, 2008

/Ev 04/ Evans, E.: Domain-driven Design, Addison Wesley, 529 pp. (2004)

/Ga 05/ Gatzemeier, F.: CHASID: A Semantics-oriented Authoring Environment, Doct. Diss. RWTH Aachen University, 284 pp. Shaker-Verlag (2005)

/GG 07/ Grammes, R./ Gotzhein, R.: Fundamental Approaches to Software Engineering. LNCS 4422, 200–214, Springer. (2007)

/GH 95/ Gamma, E./ Helm, R. et al.: Design Patterns: Elements of Reusable Object-Oriented Software, 395 pp. Addison Wesley (1995)

/GS 94/ Garlan, D./ Shaw, M.: Introduction to Software Architectures, TR CMU-CS-94-166

/Gu 76/ Guttag, J.: Abstract Data Types and th e Development of Data Structures, Comm. ACM 20, 6, 396-404 (1977)

/He 08/ Heller, M.: Decentralized and View-based Management of Development Processes across Companies (German), Doct. Diss. RWTH Aachen University, 501 pp. (2008)

/He 11/ Heer, Th.: Controlling Development Processes, Doct. Diss. RWTH Aachen University, 430 pp., AIB SE 10 (2011)

/HH 10/ Heer, Th./ Heller, M./ Westfechtel, B./ Wörzberger, R.: Tool Support for Dynamic Development Processes, LNCS 5765, 621-654 (2010)

/HJ 96/ Heimann, P./ Joeris, G. et al.: Dynamite: Dynamic Task Nets for Software Process Management, Proc. ICSE 96, IEEE Computer Society Press, 331-341 (1996)

/HJ 08/ Heller, M./ Jäger, D. et al.: An Adaptive and Reactive Management System for Project Coordination, LNCS 4970, 300-366 (2008)

/HK 07/ Hofmeister, C./ Kruchten, Ph. et al.: A general model of software architectural design derived from five industrial approaches, Journal of Systems and Software 80, 106-126 (2007)

/HP 80/ Habermann, H.N./ Perry, D.: Well-formed System Compositions,TR CMU-CS-80-117

/ICSR/ International Conference on Software Reuse, Proc. 1990 to 2017, also Wikipedia ICSR

/Ja 00/ Jazayeri, M. et al. (eds.): Software Architecture for Product Families, Addison Wesley (2000)

/JC 92/ Jacobsen, I./ Magnus, C. et al.: Object Oriented Software Engineering. 77-79, Addison-Wesley ACM (1992)

/Jä 03/ Jäger, D.: Unterstützung übergreifender Kooperation in komplexen Entwicklungsprozessen, Doct. Diss. RWTH Aachen University, 260 pp., ABI 34 (2003)

/Kl 00/ Klein, P.: Architecture Modeling of Distributed and Concurrent Software Systems, Doct. Diss. RWTH Aachen University, 237pp. (2000)

/KM 04/ Kruger, I./ Mathew, R.: Systematic development and exploration of service-oriented software architectures, 4th Working IEEE/IFIP Conf. on Software Architecture (WICSA), 177-187 (2004)

/KN 07/ Kraft, B./ Nagl, M.: Visual Knowledge Specification for Conceptual Design: Definition and Tool Support, Journ. Advanced Engineering Informatics 21, 1, 67-83 (2007)

/KS 95/ Kiesel, N., Schürr, A., Westfechtel, B.: GRAS, a Graph-Oriented (Software) Engineering Database System, Inf. Syst. 20(1), 21-51 (1995)

/Le 88/ Lewerentz, C.: Concepts and tools for the interactive design of large software systems (in German), Doct. Diss., 179 pp. RWTH Aachen University, Informatik-Fachberichte 194, Springer (1988)

/LS 09/ Land, R./ Sundmark, D. et al.: Reuse with Software Components – A Survey of Industrial State of Practice, in Edwards/ Kulczycke (eds.): ICSR 2009, LNCS 5791, 150-159 (2009)

/LZ 74/ Liskow, B./ Zilles, S.: Specification Techniques for Data Abstractions, Int. Conf. on Reliable Software, 72-87, IEEE (1974)

/Ma 05/ Marburger, A.: Reverse Engineering of Complex Legacy Telecommunication Systems, Doct. Diss. RWTH Aachen University, 418 pp., 2004, Shaker (2005)

/Me 91/ Meyer, B.: Eiffel: The Language, 300 pp., Prentice Hall (1991), 3rd ed. 2005

/Me 97/ Meyer, B.: Object-oriented Software Construction, 2nd ed., Prentice Hall (1997)

/Me 06/ Meyer, O.: aTool: Typography as Source for Structuring Texts (in German), Doct. Diss. RWTH Aachen University, 308 pp., Shaker-Verlag (2006)

/MJ 08/ Miatidis, M./ Jarke, M./ Weidenhaupt, K.: Using Developers' Experience in Cooperative Design Processes, in /NM 08/ 185-223 (2008)

/Na 90-20/ Nagl, M.: Software Engineering- Methodological Programming in the Large (in German), 387 pp., Springer (1990), plus further extensions for lecture Software Architectures 1990 to 2020

/Na 96/ Nagl, M. (ed.): Building Tightly Integrated Software Development Environments - The IPSEN Approach, LNCS 1170, 709 pp., Springer (1996)

/Na 03/ Nagl, M.: Introduction to Ada (in German), 348 pp., Vieweg (1982), /Na 03/ 6th ed. Software Engineering and Ada (in German), 504 pp., Vieweg (2003)

/Na 19/ Nagl, M.: Gothic Churches and Informatics (in German), 304 pp, Springer Vieweg (2019), see pp. 179-187

/NM 08/ Nagl, M./ Marquardt, W. (eds.): Collaborative and Distributed Chemical Engineering – From Understanding to Substantial Design Process Support, IMPROVE, LNCS 4970, 851 pp., Springer (2008)

/NW 99/ Nagl, M./ Westfechtel, B. (eds.): Integration of Development Systems in Engineering Applications – Substantial Improvement of Development Processes (in German), 440 pp., Springer (1999)

/NW 03/ M. Nagl/ B. Westfechtel (eds.): Models, Tools, and Infrastructures for the Support of Development Processes (in German), 392 pp., Wiley VCH (2003)

/Pa 72/ Parnas, D.: On the Criteria to be Used in Decomposing Systems into Modules, Comm. ACM 15, 12, 1053-1058 (1972)

/PB 05/ Pohl, K./ Böckle, G. et al.: Software Product Line Engineering, 467 pp., Springer (2005)

/PB 16/ Pohl, K./ Broy, M./ Daemkes, M./ Hönninger, H. (eds.): Adavanced Model-based Engineering of Embedded Systems – Extensions to the SPES 2020 Methodology, 303 pp. Springer (2016)

/PW 92/ Perry, D.E. / Wolf, A.L.. Foundations for the Study of Software Architecture. ACM SIGSOFT Software Engineering Notes, 17:4 (1992).

/PW 95/ Paulk, M.C./ Weber , V.V. et al.: The Capability Maturity Model: Guidelines for Improving the Software Process. SEI series in software engineering. Addison-Wesley (1995)

/PH 12/ Pohl, K./ Hönninger, K./ Achatz, H./ Broy, M. (eds.): Model-based Engineering of Embedded Systems – The SPES 2020 Methodology, Springer, 304 pp. (2012)

/PK 09/ Polzer, A./ Kowalewski, S./ Botterweck, G.: Applying Software Product Line Techniques in Model-based Embedded Software Engineering, Proc. MOMPES'09, 2-10 (2009)

/Ru 12/ Rumpe, B.: Agile Modeling with UML (in German), 372 pp. Springer (2012)

/Rü 07/ Rüppel, U.: Vernetzt-kooperative Planungsprozesse im konstruktiven Ingenieurbau, Springer (2007)

/Sc 04/ Schleicher, A.: Roundtrip Process Evolution Support in a Wide Spectrum Process Management System, Doct. Diss. RWTH Aachen University, 330 pp. (2004)

/Sc 13/ Schmidt, R.F.: Software Engineering – Architecture-driven Software Development, 376 pp. Elsevier (2013)

/SEI 10/ Software Engineering Institute of CMU: What Is Your Definition of Software Architecture, https://resources.sei.cmu.edu/library/asset-view.cfm?assetID=513807

/SG 96/ Shaw, M./ Garlan, D.: Software architecture: perspectives on an emerging discipline. Prentice Hall (1996)

/So 18/ Sommerville, I.: Software Engineering, 10th edition, Pearson (2018)

/SS 00/ Schmidt, D./ Stal, M. et al.: Pattern-oriented Software Architectures, vol. 2 Patterns for Concurrent and Networked Objects, Wiley (2000)

/SZ 19/ Sadowski, C./ Zimmermann, T. (eds.): Rethinking Productivity in Software Engineering, Springer Science+Business Media (2019)

/TP 16/ Tutorials Point: Software Architecture & Design Tutorial, 74 pp, (2016)

/We 91/ Westfechtel, B.: Revision and Configuration Control in an Integrated Software Development Environment (in German), Doct. Diss. RWTH Aachen University, 321 pp. Informatik-Fachberichte 280, Springer (1991)

/WG 84/ Waite, W.M./ Goos, G.: Compiler Construction, Springer (1984)

/Wi DA/ Wikipedia: Data Architecture, https://en.wikipedia.org/wiki/Data_architecture, 5/23

/Wi WM/ Wikipedia: Waterfall Model, https://en.wikipedia.org/wiki/Waterfall_model, 4/23

/Wi VM/ Wikipedia: V-Model, https://en.wikipedia.org/wiki/V-model, 423

2 An Integrative Architecture Language Approach

Manfred Nagl
Software Engineering, RWTH Aachen University, nagl@cs.rwth-aachen.de

Abstract

This chapter is on one hand a *survey* on /Na 90/ and newer results. On the other, it summarizes the *integrative nature* of the approach to architecture modeling presented there. Different views and aspects are brought together, which all are important, when building up or changing an architecture: the static part (how to compose components with connectors), the different paradigms and abstractions, which are used (locality, layers, object-orientation), bigger parts as subarchitectures and subsystems, and various patterns to be followed. Further and important aspects like semantics, concurrency, abstract connectors and their different realization mechanisms, distribution, and different styles are also regarded.

We follow the guideline, that if different artifacts are used, the relations between them must be clear and obvious. Furthermore, all fragments, artifacts, and documents - for architecture modeling as well as for other working areas of software development - must build up an easy to understand product model for the system to be constructed or maintained. Both ideas come from the *architecture for buildings* (standard views and building information model).

Keywords software architecture modeling, multiparadigmatic and integrative approach, clear relations between different artifacts, different views or aspects, overall and architectural configuration, analogy to the architecture for buildings

2.1 Introduction

The *term architecture* was first used for buildings. There, it denotes the overall result of the design process, which consists of surveys, floor plans, details to these plans, additions, and annotations, see sect. 2. The underlying views and notations are accepted worldwide. The architecture consists of many artifacts, aggregating different views, aspects, details, and corresponding data. However, it is always clear, how these aggregated items are related to each other, and how or why they form a description and plan for the whole building.

The *term software architecture* tries to introduce a similar understanding in the field of software system construction. We see that by looking at the covers of many books on software architectures, which mostly contain a building or a fragment thereof on the cover page (a bridge, a cathedral, a part of the outer shell). The software architecture is the essential description in the whole development process for software, it fixes the most important decisions, it determines the long-term properties of the software, and it predetermines management, quality, and documentation of the process and the final product.

Nevertheless, there are quite *different* understandings of and *approaches for software architectures* in different domains /SEI 10/ or industrial sites /HK 07/. For example, there are (a) *functional* or procedural approaches /Sc 13/, (b) *process-oriented* approaches (either (i) using processes as fundamental units, e.g. in telecom or automation software, or (ii) deriving the architecture from business processes /KM 04/, or (iii) detecting the architecture from the processes of a given program /PD 07/, or (iv) regarding the form of the design process), (c) *object-oriented* approaches /JC 92, Me 97/, or (d) *data flow* approaches, to name some of them. UML /BR 05/ (e) collects different approaches with low effort to integrate them. This is better for specific and subset situations /Ru 11, Ru 12/.

The concepts used for software architecture notations stem mostly from underlying *programming* paradigms and *languages*. In the 80ies, there were (f) books on "structured *analysis and design*" which are no longer in the focus of software architectures. A variety of books concentrate on the problem field of software architectures, (g) looking at it from different *views and perspectives*. In this chapter, we concentrate on notations for architectures and methods to use these notations.

There were a lot of *papers paving the way* to a comprehensive understanding of software architectures as /DK 76, HP 80, Pa 72/. In the history of software architecture *books* we can find /Na 90/, with predecessors /Al 78, Le 88/. Furthermore, we also see some books on programming languages, where the programming language has an architectural part, which can be regarded as a module interconnection language, as Eiffel /Me 91/ or Ada /Bu 84, Na 03/. Software architecture is still a current topic, which we see from the vast amount of available books in the field, e.g. /BK 03, Ja 00, SG 96/. The report /GS 94/ even claims that we live in the golden age of software architectures.

This chapter is a *survey* of /Na 90/ with new parts. The approach presented follows the ideas of architectures for buildings. Especially, it aims at building up artifacts where the mutual relations, inside and between artifacts, are evident. Furthermore, it should be clear what belongs to the architecture and how the parts of the architecture are built up and put together. We call the *approach integrative*. The message of this chapter is that concepts, methods, and notations integrate along different dimensions, as they combine different paradigms, different views, and different hierarchies.

There is *neither a discussion* on architectural *tools* in this chapter, nor on development tools in general, not for software construction, and not for application development, e.g. in the engineering domains. For all of that, the reader can find comprehensive collections of references in /Na 96, NM 08/.

The *contents of this chapter* are as follows: In sect. 2.2, we discuss the situation of architectures for buildings. Sect. 2.3 introduces the different static parts of software architectures, namely components, connectors, syntax rules, and subsystems. Sect. 2.4 discusses different forms of patterns, from local to global. Sect. 2.5 regards further extensions, namely for semantics, concurrency, concrete forms of connectors, and for distribution. Sect. 2.6 transforms a different notation of an architectural style (pipelining) back to the standard notation. Sect. 2.7 puts views, artifacts, relations, etc. together, which build up the architecture configuration. A summary and an outlook in sect. 8 close the chapter.

2.2 *What we can Learn from Architectures for Buildings*

Let us first have a look on the *architecture* of a building, see fig. 2.1. The architecture describes the *essential structure* and, thereby, suppresses many details, like how to build a wall, a window, or the interiors. Also, important but more technical parts are left open in the first steps, e.g. how the foundation of the house or the roof are constructed. Specialists are doing this later. Analogously, the sanitary or the electrical installation are planned and constructed later, or, in larger buildings, the engineering design for air conditioning or any kind of automation. Thus, the architecture of a building starts with a sketch and ends with a series of determinations and details. However, they all are closely and also clearly related to each other.

The architect works with a computer-aided architectural design (CAAD) system, 3- or 2-dimensional. The result of this work bridges different levels. Let us have a look on the architecture of a one family house, see again fig. 2.1. On the top level, we see 3- or 2D drawings of the *whole house* from *different perspectives*. The result of this overview might also be an animated walk through the house or an augmented flight over the house. One level down, we find the floor plans with more or fewer details, as dimensioning and possibly interior details. Further activities deliver additions, like technical details of the foundation or the roof, and installation plans for sanitary, or electricity. The architect also thinks about the use of the house, where to do what, or how to enter or leave the house, even in emergency.

There are *further artifacts* belonging to a building, which are not shown in fig. 2.1. The statics of the building has to be calculated and approved, the construction has to be planned beforehand, and the building has to be physically built. Later on, the building is changed and maintained. There are also economical aspects, which have to be noticed. The design, planning, and construction of the building have to follow legal restrictions, etc. (see /Kr 07/ for the various relations to bordering fields). The artifacts, their structure, and their mutual dependencies are put together in a database system, forming a complex overall configuration. This configuration is called the *Building Information Model* (in short BIM).

There is another topic, which we can learn. Architects in their *education* are trained by *learning from good examples*. Such an architecture example must be big enough. It can be smaller than a real-world example, as that worked out by an architectural bureau. However, it has to scale, i.e. all aspects of practice can be studied by looking on the simple example. This is often not the case for examples in the field of software architectures. They quite often are toy examples, which do not reflect the problems of practice. Whenever you see an example containing parts named like "foo", it is an example of this category.

Another aspect is that these *examples* must *reflect good practice*. The examples are carefully selected, as they should reflect a quality from which the student can learn. The examples follow a methodology, which he/ she should use, or they contain a clarity and simplicity from which the student can learn to argue. Corresponding to these goals, there is often a lack in the field of software architectures. There is a wish for this kind of examples. If you look at the cover of software architecture books, you find quite often pictures of buildings, the architecture of which is regarded to be a shining example. In some cases, you find bridges, in some other cases gothic cathedrals. The underlying relations between these buildings and software architectures are not studied. In /Na 19/ the relations between software engineering, architecture of buildings, and gothic cathedrals have been worked out.

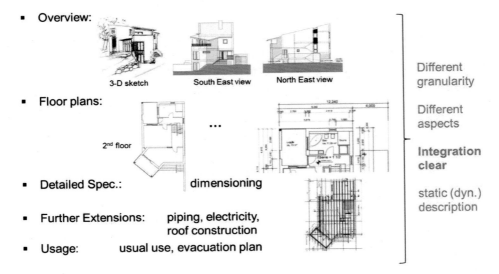

Fig. 2.1: The central role of the architecture for a family house: Overview, refinements, additions, different aspects, and their relations

What is the state in software engineering/ software architectures, and how can this situation be compared to that of design and construction of buildings? Modeling the architecture of a software system is the center of the whole design, implementation, and maintenance process, see ch. 1. The outcome of this process is a complex organization of artifacts with internal structures, built up by using different hierarchies and many mutual relationships within and between artifacts. But in software engineering, we do not have the standardization of views and aspects, the worldwide standard of notations, and the vision to put everything together to form a building model of some standardized and predefined form as BIM /ET 08/. By the way, a somewhat similar standardization approach for all facets of a product named STEP took place some time ago in mechanical engineering, see /AT 00/.

2.3 Concepts for Modeling Static Structures

In this section, we give a brief *overview* of components, connections, consistency relations, patterns, and subsystems, each within a subsection. These are the items occurring in the structural part of an architectural description.

Components

Components as modules are smaller parts of architectures, having the character of independence. We do not only introduce just units as components. Instead, we distinguish different *purposes* (cf. fig. 2.2.a): for functional or for data abstraction, for single examples or for characterizing types. So, we find function objects (abbr. fo, e.g. for a computation or coordination task), abstract data objects (ado, for complex data to forget about their internal details), and abstract data types (adt, for complex data types abstracting from details, the objects are created at runtime). Strict data abstraction means that data are always encapsulated within components. In the case of concurrent systems with processes, we also use ft (function types), see below. Modules are *atomic* design components, which are not further decomposed on design level. For subsystems as bigger components see below.

Relations between Components: Connectors

Analogously, we do not only have one *relation* between components (fig. 2.2.b). We distinguish for different *purposes*: (i) locality (thinking in decomposed specific tasks), (ii) layers of a system and placing general components on different layers, (iii) object-orientation (thinking in commonalities and differences of types).

Underlying, we find different *structure relations*: (i) a component serves as a local resource of another component (which in Pascal-like textual languages is expressed by nesting), (ii) a component is put on a layer to make use of components of deeper levels, (iii) a type, adt or ft, is the specialization of another type. Therefore, we have three *different hierarchy relations*, where all of them come from programming language concepts.

In the same way, *different and corresponding usability* relations are introduced (i.e. a component is allowed to statically make use of another): Local usability in locality structures, general usability of another component of a deeper level in layers, and usability within inheritance structures. Thus, we find different *import relations* depending on the situation (for locality, layers, and inheritance). Fig. 2.2.b gives some examples. In an architecture, we can find locality structures (specific part, only for that system), layers of general components, and also inheritance structures. All three have corresponding internal usabilities between corresponding components, and they can be connected to other structures by further usability relations.

Consistency Conditions

Consistency conditions forbid certain structures, which contain the above-mentioned components and relations. For example, it is not allowed that a component is made usable for other components both, by a local usability and at the same time by a general usability relation, see fig. 2.2.c. Thus, these two relations cannot end at the same component. Another example is that a component cannot import something from a component, which is not provided by this component. There are 28 consistency conditions of that kind. We do not discuss them here. They are the *context-sensitive syntax rules* of the graphical and textual architecture languages.

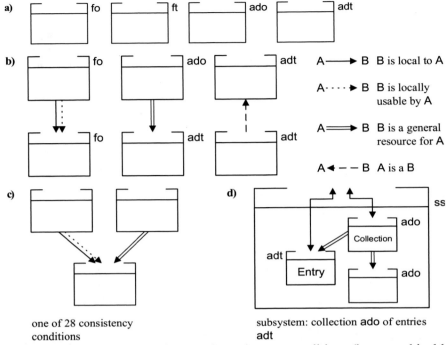

one of 28 consistency   subsystem: collection ado of entries
conditions   adt

Fig. 2.2: Components, relations, and consistency conditions (here graphical level)

Subarchitectures and Subsystems

We find *subarchitectures* within architectures. consisting of components and their connecting relations, and holding consistency conditions. A subarchitecture is a meaningful part, which is not closed and separated from the rest.

Subsystems are *bigger components*. Usually, they have an aggregated interface /HP 80/ of some of its components. In the body of the subsystem, we find a subarchitecture of inner components. This subarchitecture is separated, as it occurs within the body. In fig. 2.2.d we see a subsystem aggregating two interfaces. The corresponding components must occur in the body. The body may contain further components. The example is a collection ado of entries, of a certain abstract type adt.

There are different *granularities* in architectural artifacts in growing *complexity*: from interface parts of single modules, to their interface, to modules (interface and body, the latter not further decomposed on design level), to two modules with relations in between, to subarchitectures, to subsystems (bigger components aggregating interfaces and hiding subarchitectures), and to complete architectures. So, we also find different components w.r.t. *size*, namely modules and subsystems.

Summing up: Modules are either single *objects* or *types,* they belong to different *abstractions* (functional or data abstraction). Relations also belong to different situations, local for specific components, layers of general components, inheritance for type components. Thus, the approach for architecture modeling is *multi-para-*

digmatic. By the way, the origin of all these ideas we find in programming language concepts (nesting of components, import relations of reusable components and separate compilation, modeling similarities and differences in OO languages). They have been changed and adapted for the use in architectures.

Consistency conditions belong to the *syntax* of architectural languages. Another topic is the recommendations for how to use the language. These are *method rules*, often named patterns, which we explain next.

2.4 Different Forms of Patterns

Variety of Patterns

Rules of sect. 2.3 say what is allowed or forbidden. Patterns correspond to good/ bad usage, i.e. to methodology. *Different sorts of patterns exist*:

(a) A situation *as it should be*. That is the *usual meaning* of patterns, as coined by books like /BM 96, GH 95, SS 00/. In fig. 2.3.a, we see two fo modules A, B coupled via an ado module C, which prevents that data details of C are known in A, B.

(b) But also a bad situation (negative pattern or *antipattern*) is useful to show a situation, which should be avoided. In fig. 2.3.b two components are coupled via an open data structure, such that A and B know details of C, they should not know.

(c) There are also patterns, how to correct a bad to a good situation (*correction pattern*), as a rule with fig. 2.3.b on the left and fig. 2.3.a on the right side.

(d) There are patterns transforming an object situation to a more general type situation (*generalizing pattern*). Fig. 2.3.c gives an example of two function modules coupled by an ado module. If we need more than one coupling, we switch to an adt at the bottom. This enforces a new usability from T to C, as now in the body of T objects are created, which are passed as parameters to A, B for writing and reading.

(e) Furthermore, there are patterns transforming a fuzzy situation (e.g. many different components from different logical layers use another component of a deeper level) to a clear situation (changed by introducing intermediate abstractions to avoid the many and different uses, see fig. 2.3.d). We call them *clarifying patterns*.

(f) Furthermore, there are *experience patterns*, e.g. showing in which situations data abstraction should be used (from hiding data details, to different user interface details, or schema details in database systems, etc., thereby listing all applications of data abstraction). Another example is showing that data abstraction comes in multiple layers, e.g. the ISO/ OSI layers /Ta 12/.

All above-mentioned descriptions are *subarchitecture patterns*, how it should be, not be, should be corrected, or transformed for different goals (generalization, clarification, showing experience, or where to use data abstraction and layers).

(g) *Global patterns* in the sense of complete and recommended build plans for the whole system are even much more important. They are patterns you can trust and follow for the design and development of a whole system.

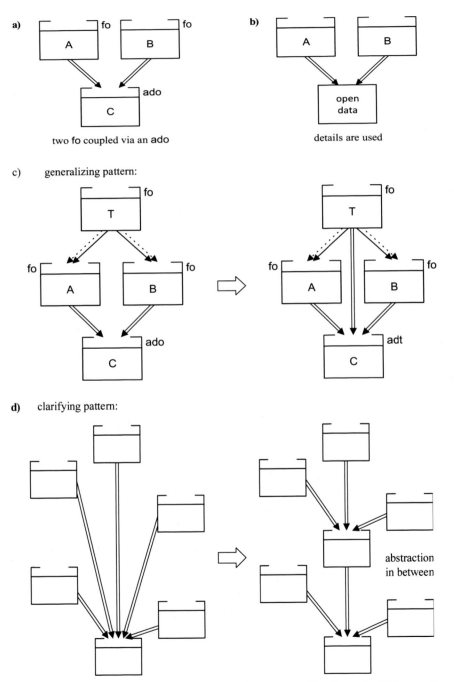

Fig. 2.3: Patterns: usual, antipattern, correction, generalization, clarifying pattern

A Global Pattern

We now explain such a global plan for a well-studied problem, namely to build a *compiler* according to the *multiphase approach* /AL 06/, see fig. 2.4. We find a control component on top, starting each of the next level *phase components* and after its end switching to the next, namely scanning, parsing (context-free syntax check), static semantics (context-sensitive syntax check), intermediate code generation, optimization, addressing and code generation, and post-optimization. These are the phases of the compiler, each of which is finished before going to the execution of the next. The first steps build up the so-called frontend, the last ones the backend of the compiler. At the bottom, we find the *data structures* which loosely couple the phase components; namely source text input, tokens (lexical units) list, abstract syntax tree, attributed tree, intermediate graph, machine code, and optimized machine code. Fig. 2.4 shows only a part of the compiler.

At the top, we have a functional object module, in the middle, we have functional subsystems, at the bottom, we find abstract data objects or subsystems. In the case of a language with separate compilation units (different source code units can be compiled in one compilation run), the bottom layer consists of abstract data type components, then with slightly different imports, see fig. 2.3.c.

Patterns (of whatever form) have *not* the purpose to *avoid thinking, arguing,* and *adapting.* They are just good examples for the architecture education as a basis for discussions, see arguments in sect. 2. In my opinion, it is a wrong perception that the complete design process can be organized in form of patterns such that the designer only has to find the right and available pattern to paste it into an architectural design and to combine it with other patterns, which are also available and pasted.

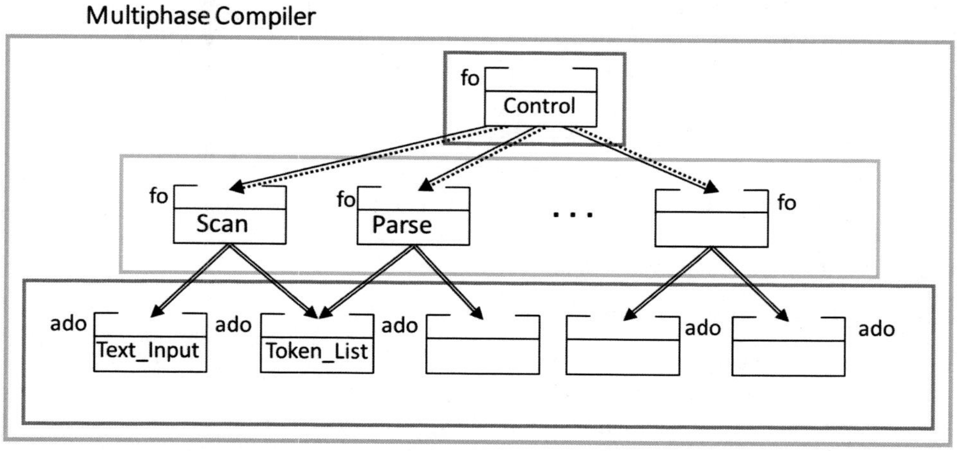

Fig. 2.4: The architectural structure of a multiphase compiler: a sketch

Design Structures for Classes of Systems

There are three basic *structure classes* of software systems (batch, interactive, and concurrent systems, the latter mostly also embedded). The above example of a multiphase compiler is a batch system. A big part of industrial systems is of one of these three forms. They define standard structures, i.e. global patterns, which are a good foundation, if a system of one of these three kinds is designed and built.

There can also be *mixtures* of these basic structure classes, like a batch system for making complex computations, which also have an interactive part to change parameters online. Then, the main part is batch, that specific part is interactive.

Application domains are business administration (BA), like calculating insurance contracts, technical computations (TC), as a crash simulation, embedded systems (ES), as automation and control of a chemical plant, systems programming (SP), like building an operating system, etc. The corresponding systems build up *application classes*. We find batch systems in BA (monthly salary computation), in SP (compiler), and in TC (crash simulation). All have a similar global structure, although they belong to different application domains. We find interactive systems in BA (change of customers' data) or SP (design tool). A concurrent system can exist in ES, but also in SP, e.g. an operating system. Therefore, from the pattern relevance point of view, structure classes are more interesting than application classes.

A further *extension* of the above classifications (structure classes, application classes, etc.) can be made, according to following *dimensions*: (a) underlying *interaction mechanisms* in systems (e.g. call vs. events), (b) *target system* platforms (mainframe, personal computer, network of machines, fine-grained sensor networks), (c) *distribution* (from bound in one computer to distributed cloud computing, or even computed on the fly /OTF 20/), and (d) how *computation is done and gained* (fixed in code, interpretation of specifications, selection of rules to be applied, code generated, tables for interpretation, machine learning from examples).

Most important of the above classifications are *structure classes* in the sense of formative experiences and examples in education. In fig. 2.4 we see an example from the systems software domain which shows the characteristics of batch systems (different computations on the second layer put together by a control component on top, which are loosely coupled via data abstraction components). This global pattern we also find in different other application domains. In the same way, we can argue about interactive systems or concurrent systems. Taking also the application classes and further differentiations into account, may refine the arguments and deliver further variations of structure classes.

2.5 Various Further Aspects are Necessary

In sect. 2.3, we have discussed syntactical and static properties of architectures, how they are denoted, and which methodological hints we can find. Now, we discuss *further aspects*, like semantics, concurrency, or distribution.

We follow the approach, which we discussed in the architectural design for buildings, see sect. 2.2. We define further refinements, views, and detail levels. However, we do not define new artifacts, where it is not clear or obvious, where they appear, and how these artifacts are related to other ones. We rather *annotate* already existing artifacts. Thereby, we define further aspects as *enrichment of the architecture* notation as explained in sect. 2.3. Therefore, it is always clear, where and in which sense the annotations deliver further information and to which part of the architecture the extended information belongs, see arguments around fig. 2.1.

Semantic Annotations

We go back to the multiphase *compiler* (fig. 2.4) and concentrate on the *scanner* (fig. 2.5.a). We assume that the underlying data structures are adt modules, which enforces a modification of the usability edges, see arguments around fig. 2.3.c.

We can specify the *semantics* of component *interfaces* by *pre-* and *postconditions*. For example, the scanner transforms a sequence of characters (precondition) into the corresponding lexical units (tokens, post condition), e.g. an identifier, a word symbol, a delimiter, a literal, etc. of the underlying programming language.

For the interface of the underlying data types (first part **operations** of fig. 2.5.b) we here use a *notation* of *functional* languages. Usually, we use an Ada-like notation for interfaces in the textual part of the architecture language. In our example, Token Streams is a queue, e.g. the scanner writes the tokens at one side, the parser reads them from the other side. Our example in 2.5.b shows a stack, relevant for the parser for generating the parse tree. For this interface of the stack, we can give a semantical description in form of *algebraic equations* (see /Gu 76, LZ 74/). In the lower part of fig. 2.5.b we find an algebraic description of the interface under the assumption that the middle part **preconditions** of fig. 2.5.b holds. By pre and post conditions or by algebraic equations, we can specify the *semantics of single components*. The specifications belong to the interfaces of components.

An even more important part of the semantical description is the *runtime semantics*, corresponding to different components. Not in all cases, this part can be formally be defined, or it is useful to do so. However, we can define the runtime semantics at least in a coarse form by *traces* /Kl 00/, see again fig. 2.5.a. The trace specification of fig. 2.5.a says that Scanner has two loops. The inner loop reads characters from TextStream belonging to a token (2.1 and 2.2), and writes the corresponding token to TokenStream (2.3). The outer loop is repeated until TextStream is completely read (2.1). At the beginning of the scanning process, TextStream and TokenStream are opened (1.a, 1.b). Then, Scanner is called from Control. The files are closed at the end (3.a, 3.b).

Traces show in which order the components are visited. They do not exactly say, what is done during the visit of a component. But traces are better than nothing. They correspond to sequence diagrams of UML /BR 05/. Introducing traces within architectural diagrams avoids defining another artifact, where its contents have to be related to the diagrams artifact. Following the argumentation of sect. 2, *traces* are *annotations* of the *diagram* and not a new artifact.

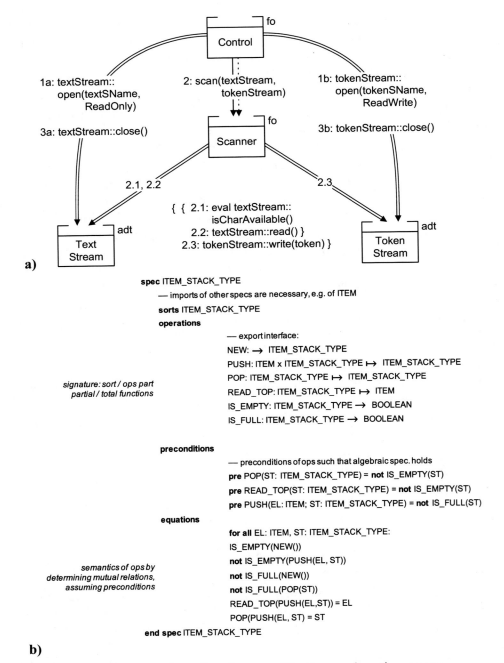

Fig. 2.5: Semantic annotations: Interface specifications and runtime traces

For the scanner of fig. 2.5.a we can even give a nearly complete semantical description, not only the algebraic interface specifications and the coarse trace specification. The behavior of the component Scanner can be described by a finite automaton (alternatively by a regular grammar) defining the lexical syntax of the programming language to be scanned /AL 06/. This corresponds to the body of the Scanner in fig. 2.5.a. This, together with the interface semantics and the traces, gives a nearly *complete and formal semantical description* of the situation described in fig. 2.5.a. We could also have chosen the parser part or the context-sensitive analysis (static semantics) part, to argue in a similar way.

We should mention that examples of such a *formal degree* (scanner, parser, context-sensitive analysis) are rather *seldom*. Software systems can depend on taste (like the user interface of an interactive system), on nonfunctional efficiency parameters (like runtime parameters of an embedded system), on restrictions of the underlying hardware (the system is to run on a special hardware system, a part of the system representing a specific component must be used, which is programmed in a specific way and only runs on certain remote hardware), and so forth. In general, formal *semantic definitions* are in most cases *only partially available*: some interfaces, typical traces, formal descriptions only for some components' behavior.

Concurrency Annotations

For inherently *concurrent problems* we need different *processes running concurrently,* the competition and collaboration of these processes, i.e. an agreement on how to synchronize for resources in the case of concurrency, competition, and collaboration. A sequential schedule makes the solution harder to understand. It also avoids that a certain part continues, if another part is blocked for some time.

In fig. 2.6, we see the well-known *producer-consumer* example as a graphical subarchitecture. Producer and Consumer are function objects (two separate single components in the architecture having the character of a function). In between, there is a Buffer component as an abstract data object, as one buffer is needed.

Producer and Consumer have to work independently. Thus, we make both to a *process*, expressed by *annotations* p at the components Producer and Consumer. As both are processes, we have to define a synchronization for the case of parallel access. It is not necessary to make the buffer to a process. This synchronization is expressed by the *annotation* Monitor (mutual exclusion of all operations of the buffer /BF 95/) as a *synchronization specification* (in short sp). The synchronization protocol could also be a protected object of Ada (mutual exclusion of writers, but parallel readers, if no writer is active /Na 03/), or anything else suitable. Again, we see that we can *annotate* an architecture diagram to express *concurrency aspects*. This avoids further and separate artifacts.

In the context of concurrency, we might have many producers or many consumers. It is not reasonable to paste as many - function object and process - components as needed. In some cases, the number of such processes cannot even be determined at program development time. For such situations, we introduce *function type components*, from which we can create as many function objects as wanted at runtime in the bodies of using components. These different processes, however, cannot be directly seen on architecture level.

For *embedded systems,* also the *explicit start* and *stop* have to be modeled. Embedded systems run "forever" until they are explicitly stopped in a controlled way. Analogously, they are explicitly started in a controlled way. Similarly, *emergency handling* has to be modeled. Both start/ stop as well as emergency handling can be modeled by the above and further annotations, which is not discussed here. This altogether explains that the productivity of developers programming embedded systems is much lower (about one third of the productivity of sequential systems), as further additional tasks have to be solved (processes and synchronization, controlled start and stop, and emergency handling).

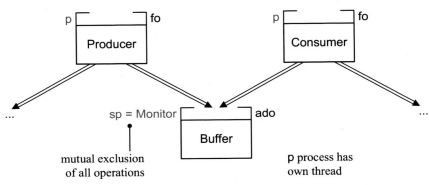

Fig. 2.6: Annotations for concurrency: processes and synchronization

Component use Connections: Abstract and Concrete

Up to now, a *usability edge* between a service user component A and a service provider component B, offering one or different services, is denoted in an *abstract form*, see fig. 2.7.a: There is a usability relation between both. It can be a local, a general, or an inheritance usability relation. It says that a service of B will be needed for A. The service use is written down in the code of the body of A. At runtime, if the corresponding part of the body of A is executed, the service is provided by B.

Up to now, we had in mind that the service is realized by a *procedure* or *function* of the interface of B and a corresponding *call*. The service provider may be a fo, ft, ado, or adt component. The caller invokes the call, the caller is stopped, and the service is called at the callee side. When the callee has finished, it stops, and control goes back to the caller.

This *abstract situation* "service of B is used from A" can be realized by *different mechanisms*. The service might be provided by a coroutine, an entry call, or a task activation. In all cases, A and B may run in parallel. A and B are synchronized later again, by language mechanisms or by means delivered by the programmer.

We discuss only three of many possible forms. In fig. 2.7.b, we see that the service of B is activated by an *activation signal*, naming the service and providing the parameters. After service completion, a *completion signal* is sent back, possibly with result parameters. In the meantime, A and B may run independently. Also, events, triggers, or interrupts may be used to handle this request and provide situation.

In fig. 2.7.c, a *callback situation* is discussed. In the left part, the situation is described: Client C would like to answer to a state change of B by doing an activity act. This happens, for example, if a user is doing something, which has to be answered by the activity act. Instead of polling (C is always asking B whether the state change has already happened), the operation act is delegated to the State component. State registers for act and gets a procedure pointer for act. Such situations are often interpreted in a wrong way. People say 'my architecture has completely inverted'. This is not the case: The abstract situation (cf. fig. 2.7.a) remains the same, the mechanism for realizing it, however, has changed, fig. 2.7.c.

An even more complicated situation we find in *event handling systems using broadcasting*, see fig. 2.7.d /Kl 00/. There are components Producer1 and Producer2 producing events e, e′ and e′′, which are sent to the Broadcasting Service. The components Comp1 and Comp2, for example, can register to get the event e to react by act1 and act2. This corresponds to the abstract situation that Producer1 or Producer2 may use service act1 of Comp1 and act2 of Comp2. Corresponding to who has currently registered at runtime, dynamic use switches are possible. This can produce a system behavior, hard to understand and even more confusing than goto-programming. It should be denoted at development time, who is possibly using whom at runtime, see green edges in fig. 2.7.d to imagine the possible switch.

Looking on all these situations, we see that the underlying *abstract situation* of fig. 2.7.a is *realized* by using quite different *concrete mechanisms* for service use. Therefore, we would rather use the abstract situation of fig. 2.7.a and provide *different annotations*, as pc for procedure call, cc for coroutine call, ec for entry call, cb for a callback, and via bc for via broadcasting. That has the advantage of abstraction (the underlying abstract situation is to be seen directly) and flexibility (the used mechanism can more easily be changed).

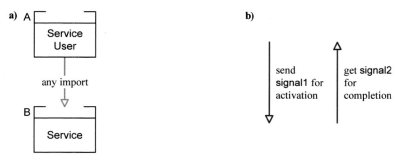

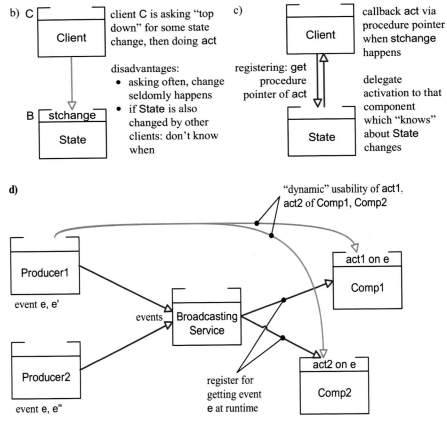

Fig. 2.7: Abstract use and three different concrete mechanisms

Distribution

A further aspect to be studied now is *distribution* and *deployment*. A software system is divided and deployed on different computers. This is done in the later stages of development, which starts with virtual and abstract notations.

Fig. 2.8.a shows the sketch of the architecture of an *interactive business administration system*, which was *reengineered* from a monolithic mainframe system /Cr 00/. It introduces subarchitectures (inner details not shown in fig. 2.8.a), which are clear areas of concern: The control part for managing the dialog, the UI part to keep all UI details away from the inner system, the main application parts determining the functionality of the interactive system, and the underlying database subsystem, which hides data and schema details. Reengineering via subarchitectures of clear concern has made the system to consist of loosely coupled parts, see fig. 2.8.a.

We now decide to put these parts on different machines: the UI part on intelligent workstations, the control, the main business functions, and the data handling each on separate function or data servers, by reasons of security or redundancy. The lines of *separation* are given as *annotations* in fig. 2.8.a, the used distribution *infrastructure*, here CORBA /COR 20/ for remote procedure calls, is also annotated.

Fig. 2.8.b shows the technical solution for CORBA /Kl 00/ for one case of the above distributions: On both sides of a cutting line and distribution, technical components are introduced, which are either provided (RPC Basic Services, Marshalling, Unmarshalling) by CORBA or are generated by CORBA from a specification (ClientStub and ServerStub). They provide that the procedure call is transformed into a data stream, sent over a connection, put together on the server side, and is executed on the server side. Similarly, it finds the way back. There are various distribution infrastructures, working similarly as CORBA, which can also be used, e.g. Remote Method Invocation for Java /WR 96/.

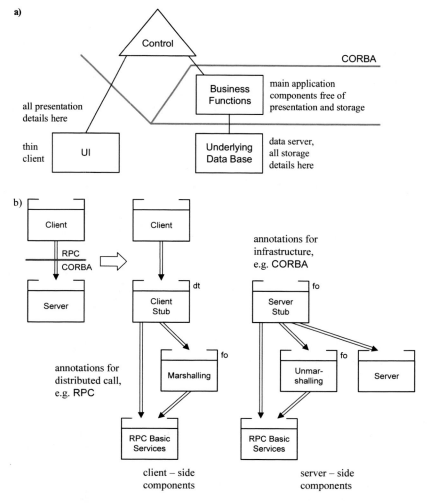

Fig. 2.8: Distribution: characterization and its realization by an infrastructure

Two remarks at the end of this short discussion: (a) Again, it should be noted that the more *abstract solution* with *annotations* says more than the detailed technical solution. It also allows to easily change the annotations and to use another distribution infrastructure. (b) Distributing software over different machines might introduce some technical concurrency, e.g. if different application functions run in parallel and have access to one data server. These accesses have to be synchronized.

2.6 Styles: Integrating Different Notations

In /GS 94/ different notations for architectures have been introduced for specific integration situations occurring in software construction. They were called *architectural styles*. Reading about these styles creates the impression that any of these styles introduces a separate notation and that these different notations have nothing to do with each other. They all lead to *separate architecture worlds*.

/GS 94, SG96/ introduce different *architectural notations*, namely (a) pipeline, (b) data flow architectures, (c) loosely coupled systems, and others. We only discuss pipeline architectures here and leave the detailed style discussions to chapter 5.

We express *pipeline architectures* by the concepts we have introduced so far. Fig. 2.9.a gives an *example* of a simple pipeline architecture. There are three components f1 to f3, executed one after the other, i.e. the output of f1 is the input of f2 and so forth. They make up one bigger component F, where the input of which is directed to f1, and the output of f3 is the output of F.

There are mainly *two* possibilities for the *semantics*. The first, called *discrete case*, works in the way that F takes the input, then executes the pipeline (functions f1, f2, and f3) and outputs the result. Then, F takes the new input. In the second possibility, called *continuous case*, the input of F is passed to f1. After f1 has produced its result, the next input of F can be taken by f1. In this case, three inputs of F can be taken and passed to f1, before the first output of f3 gives the first output of F.

Fig. 2.9.b gives the *simulation* for the *discrete case*. The control component takes the input from input, then controls the sequence of executions f1 to f3 , where for every fi an output is passed back to Control. At the end of this sequence, the output of f3 is passed by Control as output of F.

Fig. 2.9.c simulates the *continuous case*. Now f1, f2, and f3 work in parallel, so they are made to processes, see annotations p. The input is taken from f1, passed by an entry call to f2, and f1 takes the next input. It should be noted that further semantics are possible, which can also be simulated.

What we have demonstrated for pipeline architectures, can also be shown for the other style notations, as data flow architectures, loosely coupled architectures, and others. Thus, all these different notations can be traced back to the modular notation introduced above. Therefore, the style notations - as pipelining - are not really new and completely different. We can use them for architecture modeling, just as abbreviations for situations we can express otherwise in the standard notation.

Thereby, we found another *integration dimension*: We have integrated different notations by tracing them back to a 'standard' notation. As the *semantics* of the style architectures can vary from paper/ book to the next, we can *define* the semantical differences *appropriately*.

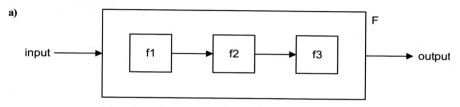

the result of f1 is input to f2; the result of f2 ist input to f3; ...

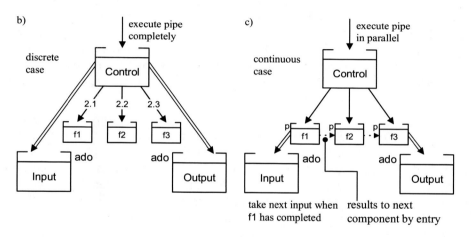

Fig. 2.9: Pipeline architecture style is traced back to the standard notation

2.7 Relations between Artifacts and Putting Together

Hierarchies and other Relations

The *architectural configuration* of a software development process *consists* of the following *artifacts*, in the sense "all is part of": overview diagram, architectural diagrams for parts of the overview diagram, architecture diagrams of subsystem bodies, text artifacts for component interfaces and also for detailed usability relations. The examples of this chapter were mostly on diagram level and there on the level of overviews. The architectural configuration is an organization relation for "collecting everything that is needed" for architecture modeling. The architecture configuration is a well-defined part of the overall configuration, see ch. 1.

Within artifacts, we find *internal diagram hierarchy relations* for expressing locality, layering, and inheritance within a diagram. Structure relations as "is local to", "located on a certain abstraction layer", or "is a" establish underlying relationships, from which we select corresponding usability relations (import relations) between components, as "locally usable", "usable between layers", or "usable within an inheritance structure".

There are *hierarchy relations for delivering details*: For example, from a shorthand notation of a subsystem to its details (the aggregated interfaces, the architecture diagram for the body), from a module to its textual description of the interface, and also to the structure and usability relations as text clauses. The relations are from a diagram to a more detailed diagram, or from a diagram to its corresponding detailed text. We also find details from an annotated diagram to the details of the annotation in another diagram, so here from diagram to diagram.

Some of the relations come from/ go to the *outside of the architectural configuration*: (a) From a requirement to the parts of the architecture realizing this requirement, or vice versa from architectural items to the requirement items they belong to. We also find them (b) from architectural items to the realization/ programming/ coding items or vice versa, (c) from architectural items to the management items organizing the work or vice versa, (d) from architectural items to quality assurance items or vice versa, (e) from architectural items to documentation items explaining the decisions or vice versa. All these relations facilitate to understand, realize, or manage the architectural configuration. They are regarded in chs. 10-14.

The architectural configuration is the *center* or the most important part of the *overall configuration*, which also contains parts for requirements, code realizations, management, quality, and documentation. The architectural configuration contains the main decisions, denotes the long-term quality properties, and the organization of the whole development process. To a big part, the overall configuration is determined by the decisions of the architectural configuration. The overall configuration contains all documents/ artifacts of the development process, together with corresponding relations inside and between the documents/ artifacts, see ch. 1.

These relations split into different *fine-grained relations* inside and outside of the architectural configuration and within the overall configuration. Examples are: (i) For an interface item of a module which is a procedure header to the procedure definition in the programming part and vice versa, (ii) for a module to its explanation in the documentation, (iii) for a module inside the body of a subsystem to the specific quality assurance measures taken for this module, (iv) from an annotation in a diagram to the corresponding detail information, etc. These fine-grained links /Na 96, NM 08/ are very important and have to be obeyed in a program systems' development. In a usual tool suite, there is usually no proper support for them.

Different Languages are Used

o *Diagrammatical* languages for overviews, *textual* languages for details. In this chapter, we concentrated on the graphical language parts.
o *Formal* languages, for the specification of an interface are used, or *informal* ones to sketch the purpose of a component in the documentation.
o Architectural *style notations* stand for abbreviations of architectural situations as sketched in sect. 2.4.
o Various forms of *consistency relations* (context-sensitive syntax) appear inside the architectural configuration.
o Different forms of *method rules* and *patterns* say what and how to design.
o The architectural languages consist of different parts along with a historical development /Al 78, Le 88, Na 90, Bö 94, Kl 00/ and this chapter.

Usable for Different Architectural Approaches, Applications, and Problems

The approach can be used in different ways:

- *Functional decomposition* with data abstraction, see the compiler example. It can also be used for *layers*, e.g. for different layers of data abstraction. We can model *inheritance* hierarchies.
- It can be used in *OO* approaches by some form of *"backward" simulation*: fo and ado components as abstract classes, inheritance inside, and layering between components outside of inheritance.
- *Style notations* can be introduced as abbreviations of modular situations, for pipeline, data flow, or loosely coupled systems.
- *Structure classes* (batch systems, interactive systems, or embedded systems) are characterized by global patterns. Further differentiation, e.g. for application domains, etc. (see discussion in sect. 2.3) can be expressed.
- The approach can be used for *new development,* for *reverse* and *reengineering,* for *maintenance,* and for *extensions* of systems. It can even be used for systems written in old programming languages, see chapter 9.

Remarkable Experience in Architecture Modeling

The software architecture *approach*, presented in this chapter, has been used for research, design, and development *tasks* of *remarkable size*. Some of them are:

The main activities were tightly *integrated tools for software development* in the IPSEN project /Na 96/, tools in *chemical engineering* in the IMPROVE project /NM 08/, and design tools for *mechanical engineering* /NW 99/. In all these cases not only tools for architectural design were regarded. Also, documentation, management, and requirements engineering have been studied. Furthermore, specialized integration tools, to keep fine-grained relations between artifacts consistent to each other, have been studied and implemented.

But there are also other and *specific applications*, as technical applications containing *expert systems* /Ba 95/, *reverse and reengineering* in *business administration*

/Cr 00/, reengineering of *telecom systems* /Ma 05, Mo 09/, tools for *authoring* /Ga 05/, and for *automotive* /Me 12/, and smart homes /Ar 10, Re 10/. Furthermore, in a project aiming at new concepts for a nonstandard database system in the *systems programming domain*, there are many architectural descriptions /Ba 00/.

Finally, in /KN 07, Kr 07/ we studied the architectural design of *buildings*. We extended CAAD systems to give specific support for the *conceptual design* of buildings and to *specialize* this support for *specific classes of buildings*, like e.g. medium size office buildings. A knowledge engineer architect develops this knowledge, which is then taken up by a traditional architect. Buildings (bridges, cathedrals) or parts of it are used as role models for good software design. In /Na 19/ the design of gothic cathedrals and its relation to software architectures has been worked out for the first time.

2.8 Summary and Open Problems

Integration w.r.t. Different Dimensions

Summary of the *static part's integration aspects* with the following *dimensions*: We have introduced different kinds of *components*, for functional and for data abstraction, as objects (fo, ado) or as types (ft, adt). Also different kinds of *relations* were introduced, namely structure and usability relations. Therefore, different kinds of *construction principles* can be applied: locality, layers, and object orientation. Different kinds of *consistency relations* are offered from the context-sensitive syntax of the underlying design languages. From the viewpoint of good and clear use of the languages, we have *method rules* (*patterns*) of different kinds: As it should be, from wrong to right, from specific to more general (as object to type), from abstract and clear to detailed or efficient, etc. We have also introduced *components* of different *size*, modules or subsystems, or *units* of the design *languages*: From interface specs of modules to complete modules, to pairs of modules with relations, to subarchitectures, to subsystems containing subarchitectures, to complete architectures. Finally, the approach unites design and *parametric* design (genericity, not discussed here). This all was presented in this chapter (sect. 2.3) using *different languages*, graphical and textual (as discussed in sect. 2.5).

Summary of *further aspects*: Further aspects have been introduced which result in *annotations* of the design artifacts, mostly together with further refinements of the artifacts in form of additional details in the same or in other artifacts. We introduced *semantical notations* for interface specifications, runtime traces, or behavioral specifications, e.g. in form of finite automata. *Concurrency* annotations denote the information for processes and synchronization protocols. Further parts for start/ stop of the system and emergency *handling* can be added for *embedded systems*. For *abstract connectors* (request and supply of services) different *mechanisms* can be introduced, from coroutine, signal, trigger, interrupt to event handling by broadcast. The *distribution* of a system can be annotated by *distribution lines* and *annotations*, or in detail by additional *components* and *connectors* of an underlying distribution *platform*. All these aspects introduce detailed views to more abstract ones. Thus, abstract and detailed views can be regarded to be integrated. In many cases, the detailed views will be developed and studied only by specialists or/ and afterwards.

Different notations from *architectural styles*, as pipeline, data flow, loosely coupled systems, etc. are *abbreviations* of our architectural notation, details in ch. 5. Therefore, they can be used together with the standard notations without leaving the conceptual framework of architecture modeling, as introduced here. Thus, we have integrated different architectural notations.

As already discussed, the architecture is the essential structure of the development process, used for decision making, arguing about structures, realization, extensions, and maintenance, explaining the structure and concepts, and also methodologies to build the system. Therefore, they integrate essential activities. The architecture is *composed* of *different views* regarding different aspects, with more or fewer details. The relations between different artifacts and units of artifacts should be clear. All the stakeholders of a system development have to do with the architecture in different degrees of detail, for writing or verifying an artifact, in other cases to roughly explain or coarsely understand it.

The *architecture* is a *configuration* of diagrams, detailing texts, annotations within a description, references to corresponding more and detailed elaborations. A part of this configuration is directly devoted to architectural views and aspects. Other parts and outside of the architectural configuration belong to quality, documentation, and management of the development process or are derived from the architecture, as the program code. In total, the architecture integrates different aspects and corresponding artifacts and is the center for integration for other aspects.

This *architecture configuration* is a part of the overall configuration of the system to be built, extended, or maintained, see ch. 1. The overall configuration contains further artifacts for requirements engineering (outside views, the system to be developed has to follow), as well as artifacts for the realization (programming, implementation). Again, the architectural configuration is the *essential part* of the overall configuration.

By the way, this role of an overall configuration we find in *all engineering domains*: outside view for requirements, essential internal view, from an abstract logical level (conceptual modeling) down to the level of describing the essence of the system as it is delivered to the customer /Na 90, Na 96, NM 08, NW 99/, and adding all details of realization (detail engineering). In this chapter, we concentrated on architecture modeling, forgetting upwards about requirements and also downwards about detail engineering. We only regarded the links from and to architectural units. The overall configuration corresponds to the BIM model for buildings, cf. sect. 2.2. We could also say, the overall configuration is our product information model for software system development.

Different Ideas in one Notation

Summaries like /SAD, SEI 10, WSA/ show *different ideas*, which came up in the context of software architectures. They present these ideas, one aside of each other. Also, in most books on software architectures usually only fragments of these ideas are presented, namely the parts favored by the author. These fragments vary from book to book or even from a version of the book of an author to the next. We hope to have shown an approach in this chapter, which overcame both problems and puts these fragments *together* to a whole in one *notation*: The notations (i) contain all fragments/ or all fragments can be expressed in the approach, and (ii) the approach integrates the corresponding ideas.

We supported the *integration of artifacts* in two ways: (a) We understand how they relate to each other in the architectural configuration and also beyond, and how they relate to artifacts outside the architectural configuration. This is (b) facilitated by the two-level approach using annotations: They are used in a more abstract form which is denoted within usual architectural diagrams, and their detailed form is mostly presented separately. In this way, the integration is easy to understand and the details can simply be exchanged. In these ways, we hope to contribute in some form to *integration* within the research *field* of *software architectures*.

Outlook

Further aspects and corresponding annotations are possible. (i) For example, we could have discussed *efficiency transformations* in sect. 2.4. There is an abstract and possible inefficient form for an architectural situation and there are possible ways to make it more efficient, but also less clear and understandable. Thus, we introduce different annotations in the abstract form and corresponding realizations by corresponding supplements.

Sect. 5 introduced several forms of further aspects and additions, as semantics, concurrency, concrete use connectors, and distribution. However, (ii) we did not discuss, how to *organize* such *additions* and in *which order*. This is, of course, dependent on the structure class, the application domain, but also the history of development in a certain company. Ch. 3 argues that there is not only one architecture but a series of architectures. Putting these architectures in some order has to be well thought-out and carefully discussed.

Sect. 2 has introduced Building Information Models as the collection and composition of all artifacts belonging to the design and construction of buildings. A similar approach (iii) should be used for the collection and composition of all artifacts corresponding to design and realization of software systems and further documents around, as e.g. technical acceptance and validation, the contract, the protocols of sessions, etc. All this information is called the *product and process model*. There is no accepted standard available for this model today. Such a standard cannot totally be fixed. It has to be flexible to allow differences of domains, of cultures of companies, of methodologies, and so on. But, there could be at least a standard, what this process and product model should address, e.g. in a checklist, or specific forms of this list for different structure classes, application domains, etc.

More research is necessary to (iv) study the *similarities* and *differences* of *design* and *development* in *different engineering domains* and to compare it with the experiences we can contribute from the software engineering side. We did some steps in this direction /Na 96, NM 08, NW 99, NW 03/. Activities are necessary to collect the advantages of different approaches and to learn from each other. There are merits in the areas of production engineering, chemical process engineering, automation and control, and communication systems, which can push software engineering forward. Conversely, the methods in direction of intelligent software construction can influence the engineering fields. There was some time at Carnegie Mellon University (CMU) where this idea to synthesize patterns and cooperations, applicable in different engineering disciplines, was very visible.

Integration of different *methods*, *models*, and *tools* are still big topics for software development in any domain, as for tools /Na 96/ and embedded systems /BF 10/. The development process has to be improved to better understand it, to make it precise, and to support novel techniques, as model-driven development /PB 16/ and generation of code. Even more ambitious is the process if we do not regard a single system but a *family of systems* /CN 07, Ja 00, PB 05/.

2.9 References

/Al 78/ Altmann, W.: Description of program modules for the design of reliable software (in German), Doct. Diss. Univ. Erlangen-Nuremberg, TR IMMD 11-16 (1978)

/AL 06/ Aho, A.V./ Lam, M.S./ Sethi, R./ Ullman, J.D.: Compilers: Principles, Techniques, and Tools, 2nd ed., Pearson (2006)

/Ar 10/ Armac, I.: Personalized eHome Systems (in German), Doct. Diss., RWTH Aachen University, 315 pp., (2010)

/AT 00/ Anderl, R./ Trippner, D. (eds.): STEP Standard for the Exchange of Product Model Data, Eine Einführung in die Entwicklung, Implementierung und industrielle Nutzung der Normenreihe ISO 10303 (STEP). 245 pp., Teubner (2000)

/Ba 95/ Bacvanski, V.:Integration and Structuring of Expert Systems in Technical Applications, Doct. Diss., RWTH Aachen University, 225 pp. (1995)

/Ba 00/ Baumann, R.: A Data Base System for Distributed and Integrated Software Development Environments (in German), Doct. Diss., RWTH Aachen University, 236 pp. (2000)

/BF 95/ Buhr, P./ Fortier, M. et al.: Monitor classification, ACM Computing Surveys 27 (1): 63–107 (1995)

/BF 10/ Broy, M./ Feilkas, M. et al.: Seamless Model-based Development: From Isolated Tools to Integrated Model Engineering Environments, Proc. IEEE, 98, 4, 526-545 (2010)

/BK 03/ Bass, L./ Clements, P. et al.: Software Architecture in Practice, 3rd ed. Pearson (2013)

/BM 96/ Buschmann, F./ Meunier, R. et al.: Pattern-oriented Software Architecture - A System of Patterns, Wiley (1996)

/Bö 94/ Börstler, J.: Programming in the large: Languages, Tools, Reuse (in German), Doct. Diss. RWTH Aachen University, 205 pp. (1994)

/BR 05/ Booch, G./ Rumbaugh, J. et al.: The Unified Modeling Language User Guide, Addison Wesley (2005)

/Bu 84/ Buhr, R.: System Design with Ada, Prentice Hall (1984)

/CN 07/ Clements, P./ Northrop, L.M.: Software Product Lines: Practices and Patterns, 563 pp., 6th ed., Addison Wesley (2007)

/COR 20/ https://www.omg.org/spec/CORBA/About-CORBA/

/Cr 00/ Cremer, K.: Graph-based Tools for Reverse and Reengineering (in German), Doct. Diss., RWTH Aachen University, 220 pp. (2000)

/DK 76/ DeRemer, F./ Kron, H.H.: Programming in the Large versus Programming in the Small, IEEE Transactions on Software Engineering, SE-2, 2, 80-86 (1976)

/ET 08/ Eastman, C./ Teicholz, P. et al.: BIM Handbook. John Wiley & Sons, 2008

/Ga 05/ Gatzemeier. F.: CHASID: A Semantics-oriented Authoring Environment, Doct. Diss., RWTH Aachen University, 284 pp. (2005)

/GS 94/ Garlan, D./ Shaw, M.: An Introduction to Software Architectures, TR CMU-CS-94-166 (1994)

/GH 95/ Gamma, E./ Helm, R. et al.: Design Patterns: Elements of Reusable Object-Oriented Software, 395 pp. Addison Wesley (1995)

/Gu 76/ Guttag, J.: Abstract Data Types and the Development of Data Structures, Comm. ACM 20, 6, 396-404 (1977)

/HP 80/ Habermann, H.N./ Perry, D.: Well-formed System Compositions, TR CMU-CS-80-117, Carnegie-Mellon University (1980)

/HK 07/ Hofmeister, C./ Kruchten, P. et al: A general model of software architectural design derived from five industrial approaches, Journal Systems & Software 80, 106-126 (2007)

/Ja 00/ Jazayeri, M. et al. (eds.): Software Architecture for Product Families, Addison Wesley (2000)

/JC 92/ Jacobsen, I./ Magnus, C. et al.: Object Oriented Software Engineering. 77-79, Addison-Wesley ACM Press (1992)

/Kl 00/ Klein, P.: Architecture Modelling of Distributed and Concurrent Software Systems Doct. Diss. RWTH Aachen University, 237pp. (2000)

/KM 04/ Kruger, I./ Mathew, R.: Systematic development and exploration of service-oriented software architectures, 4th Working IEEE/IFIP Conference on Software Architecture (WICSA), 177-187 (2004)

/KN 07/ Kraft, B./ Nagl, M.: Visual Knowledge Specification for Conceptual Design: Definition and Tools Support, Journ. Adv. Engg. Informatics 21, 1, 67-83 (2007)

/Kr 07/ Kraft, B.: Semantical support for the conceptual design of buildings (in German), Doct. Diss., RWTH Aachen University, 381 pp. (2007)

/Le 88/ Lewerentz, C.: Concepts and tools for the interactive design of large software systems (in German), Doct. Diss., 179 pp. RWTH Aachen University, Informatik-Fachberichte 194, Springer (1988)

/LZ 74/ Liskow, B./ Zilles, S.: Specification Techniques for Data Abstractions, Int. Conf. on Reliable Software, 72-87, IEEE (1975)

/Ma 05/ Marburger, A.: Reverse Engineering of Complex Legacy Telecommunication Systems, Doct. Diss., RWTH Aachen University, 418 pp. (2005)

/Me 12/ Mengi, C.: Automotive Software – Processes, Models, and Variability (in German), Doct. Diss., RWTH Aachen University, 350 pp. (2012)

/Me 91/ Meyer, B.: Eiffel: The Language, 300 pp., 3rd ed. Prentice Hall (2005)

/Me 97/ Meyer, B.: Object-oriented Software Construction, 2nd ed., Prentice Hall (1997)

/Mo 09/ Mosler, Ch.: Graph-based Reengineering of Telecommunication Systems (in German), Doct. Diss. RWTH Aachen University, 268 pp. (2009)

/Na 03/ Nagl, M.: Introduction to Ada (in German), 1st ed. 348 pp., 6th ed. Software Engineering and Ada (in German), 504 pp., Vieweg (2003)

/Na 90/ Nagl, M.: Software Engineering- Methodological Programming in the Large (in German), 387 pp., Springer (1990), as eBook available, plus further extensions for a lecture on Software Architectures between 1990 - 2020

/Na 96/ Nagl, M. (ed.): Building Tightly Integrated Software Development Environments - The IPSEN Approach, LNCS 1170, 709 pp., Springer (1996)

/Na 19/ Nagl, M.: Gothic Churches and Informatics (in German), 304 pp., Springer Vieweg (2019)

/NM 08/ Nagl, M./ Marquardt, W.: Collaborative and Distributed Chemical Engineering, From Understanding to Substantial Design Process Support, IMPROVE, LNCS 4970, 851 pp., Springer (2008)

/NW 99/ Nagl, M./ Westfechtel, B. (Eds.): Integration of Development Systems in Engineering Applications – Substantial Improvement of Development Processes (in German), 440 pp., Springer (1999)

/NW 03/ Nagl, M./ Westfechtel, B. (eds.): Models, Tools, and Infrastructures for the Support of Development Processes (in German), 392 pp., Wiley VCH (2003)

/OTF 20/ Collaborative Research Center 901 "On the Fly Computing", University of Paderborn, https://sfb901.uni-paderborn.de/de/

/Pa 72/ Parnas, D.: On the Criteria to be Used in Decomposing Systems into Modules, Comm. ACM 15, 12, 1053-1058 (1972)

/PB 05/ Pohl, K./ Böckle, G. et al.: Software Product Line Engineering, 467 pp., Springer (2005)

/PB 16/ Pohl, K./ Broy, M./ Daemkes, M./ Hönninger, H. (eds.): Adavanced Model-based Engineering of Embedded Systems – Extensions to the SPES 2020 Methodology, Springer, 303 pp. (2016)

/PD 07/ Pollet, D./ Ducasse, S. et al.: Towards a Process-Oriented Software Architecture Reconstruction Taxonomy, Proc. 11th European CSMR 07, 137-148 (2007)

/Re 10/ Retkowitz, D.: Software Support for Adaptive eHome Systems (in German), Doct. Diss. RWTH Aachen University, 354 pp. (2010)

/Ru 11/ Rumpe, B.: Modeling with UML (in German), 293 pp., Springer (2011)

/Ru 12/ Rumpe, B.: Agile Modeling with UML (in German), 372 pp. Springer (2012)

/SAD/ Software Architecture and Design Tutorial, TutorialRide.com, https://www.tutorialride.com/software-architecture-and-design/software-architecture-and-design-tutorial.htm

/Sc 13/ Schmidt, R.F.: Software Engineering – Architecture-driven Software Development, 376 pp. Elsevier (2013)

/SEI 10/ Software Engineering Institute of CMU: What Is Your Definition of Software Architecture, https://resources.sei.cmu.edu/library/asset-view.cfm?assetID=513807

/SG 96/ Shaw, M./ Garlan, D.: Software architecture: perspectives on an emerging discipline. Prentice Hall (1996)

/SS 00/ Schmidt, D./ Stal, M. et al.: Pattern-oriented Software Architectures, vol 2 Patterns for Concurrent and Networked Objects, Wiley (2000)

/Ta 12/ Tanenbaum, A.S.: Computer Networks (German edition), 5th ed., Pearson (2012)

/WR 96/ Wollrath, A./ Riggs, R. et al.: A Distributed Object Model for the Java System, Computing System 9, 4, 265 - 289 (1996)

/WSA/ Wikipedia: Software Architecture, https://en.wikipedia.org/wiki/Software_architecture

3 Sequences of Architectures from Abstract to Details

Manfred Nagl

Software Engineering, RWTH Aachen University, nagl@cs.rwth-aachen.de

Abstract

The architecture of a software system consists of different artifacts with hierarchy and other dependency relations between them. This architecture is developed in stages. It starts with an abstract and conceptual form and ends with a concrete form with many details, describing various technical topics of the shipped system.

This chapter deals with the specific question, how these stages of the architecture have to be organized. What is the order of these architectures and what are the relations between them? The order is connected to the methodology of the design process, to the properties of the resulting design (e.g. adaptability), and also the type of system to be developed. The underlying architectural language should be able to express these relations. Two examples are discussed, one from business administration and one from embedded systems.

Keywords: software architecture modeling, different stages of the architecture and mutual dependencies, order of the stages and adaptability, desirable uniform architecture language and methodology for the stages

3.1 Introduction

What is a *software architecture*? It is a collection of artifacts, which (or some of which) correspond to different goals, as overview/ detailed, according to hierarchical relations as e.g. layers, according to different degrees of detail, according to the art of presentation (graphical or textual), according to the type of description as static (structure) or dynamic (execution), etc.

All these artifacts are related to each other and are aggregated in the *architectural configuration*. This architectural configuration is part of the *overall configuration* of the complete development process, which, in addition, contains all the artifacts belonging to requirements, programming, quality assurance, documentation, and management, see ch. 1.

This is rather similar in all *engineering design and development processes*. What we call architecture modeling in the software business is there called conceptual design/ modeling, what we call programming or implementation is there called detail design or engineering. This view of the overall configuration, having different *technical parts* and *others for management, documentation, or quality assurance*, exists also in the field of architectures for buildings and civil engineering. There, the overall configuration is called "building information model" (in short BIM /ET 08, KN 07, Kr 07/).

This chapter concentrates on the architectural configuration and there on the statement that there is not only one architecture. The architecture runs through different stages from abstract to concrete and detailed. The question "What are these *stages*

M. Nagl, B. Westfechtel, *Software Architectures*, https://doi.org/10.1007/978-3-031-51335-0_3

and *how should they be ordered* in the design process?" is the topic of this chapter. We assume that the underlying architecture language is able to express a variety of concepts, see ch. 2.

The architectures of the series belong to different stages of development. These different stages correspond to different *aspects and views*. The *order*, in which these architectures appear, should be *carefully organized*. The architectural *language,* in which these different architectures are denoted, should be able to *cover* these *different aspects*, it should be universal /Na 90-22/ in the sense of integrating these different aspects and views. This avoids that different architectural languages are used, where it is not clear, how they are combined w.r.t. syntax, semantics, pragmatics, and methodology.

This chapter is structured as follows: We start in sect. 3.2 with examples in order to show the different stages for two scenarios, which belong to different application domains. Sect. 3 3 discusses the rules to apply on the way to find a suitable order of architectures. Using these rules, sects. 3.4 and 3.5 explain the order we have found for the scenarios of sect. 3.2 and sketch the contents of the different architecture stages. Sect. 3.6 sums up, which different aspects the universal architecture language should cover, thereby defining the requirements for the architecture language. Sect. 3.7 summarizes the findings.

3.2 Scenario Examples

Before going into details, we discuss *two example scenarios* as introduction to the main part of this chapter. Both are valuable scenarios, others are also possible.

A Business Administration Application

We regard a *business administration application*, e.g. a system in an *insurance company*, which supports employees in preparing an insurance contract for a client, who is interested in getting such a contract. We do not look deeply into the application system, we only sketch the examples of the different stages, the architecture of the system could go through, see fig. 3.1.

We first assume that the *system is new*. The architecture is carefully designed, but in an abstract way. The services are planned, the main components have been found, and the system is divided into different layers. The result is the *logical architecture*, reflecting an idealized build plan. This is the first step.

In the next step it might be useful to precisely specify at least some components, for example the *components* which are mostly *important* for the success of the system. Thus, we define their *semantics*. It might be desirable to specify the semantics of the whole system. However, this can get complicated or impossible (as formulating the taste of the UI interface, or nonfunctional parameters of the requirements make it difficult). Therefore, often only the semantics of some of the main components are defined formally. This is done by annotations to the interface of these components. This is the second step.

Such a system runs on different machines. Client machines process the inputs of external company employees, i.e. check them for plausibility or mutual dependency. The main functionality is executed on a mainframe, possibly on different mainframes by reasons of flexibility, redundancy, safety, and security. The underlying data are stored on a data server or different ones, again due to redundancy and security, being located behind thick concrete walls. *Distribution* is described by *annotations*. A methodology can help later by *realizing the distribution* of the system (deployment), using a specific platform. We put these two tasks together and regard the distributed and deployed architecture as step 3.

Distribution induces *concurrency*. For example, different parts of the system might be executed concurrently. The accesses to common resources, therefore, have to be synchronized. Although the whole system is not concurrent by its nature, concurrency here comes with distribution as a technical aspect. The result is step 4.

Finally, it might become clear that the system must be modified in order to fulfill the demanded efficiency parameters. So, *efficiency transformations* are used. They usually are done only, if absolutely necessary. We get step 5.

Summing up: We started with an abstract system's architecture, and with an understanding of modular architectures as usual /Bö 94, GS 94, Le 88, Na 90-22/, see chs. 1 and 2. After five steps - logical architecture, adding semantics, determining distribution and deployment, adding induced concurrency, and making efficiency transformations - our example system looks rather differently. We call the result of all these transformations the *physical* or concrete *architecture*. This architecture describes how the final system looks like on architecture level. The regarded example could even have run through further transformation steps.

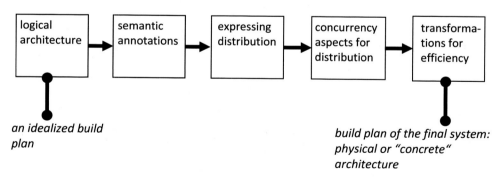

Fig. 3.1: Architecture sequence for an example from business administration

Now we change our scenario. We start with an *existing* and *old system*. This old system was developed without an architectural design. Therefore, the first step is to find out what the architecture of the program system could be (*reverse engineering* /PD 07/). This result is usually not a clean architecture.

The following step finds a new and suitable form of the architecture (*reengineering*) and tries to modify the program according to this new architecture. The architectural and program modifications do not try to make the system completely new. We are glad, if we have eliminated the most important weak points and, furthermore, if we have a chance to make future modifications in direction of extending the system, integrate it with other systems, or alike.

We call this approach *modification in the large* (or *coarse*). It was shown that by reverse and reengineering we get rid of many unnecessary technical details /Cr 00/, which hinder adaptability and further maintenance, see ch. 9. Now, the above steps of fig. 3.1 can possibly follow.

Embedded Systems

As second example we regard a possible *architecture sequence* from the domain *embedded systems*, see fig. 3.2. The first step again is to design the logical architecture, which is free from details. Then, the sequence of changes in direction of details can start.

Embedded systems are usually concurrent from their nature. So, the second step is to specify which parts of the architecture may run concurrently. Thus, we add annotations which parts are *processes* and which other parts need a *synchronization* protocol /BF 95/, as they are accessible by these processes.

Embedded systems usually run forever. Thus, they have to be explicitly started and they have to be explicitly shut down. Starting means to wake up and start the internal processes and shutting down to finalize them and to stop them. Therefore, *explicit start* and *explicit stop* need further technical processes and further communication in order to do the job. The design of that part is done in step 3.

An embedded system may also need an *emergency handling*, which immediately shuts down the system in dangerous situations. This avoids that the underlying technical system (a chemical plant, a production line, etc.) gets damaged. The emergency handling cares about these situations (pressure too high, temperature out of limit), shuts down the usual execution in order to care about these possible damages. Therefore, it acts according to the scheme to minimize the damage. The result of step 4 includes this emergency handling.

Embedded systems usually run on a distributed infrastructure. This *distribution* has to be specified. So, we define distribution lines and the *deployment* of the different parts in step 5.

As mentioned above, due to distribution *technical concurrency* may come up (further processes, further synchronization), which is formulated in step 6.

Finally, having the system deployed and integrated and carried out the first efficiency test, it becomes clear that some efficiency transformations must be done. If they are not restricted to the bodies of components, then the architecture of the system has to be modified in step 7.

At the end of this transformation sequence, we see again how the final architecture looks like. This final architecture shows the technical details of the system, which is shipped to the customers.

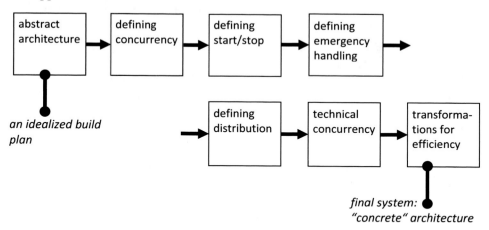

Fig. 3.2: Architecture sequence for an embedded system

Using processes and synchronization has advantages: We can better control the concurrency at runtime. The disadvantage is that this type of development is rather complicated. Therefore, in practice solutions are built, which often use a *fixed scheduling* by *fixed control loops*. In this case, a control process masters all the interactions of the child processes. This usually makes handling of start/ stop and also of emergency handling easier. By using fixed control loops, we get a different architecture in step 2, and also a different architectural sequence from this step on. We do not discuss this here.

Summing up: Again, similar to the BA example of above, we get a sequence of steps, starting from the logical architecture and ending with a physical architecture. Comparing to the steps of fig. 3.1 we see: The steps are different, and also how they are ordered.

In the above discussions of figs. 3.1 and 3.2, we have a *linear* development on architecture level from left to right. The architectures are developed in a *top-down* manner, from abstract to detailed. This is never the case in practice. There, we find backtracking steps (going back to try something different) and iterations (cycles, until the right solution is found). Therefore, the above discussion describes an ideal situation.

Again, there might be *further steps*, before we can start with the abstract software architecture of the embedded system. If the automation and control software is for a new and specialized chemical plant, the *design of this plant* has to be started in advance. It also consists of different steps, from abstract to detailed and concrete.

Alternatively, an embedded system for a specific production line has been built several times. However, it has to be extended. Furthermore, there are demands for quality improvements. So in this case, some *reverse and reengineering steps* have to take place before the *extension*. After the extension, the architecture sequence according to fig. 3.2 can start.

There are two further extensions, we do not discuss here. (a) One is that we do not develop one system, but a family of systems /Ja 00, PB 05/. Any member of the family will have a different and specific architecture sequence, as that of fig. 3.2. In addition, there is the *family architecture*, expressing the commonalities of the family. There are specific considerations afterwards to *derive the member of the family*.

(b) Embedded systems in the automation and control domain are in close connection to other systems for monitoring, for quality control, for integrating the embedded system into the company organization, etc. Therefore, the embedded system is connected upward to *further layers* building up the automation pyramid, see ch. 4. The architecture of the embedded system is connected to other architectures via *corresponding interfaces*.

3.3 Characterization: Order, Rules, and Consequences

Technical Details Should not Drive the Design

In industrial practice, we find quite often that (*technical*) *details* drive the development of systems, especially in the case of embedded systems. The problem is that these details might change. In this case, the development and – especially the design – has to be backtracked. Changes occur more often than forward development. So, *changes* of these technical details, cause many *problems* and consequently *costs*. Therefore, the underlying principle of the order in the above sequences is that details do not determine the solution.

This does not mean that details are unimportant. It only means that *details* should be introduced in the *right place* and at the right time. Furthermore, we should mention, that a solution is rarely found in a top-down and linear way, as both figs. 3.1 and 3.2 suggest. There are backtracking, cycles and spirals, as known in software engineering. Both figures describe the *ideal situation*, which rarely exists in practice.

The important *aspects*, which play a role in both examples, are structure, semantics, concurrency, explicit control, distribution, deployment, and efficiency.

Order and Principles

What are the underlying *principles*, which determine the order of the architectures in the sequences of figs. 3.1 and 3.2? What is left of what and what is right of what? What are the corresponding *rules* we should apply to determine the order of architectures within the sequences?

(A) From more *abstract to* more *concrete*

The logical architecture is the most abstract form in both examples. Therefore, it appears on the left side of figs. 3.1 and 3.2. An abstract architecture can have different concurrency solutions, a concurrency solution may have different solutions for explicit start/ stop, and so on. Thus, they are placed at the right side. Also, defining concurrency, explicit start/ stop, and emergency handling is left of defining distribution in fig. 3.2.

(B) From *basic* knowledge *to additions* in form of annotations or supplements

Defining distribution in fig. 3.1 depends on the logical architecture and there might be different ways for defining distribution for the same logical architecture. To explicitly organize start/ stop, we need the concurrent architecture. Defining explicit emergency handling needs start/ stop definition before, as an emergency case might appear in the initialization. Additions can have quite different purposes: It might be that the addition gives more *preciseness* (e.g. semantics), it might indicate a *way to follow* (annotation), or it might realize a certain way *for a solution* (thereby introducing the corresponding realization details).

(C) From less to more probable to change, so from *stable to more changeable*

A transformation to improve efficiency is more probable to happen than defining distribution. The latter is more probable than defining concurrency. Most stable is the logical architecture. We see: Stability appears left, changes appear right.

(D) From an *artifact to* a *depending one*

Technical concurrency depends on how the distribution was defined, see fig. 3.2. Defining concurrency depends on how the logical architecture was designed. Many further examples exist.

(E) From *early to late decisions*

The best examples of figs. 3.1 and 3.2 for late decisions are the efficiency transformations. They are placed at the right side, as they should be addressed at the end of the development process: On the one hand, because they should be applied late, as any change induces that they probably have to be done again. On the other hand, all efficiency transformations take all architectural aspects into account, which have been regarded before.

Consequences

Following the above rules by ordering architecture sequences has some *implications*. We mention two of them.

They *lessen* the *width of backtracking*. Backtracking means to go back to the place where a change has to take place and to modify from this place on. As more probable changes are right of less probable ones, we reduce the width of a backtracking step. Looking on fig. 3.2: If the efficiency transformation was wrong, the probability is high that we take another one. This is more probable than defining the distribution/ deployment differently. This, again, is more probable than modifying the logical architecture.

The order of the architectures *delivers* what is *more general* (more left) or what is *more specific* (more right). Thinking in these categories "general" or "specific" improves the design and development process. The more general aspects are concentrated at the level of logical architectures. All aspects of the following architectures at the right should not be covered or predetermined by the logical architecture. This argument can be applied to all of the following architectures. For example, defining concurrency should not care about start/ stop or emergency handling.

3.4 The Refined Business Administration Example

The Logical Architecture in a Sketch

The logical architecture of the BA example was worked out in a cooperation with Aachen Münchener Insurance Company (now Generali), especially those parts which are described below. The example is an *interactive system*, preparing and completing an insurance contract in the back office of the company

We present the structure of the logical *architecture* here only as a *sketch* to keep it simple, see fig. 3.3. It consists of an UI part, a dialog control part, the main business functions, and the access to data stored in specific files or in the underlying data base system.

(i) The *UI part* is responsible for inputting the data of the insurance customer. Usually, the data are checked for correctness or plausibility. The other parts of the system should not know anything about the UI layout and other specifics. Only the selected command and its parameters for IO should be visible.

(ii) The *dialog control part* of the system is independent of the UI part, but also of how the business functions are realized.

(iii) The main *business functions* are independent of the way they are invoked (UI and Control) and independent of how the data of the system are internally stored. They see the data in a realization independent form via data abstraction interfaces.

(iv) The *data* are finally stored in specific *files* and/ or in a *data base system*, following a certain data base approach and stored in a specific way. This should not be seen at the interface.

(v) Trivially, the UI part and the data part are separated.

The *logical architecture* of fig. 3.3 was the result of a *reverse* and a *reengineering* step /Cr 00/, which is discussed later in ch. 9. The aim was to overcome the following weaknesses of the old system: (a) The primitive UI specifics were visible within the business functions, (b) control of the dialog and business functions were not clearly separated, (c) the specifics, how the data are stored were visible within the functions. The original 'architecture' (the structure of the program) was by no means an abstract one. The reverse and reengineering steps delivered the logical architecture of fig. 3.1 in the form sketched in fig. 3.3.

A *semantics definition* could have been used in the example, as shown in fig. 3.1. The semantics of (some of) the main business functions in a pre and post condition form could have been specified. Furthermore, a trace semantics for the system could have been used to define the execution paths. Finally, algebraic semantics /BH 85, EM 89, Gu 76, LZ 74/ could have been used for some parts of the data interface.

In step 3 of fig. 3.1 the *distribution of the application* is determined. (i) We specify the possible distribution lines between the separate parts by annotations, see again fig. 3.3 and there the yellow lines. (ii) Then, we add the corresponding components, either basic or generated, according to a distribution platform, as e.g. COR-BA /COR 20/, in fig.3.3. The resulting distributed architecture is not shown. Finally, we (iii) deploy the different parts on different computers. Typically, the UI part is placed on a thin client, the control part and the business functions on a function server (mainframe) and the data part on data servers (mainframe). This distribution is possible for the abstract architecture as we separated the different aspects of the dialog system (parts for UI, control, business functions, and data). This would not have been possible for the 'architecture' of the original system (the code structure) before the reverse and reengineering steps, due to their unnecessary and tight coupling and corresponding dependencies due to many details. In addition, it may be necessary that the functions or the data services are replicated and placed on different machines, due to reasons of security or efficiency. In this case, we might have different function servers and different data servers.

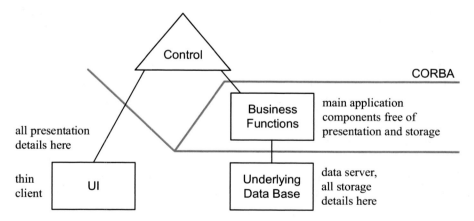

Fig. 3.3: A sketch of the business administration system: logical architecture with distribution annotations

As now different function(s) may be on different machines and try to get access on data services on other machine(s), we get into concurrency problems, although the application is not concurrent from its nature. We called this *technical concurrency* (step 4 in fig. 3.1). We have to define a synchronization protocol. This, again, is not shown in fig. 3.3.

Fig. 3.3 contains a sketch of the logical architecture with distribution annotations. The CORBA components according to deployment on different machines /Kl 00/ are not shown. The same is true for the concurrency aspects due to distribution.

Eventual Changes

The *UI part* can have different forms: other UI style, a different UI management system, other commands of similar form, other client (e.g. thick client for extensively checking data). This all should not (or only little) affect the main part of the application. Therefore, the UI part should abstract from these details.

In the same way, the *data part* should be freed from details: How are the underlying data built up in files, which database systems are used, which schema is used for the data, and alike. There should be a data abstraction interface, which hides all these details. The main part of the program should only know what is necessary from the application side. So, we use data abstraction of different forms.

As already told, we may have different function and data servers, and also the distribution of them on different machines. *Distribution* and *change of distribution* is only possible, if there is loose coupling between the parts on different machines. This loose coupling is achieved by the various forms of abstraction being applied to both sides of a separation line, as sketched above.

Another possibility for a big change is the cooperation of a *program for insurance agents* and the *back office solution* of above. The agent gets the available and interesting information of the back office, enriches this information, and delivers is back to the back office as preliminary and not completely verified. This avoids that the back office has to input these data again. It now concentrates on the verification of the input data and the completion part for the contract.

Adaptability, which was discussed in this subsection, demands for abstraction. Not important details should be hidden, as data, layout, style, UI systems used, schema definition details, etc. This all is *data abstraction* if we define "data" in a more general sense.

Starting with an Existing Program

As already mentioned, the starting point of our cooperation with the insurance company was not the logical architecture of fig. 3.3. We now shortly characterize the reverse and reengineering activities. We *started with* a huge and *old COBOL program* on the mainframe, being connected to hundreds of "non-intelligent" terminals, all UI properties and details to be seen in the program, main business functions appear within the interwoven program, and the program knew all the details of the underlying storage of data. How to reorganize this program without to start to program completely new from scratch. The investigation was carried out within a Doctoral Thesis /Cr 00/, see ch. 9.

It started with *reverse engineering*, i.e. understanding the big program and finding out the 'architecture' and its essential parts. The aim was to preserve these parts and to reuse them, without using the evident weaknesses of it.

Then came the important part of *reengineering*: (a) building a *new UI part* and make it in a way that all details are in the UI system. The interface of it is completely free of details (how to invoke a command and to get its data) and makes the rest of the program UI independent. (b) The *data* part got a *new and abstract interface*. (c) The COBOL program was freed from UI and data access details and separated business functions from control of the dialog. So, we could identify the essential business functions. They all got a new interface.

Reengineering was applied by reorganizing the program and making it better in its internal structure. At the same time, we aimed at getting the code of the old program which we can reuse. We called this approach „Reverse and Reengineering in the Large (or in the Coarse)". Big parts of the COBOL program are saved but in another form (without UI details, without data details, clear separation of functions (activities) and manipulation of the underlying data).

All the *reorganization* steps of this subsection *yield the logical architecture* of fig. 3.3. However, the internal structure of the business functions and the data access was to a big part saved from the COBOL program, we started with. So, they were not completely reengineered.

3.5 A Refined Embedded Example

We take an *example*, now from the system class embedded systems. We look on the architecture of this example and give a sketch of some of the *architecture's forms* of the sequence in fig. 3.2. The example is from the *automotive* domain and contains some simplifications. In this section, we discuss the relation to architectural series. For other aspects of embedded systems, as adaptation, see ch. 4.

The domain is quite specific which makes it interesting for the argumentation of this chapter. In ch. 4 the case of embedded software for mechanical or chemical production is studied. In /NW 99, NM08/, tools for production processes are studied, which are not regarded here. We come back to the specific characteristics of automotive embedded systems after we have discussed the corresponding sequence of software architectures.

Software Architectures

The *logical software architecture* of the embedded system (step 1 of fig. 3.2) contains components and their dependencies. It is *abstract*, i.e. the architecture contains no specifics, they are determined later, see fig. 3.2 and ch. 4. Abstractions correspond to functional abstractions or data abstractions, i.e. the realization in both cases is below of a *clear* functional or data abstraction *interface*. Later on, we discuss that this logical architecture is the result of a transformation process.

Step 2 of fig. 3.2 determines the *concurrency properties* of the system. This is specified by saying, which components are processes (potentially parallel) and determine their cooperation and competition by synchronizations. For example, if different processes try to get access to some data component expressing a state information, we determine a synchronization protocol for the accesses to that component (e.g. mutual exclusion of the operations).

In embedded systems in the automotive domain, often a *simpler process and synchronization scheme* is applied, as these processes are assigned to different control units to be executed there. The reaction of a process in a certain time is guaranteed by counting the execution times of dependent components and assuring that the sum of these times is less than the wanted execution time. Furthermore, priority rules are defined in order to avoid that an urgent or critical process is hindered.

A *simpler* scheme is also used for *start/ stop* (step 3). Whenever the car is unlocked, the components of the body part of the software are waked up, when it is locked, the body part of the car is switched off. Whenever the engine part is started, the corresponding components of motor control, drive control, etc. are waked up. Whenever the motor is switched off, the corresponding components are switched off. This scheme works quite well as the components belong to different areas (body, motor, driving), which are separated and work together via clear interfaces.

Emergency handing (step 4) is also realized in a *simpler* way, either by a stable mechanical solution, e.g. for steering or braking the car. The car has to be stopped immediately and the driver gets an alarm. It is more sophisticated, if steering or braking is done by wire.

Distribution and Deployment

After the modifications as described above, the logical architecture is transformed into a distributed solution (step 5 of fig. 3.2). After the *distribution* lines are identified (analogous to those of fig. 3.3), the architecture is deployed on the so-called *physical architecture*. This physical architecture consists of control units, connected by buses. The control units are different, on one hand because they realize quite different functionalities in size and corresponding requirements. On the other hand, they are determined by subcontractors of the OEM. Control units belonging to one problem area (as motor control) build up a subnet, which might have a specific form and protocol. These subnets are connected by gateways.

The physical architectures can *vary*, even for the same model of a car. There are different variants according to the number of features of this variant. There may be more or fewer control units or such of possibly different computational power, and more elaborated or poorer subnets. So, there are *software architectures* which reflect a *rich functionality* and, accordingly have a *rich physical architecture*. Similarly, an architecture with a poorer functionality can have a poorer related physical architecture.

In any case, there is a balance between the software architecture and its related physical architecture. They are usually *developed "in parallel"*. The physical architecture has to answer physical, efficiency, and security aspects and restrictions. The physical architecture is built up according to *experiences* gained in the *past*.

Different parts of the software architecture are usually *distributed*. The first step is to determine, which parts are to be placed on different hardware. In this first step, we do not say on which hardware the components are deployed. Instead, we determine by an *annotation*, that a subarchitecture or software component is placed differently, but possibly nearby.

In the next step, a subarchitecture or a software component is assigned to a certain control unit of a certain bus to be placed there, which is called *deployment*. It may be, due to logical relationship (like for motor control), due to efficiency (this part has a higher internal traffic, or this subarchitecture is too much for one control unit), or due to economic reasons (a control unit has open place and available runtime resources) that this assignment is split: one part on this control unit, the other on another unit. Therefore, this deployment is complicated and error-prone if it is made manually. Please recall that this deployment can be different for different variants of a model.

Deployment is facilitated by the AUTomotive Open System ARchitecture (*AU-TOSAR*) *approach* /AU 20/. Here, several programming tasks (as routing through the network, introducing the program parts for a control unit which listen to the bus to find out, what is essential for this unit or, conversely, to put results of a unit computation on the bus again) are done in a semi-automatic way, i.e. the code is generated according to some specifications by AUTO-SAR. That is an enormous progress to the situation before, where these code parts had to be written and deployed individually.

This approach provides *flexibility in the deployment subprocess*. This flexibility is necessary to handle the many variants of deployments according to the variants of functionality. It also makes backtracking steps easier, which occur after detected errors in a development process. Finally, it also eases reuse in the software between car model families.

Characteristics of the Domain and Different Starting Points

There are *various internal problems* connected to *automotive systems*: The target system (hardware architecture /Ta 12/) consists (a) of about 50 or more control units. These control units are connected (b) by different networks, for example for body control, motor control, drive control, etc. These networks have different protocols and are connected by gateways. Due to the big number of variants (many or few features) of a model, (c) the hardware architecture can vary as well (number of control units). This is also true for the software (number and size of software components). A general problem, therefore (d) is the distribution (together or distributed) and where to be located (deployment). Thus, (e) it is an enormous problem to keep the development of solutions together, from the capability and efficiency point of view. Even harder (f) is the reuse problem, namely to save and apply the knowledge of solutions from one model change to the successor or from model to another model, as OEMs usually start first with more expensive models and later transfer to cheaper ones. Finally, (g) there is a current trend to reduce the number of control units (less and bigger ones) in connection to electrification of cars. Another trend is to produce uniform solutions in big automotive companies, which have different brands. In the long run, this might simplify the solutions, in the short run, it produces further problems as a complex solution has to be transformed to another structure.

How to solve such a complicated problem? It seems reasonable to start with an abstract description of the solution, which is free of the specific details of (a) to (g). We call this a *conceptual architecture*. This architecture is a *network* of functionalities/ *services*, where the connections correspond to data transfer of parameters, to control transfer (subfunction of, or one function after the other), and to synchronization (all next functions in parallel or in a controlled schedule). Thus, connections represent dependencies, the network is a dependency graph (a dataflow-oriented approach). This network should be abstract, i.e. independent of how to transform functionalities and connections into software and where to place it on hardware.

Now, the *logical architecture* is developed (step 1 of fig. 3.2), which *transforms* the conceptual architecture to a software architecture consisting of components and relations. This software architecture has at the beginning an abstract form, and gets more and more detailed and concrete, see above.

What are the *transformation rules* between the conceptual architecture and the (abstract) software architecture? A functionality of the conceptual architecture can be mapped on a software component. It can also be that a function is mapped on more software components together with the relations between these components, so on a software subarchitecture. Finally, different functionalities together with their relations (a subarchitecture of the conceptual architecture) can be mapped on one software component. Thus, the transformation is not necessarily one to one. The reason is that the conceptual architecture contains services, whereas the software architecture delivers the structure of a program system, which realizes these services.

Modeling on the level of services (conceptual architecture) and on the level of software components (logical architecture) should have a *similar granularity*. The conceptual model should not contain functionalities of a fine-grained level. In that case, the model is more a too detailed requirements specification or a detailed realization and not a conceptual model. Thereby, the software architecture would contain many software components, which compose the realization of conceptual components.

Again, we could have started with an *existing solution*, as above in the BA example. Then, reverse and reengineering steps would be necessary, to improve the solution and to make it ready for modifications and extensions. This way was followed for an embedded system from the domain communication systems for cell phones in /Ma 05, Mo 09, Re 10/, see ch. 9.

In /Me 12/ there is another starting point by looking on different *feature variants* and developing different conceptual architectures for these variants. The start with a variability model helps in finding out the commonalities and differences of variants. The focus of /Me 12/ was to master the variability problem. A further and *bottom-up approach* was taken in /Ar 10, Ki 05, No 07/ for embedded systems in the field Smart Homes. Different eHome systems were built, on top of simple functions/ features offering novel functionalities.

3.6 Requirements for the Underlying Architectural Language(s)

If we look on different software architectures /SAD, Sc 13, SEI 10/, there are *obvious requirements* for the used and underlying architecture language(s). (a) The language(s) should contain elements to express all the different aspects and views, as discussed here in sects. 3.2 to 3.5, see also ch. 2. (b) It should be clear how these different aspects/ views are related to each other. This is not the case for UML /BR 05/, which is a collection of separate and rather nonrelated languages. The situation is much better for subsets /Ru 11, Ru 12/ (c) The best is, if the language elements belong to one and uniform architecture language, se again ch. 2. If we have different languages, e.g. another language for annotations, it must be clear and obvious, to which part of an artifact the annotations belongs.

Within the architectures discussed above we find different parts; see /Na 90-22/ and chs. 1 and 2. The biggest and basic part belongs to *modeling* the *logical architecture* and there to *define the static structure*. For that static structure we have *components* of different kinds (functional or data abstraction, objects or types) and of different size (modules or subsystems). Components have interfaces according to kind and size. Between components we have different *structure* relations (local to, is a), and also different *import relations* (local, general, and inheritance import). Consistency conditions define the context sensitive syntax rules. There are *method rules* and *patterns* of different kinds giving hints how to use the language. The pattern discussion is broader than usual /BM 96, GH 95, SS 00/, as here different architectures (fig. 3.2), changes within a specific form and changes from form to form, are involved. The presentation is *graphical* for surveys and *textual* for details.

Further notations are necessary, for defining the *semantics*, for *concurrency*, for *distribution, deployment*, etc. It can even be shown that the notations for architectural *styles* /SG 96/ can be expressed by the aforementioned language concepts, see ch. 5. Therefore, these style notations can be used as abbreviations without escaping from the architecture language concepts.

In ch. 2, it was also shown that the above language and methodology *approach* is *integrative* in its nature. Many of the different and necessary parts for expressing aspects and views are found within one architecture language. The others are expressed by annotations inside of artifacts written in the language. It is always clear what these annotations belong to.

3.7 Summary, Messages, and Outlook

Summary and Messages

The output of a design and realization process for a software system is a *complex configuration* containing different abstractions, views, enrichments, which all deliver different information and details, see ch. 1. We find also different hierarchies within artifacts and between artifacts. In this chapter, we *concentrated* on the *architecture part*, which, although being a part of the overall configuration, has the same characteristics as the overall configuration.

That architectural configuration contains *more than one architectural description*. We have shown that the descriptions should be organized in different stages and that the order of these stages must be planned carefully. The order reflects abstraction, probability of changes, minimization of backtracking steps, and alike.

In this chapter, we have discussed *two examples*, one from the domain business administration and one from the domain embedded systems. In this sense, this chapter is the application of chs. 1 and 2, where we introduced the integrative approach for architecture modeling, as the architecture sequence for reflecting different aspects is one of the integration dimensions, which need different notations which are also integrated. This means that different aspects of an architecture have to be denoted and that the mutual relations of these parts have to be obvious. We call this *integration* within an *architectural language and methodology*.

We also gave some *rules* in order to find the order in the architecture sequences. The right *order supports* the *adaptability* of the system and the *consistency* of the different architectural descriptions.

Further problems, which also have to do with different aspects of architectures were not addressed in this chapter: as (i) *families of systems*, where we have to master their commonalities and differences, (ii) libraries of *reusable components* and their organization, or (iii) organizing *reuse* in building successively systems of a *certain application domain or structure*.

Outlook

The order of sequences in figs. 3.1 and 3.2 obviously depends on certain *aspects*: (a) What is the *structure class* of the system to be developed or maintained (batch, interactive, embedded)? (b) What is the *application domain* (business administration, etc.)? What is the hardware and software *infrastructure* (from one big computer to somewhere in the internet) the system is to run on? See the classification discussion in sect. 4 of ch. 2. For all these aspects: Can we give more *specific rules* to *order the sequences of architectures*, than those given in sect. 3?

In this chapter, we argued in a rather statical manner by looking only on one system. However, there are *dimensions*, which have a longer range of time and, therefore, also their architectural sequences: (i) Discuss *maintenance/ extension*, by looking not only on one system, but also on the history of a system in a longer period, from reverse engineering, ..., to integrating the system with others to extend the system. (ii) Do not regard only one system, but a *family of systems*. Essential knowledge you do not get top-down, you get it bottom-up. Starting with one system, you recognize a similarity within following systems until you end up with a clear family development approach. (iii) The same is true for *reuse*, especially if you try to abandon shallow reuse (like doing it the same way as the last time) and to reach *deep reuse* (like generation of code instead of handcrafting the code). In all these cases (i) to (iii), you have many architectures in a long-term maintenance/ family/ reuse project. What is the *effect on the architectural sequences*?

3.8 References

/Ar 10/ Armac, I.: Personalized eHome Systems (in German), Doct. Diss. RWTH Aachen University , 315 pp., (2010)

/AU 20/ AUTOSAR: Automotive Open System Architecture, http://www.autosar.org/ (2020)

/BF 95/ Buhr, P./ Fortier, M. et al.: Monitor classification, ACM Computing Surveys 27 (1): 63–107 (1995)

/BH 85/ Bergstra, J.A./ Heering, J./ Klint, J.: Algebraic Specification, EATCS Monographs on Theoretical Computer Science, Vol. 6, Springer 1985)

/BM 96/ Buschmann, F./ Meunier, R. et al.: Pattern-oriented Software Architecture- A System of Patterns, Wiley (1996):

/Bö 94/ Börstler, J.: Programming in the large: Languages, Tools, Reuse (in German), Doct. Diss. RWTH Aachen University, 205 pp. (1994)

/BR 05/ Booch, G./ Rumbaugh, J. et al.: The Unified Modeling Language User Guide, Addison Wesley (2005)

/COR 20/ https://www.omg.org/spec/CORBA/About-CORBA/ (2020)

/Cr 00/ Cremer, K.: Graph-based Tools for Reverse and Reengineering (in German), Doct. Diss., RWTH Aachen University, 220 pp. (2000)

/ET 08/ Eastman, C./ Teicholz, P./ Sacks, R./ Liston, K.: BIM Handbook. John Wiley & Sons, 2008

/EM 89/ Ehrig, H./ Mahr, B.: Algebraic Specification, Academic Press (1989)

/GH 95/ Gamma, E./ Helm, R./ Johnson, R./Vlissides, J.: Design Patterns: Elements of Reusable Object-Oriented Software, 395 pp. Addison Wesley (1995)

/GS 94/ Garlan, D./ Shaw, M.: An Introduction to Software Architectures, TR CMU-CS-94-166 (1994)

/Gu 76/ Guttag, J.: Abstract Data Types and the Development of Data Structures, Comm. ACM 20, 6, 396-404 (1977)

/Ja 00/ Jazayeri, M. et al. (eds.): Software Architecture for Product Families, Addison Wesley (2000)

/Ki 05/ Kirchhof, M.: Integrated Low Cost eHome Systems – Processes and Infrastructures (in German), Doct. Diss. RWTH Aachen University, 331 pp. (2005)

/Kl 00/ Klein, P.: Architecture Modeling of Distributed and Concurrent Software Systems Doct. Diss. RWTH Aachen University, 237pp. (2000)

/KN 07/ Kraft, B./ Nagl, M.: Visual Knowledge Specification for Conceptual Design: Definition and Tools Support, Journ. Adv. Engg. Informatics 21, 1, 67-83 (2007)

/Kr 07/ Kraft, B.: Semantic support for the conceptual design of buildings (in German), Doct. Diss., RWTH Aachen University, 381 pp. (2007)

/Le 88/ Lewerentz, C.: Concepts and Tools for the Interactive Design of Large Software Systems (in German), Doct. Diss., 179 pp. RWTH Aachen University, Informatik-Fachberichte 194, Springer (1988)

/LZ 74/ Liskow, B./ Zilles, S.: Specification Techniques for Data Abstractions, Int. Conf. on Reliable Software, 72-87, IEEE (1975)

/Ma 05/ Marburger, A.: Reverse Engineering of Complex Legacy Telecommunication Systems, Doct. Diss., RWTH Aachen University, 418 pp. (2005)

/Me 12/ Mengi, C.: Automotive Software – Processes, Models, and Variability (in German), Doct. Diss., RWTH Aachen University, 350 pp. (2012)

/Mo 09/ Mosler, Ch.: Graph-based Reengineering of Telecommunication Systems (in German), Doct. Diss. RWTH Aachen University, 268 pp., RWTH Aachen University (2009)

/Na 90-22/ Nagl, M.: Software Engineering- Methodological Programming in the Large (in German), 387 pp., Springer (1990), plus further extensions for a lecture on Software Architectures 1990 - 2020

/Na 99/ Nagl, M. (ed.): Building Tightly Integrated Software Development Environments - The IPSEN Approach, LNCS 1170, 709 pp., Springer (1999)

/NM 08/ Nagl, M./ Marquardt, W. (eds.): Collaborative and Distributed Chemical Engineering – From Understanding to Substantial Design Process Support, IMPROVE, LNCS 4970, 851 pp., Springer (2008)

/No 07/ Norbisrath, U.: Configuring eHome Systems (in German), Doct. Diss. RWTH Aachen, 286 pp. (2007)

/NW 99/ Nagl, M./ Westfechtel, B. (eds.): Integration of Development Systems in Engineering Applications – Substantial Improvement of Development Processes (in German), 440 pp., Springer (1999)

/PB 05/ Pohl, K./ Böckle, G. et al.: Software Product Line Engineering, 467 pp., Springer (2005)

/PD 07/ Pollet, D./ Ducasse, S. et al.: Towards a Process-Oriented Software Architecture Reconstruction Taxonomy, Proc. 11th European CSMR 07, 137-148 (2007)

/Re 10/ Retkowitz, D.: Software Support for Adaptive eHome Systems (in German), Doct. Diss. RWTH Aachen University, 354 pp. (2010)

/Ru 11/ Rumpe, B.: Modeling with UML (in German), 2nd ed., 293 pp., Springer (2011)

/Ru 12/ Rumpe, B.: Agile Modeling with UML (in German), 2nd ed., 372 pp. Springer (2012)

/SAD/ Software Architecture and Design Tutorial, TutorialRide.com, https://www.tutorialride.com/software-architecture-and-design/software-architecture-and-design-tutorial.htm

/Sc 13/ Schmidt, R.F.: Software Engineering – Architecture-driven Software Development, 376 pp. Elsevier (2013)

/SEI 10/ Software Engineering Institute of CMU: What Is Your Definition of Software Architecture, https://resources.sei.cmu.edu/library/asset-view.cfm?assetID=513807

/SG 96/ Shaw, M./ Garlan, D.: Software architecture: perspectives on an emerging discipline. Prentice Hall (1996)

/SS 00/ Schmidt, D./ Stal, M. et al.: Pattern-oriented Software Architectures, vol 2, Patterns for Concurrent and Networked Objects, Wiley (2000)

/Ta 12/ Tanenbaum, A.S.: Computernetzwerke, 5th ed., Pearson (2012)

4 Embedded Systems: Rules to Improve Adaptability

Manfred Nagl

Software Engineering, RWTH Aachen University, nagl@cs.rwth-aachen.de

Abstract

Embedded systems have specific properties, which are consequences of the application domain, namely the close connection to the underlying technical system, the specific challenges of the development process, the mixture of persons involved in their development, etc. Thus, adaptability (portability, extensibility, and changeability) is more difficult compared to other types of software systems.

The chapter addresses the question, what we can be do to improve adaptability of embedded systems. We study different examples of embedded systems. A series of hints is given. Most of them are related to the abstract architecture, i.e. the first result of the design process. The hints are also helpful for other higher-level tasks, such as integration of embedded systems, developing families of embedded systems, finding opportunities for reuse, and alike.

Key words: embedded systems, dependency of the technical system, adaptability of corresponding software architectures, data and functional abstraction in a generalized sense, variability of the solutions, list of hints for adaptability and variability

4.1 Introduction

Embedded software systems /BL 18, Ma 21/ have specific *characteristics*: (i) They live for a long time (20 years and more), they (ii) run "forever" (until they are explicitly stopped, accordingly they have to be started explicitly), they are (iii) highly dependent on the surrounding technical system they are controlling, and they sometimes have (iv) specific parts for emergency handling. They have (v) to be efficient and react in short time, they (vi) mostly have to address concurrency. They (vii) are developed together with engineers, in some cases only or mostly by engineers. There are (viii) many technical details in the hardware/ software solution, which dominate the solution, as corresponding abstractions are not introduced in the design and development of the system. Finally, (ix) many variations corresponding to functionality, structure, and realization of the technical system are possible. The same applies to the software part. (x) Families of systems and not only one system are sometimes the goal.

Adaptability is difficult for *hardware*. Hardware is not easy to change, in many cases it is easier to build it newly. *Software* can more easily be changed, if it is built in the right way. In many cases, software is designed and constructed in too close connection to hardware, and thereby inherits the property of inflexibility. This chapter gives some hints in the direction, what has to be regarded to make the software part adaptable, thereby also improving the adaptability of the overall embedded system. The key are suitable activities on architecture level /BK 03, GS 94, HK 07, KM 04, Ru 12, Sc 13, SEI 10, SG 96, SS 00/.

Engineers on one side and IT specialists/ computer science people on the other have run through a different education. Therefore, they follow a different mental approach to achieve a solution. A combination of both approaches – thinking in complex technical details on one hand and trying to abstract from details to cover situations, where changes are probable, does improve adaptability. To demonstrate this, is the most important goal of this chapter. The problems adaptability, flexibility, and variability have to be addressed at the beginning of the design and development process. They cannot be added afterwards.

This chapter has a specific goal and thus a special motivation, namely to give some hints for embedded systems' development in direction of achieving adaptability and mastering variability. There are many publications and books for general knowledge on the fundamentals, foundations, and methodology of new modeling approaches, as e.g. /PB 16, PH 12/. This chapter is the embedded systems' supplement of a general software architecture approach /Na 82-03, Na 90/.

The *chapter is structured as follows*: In sect. 4.2, we discuss a small embedded system on one microcontroller (programmable logical controller, in short PLC) and show, what has to be done for adaptability. Then, we step forward to more complex systems: (a) connected and distributed systems in sect. 3 (as software in automotive), (b) layered systems (like software for a chemical plant) in sect. 4. The summary of sect. 5 contains a list of problems to be addressed in embedded system construction for adaptability in an improved process. The hints given here are important when designing the more abstract logical architecture, before technical details are studied. All hints are of specific value for a mixed developer crew of engineers and IT specialists. In sect. 6, we discuss lessons learned and open problems.

4.2 Simple Example: A Coffee Maker

The Design as Usual

We start out with a *simple solution*, a coffee machine where the control hardware is only one microcontroller. You see the hardware solution in fig. 4.1.a, the software design as usual in 4.1.b, and the design regarding adaptability in fig. 4.2. Although the example is small, we can learn some basic rules from it.

The *hardware* is shown in fig. 4.1.a. There is a grinder to provide coffee powder. The amount is regulated by a volume sensor. A tilter transports the powder down to the brewing region. Water is contained in a reservoir, where a water level sensor says, when to refill. A pump takes the water out of the reservoir, such that it flows through a heating pipe, regulated by a flowmeter. The plunge opens the way for the hot water to flow through the powder, in order to brew the coffee. After brewing, the used coffee falls down into the tray container. The open tray sensor indicates, when it has to be emptied.

The *user panel* consists of four function buttons: To start the machine, to produce a small or a big cup, and to clean the machine. There are four warning lamps: coffee beans missing, water missing, the tray container full, and clean machine.

Fig. 4.1.b shows a *(wrong) software solution, without* looking for *adaptability*. We recognize that the software 1:1 maps the hardware. On the bottom level, we see the components as used physical devices, or corresponding sensors/ actuators. The hardware solution can easily be seen from the software solution.

What is wrong? All components are functional units, organized in a tree. Tasks are split into simpler tasks. Units reflect physical realizations, not abstract functionalities. Hardware is directly used, either by sensors, actuators, or physical components: water level sensor, pump, water container, etc. For these components, the very specific interface of the corresponding vendor is used. Standard user functions (order a small cup) are not separated from special functions (provided by the user, as "refill coffee beans" or "clean machine").

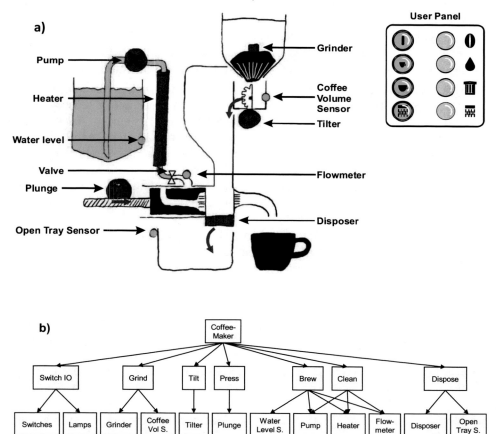

Fig. 4.1: A simple coffee maker: hardware outline and wrong software design

Changing Device Infrastructure, Physical Realization: Adaptable New Architecture

We now discuss *changes* of the machine's realization and their effects on the software solution of fig 4.1.b. We discuss the new software solution, see fig. 4.2.

Sensors and *actuators* usually have a *specific* and *vendor-dependent interface*. As no coffee machine producer likes to be bound to one producer for a part of the machine, the exchange of such sensors/ actuators should be simple. This is not the case in the design of fig. 4.1.b. The solution for this problem are abstract sensors/ actuators with physical or Boolean values at the interface (like temperature in degrees of Celsius, or is full, or grind 5 g). In the body of the component, we connect to the cryptic and vendor-specific interface form. Thus, the exchange of a device to that of another vendor is handled internally in the corresponding *abstract sensor/ actuator* component and, therefore, has no effect on upper components. By the way, all such sensor components are abstract data object (ado) components, as they organize a state. Actuators are functional components (fo). In /PK 09/ we find similar ideas, not for software architectures but for models in a model-driven scenario.

Also, the *physical realization* of the machine *might change*. For example, measuring coffee powder can alternatively be realized by a timer and a sensor for the speed of rotation, which goes up, if the container for beans is empty. Analogously, the amount of hot water can be measured by a timer instead of a flowmeter, if the water flows continuously. Or, the grinder part can be replaced by putting in a coffee tab. All such realization changes induce heavy changes in the wrong software design of fig. 4.1.b. The solution for such problems is to define *abstract functionality*. In this case, the realization can be replaced by a corresponding different one below of the interface. Again, the change does not go up in the architecture. An example is the preparation part, consisting of grinding, tilting, and plunging, see fig. 4.2. If we now use pads, then the components below of Preparing have to be exchanged, i.e. the subtree is exchanged. Of course, this means a bigger change of the hardware. In the software solution going up, the rest remains unchanged.

Changes of the *user interface* will also happen. There are trivial changes as, other invocation of user functions, by text, number, menu selection, speech input, etc. In the same way, warnings and messages can be output as texts, spoken words, warning signals, or melodies. More complex user interfaces can be built by making use of User Interface Management Systems, UI realization can go over different layers, and so on. This all is not regarded in the software design of fig. 4.1.b. The right solution also orders *input* and *output* in different *categories*, as user function input, warning output, waiting for user repair, or cleaning. Furthermore, there is a component for initialization and shutdown. These abstract inputs and outputs can be realized differently, which again, means to replace realizations in fig. 4.2. The three dots in fig. 4.2 indicate that further usability edges are necessary to realize the three functional components.

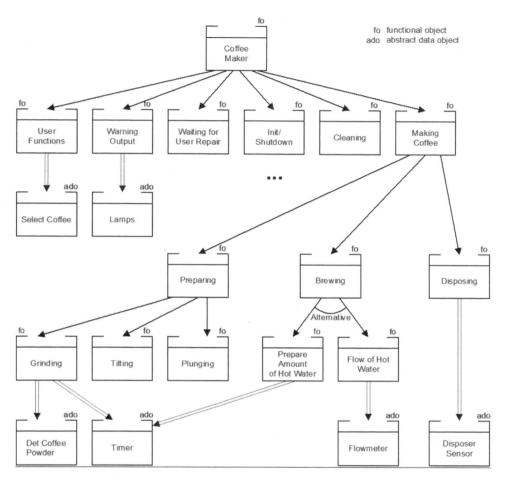

Fig. 4.2: The architecture regarding adaptability

A further goal is to have an architecture, which is also prepared for *bigger changes*, as to be *integrated* with others, or to be specialized such that specific *variants* can be easily built. Especially, the new architecture should open the way to *think in families* of systems and not only on one specific system. There is no producer of coffee machines, who only produces one type. They usually have different models in their catalog, which differ in functionality, realization, UI handling, and price. But the corresponding software systems share more or fewer parts. A good software architecture is the basis for thinking in and realizing families, and the family and its members are the basis for improving the software architecture. In the architecture, we should be able to identify the common parts of the family and to identify the specific and replaceable parts of the different family members.

Summing up, we see *improvements*: (a) by localizing the vendor details of sensors or actuators, (b) and by making such components' interfaces purely problem-dependent (as temperature values in °C). (c) We also use abstractions in the IO interfaces (independence of IO devices, of style, used UI systems, and grouping user activities). (d) We facilitate small changes of the physical realization (e.g. for the suitable weight of powder in grinding), or larger ones (different ways for brewing). Both, we get by finding abstract interfaces, below of which we can change. The change details do not go up. Altogether, the design of fig. 4.1 is tightly bound to details, which are likely to change.

The embedded system of above is trivial. We only have one control unit together with sensors and actuators for corresponding devices. Practical Solutions are bigger and much more complex: We might have a distributed solution across different hardware components, reaction time plays an important role, the solution for the embedded system can have concurrent components and thus need synchronization of these components in certain steps. We sketch examples of bigger systems below.

Conclusions

The key is to introduce *abstractions*. That means to introduce an *interface* for a component C in the architecture (see fig. 4.2), which does not rely on details and provides for *exchanging* the corresponding *realization* (in the body of C and the needed infrastructure below). This is used for abstractions of state details (how it is represented internally). This is called *data abstraction* (abstracting from the specific representation of values of sensors or UI structuring details). This is also used for abstracting from details of actuators and of physical realizations (grind 5 grams and leave it open, how this is physically realized). This is called *functional abstraction*. We see that any abstraction has two aspects: an abstract interface and a realization below of the interface. We also see that the realization is not restricted to the body of the C component, it can also include the realization infrastructure.

4.3 Realistic Example: Automotive Distributed Systems

All *aspects of above* are also *important* for more complex systems. The hints of above apply to them as well. Again, functional and data abstractions have to be applied in the right way. We find further and new aspects, for which we have to find solutions.

Multiply Connected Systems

We regard as an example the software in a car (*automotive software*). This example is *interesting* from the *outside perspective*, as (i) a car is a mass product, which has to be inexpensive, (ii) every car producer offers a variety of models and any model has a huge amount of variants, (iii) the solutions are a product of many delivering companies and the original equipment manufacturer (OEM). Therefore, (iv) the solution is distributed, and the solution is also developed in a distributed way.

It is a miracle that this kind of software works quite well in general. One important reason for this is that *user functions* are *clearly separated*, e.g. to lock/ unlock a car, to start/ stop the engine/ to drive, e.g. go with more or less speed, to steer a car/

to accelerate/ to brake, etc. These categories have connections, but they are not tightly interwoven. In this section of the chapter we regard a part of the car body system, namely to *unlock* or *lock the car*. The example is small, but it is big enough to learn about embedded systems.

There are *various internal problems* connected to automotive: The target system for the software (hardware architecture) consists (a) of a bigger number (about 50 or more) of control units. These control units are connected (b) by different networks, one network for motor control, for drive control, etc. These networks can be different (CAN, LIN, etc.) and are connected by gateways. Due to the big number of variants (many or few functions) of a model, (c) the hardware architecture can vary as well (fewer number of control units, smaller subnets). This is also true for the software (different number and different sizes of software components). A general problem, therefore (d) is the distribution (software together or distributed) and where to be located (deployment). Thus, (e) it is an enormous problem to keep the development of the various solutions together, from the capability and efficiency point of view. Even bigger (f) is the reuse problem, namely to save and apply the knowledge of solutions from one change of a car model to the successor, or from model to model. OEMs usually start first with the more expensive models and later transfer to cheaper ones. Finally, (g) there is a current trend to reduce the number of control units (less and bigger ones) in connection to electrification of cars. Another trend is (h) to produce uniform solutions in big automotive companies, which have different brands. In the long run (see (g) and (h)), this might simplify the solutions. In the short run, it produces further problems, as a complicated solution has to be transformed to a different one.

Conceptual Architecture and Feature Model

How to solve such a complicated problem as indicated in the last subsection? It seems reasonable to start with an abstract architectural description of the solution, which is free of specific details (a) to (h). We call this the *conceptual architecture*, as it is a solution (can be executed/ interpreted in some way) and not only a specification (only specifying the problem).

This solution is a *network of functionalities/ services*, where the connections correspond to data transfer of parameters, to control transfer (subfunction of, or one function after the other), and also to synchronization (all next functions in parallel, in a controlled schedule, or having situations, where explicit synchronization is necessary). The resulting description is often a function block model, SysML model, or alike. So, connections represent dependencies. In other words, the network is a dependency graph (flow-oriented approach). It also describes the execution order.

This architecture network is *abstract*, as it is independent of the steps following below, as how to transform functionalities and connections to software, and where to place it on hardware. It is important that we do *not model details*, which *belong to* the *realization* or *implementation* (code level of component bodies) and not to the architecture view. Thus, a conceptual architecture should not contain details of hardware or software.

It is even better to start with a variation model. We introduce a *feature model*, describing the "outside" commonalities and the specifics of the different variants of the car model. This feature model describes the *family of cars* connected with a model of a car, e.g. the 3 series of BMW. That feature model helps to find core functions, which are common for all variants, functions which are specific for a variant, and also how functions are built up from common or specific parts. It also helps to find out, which parts are placed in the conceptual model, in the software architecture, or hardware architecture. Furthermore, it helps to model in the right way, by separating common parts from specific parts.

It also helps to find the *right granularity* to model the *conceptual architecture*, and also for the *subsequent architecture models*. By the way, the feature model is not only important for the embedded software, but also for the complete design of the car, the mechanical/ electric construction, and also for the necessary IT hardware of the car in form of sensors and actuators.

In the following, we sketch a rather *small part* of the automotive *functionality*, namely the *access to the car*, i.e. to lock and to unlock the car /WR 11/. Even this part is noticeably simplified. We regard and discuss the example here only to invent rules for adaptability.

The example *conceptual architecture* works *in two steps*, see fig. 4.3: (i) Outside the car and from the user side to lock/ unlock, where a component Authenticate is necessary (left part) to validate the user. The corresponding status information is presented by the component LU_Request (LU for Lock or Unlock). (ii) Inside the car or in automatic mode, where this authentication is not necessary, the corresponding status information is delivered by Vehicle_Info. Both inputs (authentified LU_Reqst and Vehicle_Info) are put together (component Combine). Then and in case of contradictions/ different priorities, it has to be decided (component Arbitrate). Afterwards, the decided action takes place, see component Door Locker.

The conceptual architecture regards the *feature model*, which determines that we regard lock/ unlock in *two variants*. On the one hand, the user can lock/ unlock from outside by using a remote radio key. The other variant is to use an electronic passport: Whenever he/ she gets near to the car, the car unlocks, if the grip is touched at the driver side. Locking is done by the radio key (simple variant), or if the passport holder has a certain distance to the car (passport variant). In both variants, the functionality as presented in fig. 4.3 is the same. The variation here only corresponds to the realization of the lock/ unlock mechanism and the comfort of the user interface. Lock/ unlock can also come from inside, as a car has an in-button for lock/ unlock.

Information has to be checked *dynamically*: (a) A door is locked automatically for a running car to prevent that somebody opens from outside (robbery in a dangerous city). It is unlocked automatically, if the speed is higher than 40 km/ h. The user can configure such situations for more expensive cars. (b) In all cars, a car cannot be locked, if a door is open. (c) In all cars, a car is automatically unlocked in case of a crash. This information according to (a), (b), and (c) is collected in the component Combine. The component Arbitrate decides situations of conflict. Here, we can differ according to variants: Door_Status and Crash_Status are regarded in all variants, the status information Vehicle_Speed only in the expensive variant.

So, for Arbitrate there can be *different information* available, which then is *decided* by this component: A lock request from outside or inside is ignored, if a door is open or there is a crash. Vehicle_Speed can be the reason of locking/ unlocking (only implemented for expensive cars), but explicit lock/ unlock from inside has higher priority. And so on.

State information as LU_Request and Vehicle_Info are *connected* by *undirected edges* in fig. 4.3 with the corresponding function. They deliver information, as e.g. CL_Reqst for Authenticate. This can be done by two mechanisms: Either Authenticate asks LU_Request, or LU_Request in case of a state change causes an interrupt (and activates Authenticate). Both mechanisms mean the same disregarding details.

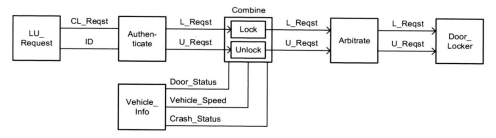

Fig. 4.3: Conceptual model for the access to the car

We have seen from this even small example: The *model* can be *independent of details* (as the concrete locking mechanism). But it can *regard the different variants* and use their information, as common features for all cars and specific ones for a variant. We have this distinction – common or specific – in mind, and use it for subsequent models.

Software Architecture and Mapping

The conceptual architecture is the guideline for the *software architecture* to be developed. It is the blueprint to transform the conceptual architecture to software components and relations between these components. This software architecture has at the beginning an *abstract form*. For example, *no specifics* of distribution and following deployment are contained in it. Later forms of this software architecture contain these specifics, see ch. 3.

How does this abstract form of the software architecture look like, and what are the *transformation rules* between the conceptual architecture and the (abstract) software architecture? A functionality of the conceptual architecture can be mapped 1:1 on a software component. It can also be that a function is mapped on more software components together with the relations between these components, so on a software subarchitecture. Finally, different functionalities together with their relations (a subarchitecture of the conceptual architecture) can be mapped on one software component, especially if they rely on the same or a similar realization infrastructure.

Thus, the *transformation is not necessarily one to one*. The reason is that the conceptual architecture contains functions/ services (what to do, driven by requirements), whereas the software architecture delivers the structure of a program system, which realizes these services (how to do in the form of a software build plan). Especially, the software architecture also contains components, which cannot be derived from the services, as they belong to deeper layers of the architectural structure. These *deeper components* or *layers* are necessary to realize the abstract components, which are derived from the conceptual model.

In the *example of above*, the **Authenticate** component in reality is more complex, as there are different further ways to request for lock/ unlock, which are not explained above, e. g. there is the mechanical key for worst case handling, etc. Analogously, the **Arbitrate** component has to check dynamic situations, which depend on many state values, e.g. in order to check for an accident. Therefore, in both cases the software architecture might contain more than one component for each of both conceptual components. Furthermore, there might be separate infrastructure components in the software architecture, to avoid that the corresponding code for these components is found multiple times in other components. Together, the *software architecture* can look differently, it is *not a 1:1 image* of the conceptual architecture.

Physical Architecture

The *physical architecture* (hardware architecture) consists of connected control units. The control units are different, because they shall realize quite different functionalities in computational demand and also corresponding related requirements. Furthermore, they are determined by subcontractors of the OEM. Control units belonging to one problem area (as motor control) build up a subnet, which might have a specific form and protocol. The different subnets are connected by gateways.

Physical architectures can vary, even for the same model of a car, as there are different variants of the model, according to the number of features. There may be more or fewer control units, or of possibly different computational power, and more extended or simpler subnets. So, there are conceptual architectures which have a *rich functionality* and, accordingly, a *rich physical architecture*. Similarly, a conceptual architecture with a poorer functionality will have a poorer related physical architecture. The same is true for the software architecture.

In any case, there is a balance between the software and the physical architecture. Both are usually *developed "in parallel"*. The physical architecture has to answer physical, efficiency, security aspects, and restrictions. The physical architecture is usually built up according to *experiences* gained in the *past*: It is usually an extension and modification of a former physical architecture. This is not true if a new situation for the physical architecture is planned (electric car, new car model, new approach with fewer control units).

Modeling on the level of services (conceptual architecture) and on the level of software components (software architecture) should have a *similar or comparable granularity*. The conceptual model should not contain functionalities of a fine-grained level. Then, the model is a too detailed requirements specification and not a conceptual model. The same is true for the software architecture. If low-level details were expressed on architecture level, the software architecture would contain components, which compose the realization of conceptual or software components and describe implementation details. Such details should be described inside of components, i.e. in their bodies and should not appear on (conceptual or software) architecture level. Or, they should appear as connector components to the hardware (see abstract sensors or actuators in the coffee machine example). Thinking too fine-grained makes the software architecture also too fine-grained and thus not adaptable.

Distribution and Deployment

Different parts of the software architecture are usually *distributed*. The first step is to determine, which parts can be placed on different hardware. In this first step, we do not say on which hardware the components are deployed. Instead, we determine by an *annotation*, that a subarchitecture or software component is placed differently. Distribution is one aspect, which makes the architecture more concrete. Other aspects are concurrency, efficiency transformations, etc. So, the abstract architecture undergoes different stages, see ch. 3.

If we have specified distribution, in the next step, which is called *deployment*, a subarchitecture or software component is assigned to a certain control unit to be placed there. It may be, due to efficiency (this part has a higher internal traffic, or this subarchitecture is too much for one control unit) or due to economic reasons (a control unit has open storage place and available runtime resources) that this assignment is split: one part on this control unit, the other on another unit. Therefore, the deployment task is complicated and error-prone, if it is made manually. Please recall that this deployment can be different for different variants of a model.

For our example of above, the components of the software architecture can be deployed to one and *bigger* control unit, or to *different smaller* control units. The parts deployed to a control unit should have a tighter logical coupling compared to those being deployed on different control units. If the code for the car body functions is deployed on different control units, these body components are located on the *same bus*. Therefore, the deployment maps the parts of the software architecture, which are closer related to each other, to a related part of the hardware architecture.

Deployment has been facilitated by the AUTomotive Open System ARchitecture (*AUTOSAR approach*) /AU 20/. Here, several program tasks (as routing through the hardware network, introducing program parts for a control unit which listen to the bus to find out, what is essential for this unit or, conversely, to put results of a unit computation on the bus again), are done in a semi-automatic way. I.e. the code is generated according to some specifications by AUTOSAR. That is an enormous progress to the situation before, where these code parts were written individually and manually.

This approach provides *flexibility in the distribution and deployment tasks*. This flexibility is necessary to handle the many variants of deployments according to the variants of software functionality and the availability of hardware. It also makes backtracking steps easier, which occur after detected errors in every development process. Finally, it also eases reuse in the software between car model families.

The *discussion* of above is *simplified*: AUTOSAR also helps in the scheduling of software parts on a control unit e.g. according to different priorities. Scheduling was not discussed here. Also, security and safety aspects of software in the car were not addressed.

The Role of Formal / Behavioral Models

For the construction of embedded systems, sometimes *formal models* are used. Usually, they specify the behavior of parts of the system, e.g. in form of *Simulink models* /Si 20/. The question now is, what are the units, the behavior of which are to be specified? Are the units the services of the conceptual model or the components of the software architecture? In our view, the right units are the components of the software architecture. The Simulink models then specify the behavior of the bodies to these components.

From a Simulink specification, *code* can be *generated*. This code belongs to the body of the component and specifies the behavioral semantics of this body. The architectural level delivers the glue to *combine* these different Simulink *models*. For this kind of integration, the different models need not be formally integrated and the generator need not generate code for a large and integrated formal model across different software components. Furthermore, we can integrate components coming from outside, which are not generated, and we can integrate components, which are manually developed, because no model is available, or the generated code was not efficient enough.

Integration of formal models to an integrated formal model is *complicated*, as models can have different forms and also different underlying languages. An integrated model gets large and complicated, and no suitable tools are available /BF

10/. Furthermore, the code for the integrated model would have to be separated for deployment.

Summary and Conclusions

The *hints of section 2* of above corresponding to sensors, actuators and data or functional abstraction also apply here. Further hints follow now.

We start with the *variability model*. That helps to find similarities and differences. The variability model *drives* the following *conceptual* and *software models* and also the distribution and deployment process. The developers rather think in *families* of *solutions* than in solutions for one single single variant.

For architecture modeling, *think* first *in functionality*, not in devices and not in hardware networks. They come later. The conceptual architecture should be free of details; they are probable to change. This architecture is not a detailed requirements specification, where outside functionality is described in detail.

Modeling the corresponding software *architecture* has to be done clearly, and also in *controlled stages* from abstract to detailed, see ch. 3. This should be supported by tools, and available suitable software should be used. As the software architecture is a build plan, it also contains common components. This is necessary to avoid repeated development.

In the automotive domain, for *conceptual models* often data flow networks are used (function blocks, SysML, etc.). Mostly thereby, *control loop models* are used, e.g. for cruise control. But, it can also be an *automata model* (Statechart, for describing unlocking and locking of doors), a *communication* model (for communicating with peer cars or infrastructure), an *abstract component* model (for infotainment or for integrating an overall solution with parts outside the car). Therefore, the specific models should not be constrained.

The solution of the past and in many cases of today is that the *design process* is driven by an enormous amount of *problems*: the variation problem, the distribution and deployment problem, the selection of control units and the network structure. These problems are often solved at the *same time*. That makes the design and realization process difficult. It also makes the resulting software system not adaptable. Consequently, the maintenance, reuse, and variation problems are more complicated than needed.

The *solution* is to define the conceptual architecture first (directly after the variability model) and make it free of realization details. The (abstract) software architecture is developed next. Using experience from the past, the hardware architecture is modified and extended. Thereby, also a clean structure of the hardware structure should result. The approach AUTOSAR helps for distribution and deployment, i.e. where to place the software components and helping for the details. Thus, for example, modifying the deployment is much easier.

The *conceptual architecture* and the *software* architecture should have the *right granularity*. To develop a feature model - for describing the commonalities and differences of different cars from a family at the beginning - can help to find the right granularity. It also helps to improve reuse, by avoiding that common parts are realized repeatedly. The conceptual and the software architecture should be free of those details, which should be described inside a component, i.e. in the code of the body. Formal and behavioral models as Simulink models should be related to these bodies. In this way, the *integration of different models* is given by the architecture approach described above, see ch. 8.

There are strong *similarities* of *embedded software solutions* in trucks, rail vehicles, and also somewhat in aircrafts. However, in aircrafts much more powerful and expensive hardware control units are used. The price of an aircraft is much higher than that of a car, and the demands for security and process regulations are much higher.

In all these cases, there is also an *outside connection* to other systems (car and truck: planning and guiding a travel, emergency handling after an accident, automatic drive using an infrastructure; aircraft: automatic flight control, planning and optimizing the route using weather data). These outside systems and their connection are not studied here. The *interface* of the system *to these outside parts* should also be clear and free of internal realization details.

4.4 Processes and Layered Systems

Embedded Systems have Further Challenging Aspects

We now *switch* the *scenario*. We have a look on the embedded system inside of a *plant*, for example in the field *chemical engineering* or *mechanical production*. The underlying technical system (chemical or production plant) has been developed beforehand, again in different steps starting with the conceptual design and ending with detailed design of the plant. Then, the development of the embedded software/ hardware system controlling the plant can start.

The embedded software system is usually a *concurrent* one. That means that we find processes (different threads running potentially in parallel), which cooperate with others or compete against others. Synchronization and protection have to be *specified* and later *implemented* by software. The solution might be simplified by fixed control loops.

In addition, embedded systems run „forever". They are *explicitly started* and *shut down*. This is organized by software. In cases of emergency, the system is stopped immediately to prevent damages of the plant/ factory. Further software is necessary to organize *emergency handling*.

Summing up, developing the concurrency/ fixed control part, explicit start/ stop, and emergency handling, causes additional effort compared to other software. Thus, *embedded software* is *more complicated* and the productivity in code lines per time unit of a developer is much lower. The above remarks also make clear that the design process has to be clearly organized and that the architecture runs through different stages, from abstract to detailed and technical (cf. ch. 3 for rules how to organize these stages).

Layered Systems

Communication and *cooperation* in a plant and in the corresponding company are organized in *layers*. This also applies for the corresponding hardware and especially to the software for automation control and process support /Po 94/. There are many variants of such layer models and the corresponding terminology, see /MP 17/. Fig. 4.4 shows a variant following /Si 16/. The picture and its terminology is from the mechanical production domain.

We now shortly *explain the layers*. The lowest level (level 0 in fig. 4.4) is on top of the *production devices*. We get sensor data and send actuator data usually in binary form. On level 1, we find *sensing and manipulating* by programmable logic control (PLC) units. They control and steer a production machine to do complex actions. PLCs and also machines are nowadays connected by a fieldbus (Profibus, Profinet, Modbus, etc.) to avoid tedious wiring. On the next level 2 we *monitor and supervise* (supervisory control and data acquisition, SCADA), thereby also possibly using human machine interfaces (HMI). On level 3 *complex production steps* are integrated by using a manufacturing execution system (MES). As a plant usually produces different products, *business planning and logistics* are relevant, also because an enterprise has different plants working together. This is supported by an enterprise resource planning system (ERP). In upper levels, we often find Ethernet for communication.

We have seen above that an embedded system is connected to its environment, see remarks for vehicles and aircrafts of above. This is also true here. However, the connections are tighter in the fields of production and chemical engineering. Control and automation goes up in the same enterprise from the sheer technical levels of single machines to the level of strategy and financial performance of the whole company. Again, we have different networks, as ProfiBus, Profinet, etc. in lower levels, and Ethernet in upper levels. Time slices from 10^{-6} sec to one sec we find on level 0 and 1, up to days and even months on level 3 and 4.

For the *lower levels* 0 to 2 of fig. 4.4, the *arguments* are *similar* to those presented in sects 4.2 and 4.3, for the simple example and for the automotive example. The production process has to be planned carefully and, correspondingly, the supporting software for automation and control. You should start by thinking in services and software architectures, distribution of their realization, try to keep in mind upcoming changes and adaptability of the realizations. Therefore and again, we find architectures of different degree, abstraction (at the beginning) and technical details and realization (in later stages).

It is clear that a top-down procedure (planning a new factory and going down until you end by the newest production machines, and then starting to develop a new solution for automation and control) is rather seldom in practice. A factory lives long and is changing all the time: It produces new products, the software and hardware is updated, at the level of production machines, old machines are replaced by modern ones, etc. Nevertheless, the arguments for adaptability and the rules to get it still apply.

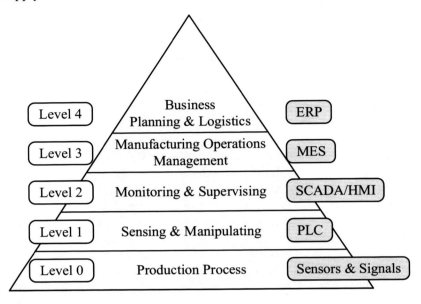

Fig. 4.4: The automation pyramid: different levels within one company

The above example was from production engineering. The situations in chemical engineering and in *automating and controlling a chemical plant* are the same, regarded on a coarse level, as done in this chapter. The underlying machines now are the parts of a chemical plant: vessels with valves, pipes with regulators, etc. Here, designing and planning the plant may also lead to a design of new parts, as vessels, pipes etc., if the plant produces new chemical substances.

There is a *trend* towards *decentralization* and more *intelligence* on lower levels compared to the past. In former times, there was an automation and control computer, being connected by wires to many sensors and actuators of different parts of the plant. Already nowadays, production machines or vessels of the chemical plant have a local hardware and software, which makes them more intelligent. That is also true for bigger parts of the factory/ plant. This facilitates to think in levels of automation and control. This more applies to chemical than to production engineering, as a production machine is usually engaged in processes for different products, whereas a part of a chemical plant is more specific to suit for a chemical process.

Reuse, Simplifications, and Specifics

In *informatics*, a *strict object-oriented program* consists only of classes, i.e. components describing a type. The objects of that type are created at runtime, the body of the class describes their behavior, also at runtime. That means that the program code has to determine the behavior of all runtime situations.

In the *domain process engineering and control*, but also in other domains, there is sometimes a different development process, which is also named "object-oriented". The process falls into two parts. In the first part, called *knowledge* or domain development or *design*, the different types of object of that domain/ company/ department are built up as classes, together with their similarities and differences. The result is an inheritance and classification hierarchy.

In the second step, a *specific solution* for a problem is constructed by taking objects of these classes and connecting them to a solution. That is again a design process. Therefore, two different roles are involved in this two-level design process: the knowledge engineer for the domain and the designer for a specific solution in the domain. Please note, that the two-level process can be used for process design (chemical plant, production factory) as well as for the automation and control of this process (a program and its components controlling the plant).

In the field automation and control *libraries* of many software *components* are available, to be used for an automation and control solution, see standards of IEC or DIN. These are typical components for different forms of controllers in graphical or textual forms. In addition, there are components and *tools* for connecting controllers to bigger automation & control solutions. The motto of this approach is configuration instead of programming a solution.

The two-level design process, the libraries for process control elements, as well as the tools for their construction and combination are valuable *reuse approaches*.

At the beginning of this section, we mentioned that processes with different threads and synchronization of these processes are typical units of an embedded system. In practice, the *solution is often simpler*. This is true for automotive solutions (sect. 4.3) as well as for layered solutions (this section). A task and its subtasks are carefully investigated according to their runtime demands. If they all together are below of the wanted reaction time, they are regarded as a sequence with a fixed schedule. A loop is regarded as a repetitive sequence, etc. The control flow can also be organized via signals (see automotive). This simple solution works well, if the necessary precautions are taken.

We have only sketched two examples of more complex and practical embedded systems in the last two sections, namely highly distributed (automotive software systems) and layered software systems (chemical plant, production factory). Any *further application domain* introduces *specifics and solutions*, which *deliver further hints*, how to build a solution.

Section: Summary and Conclusions

An automation and control system is tightly connected to the underlying technical system. Therefore, this underlying system should have a clear structure. The automation and control *solution* refers to this *structure*, but it should *not* depend on its *internal details*. Embedded systems are *more complicated* than other software systems (start/ stop, emergency handling, concurrency). Instead of processes and explicit synchronization, simpler solutions with a *fixed schedule* are often found in practice. They demand for precautions to assure reaction time and synchronization constraints.

Communication, automation and control, and also the corresponding solution in hardware and software are organized in *layers*, see the automation pyramid. It has to be decided, on which level a certain functionality is placed. The *interfaces between the layers* have to be carefully designed. From above, one should not see the details of lower levels, i.e. details should never go up.

Connections to outside should also use clear interfaces. For example, planning a route for trucks can use constraints of the truck as the steepness or the tight turning cycle of a street the vehicle can go. It should not use details of the truck itself or of its control system.

In layered systems (see pyramid) "outside" connections are within the *same company*, but possibly at different sites. Then, clear interfaces and abstraction from details are even more important. In layered systems, we find the *architectural problems* on *different layers* and, in addition, we find it *between* these layers.

The design and development of the embedded software system depends on the *technical system*. The latter has to be clear beforehand. This technical system has been designed and *developed* specifically (a new plant for novel chemicals) or is *configured* from bought production machines (factory). In both cases, the technical system can change and also the requirements for the embedded system (hardware and software). The trend for solutions of the hardware and software for automation and control is decentralization and non-monolithic solutions. *Machines/ devices and bigger parts* of the plant/ factory get *more intelligent. Adaptability and variability* is important for all the parts of the automation and control solution to answer changes of the underlying technical system.

Reuse is also important for solutions of a specific domain, if the solutions are built quite often. A *two-level design and realization* process (knowledge design and specific solution design) is helpful, as the knowledge part sums up the experiences of former solutions. That can directly be reused. *Libraries* of parts for solutions and *tools* to combine components to solutions are helpful, too. Then, building a solution is more a configuration than a programming task.

4.5 Summary of this Chapter

We now *summarize* the *hints* and *rules* we have discussed for the examples of above in form of a memory list. Where should we pay attention in a development process for embedded systems on architecture level, in order to get adaptable systems and to master the variability due to the many technical details?

Coffee Machine – an Introductory Example

- Sensors and actuators should not have a *vendor specific form*: *abstract from* this.
- Clear *physical* and *logical values* should appear in interfaces of sensors, actuators (but also other components), temperature in C or K, pressure in bar, logical value as true or false, etc. In the body of the component you connect to specific sensor or actuator values in some way. This is easier to change.
- For any physical subprocess (as melting or brewing in the coffee maker example) *abstract* from the underlying *physical hardware realization.*
- Separate *usual functions* from *error* handling/ *reacting* on errors/ *start* or *stop*.
- Make the *user interface independent* of how values and decisions are input. Thus, make the IO part adaptable: abstract from the form of text, clicking in a menu, number, or any other input, abstract from UI system style of input, etc. The client components of the UI system should only know, what has been selected, what has been put in or out, but not how this is done, styled, or layouted.
- Altogether, use data (*detail*) abstraction and *functional* abstraction wherever possible.

Automotive

- Start with a *variability model*, e.g. a feature diagram. That helps to identify the common parts and the specific parts of following architectures. It helps to find family characteristics. It is useful to find the units, which should appear in the architecture.
- Make the *conceptual architecture* as a network of *services* (what to do but not how in detail): Find the right abstraction level for these services, which corresponds in its granularity to that of software architecture components. No details (technical details, software realization details) should appear here.
- The *software architecture* in its first form is *abstract*, free of specifics as distribution, concurrency, efficiency, etc. These specifics come in later stages. In a software architecture, there is tight coupling in components and looser coupling between components.
- Clearly *distinguish* between the *architecture* level and the later *implementation* level. Also, clearly distinguish between conceptual and software architecture level. Realization components, e.g. infrastructure components or layers, should appear in the software architecture but not in the conceptual architecture.
- Think about software components according to the services. The *mapping* from *conceptual architecture* to the *software* architecture can be *different*: Services

are 1:1 mapped, bundled, or services are split in order to get the components of the software architecture. There should be clear decisions for the mapping from the conceptual to the software architecture.

- In the conceptual architecture and in the software architecture do not model behavioral details, which correspond to the internals of the corresponding software units (the bodies). So, do *not model* realization and implementation details (which correspond to the code level) in *architectures*. This also applies to hardware details.
- *Formal models*, like Simulink models, in our view correspond to *components* of the conceptual and even more likely to those of the software architecture. They correspond to the behavior of these components, i.e. to their bodies. By code generation you can get the code for these bodies. The *integration* of the different components is ensured on *architecture level*, not between the formal models. The models can have different underlying notations (Statechart, control loops, communication protocols, etc.).
- The software architecture has to offer *interfaces* for the integration of *external parts*, e.g. for functionalities in the case of accidents (delivering information for rescue organizations, announcing serious injuries to hospitals, sending warnings to cars behind a curve that an accident has happened, etc.).
- *Forget* in the first steps about the underling network of control units, their sub-networks, their protocols (altogether the *hardware architecture*): We are first handling the abstract software architecture.
- Think about *distribution*, where to group or where to distribute software components.
- Think about the *hardware architecture*, which control units, which networks are available, and which gateways to combine subnets. What preparations have to be made for safety and security. The hardware architecture is usually developed "in parallel" to the software architecture. This demands for hardware architecture experience to avoid big changes, such as the hardware architecture does not fit, the hardware architecture cannot handle the variability.
- Think about *deployment* of software components or groupings of such components into the hardware architecture. Tight coupling has to be answered by putting coupled components into one control unit or putting them to another control unit on the same subnet.
- Approaches like *AUTOSAR* /AU 20/ make the above steps distribution and deployment easier and make the mapping more flexible.
- Introducing *abstractions begins* already in the feature model, *continues* in the conceptual architecture, and has to be applied for all the steps of above.

Layered systems; Production or Chemical Plants

- The *plant/ factory design* must be *fixed* before starting the design of the automation & control part, either in hardware or software. If a plant/ factory of a certain kind is often realized and in different forms, start with a variability model to find out family characteristics.
- There should be a *clear structure* of the underlying *technical system*, either plant or factory. Otherwise, automation and control cannot get clear. Software cannot repair a bad plant design. Otherwise, it is also getting bad.
- The *software* part of the embedded system should start with a logical and abstract form, then introduce concurrency, then start/ stop, then emergency handling, as any further form relies on the preceding ones. The *sequence* should be *organized* according to, abstract is left, aspects more likely to change are right, see chapter 3.
- A solution might not use processes and synchronization but a *simplification* with a fixed schedule. *Precautions* in direction of efficiency and security have to be made.
- The solution is *organized* in layers, see the automation pyramid, fig. 4.4. Make clear that the *functionality* of automation and control you are realizing, is on the *right layer*. It is not using higher functionality, and also not indirect lower realization functionality. It may use the interfaces of the next layer.
- For the *lower layers* 0 to 2 the above *rules* (simple or automotive example) *apply* too.
- The components needed in higher levels of a layer should have *clear interfaces*. Realization *details* should not go up or, i.e. they should *not be accessible* from higher layers.
- From layer to layer upwards: Do *not spread lower level knowledge upwards* and *upper level knowledge downwards*. In both cases you hinder flexibility. The presented approach is based on a clear layering of control functionalities: Who is controlling what, and determines the considerations of actions in a control loop and loops of loops.
- Do *not intermix* technical automation knowledge (lower and technical levels) with quality assurance, strategy development, business administration, etc.
- If embedded systems of this kind are *integrated*, be careful which *knowledge* is visible on both sides of integration. Have *clear interfaces* on both sides.
- Think about *possible changes to happen* on all layers and make sure that these changes do not have global consequences. Any severe change of functionalities (other grouping, shift to another level, etc.) means that you run into a big rearrangement problem.
- If you regard an *OO design*, use the *two-level* approach, separating domain knowledge design from design of specific solutions.
- If there are *libraries* for parts of an automation and control solution, use them if they are appropriate. If *tools* to combine such solutions are available, use them.

If there are possibilities to *generate code* from a specification (available usually only for parts of the solution) make use of it. All these means are *good for reuse*.

There are *further rules* if we regard other and *further domains*. Therefore, the above set of hints is not complete. However, the argumentation will go along the same lines of thought, as that of the three examples of above.

Although we *did not go deep into technical problems* of embedded systems in this chapter, neither in the automotive example nor in the layered example (production factory or chemical plant), we detected a *valuable list of rules and hints* to improve adaptability. Going deeper will create further hints and rules to apply.

4.6 Lessons Learned and Open Problems

Experiences and Expectations

Our group has *experiences* with *embedded systems*: We worked about smart homes /Ar 10, Ki 05, No 07, Re 10/, about telecommunication systems /He 03, Ma 05, Mo 09/, automotive /Me 12, MN 12/, general distributed & concurrent systems /Kl 00/, technical systems with expert systems /Ba 95/, and modeling of automation systems /Mü 03/. Furthermore, there were publications on informatics and mechanical engineering (e.g. /NW 99, NW 03/), chemical engineering (e.g. /NM 08/), and others, mostly on tools for the design and development process.

These experiences but also the contents of books on embedded systems led us to study the adaptability of embedded systems or to master the variability of embedded systems. The key to solve these problems is to *introduce abstractions*, see the lists in section 5.

By the way, embedded systems are an ideal discipline for *cooperation* between *computer scientists* and *engineers*. There are many technical problems to solve, where expertise from the application domains is necessary to achieve a solution. On the other hand, modeling and introducing the right form of abstractions is the key to master adaptability and variability. Also, efficiency of the solutions is necessary, which demands knowledge from engineering domains and also informatics. Engineers and IT people have different approaches. The combination of these approaches is the right way for the solution of embedded systems.

Open Problems

Reuse in embedded systems is more difficult than in other systems, due to the many technical details, which appear in any system. Therefore, there is no uniform structure class build plan describing how an embedded system should be built up. Instead, we have different forms, like (a) small systems which can be controlled by one control unit, (b) systems which have a hardware architecture of many and cheap CUs (like automotive of above), (c) those which have powerful and connected control hardware (as in aircrafts), (d) those for big technical plants as chemical or manufacture plants with a layer structure. There exist decentralized forms (every vessel already has a control unit) and more centralized forms (big control hardware with many sensors/ actors connected to it), and so on. It would be nice to find *abstract build plans as global patterns* for all these specific forms, or methodologies to build them up, such that every design delivers experience for next designs.

If there were such a series of global patterns, then it would be much simpler to decide what you can take as ideas from a given embedded system, if a system in the same or in a similar domain is developed. Even more, one could take parts of the solution (basic layer, some important components, the methodology to develop essential parts, and so on). Thus, *reuse of any kind* would be *easier*.

To look on different systems from an abstract view would also make another problem easier, namely to *develop system families* or *product lines* /CN 07, Ja 00, PB 05/, which may evolve over the time /LR 19/ or which may even be configured dynamically /LB 17/. For system families, you have to detect similarities in a systematic way. We see which differences are less important as coming up only in a member of the family, which parts are essential and characterize the family. To develop one embedded system in a clean way is complicated, as we see from this chapter. To develop a set of systems in a clean way with an underlying view of the whole family is even more complicated. The build plan for the family must contain the commonalities of the whole family, and at the same time indicate the differences between the members of the family. In the best case, the members are configured automatically from a variant and configuration model.

A specific *problem for families* we find in automotive. The development time of a car is about 6-7 years. There is a pressure to have less. A car producer usually has several models (and each, as already told, with many variants). So, the embedded system of different models is developed in some order, to avoid to overload the developers on the one hand and to keep them busy on the other. Let us call this order the big cycle. At BMW, for example, the development cycle starts with the big 7 model, then comes the 5 model, and so on. At the beginning of this big cycle, the company has to decide, what to *reuse from the last big cycle* (more methodology than direct product reuse, as the design of the old 7 model is more than 9 years old and many things have changed, either on the feature side, or on the methodology, and also development side). The same holds for the other cars which have been developed after the 7 model, so *within the big cycle*. Therefore, there is a nice problem in system families, which consist of smaller families: How to organize the results and *how to exhaust the knowledge* gained in this big cycle for the rest of the cycle but also for the next big cycle.

Model-driven Development (MDD) /PB 16, PH 12, PK 09/ is a *more ambitious* approach compared to the approach described in this chapter. In MDD we start with abstract models denoted in a suitable language and transform these models into software, ideally in an automatic way by generating the code. This model can be a control loop Simulink model /Si 20/, e.g. for cruise control, which automatically maintains the speed of a car. It can be a Statechart model /Ha 87, St 20/, for example for opening or closing the doors of a car. It can be a specification for the communication of the car with other cars, or with the road infrastructure.

In all these cases, the generator has to be written such that it automatically and always watches the hints given in this chapter to produce adaptable software. Or, the generated code is put into a framework for components which fulfills the hints. Today we find the *generation approach more for partial solutions* within an automation and control system, as door locking/ unlocking, cruise control, etc. Therefore, the generation approach has to be integrated into the design and realization process of the whole system, as the control of an automobile or a chemical plant. Integration of all models in one overall model and then generating the code out of this integrated model is not realistic /Me 12/. Neither the models, nor the corresponding tools for different models are integrated /BF 10/, nor the generation processes. Therefore, there is some gap between the current state of the art and a *smooth integration of the model-based and* the *adaptability/ variability architectural approach* presented in this chapter.

In our approach, in every step a *person* is involved. He/ she (the designer, programmer, etc.) follows the hints given above and by the way he/ she *makes architectural decisions,* achieves adaptability, and masters variability for the resulting system. This is much simpler than a global MDD approach, where the machinery has to be built in such a way, that all these decisions can be made automatically by the generator. In addition, as sketched in the last paragraph, the models can be very different or even might be determined from outside. In a solution, the generated code for the different models has to work smoothly together and the architecture should look, as if it were designed by an experienced designer.

Acknowledgement. The author is indebted to C. Mengi for valuable discussions and proofreading.

4.7 References

/Ar 10/ Armac, I: Personalized eHome Systems (in German), Doct. Dissertation, RWTH Aachen University, 315 pp., (2010)

/AU 20/ AUTOSAR: AUTomotive Open System ARchitecture, http://www.autosar.org/, access 12, 2020

/Ba 95/ Bacvanski, V.: Integration and Structuring of Expert Systems in Technical Applications, Doct. Dissertation, RWTH Aachen University, 225 pp. (1995)

/BF 10/ Broy, M./ Feilkas, M. et al.: Seamless Model Based Development: From Isolated Tools to Integrated Model-Based Developments, Proc. IEEE of the IEEE, 98, 4, 526-545 (2010)

/BK 03/ Bass, L./ Clements, P. et al.: Software Architecture in Practice, 2nd ed. Addison Wesley (2003), 3rd ed. Pearson (2013)

/BL 18/ Bringmann, O./ Lange, W. et al.: Embedded Systems (in German), De Gruyter/ Oldenbourg, 3rd ed. (2018)

/CN 07/ Clements, P./ Northrop, L.M.: Software Product Lines: Practices and Patterns, 563 pp., 6th ed., Addison Wesley (2007)

/GS 94/ Garlan, D./ Shaw, M.: An Introduction to Software Architectures, TR CMU-CS-94-166 (1994)

/Ha 87/ Harel, H.: A Visual Formalism for Complex Systems, Science of Computer Programming, 231-274 (1987)

/He 03/ Herzberg, D.: Modelling Telecommunikation Systems: From Standard to System Architectures, Doct. Dissertation, RWTH Aachen, 305 pp. (2003)

/HK 07/ Hofmeister, C./ Kruchten, Ph. et al: A general model of software architectural design derived from five industrial approaches, Journal of Systems and Software 80, 106-126 (2007)

/Ja 00/ Jazayeri, M. et al. (eds.): Software Architecture for Product Families, Addison Wesley (2000)

/Ki 05/ Kirchhof, M.: Integrated eHome Low Cost Systems: Processes and Infrastructures (in German), Doct. Dissertation, RWTH Aachen University, 331pp. (2005)

/Kl 00/ Klein, P.: Architecture Modelling of Distributed and Concurrent Software Systems, Doct. Dissertation, RWTH Aachen University, 237pp. (2000)

/KM 04/ Kruger, I./ Mathew, R.: Systematic development and exploration of service-oriented software architectures, 4th Working IEEE/IFIP Conference on Software Architecture (WICSA), 177-187 (2004)

/LB 17/ Lochau, M./ Bürdek, J./ Hölzle, S./ Schürr, A.: Specification and automatic validation of staged reconfiguration processes for dynamic software product lines, Softw. Syst. Model 16, 125-152 (2017)

/LR 19/ Lochau, M./ Reuling, D./ Bürdek, J./ Kehrer, T./ Lity, S./ Schürr, A./ Kelter, U.: Model-Based Roundtrip Engineering and Testing of Evolving Software Product Lines, in R. Reussner et al. (eds.), Managed Software Evolution, Springer (2019)

/Ma 05/ Marburger, A.: Reverse Engineering of Complex Legacy Telecommunication Systems, Doct. Dissertation, RWTH Aachen University, 418 pp. (2005)

/Ma 21/ Marwedel, P.: Embedded System Design, 4th ed., Springer (2021)

/Me 12/ Mengi, C.: Automotive Software – Processes, Models, and Variability (in German), Doct. Dissertation, RWTH Aachen University, 350 pp. (2012)

/MN 12/ Mengi, C./ Nagl, M.: Refactoring of Automotive Models to Handle the Variant Problem, Workshop „Modellbasierte und modellgetriebene Software-Modernisierung" (MMSM 2012), Softwaretechnik-Trends 32, 2, 11-12 (2012).

/Mo 09/ Mosler, Ch.: Graph-based Reengineeing of Telecommunication Systems (in German), Doct. Dissertation, RWTH Aachen University, 268 pp., RWTH Aachen University (2009)

/MP 17/ Meudt, T./ Pohl, M. et al.: Die Automatisierungspyramide – Ein Überblick, TU Prints, TU Darmstadt (2017)

/Mü 03/ Münch, M.: Generic Modeling with Graph Rewriting Systems, Doct. Dissertation, RWTH Aachen, 242 Spp., Shaker-Verlag, Aachen (2003)

/Na 82-03/ Nagl, M.: Introduction to Ada (in German), 348 pp., Vieweg (1982), /Na 03/ 6th ed. Software Engineering and Ada (in German), 504 pp., Vieweg (2003)

/Na 90/ Nagl, M.: Software Engineering- Methodological Programming in the Large (in German), 387 pp., Springer (1990), plus further extensions for a lecture on Software Architectures, 1990 - 2020

/NM 08/ Nagl, M./ Marquardt, W.(eds.): Collaborative and Distributed Chemical Engineering – From Understanding to Substantial Design Process Support, IMPROVE, LNCS 4970, 851 pp., Springer (2008)

/No 07/ Norbisrath, U.: Configuring eHome Systems (in German), Doct. Dissertation, 286 pp. (2007)

/NW 99/ Nagl, M./ Westfechtel, B. (eds.): Integration of Development Systems in Engineering Applications – Substantial Improvement of Development Processes (in German), 440 pp., Springer (1999)

/NW 03/ Nagl, M./ Westfechtel, B. (eds.): Models, Tools, and Infrastructures for the Support of Development Processes (in German), 392 pp., Wiley VCH (2003)

/PB 05/ Pohl, K./ Böckle, G. et al.: Software Product Line Engineering, 467 pp., Springer (2005)

/PB 16/ Pohl, K./ Broy, M. et al (eds.): Adavanced Model-based Engineering of Embedded Systems – Extensions to the SPES 2020 Methodology, Springer, 303 pp. (2016)

/PH 12/ Pohl, K., Hönninger, K. et al. (eds.): Model-based Engineering of Embedded Systems – The SPES 2020 Methodology, Springer, 304 pp. (2012)

/PK 09/ Polzer, A./ Kowalewski, S./ Botterweck, G.: Applying Software Product Line Techniques in Model-based Embedded Software Engineering, Proc. MOMPES'09, 2-10 (2009)

/Po 94/ Pohlke, M.: Prozessleittechnik, 2nd edition, Oldenbourg (1994)

/Re 10/ Retkowitz, D.: Software Support for Adaptive eHome Systems (in German), Doct. Dissertation, RWTH Aachen University, 354 pp. (2010)

/Ru 12/ Rumpe, B.: Agile Modeling with UML (in German), 2nd ed., 372 pp. Springer (2012)

/Sc 13/ Schmidt, R.F.: Software Engineering – Architecture-driven Software Development, 376 pp. Elsevier (2013)

/SEI 10/ Software Engineering Institute of CMU: What Is Your Definition of Software Architecture, https://resources.sei.cmu.edu/library/asset-view.cfm?assetID=513807

/Si 16/ Siepmann, D.: (2016): Industrie 4.0 -Technologische Komponenten, in: Einführung und Umsetzung von Industrie 4.0, in A. Roth, (Hrsg.), Berlin Heidelberg, Springer Gabler Verlag, S.47-72 (2016)

/Si 20/ Wikipedia Simulink: https://en.wikipedia.org/wiki/Simulink und http://www.mathworks.com/products/simulink/ , access 11,2020

/SG 96/ Shaw, M./ Garlan, D.: Software architecture: perspectives on an emerging discipline. Prentice Hall (1996)

/SS 00/ Schmidt, D./ Stal, M. et al.: Pattern-oriented Software Architectures, vol 2 Patterns for Concurrent and Networked Objects, Wiley (2000)

/St 20/ Wikipedia Statechart: https://en.wikipedia.org/wiki/State_diagram, access 11, 2020

/WR 11/ Wallentowitz, H./ Reif, K. (eds.): Handbuch Kraftfahrzeugelektronik, Section 6.2, Zugangs- und Berechtigungssysteme, 369 – 379, Springer Vieweg (2011)

5 Architecture Styles: Do they Need Different Notations?

Manfred Nagl

Software Engineering, RWTH Aachen University, nagl@cs.rwth-aachen.de

Abstract

Styles or patterns for software architectures look very different. Any of them seems to open a new world. We try to discuss the commonalities by tracing them back to the traditional approach for software architectures used in this book. We do this for some cases and hope that the reader is convinced that it can also be done for the remaining ones. We are sure that the discussion how to trace back can also be conducted for other approaches of 'standard' software architectures. As a result, we see that styles/ patterns, although looking different at first sight, have a lot in common with classical concepts.

In this chapter, we concentrate on styles. Tracing back a style notation N to a 'standard notation' N_S is done for three different modes: In some cases (example data flow) the notation N_S is more detailed and delivers more accuracy than N. In other cases (event or distribution architectures) written down in a more technical notation, N_S is more abstract. Finally, N and N_S can be on a similar level of abstraction (N-Tier, Blackboard), but N_S is again more precise. So, the answer to the question of the title is No <u>and</u> Yes.

Keywords: Architectural styles/ patterns, different and specific notations, simulation by classical architectural concepts, language integration, patterns on different levels, examples: data flow, technical (event-based, distribution) and global styles/ patterns

5.1 Introduction

There are rather different *approaches* and *notations* for *software architectures* /BK 03, Bö 94, CB 02, HK 07, HP 80, Le 88, Na 90-20, Pa72, PW 92, SAD, SC 06, Sc 13, TP 16, Wi SA/. We find approaches coming from the programming language side /Bu 84, Me 91, DK 76, Na 82-03/, those coming from theory /Gu 76, LZ 74, BH 85, EM 89, ST 12/, more industry-like approaches /BK 03, BR 05, HK 07, Sc 13, Ru 12, TP 16/, those coming from an underlying paradigm as service-oriented /KM 04/, object-oriented /JC 92, Me 97/, and so on.

Looking on the *character of approaches*, we can find functional and modular ones, abstract data object and type notations, object-oriented ones (adt-based together with modeling the similarities and differences), data flow-oriented approaches, event-based approaches, global approaches etc. We find approaches concentrating more on an abstract level and those mainly caring about technical details as event or distribution handling. There are some with more theoretical and some with practical and industrial impetus. In ch. 2 we have attempted to show, that different aspects/ approaches/ notations/ annotations can be used *in one architecture* notation.

© The Author(s), under exclusive license to Springer Nature Switzerland AG 2024
M. Nagl, B. Westfechtel, *Software Architectures*, https://doi.org/10.1007/978-3-031-51335-0_5

In /GS 94, SG 96/ and other sources different notations for *architecture styles* have been introduced. Reading about styles creates the impression that any of them introduces a separate notation and that these notations have nothing to do with each other. It seems that any of these styles introduces a *separate world*. The notations, in which they are expressed, as well as the models and methodologies, which are built or used using these styles, disintegrate into disjoint areas. To verify this impression, the reader is invited to look on figs. 5.2 to 5.4 of this chapter, which show different forms of a data flow, event-driven, distribution, and global architecture.

Architectural styles are in literature not clearly distinguished from architectural patterns. In analogy to the use of these terms for buildings, we *distinguish* between a *style* as a certain way or fashion to model on one hand, and a *pattern* as an accepted solution or an accepted part of a solution on the other. In this way the gothic style intends to build high and filigree churches by using columns, vaultings and tracery windows as central elements, whereas the pattern of classical gothic French cathedrals defines a certain structure and form (main house and transept with three naves, round choir with 5 naves, and west towers) applying this style /Na 19/. In this sense, a pattern is more specific: It is an existing church, a part of it, or the way to model churches from a specific class. Any style or pattern needs a *notation* (language) to be written down and explained. This notation usually follows *paradigms*.

The *aim of this chapter* is to look at different styles, to extract specific characterizations, commonalities and differences, thereby getting knowledge about these styles. We deal more with styles than with patterns. Especially, we relate these styles to concepts of traditional architectural design concepts, as e.g. /Na 90-20/. This tracing back and relating can be done also for other architecture concepts (object-oriented, service-oriented, etc.). Thereby, the traditional concepts can be more detailed or more abstract, depending on the style which is discussed.

From the *variety* of styles, we *discuss* only a *selection*. The discussion of the others not discussed should be possible and go similarly as those presented here. In this way, we hope to convince the reader that the discussion is 'complete'. Discussions of other styles should not change the line of thought and the essentials of this chapter.

5.2 Clarification of Terms

Clarification

Using /GS 94, MP 10, SG 96/ we give in table 5.1 a coarse enumeration and a rough 'classification' of styles, which is not complete and not free of redundancy.

components
components in form of modules, packages, services, etc.
processes, threads, synchronization, and concurrent processing
interacting processes, e.g. by event-based mechanisms
OO: classes, message passing, and dispatching

connectors (use relations)
> call and return, functional or task decomposition
> general resources (abstract data objects, types, etc.) one or more levels down
> object-oriented modeling: detecting similarities and differences of types
> abstract uses (behind technical bindings)

technical bindings between components
> events, interrupts
> callbacks
> publish- subscribe, broadcasting
> variations: further and different mechanisms

dataflow/ motion of data from component to component
> batch
> pipe and filter
> control loops in automation and control
> variations: push vs. pull, topology, degree of concurrency, consumption discrete
>   or continuous, start of next input before end of computation, etc.

data-centered
> data bases and repositories
> blackboard architectures

hierarchical, any layer delivers an abstraction
> layers and protocols between layers
> n-Tier
> strict vs. non-strict hierarchies

distribution
> client-server
> peer-to-peer (each component is both client and server)

other kind of execution
> interpreters of a specification
> rule-based programming and trying to apply rules
> training a ML network by data and later decision making

Table 5.1: Different Styles: An enumeration, not complete

To give just a *few examples*: Fig. 5.2.c shows a data flow system with a loop, where the connectors have ports. Fig. 5.3 shows how a broadcasting service works via a service in the middle and with events caring for connections. Fig. 5.4 shows a 4-Tier architecture and a blackboard architecture. We immediately see that fig. 5.2.c is on a conceptual, fig. 5.3 on a technical, and figs. 5.4.a, b on a coarse and sketchy level.

Which Kinds of Styles/ Patterns?

Despite of the difference we made above between styles and patterns, we can classify them in a similar way: (a) *Global* styles and patterns are applied for the architecture of complete software systems or kernel parts of them. (b) Styles or patterns for *coupling* systems, which are described elsewhere, can have different forms. (c) Styles/ patterns appear also for *essential parts* of a system as frameworks, basic layers, UI handling parts, data access parts, and (d) local architectural situations within complete systems, like a few components with specific mutual relations, as the model view controller pattern. The latter we call here *micro patterns* as they appear inside of architectures or big parts thereof. Micro patterns are what most people think, if they mention the term pattern, see e.g. /BM 96/.

Finally, (e) for single *components* we can regard interface design, realizations' design, imports, and differentiate again different patterns, e.g. for known data structures as stacks, queues, lexicons, trees, or graphs.

In this chapter, we *concentrate* on (a), (b), and (c). The cases (d) and (e) are not regarded, as they either are well-studied micro patterns or they are below of bigger architectures (interfaces, bodies, and how to define and use imports).

Which of these cases is *most important*? *Patterns* are more important than styles, as they represent a solution or a part of it, which can be taken to build another solution. Regarding patterns, *global* patterns are the most interesting form. They are a blueprint for a complete system to be built, or its kernel or framework. The next are patterns for *coupling* systems, those for *big parts* of systems as, for example, basic layers for systems, or patterns how to build the UI part of an interactive system.

Less important for this chapter are *micro patterns* /BM 96, Ev 04, GH 95, SS00/. They are applied inside of a software architecture. They are well studied, such that there is no need to look at them here. On the other hand, they have two disadvantages: (i) Using them to build the internals of an architecture means to combine those patterns. There is the possibility of big multiplicity and redundancy. (ii) Books on micro patterns give the impression that argumentation and discussion on architectural design are not necessary. You take the ‚right' patterns out of suitable drawers and just use them. The reality, however, is different: You have to find the right ones, they often have to be modified, and their combination is not trivial. Sometimes, you have a situation, where there is no pattern. You have to invent a solution, which possibly later becomes the extension of an existing pattern, or even a new pattern.

Another classification of patterns looks at the *character of patterns*: Patterns are either creational, structural, or behavioral /Wi SDP/. A further and different way is to look at the core of a solution, as components around a repository (blackboard, see fig. 5.4.b), or the taken approach, as the service-oriented approach /KM 04/ or the object-oriented approach /BR 05, JC 92, Me 91, Me 97/.

There is no way to have the variety of terms fully clarified. The purpose of the chapter is a different one: We want to look on patterns and styles and we want to show their commonalities, what they have to do with each other, and also their relation to usual architectural concepts. For that purpose, it is not necessary to look on all patterns and styles. It is sufficient to look on some and discuss them. Thereby, we hope to convince the reader that the remaining ones can be treated in the same way.

5.3 Examples for Different Styles/ Patterns

We start with a short survey and give some examples of the variety of styles or patterns, see figs. 5.2, 3, and 4. From the range of categories, we only introduce examples from the categories data flow systems, event-based systems, and global styles.

Pipes and Filters, Data Flow Systems

We start with pipe and filter systems, which consist of *components*, called filters, and *connectors*, called pipes, see fig. 5.2. Both can have specific names.

Such a model can be *hierarchical*, as the first part of fig. 5.2, where three filters f_1 to f_3 are connected. They altogether are combined to a filter F.

Fig.5.2.b contains a *non-hierarchical* model, which has a *loop* in the lower part. Loops are important for automation and control. We also see sequences, splits, joins.

The third part, fig. 5.2.c, shows a model with so-called *ports*. Ports allow to structure the input as well as the output into different parts. Thereby, we can specify, which part of the output of a component is connected to which part of the input of another component. Modeling is more precise and clearer compared to that without ports.

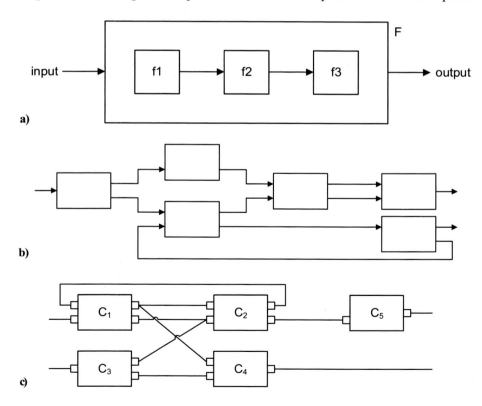

Fig. 5.2: Pipes and filters/ data flow systems without and with loops or ports

Event-based and Distributed Systems

In fig. 5.3.a, we see an *event based system* with a *broadcasting mechanism*. The component `Producer1` sends event e to a `Broadcasting Service`, the component `Comp1` as well as `Comp2` have registered for it. Therefore, both `Comp1` and `Comp2` get the event, react on it, and do something. Later in time, `Producer1` does not send the event e, `Producer2` does, `Comp1` has unregistered. Now `Comp2` reacts alone.

We see that registration can change at runtime, also sending out of events. Then, the bindings from senders to reactors change. That corresponds to an activation of a service, which can be changed at runtime to a new producer and reactor. Approaches, where you can *change the call structure* are dangerous. Much less dangerous is it to use a structure differently at runtime, determined at design time.

Architectures like that of fig. 5.3 use and are determined by technical mechanisms, as event handling. Another example of such a *technical pattern* describes a client server situation, where the client and the server are placed on different machines. For *distribution*, we can use a distribution infrastructure, as CORBA, see sect. 5.

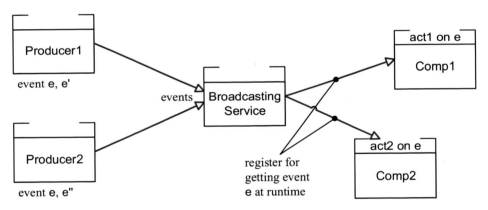

Fig. 5.3: Broadcasting system (pattern) as the core of component interaction

Global Approaches

A *global style/ pattern* helps to structure a complete system or an essential part thereof. It is on a coarser level. So, it is more a sketch than a detailed build plan.

In fig. 5.4.a, we see the *n-Tier style/ pattern*, for n=4. It says that the design should be structured using a hierarchy of different layers, here of 4 layers. The advantage of these layers is that it should be easier to extend the hierarchy with further layers. A necessary condition for that is that the layers are connected by clear interfaces.

The second example of fig. 5.4.b is the so-called *blackboard style/ pattern* (/MS BD, SG 96/, other names data-driven or data base-driven style/ pattern). It shows a number of components ksi doing some computation and using a data base/ data structure for delivering or using (intermediate) results. There are no direct connections between the components ksi. All of them have direct access to the blackboard.

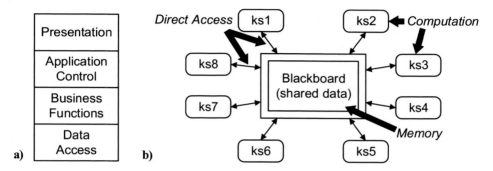

Fig. 5.4: Two of many global styles: a) N-Tier for N=4, b) Blackboard architecture

The above examples of figs. 5.4.a and 4.b are on a level that they do not relate to components (modules or aggregated subsystems). Instead, they show the big chunks of a system. The simulation (sect. 5.6) also contains parts of this granularity.

Tracing back for what?

Looking on the above examples, we give some summarizing remarks. In the following, we *trace* the examples of figs. 5.2, 3, and 4 *back* to the *traditional architectural notation* of this book. What do we intend, when we trace style notations back? This means that we give an explanation using another architectural design notation. We show that the above styles can be expressed or explained using the other notation. In this way, we show that the different kinds of notations/ languages, and methods how to use them are not far away or even completely separate. Instead, tracing back emphasizes what they have in common.

We take the examples of figs. 5.2, 3, and 4 as examples from the wide range of style/ pattern possibilities. We also give an explanation, why we chose these styles and not others. The taken examples are *representatives*. They on one hand *cover a part* of the range of possibilities. On the other hand, they indicate how the *discussion for the remaining* styles not discussed should or could be *handled*.

The consequences of tracing back are different: (a) Having shown how to simulate, allows to use the styles as shorthand and further notations. (b) If there are different possible semantics for a style, tracing back can give a precise semantics. (c) The trace can also go in the other direction, arguing that the style has too many technical details, the architect should abstract in the first run and add the details later. We now discuss the different styles of sect. 5.3 in in the following three sections.

5.4 Data Flow Architectures: From Pipes / Filters to Embedded Systems

In this section, we discuss the style of data flow architectures, which exist in different forms and notations. It is a rather old concept for architecting and programming, see

/De 74, Wi DFP/. Later on, these diagrams were very fashionable at the time of structured approaches, see /DM 78/ or /MM 87/. They are still used in embedded systems. There, they have a big importance in the real time part of UML /BR 05, RJB 10/. We start with the simplest form and end with the more complicated ones.

Pipes and Filters

Fig. 5.2.a gives a first and simple *example*, of a *pipeline architecture*. There are three components f_1 to f_3, called filters, connected by pipes, and executed one after the other. This means that the output of f_1 is the input of f_2 and so forth. They are composed to one bigger filter component F, the input of which is directed to f_1, and the output of f_3 is the output of F.

There are mainly *two* possibilities for the *semantics* of this hierarchical component F: (i) The first, called *discrete case*, works in the way that F takes the input, then executes all pipeline functions f_1, f_2, and f_3, and outputs the result. Then, F takes the new input. (ii) In the second possibility, called *continuous case*, the input of F is passed to f_1. After f_1 has produced its result, the next input of F can already be taken for f_1. In this case, three inputs of F can be taken and passed to f_1, before the first output of f_3 gives the first output of F.

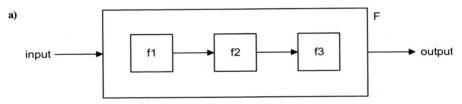

the result of f1 is input to f2; the result of f2 ist input to f3; ...

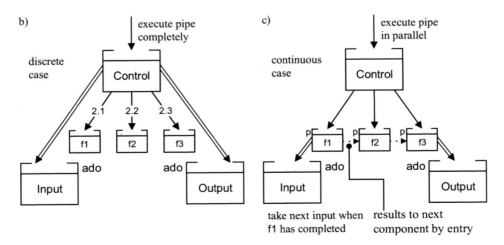

Fig. 5.5: Simple pipeline architecture with discrete or continuous semantics

Fig. 5.5.b gives a *simulation* for the *discrete case* using 'classical' architectural concepts. The control component takes the input from input, and then controls the sequence of executions f_1 to f_3, where for every f_i an output is passed back to Control. At the end of this sequence, the output of f_3 is passed by Control to output. Another simulation uses data between the f_is, see next subsection.

Fig. 5.5.c *simulates* the *continuous case*. Now f_1, f_2, and f_3 can work in parallel, so they are processes, activated by Control. The input is taken from f_1, the result of f_1 passed by an entry call to f_2, and f_1 immediately takes the next input. In this case, f_2 and f_1 for the next input now work in parallel. In the next run, f_1, f_2, and f_3 work in parallel. Again, there is a simulation with (synchronized) data between the f_is.

It should be noted that further and specific semantics are possible, which are related to how data input or output are handled. Moreover, control loops in data flow diagrams are possible. We give some examples later.

Special Cases: Batch Systems and Loosely Coupled Systems

A special case of a style – here more specific a pattern – is a *batch system*. A prominent example is the *multiphase compiler* /AS 06, WG 94/, where the number and functionality of the processing units is exactly defined: scanning, context-free syntax analysis (parsing), context-sensitive syntax analysis (static semantics), intermediate (graph-like) code generation, optimization on this intermediate graph code, addressing and machine code generation, and post optimization, see fig. 5.6.a.

Analogously, the *data* in between are *standardized* (token list, abstract syntax tree, plus symbol list or alternatively attributed syntax tree, graph-like intermediate code, which is changed by the following optimizations, machine code with addresses, and post-optimized code). Here, we can clearly speak of a *pattern* for the whole compiler and *specific system*. The underlying style is clearly defined, namely as precise functional units being coupled by precisely defined files.

In the compiler example, we find a loose coupling of phases by files and a *complete* and *sequential execution* of the phase sequence (discrete case). Every phase produces a file, taken up by the next phase. The phase sequence is completely run through. However, it is possible but seldom used that a compiler starts the first phase of the next program unit, when the previous compilation unit has been finished by the scanner (continuous case and concurrent execution of compilation units).

The compiler is also a special case of *loosely coupled systems*, which is also regarded as a style or pattern in literature, cf. fig. 5.6.b. Here different application systems (of any internal form) are coupled by a file in between. The first ends with producing the complete file, the second takes the resulting file as input. They are called loosely coupled, as coupling is done by a file and not directly by coupling the items of the file. There can be some time between the end of the first application and the start of the next. Often different systems are coupled in this way, as it is the simplest form.

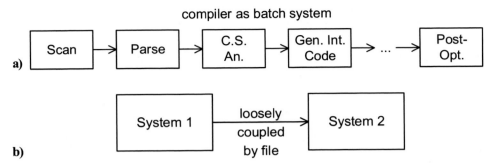

Fig. 5.6: Patterns: a) Compiler as a batch system, b) Loosely coupled systems

The *simulation* of the *sequential batch* compiler is done in the same way as already discussed in fig. 5.5.b. Also, the simulation of loosely coupled systems is easy, see again fig. 5.5.b. The control unit starts System2 only, after System1 has completely done its work and the corresponding file is available. The transmission of the results of System1 is done via the file in between.

Of course, also *other forms of loose coupling* can be simulated. For example, a compiler could also work in some pipeline-coupling mode, i.e. it translates series of programs or program units. When the first program or unit has been scanned, the next phase can start for this part. At the same time, the scanner starts to scan the second program or program unit. Here the coupling is done for the phases and not for the whole compiler. The simulation would be the same, as shown in fig. 5.5.c.

Data Flow Architectures: The General Case

Pipes and filters models can have loops, see fig. 5.2.b. Fig. 5.7.a gives the special case of a *hierarchical* unit, where the loop is inside F. If the model is *discrete*, the hierarchical unit F starts the sequence f_1, f_2, f_3, and also controls the interaction. If the iteration stops, Control produces the output.

The simulation of the *discrete case with a loop* is nearly as above in fig. 5.5.b. The component Control decides, whether to iterate by starting the sequence again, or to close the iteration and to output the result. That is, it decides inside of Control which, therefore, cannot be seen from the architecture in fig. 5.7.b. Similarly, the case is handled that the component F iterates and outputs any intermediate result.

Loops can also appear in data flow *diagrams*, which are *not hierarchical*. In this case, we add a control unit for any part of the model representing a loop. If loops contain other loops, then the inner control units are a part of outer ones. The simulation is a bit more complicated but can be handled analogously.

If the model of fig. 5.7.a is now *continuous*, then we act similarly to fig. 5.5.c, regard fig. 5.7.c. Remember that f_1, f_2, and f_3 are now processes, which run concurrently, and the connections between f_1, f_2, and f_3 is now realized by an entry, which has a data transmission and also a synchronization aspect. The backward connection between f_3 and f_1 can be realized by Control – the result of f_3 goes to Control and is delivered for f_1 again. Control also decides whether the iteration continues or stops. The continuous behavior is only inside F.

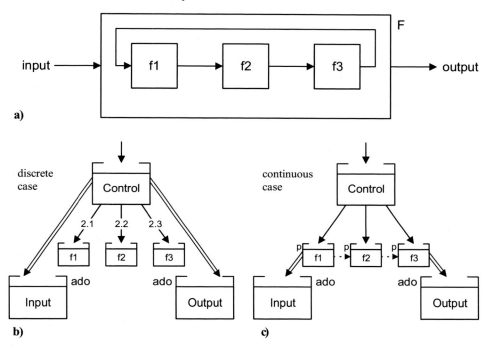

Fig. 5.7: Data flow architectures with loops traced back

There are also approaches, which distinguish between *data* and *control* channels. The first ones deliver only input and output data, the second signals for start, stop, synchronization, etc. We do not discuss this further here, as the discussion is similar. On the other hand, the differences come more from the internal behavior of components, which are not to be seen on the architecture diagram level.

We have sketched above that there are various *runtime semantics* in connection with variations of data flow diagram forms, which induce differences for their styles and also patterns. We discuss them in the next subsection. We hope that the above discussion has convinced the reader that they can be discussed/ solved in a similar way.

Specific Semantics

Above, we have learned about *data flow architectures*, starting from the simplest case (discrete and sequential case) and extending the examples to more complicated forms (continuous, with loops, etc.). They consist of functional units for *components* being connected in a graph-like form by *channels*, cf. figs. 5.2, and 5.5-7.

Above, we have recognized that there are quite *different* cases for the *semantics* associated with production/ consumption of data on channels, see e.g. /Ko 96, vB 95/: Channels can store from 1 to n tokens, i.e. the capacity is 1 or n.

A new token (data portion) destroys an old one on the channel with capacity 1, if the old one was not consumed. Alternatively, the unit trying to write on the channel is delayed.

In the case of a channel with capacity n, the new token is stored, if the channel has available capacity. Otherwise, the last token is destroyed, or the writer is delayed.

A unit can write on its output channel, although the input was not completely consumed. Alternatively, the output has to wait until the input is completely consumed, A consumed token is deleted automatically after consumption, or it remains on the input until it is explicitly deleted by the reading unit.

Tokens are produced or consumed either in a discrete or continuous way. Else, a unit may consume all or only some of the input tokens in order to start.

The information on channels may contain a mixture of data or signals. Data are necessary for the algorithmic execution of units, signals trigger the execution. Alternatively, only data are allowed on data channels. Then, there are further signal channels for the control of units (start, stop, wait, resume, synchronize, etc.).

There are even more details which could be determined and defined differently. All of these details can be regarded, if we make a suitable simulation. In this way, *via the simulation* the above *cases can be precisely determined.*

However, the details of the simulation cannot be completely seen on the level of the simulating architectural and graphical description. Many of the details are determined by the *behavior* of the *components* of the *simulation* for *data flow components*, by the behavior of the components simulating the *channels*, or by the behavior of control components. For example, a data flow component, which is writing on a channel with capacity n, can delay this writing if there is something on the channel, it can write on the channel, if the channel has less than n items, it can replace the last item and so forth. The cases depend on the behavior of the writing component and the behavior of the channel accepting an item.

Ports

Channels can start and end at *ports*. There are input ports at the left side of data flow components, and output ports at the right side. Channels connecting components can have finite (a certain number of data tokens) or potentially infinite capacity (unbounded capacity). Channels transport *data*, in some approaches also *control tokens*, in some other approaches there are different ports and channels for data and control. We now briefly discuss an example containing some of these cases. The example is a cutout and simplification of the diagram of fig. 5.2.c.

The *simulation* of data flow *with ports* is similar to the situation without ports. The simulation even remains similar, if the diagrams contain loops. Therefore, it suffices for our discussion to regard a part of fig. 5.2.c containing ports. This part is shown in fig. 5.8.a. Fig. 5.8.b gives a simulation of this part in our 'standard' notation.

There is an explicit control unit Control on top. The units C_1 to C_4 of fig. 5.8.a are fo components (functional objects) characterized by the annotation p for processes in fig. 5.8.b. The channels in the diagram of fig. 5.8.a are now denoted by ado (abstract data object) components with a synchronization protocol, e.g. mutual exclusion in fig. 5.8.b, and not by entries, as it was done in fig. 5.5.c. These channel components may have a guard to control that a channel with finite capacity can store a new item. This guard also prevents that an empty channel is read.

The port P_w^1 of fig.5.8.a is an *output port*, so indicated by w for write. The port P_r^3 is an *input port*, characterized by r for read. These ports in the data flow diagram *belong to the components* C_1 and C_2. However, they *also belong to the channel* Ch_1, the one for enqueuing, the other for dequeuing the items transported by the channel. In the simulation of fig. 5.8.b the output port is represented by a write (enqueue) operation of the ado Ch_1, the input port by a read operation (dequeue) of the ado. Both operations are connected to the corresponding components C_1 and C_2 by a corresponding import. The channel is represented by the ado Ch_1. In both representations - data flow as well as classical architecture diagram - we can argue that ports belong to both, the components and the channels. They define which way to go for a token written by a component via a channel to another reading component.

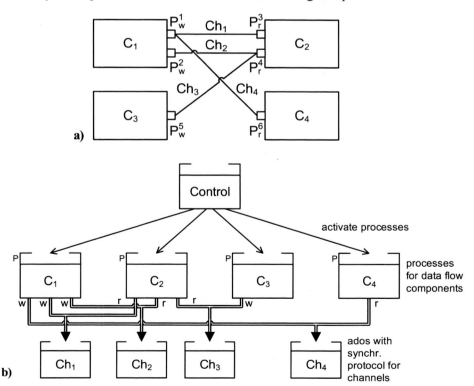

Fig. 5.8: a) Data flow diagram with ports, b) simulation of channels with ports

The *specific semantical behavior* chosen from the many possibilities of above can be realized in the simulation by the behavior of control, determined for both processes and the ado in between with synchronization and guards.

The reader should note that in this way also data flow networks with ports and loops can be simulated. As already told, such *diagrams* are quite common in *automation and control* and industrial practice /RJB 10/.

If we allow data flow diagrams with *separate channels* for data and for control, then we can take different ports, data ports and control ports. The simulation uses data and control channels. The simulation is similar but more complicated.

Again, data flow architectures are not completely new. As they can be simulated, they can be regarded as *abbreviations* of situations built up by our 'standard' notation. Parts of a system to be modeled can now be defined by a data flow notation, as we know how to interpret the connection of different diagrams.

Summary of this Section and Underlying Ideas

We have shown that the different notations of this section can be traced back to the modular notation introduced above. Thus, the notations are *not* completely *new* and *different*, as it appears at the first glance. They are not opening a new world. The simulations say that they are a different view of the same world.

Therefore, we can use the flow notations for architecture modeling, as *abbreviations for situations* we can express otherwise in the standard notation.

The *notations* can be *mixed*, as we know to interpret and understand them, a *comfort* advantage. A notation might be easier to understand for this or the other purpose.

Thereby, we found another *integration dimension*: We have integrated different notations by tracing them back to a "standard" notation. The same can be done for other style-specific architectural notations, which we do not discuss here.

Furthermore, as the *semantics* of the style notations can vary from one book to the next, we can *define* the semantical differences *precisely* and *appropriately*. This is usually not only seen on architecture diagram level. If we look inside components, we see how they react and how they act with data, control signals, and synchronization rules.

5.5 Event-based Architectures and Distribution

Event-based Architectures

If a service is being used from a component B, then the situation is as in fig. 5.9.a. The service user A wants to get a service of the service provider B. We have an import relation between the two components, allowing to use the service at development time. At runtime, the service user A initiates the service, the corresponding service of B is executed, and the result goes back to the User A. The *abstract* situation is like a *service call*, i.e. A calls a service from B.

In fig. 5.9.b we see that the abstract situation is *technically realized by signals* or events. We call this event-based programming and, correspondingly, the architectures event-based architectures /Wi EDA/. We do not clearly distinguish between events and signals. (To be more precise: A signal is exchanged between processes and an event is the cause, why the signal is sent.) In fig. 5.9.b a signal is sent to Service B saying what to do together with the parameters. This component B does something and sends the results back to A as a signal.

This more technically realized implementation of a service call can also be expressed in other ways: A and B can be processes, which can communicate via more high-level communication concepts, like entries. The communication can happen via more low-level concepts like task activation of B and following low-level communication via events, triggers, or interrupts for delivering the result. We see, there is a *range of technical possibilities* for the abstract service call.

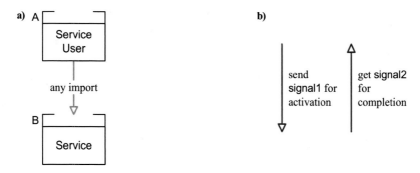

Fig 5.9: Technical use relations: What do all of them mean?

We now look on two examples using such technical means. The first is a *remote reaction*, see fig. 5.10.a. A client C is watching a state S and wants to react by the operation act, when the state change stchange happens. The obvious solution, namely for C to look frequently and wait for the change (*polling*) and then doing act is evidently *inefficient*, see fig. 5.10.a left side. A more *efficient solution* is the *callback*, see the right side of fig. 5.10.a: Client C delegates the act operation to state S, which knows about stchange. The delegation is realized by S registering for act, and S getting a procedure pointer for act from client C /Kl 00/.

Looking on the technical solution of a callback in the technical way leads to a *wrong interpretation*: You might think that the solution has completely changed. People say 'my architecture has completely inverted'. Looking more clearly, we see that is not the case, as the solution is the same from a more abstract point of view. The abstract situation (cf. fig. 5.9.a) remains the same, the mechanism for realizing it, however, has changed.

The second example, what we discuss, is *broadcasting*. We have already learned about the technical solution in fig. 5.3.a. There, a broadcasting *service* is used as a central *mediator* component. A producer Producer1 would like to have act1 exe-cuted, and Producer2 also wants act 2. Both operations can be executed 'anywhere'. This is solved by Producer1 emitting event e and Producer2 emitting the same event e. Comp1 has registered for e as well as Comp2. They get the events and act corre-spondingly. Producer1 has activated act1, and Producer2 has activated act2, without knowing, where these activations take place. This is shown by green connections in fig. 5.10.b to indicate the more abstract situation.

Later in time (not shown in fig. 5.10.b), Producer1 stops to send the event e, and Comp1 deregisters. Producer2 now sends the event e". Comp2 has deregistered for e and registered for e". Then, Producer2 and Comp2 are *now connected by a green dynamic* use edge.

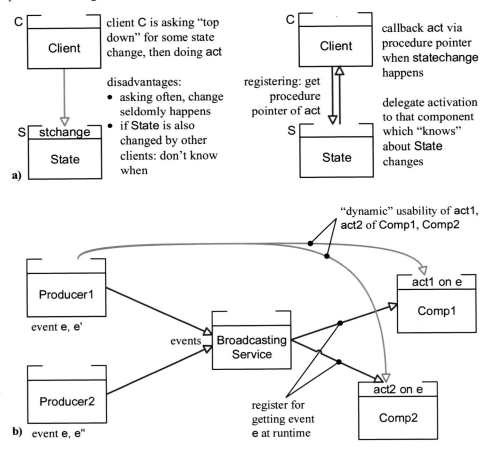

Fig. 5.10: Technical architectures and their abstract forms: a) Callback and b) Broadcasting

Registering and deregistering happen at *runtime*. Of course, it should be planned at architecture *design time*. Depending on runtime behavior alone, creates systems, which are hard to understand, even more confusing and error-prone than programs with many gotos.

A dynamic situation at runtime, which is still quite *safe* is *handling redundancy*: We need a special service multiple times, for example, depending on the load. Then, we create or activate multiple components at runtime for this service.

Another safe situation is to have *flexibility* about, *where* the *service is delivered*. This corresponds to a virtual service, where it is irrelevant, where it is provided.

A further situation is *load balancing*, i.e. many components are necessary to achieve the load. Another example is to *exchange* at runtime an *invalid component* (erroneous, blocking, etc.). There are *further examples* of and remarks for such more 'safe' situations.

In any case, the logical *goal* of a service provider should be *fixed at design time*. The provider can be virtual, anywhere but doing the corresponding job. This avoids drastic behavioral changes at runtime by events. The green connectors of fig. 5.10.b represent such an abstract situation, the red ones are suitable technical descriptions by event handling for this abstract situation. Of course, there are further possible technical descriptions for the abstract situation.

Looking on both situations of callback and broadcasting, we see that the underlying *abstract situation* of figs. 5.10.a and 5.10.b given by green connectors can be realized by using quite different concrete and technical mechanisms for service use. Therefore, we would prefer to use these abstract situations and provide *different annotations*, as cb for a callback, or via brc for via broadcasting. These abstract notations with annotations are on one side easy to understand and the annotations refer to the concrete realization. That has the advantage of *abstraction* (the underlying abstract situation is to be seen directly) and *flexibility* (the used mechanism can more easily be exchanged).

Of course, we can find more examples, not only callback and broadcasting. Above, we have given a *way to follow*, whenever complicated technical solutions are used: (a) Think in *abstract* styles, patterns, and architectures, (b) *annotate* which technical solutions you are going to use, (c) build up the corresponding detailed *technical solutions*, and later on (d) *extend* or *exchange* this technical solution.

The solution given in this section is different from the solution presented in sect. 5.4: In the last section we presented styles/ patterns and then *traced* them *back* to 'standard' architectures (simulation). The simulation was that the 'standard' architecture is more detailed.

In this section we abstracted from a more technical style/ pattern to find the underlying abstract architecture style pattern and to annotate it. Thus, here we have some *backward simulation*, from concrete and technical patterns/ solutions to their more abstract form. By *annotations* we indicate the technical/ detailed form and later insert the details of this technical form.

The *advantage* is better understandability, openness and flexibility for other technical solutions. We thereby avoid that technical details restrict the solution space.

Distribution

This *backward simulation* approach we also apply for the next category of patterns/ styles, now dealing with distribution. Therefore, we can shorten the explanation and discussion. In the last subsection we have discussed event mechanisms, we use other technical means now for *distribution patterns*.

The first example is the CORBA distribution pattern, see fig. 5.11.a. It shows, how a *remote procedure call* can be *technically realized using the CORBA infrastructure* /KL 00/. The CORBA mechanism /COR 20/ acts in the following way: For a call from a Client to a Service, a server stub is automatically generated by using the syntactic form of the procedure call. A Marshalling component (which makes from the actual parameter list a stream) and an Unmarshalling component (making the reverse) is used from the infrastructure, as well as the component RPC Basic Services, which makes the transmission in the distribution network in both ways.

We see immediately that the solution – the technical pattern – is quite specific and is likely to be changed, if we take the distribution infrastructure of another vendor. The other solution making use of the other infrastructure is quite *similar*, but we *cannot make use of this similarity*. We also see that a lot of technical aspects hide the underlying logical situation.

So again, we prefer to use the *abstract pattern*, which is shown on the right side of fig. 5.11.a. This pattern, again, gets an *annotation*, namely that a CORBA Remote Call is intended for distribution. That indicates that we make the design having a specific technical solution in mind, but also want to have flexibility, to exchange this technical solution. It is evident that this flexibility can only be achieved, if we *start with a more abstract design* and later on insert the specific and detailed design for a technical solution.

Fig. 5.11.b shows how such an *abstract design* can be used with a *distribution annotation* for the sketch of an *interactive system*. By brown distribution lines as annotations we show the possibilities of distributing the system. The black lines indicate the logical connections of the system. If there are *many interactive workplaces*, then there might be many thin clients for UI handling together with simple user checks, and one control instance for controlling all these interactive workplaces. Furthermore, there is one instance for the business functions and one for the data access. By reasons of load balancing and also handling problems, the business function instance as well as the data access instance might be realized multiple times or even multiplied at runtime (redundancy).

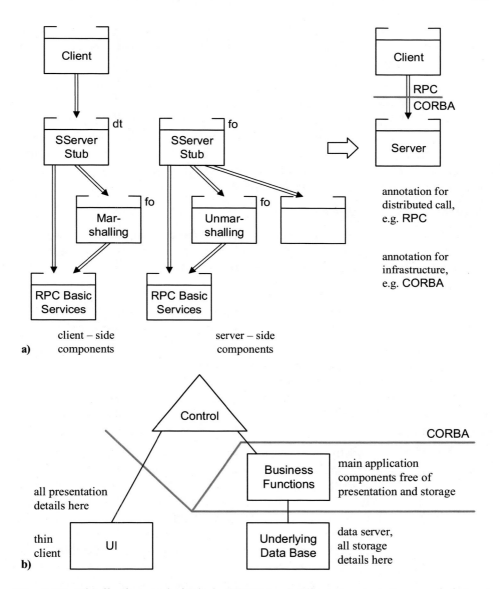

Fig. 5.11: Distribution, technical via CORBA, a) Client Server pattern, and abstract distribution, b) abstraction with annotations

Summary of the Section and Ideas Behind

As already discussed, we *proceeded differently* in this section, just the reverse direction of what we did in sect. 5.4. A technical situation was abstracted to get the essentials. Only an annotation now refers to the technical situation. We called this approach *backward simulation*. We showed this for the examples callback, broadcasting, and distribution via CORBA RPC. There are numerous further examples. Essentially, this proceeding should be applied, whenever technical details can make us blind in finding flexible and clear solutions.

The *technical solution* can more easily be *substituted* or *extended* afterwards, if we start with the abstract situation in the development process. We do not rely on the technical specifics from the beginning and we do not use them at the beginning.

Only the *annotation* refers to the technical solution. We get more *flexibility* in direction of extensions and substitution of technical details. This is specifically important in the application domain of embedded systems, which come with many details from the environment, its solution, and their impact on other details.

5.6 Global Patterns for Systems

The last *section* of this chapter is rather *short*. On the one hand, because we have already discussed some time about patterns. On the other hand, because the discussion is quite trivial. Again, we do not strive for completeness.

N-Tier Pattern

We deal with *global patterns*, which - from their definition in sect. 5.2 - determine the overall solution for a software system. We only look on two examples.

The first is the pattern *N-Tier*, also called Multitier or Multilayer Pattern /Wi Ma/. In general, an N-tier architecture is a client-server architecture, which 'divides an application architecture into logical layers and physical tiers, and thereby distinguishes between presentation, application processing, and data management functions'. The purpose is to create a flexible solution, such that layers can easily be modified or new ones inserted.

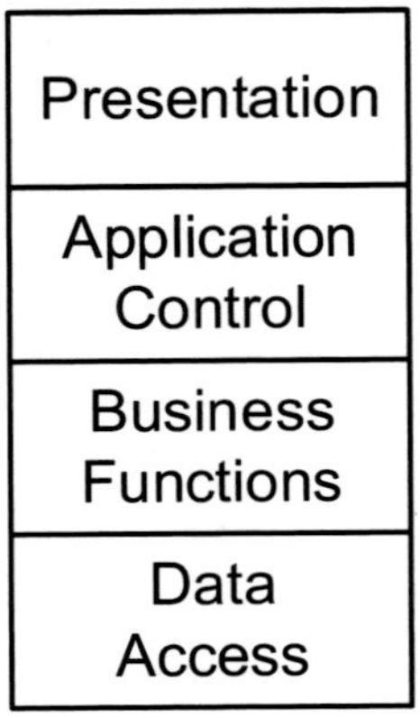

Fig. 5.12: 4-Tier global pattern (modified hierarchy, cf. fig. 5.11)

Mostly cited and used are the cases for n equal to 3 or 4. We look at the case *4-Tier for an interactive system*, see fig. 5.12. It distinguishes between a presentation layer, an application control layer, a business layer, and a data access layer. The upmost level is for the UI structure, the second for structuring the command control loop (input, internal change, changed presentation) by using corresponding services, the third to describe how the services are internally structured by using business components, and the last for the underlying data access, usually in a data base system.

The presentation layer is drawn upside, as it is 'nearest to the user'. The presentation (how commands look like and how the presentation of the intermediate results of the dialog look like) should be adaptable. The system should not heavily change if commands are differently presented (another UI management system is used, another style of UI handling, or just a primitive pure textual form for commands). The same applies for the textual and/ or graphical form of the intermediate state of the dialog results. They also can vary, and this should not heavily change the interactive system. That means that the *presentation layer comes in different sublayers*, e.g. from abstract down to one composed of simple and technical structures.

These all are arguments that the sketch of an architecture as shown in fig. 5.11.b is more appropriate than that of fig. 5.12. It regards that the UI (and also the data access as well as the business functions) have to be structured and divided into different sublayers, and that the use of these big parts of the system should not know anything about theses internal structures of sublayers.

The client server pattern is also applicable here, and also the separation of presentation (internals of UI) in a separate and usually thin client is possible. The separation line is between UI handling and Control, also between Control and Business Functions, and Business Functions and Underlying Data Base, cf. fig. 5.11.b.

Blackboard Pattern

The second example is the *blackboard pattern*, a special case of the data-centric pattern (fig. 5.13). The data- or *database-centric pattern* characterizes that different applications or part of applications (services) ksi have access to common data, usually stored in a database system or a specific data structure.

This usually means that the applications are *separate clients*, which do not exchange data directly. The blackboard is the *common memory*. No other data access is intended. This pattern is used in embedded systems: For example, there are technical data (for parts) of a plant, which should not be directly seen by the applications, but only via a data abstraction interface. Different parts can have different blackboards.

In the case that the applications are *interactive* (for an operator of a part of the plant), the applications should not know about the presentation details (commands, forms of intermediate results, see above). We have to *abstract* from all these *details*.

Especially, we have to take care that the *details of data* are *not used* in the applications and their services. In the case of a data base system, even the way the schema has been built up, should not been seen. So, data abstraction via a problem-oriented interface should be provided. This interface may be different for the different applications, as they may be interested in different parts of the information or in different ways how to access them. The right form is again delivered by fig. 5.11.b. Especially, the interfaces for the data accesses by the business functions should be designed clearly, as well as the internal structure of the data base system.

The arguments can be continued. The interactive applications ksi should *not use details* of Application Control and also not of Business Functions, and vica versa. That is demanded for any ksi but also between the different ksj.

Now we sketch and summarize some *special forms* of the blackboard pattern: If the different applications need different *views of the data*, different data abstraction interfaces have to be provided for the views. If the different applications are interactive

and have *specific presentation forms* (user interfaces, control, and application functionality), then the upper part of fig. 5.11.b (UI, control, and business functionality)
has to be multiplied for every client. If we have different applications which *share*
one and the *same presentation* (this is one form of understanding the blackboard
pattern), only the business functions are multiplied. Further interpretations of the
blackboard pattern are found in literature /MS BD/.

We see that the different situations are *clearer* and the different situations are more
precisely separated, if we trace global design patterns (as N-Tier or Blackboard)
back to more traditional architecture concepts.

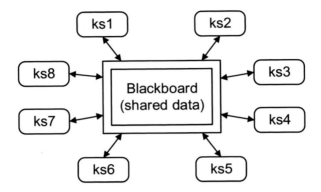

Fig. 5.13: Blackboard pattern original form /SG 96/ (and modified sketches)

Summary of this Section and its Central Ideas

Two examples of many possible ones have been studied, namely the N-Tier and the
Blackboard pattern. Both come in various forms. In both cases, the *client-server* situation may be applied and in both cases also many *presentation details* have to be
hidden from the application core. Further examples of global patterns are the ECMA
toaster for the support of automotive software /EN93/ or the control loop of automation & control applications /SG 96/.

Tracing both examples of above back to more 'classical' architectures not only
makes them *more precise*. As we have argued: The presentation layer cannot be more
abstract than the control functionality. From the discussion of internal sublayers of
the presentation layer, which range from an abstract interface down to primitive or
technical details, it is clear that the presentation has to be placed aside and not on
top. Similarly, we have discussed different layers for data access. Finally, tracing
back also allows to characterize the *different variants* of these patterns.

In this section, we have traced back to a coarse architecture level, which we call
architectural sketch level. Nevertheless, it provides more preciseness and allows to
differentiate more clearly between the variants.

5.7 Conclusion: Integrating Different Notations

After having discussed architectural styles/ patterns and their relations to traditional architectural notations, we summarize: The patterns *no longer* belong to *disjoint worlds*. We detect similarities and mutual relations.

The patterns are no longer conceptual pictures, which are open to different interpretations. Instead, they are *unambiguous* architectural *solutions* or parts of such solutions, or *styles* to work out corresponding solutions.

We have studied three different *classes of patterns/ styles*.

1 *Data flow patterns/ data flow styles* in sect. 5.4: There, we started with the simplest forms and ended with general forms. We discussed four examples. We used *forward simulation*. We can precisely define, which specific form we would like to regard: precise *semantics*. We can also discuss *variations* of these diagrams.

We now can use data flow diagrams as *abbreviation* for classical architectural solutions. We can *mix* both *notations*, e.g. architecture diagrams with data flow parts.

2 *Technical architectures* and patterns/ styles, which are heavily dependent on specific mechanisms in sect. 5.5: We discussed two examples for *event-* or signal-*based architectures*, callback and broadcasting. We discussed one example of an architecture, which is determined by a *distribution infrastructure*, namely CORBA. Here we used *backward simulation*.

We looked for a more *abstract notation*, which neglects the technical details. That notation fits better for architectural discussions to start with. *Annotations* then refer to the technical solution, which is to follow. That makes extending or exchanging technical solutions much simpler, if we start architectural design on an abstract level.

3 *Global patterns/ solutions* of sect. 5.6. They are patterns on a coarser level of granularity. We studied the example N-Tier and Blackboard. We used again forward simulation but now on a coarser level. The results of that simulation are more architectural sketches.

The approach delivered a clear demarcation between architectural pictures (as figs. 5.12 and 13) on one side and *architectural sketches* on the other (see fig. 5.11.b). We see the *advantages* of the latter: We identified a false hierarchy in N-Tier architectures, we discussed the importance of clear interfaces - UI and the data access part - and we also discussed variations of the blackboard pattern on the base of the coarse pattern of fig. 5.11.b.

5.8 Summary and Outlook

We argued at the beginning that *different styles/ patterns* introduce different *worlds*. We can discuss this on two levels: (a) The *notations* of patterns are different, or (b) the *patterns or styles* are different. We contributed to both dimensions.

On the one hand, we traced different notations back to a more traditional architectural notation thereby contributing to *integration* of different *architectural notations*. Now we better understand the commonalities and differences of notations.

On the other hand, after having expressed the different patterns to some 'standard', we can now discuss more precisely the *differences of patterns*.

The argumentation does *not* cover *all patterns* or styles. We hope to have convinced the reader that for the remaining patterns/ styles the corresponding discussion and explanation can be delivered as well.

We have also learned – especially in the discussion of data flow approaches – that there are *different semantics*, which can be assigned to a notation. Here also, it should be clear that any of them can be expressed by a suitable 'standard notation'. So, the approach presented in this chapter can be used for differentiating the variety of possible semantics.

In general, we have contributed to a better understanding of / and a better *integration of different architectural approaches* in the field of Software Engineering.

There are *further integration dimensions* we discuss in other chapters: (i) In chapter 2, we discussed which notations for different *aspects/* on different *levels/* in different *stages* of architectural design we need, from an abstract form to a concrete form. (ii) In chapter 3, we discuss in which *order* the different aspects should be introduced in order to gain as much flexibility as possible in the design process. (iii) In chapter 4, we discuss which *rules* we can find and apply in the development of embedded systems to assure adaptability. (iv) In chapter 6, we introduce a new *notation* for coupling processes, more general than the usual output input relation. (v) In chapter 7, we explain demarcations and integration of *reuse* approaches, for which we need the process notation of chapter 6. (vi) This chapter introduced the integration of different patterns/ styles. (vii) The integration aspects of software development and corresponding tools were discussed carefully in /Na96, NM 08, NW 99, NW 03/.

Going back to the title of this chapter and the question, whether we need *different notations for patterns/ styles* there are two answers. The first is *no*, as we can trace back different notations to one 'standard notation'. The other answer is *yes*. We can use different notations, as the integration has become clear. In some cases, it is nice to have different abbreviations.

There are many further approaches besides styles and patterns in order to support the development of large software systems, or to elevate it to a higher level. We find the *model-driven* approach where we first try to find a formal model and in many cases generate the solution automatically /BF 10, PB 16, PH 12/. Another approach is to think not in single solutions but in *families* of systems or *product lines* /CN 07, Ja 00, PB 05/. A very specific way is to *build* such systems *by configuration* /No 07/. More general and unspecific is to apply *reuse* techniques wherever possible /Co 98, LS 09, ICSR/. It is in general not clear how to *combine* the style or pattern approach with all these advanced approaches.

There are application domains where specific problems occur. In the development of *embedded systems* /BL 18, Ma 21/, we often find the mistake that solutions are *bound to technical* and *detailed items* of the technical target environment. We have discussed this in sect. 5.4, where we argued for first making an abstraction. Especially in embedded systems but also in others, we find the task of changing given systems by *reverse* and *reengineering* /Cr 00, Ma 05, Mo 09/ to make them understandable, or to make systems more flexible and adaptable /Me 12, Re 10/. Again, the question is how to *combine* such objectives and approaches with styles or patterns as discussed in this chapter.

In *development processes* of software engineering but also of other engineering processes, there is a lack of tools which serve for the *integration* of the different working areas, for example between requirements engineering and software architecture modeling, or architecture modeling and organization/ management of the process. Solutions are more in academic projects, e.g. /Na 96/ for software development, /NM 08/ for chemical engineering, or /KN 07/ for architecture and civil engineering. Even more evident for this chapter is that there are few tools for supporting the *approaches addressed* above (model-driven, product lines, generation, etc.). Even more missing are tools for *integrating* these new approaches with the application of *styles and patterns*. So, there are many problems and tasks open for future work on tools.

5.9 References

/AS 06/ Aho, A.V./ Lam, M.S./ Sethi, R./ Ullman, J.D.: Compilers: Principles, Techniques, and Tools, Addison-Wesley, 2nd ed. (2006)

/BF 10/ Broy, M./ Feilkas, M. et al.: Seamless Model-based Development: From Isolated Tools to Integrated Model Engineering Environments, Proc. IEEE, 98, 4, 526-545 (2010)

/BH 85/ Bergstra, J.A./ Heering, J./ Klint, J.: Algebraic Specification. EATCS Monographs on Theoretical Computer Science. Vol. 6. Springer (1985).

/BK 03/ Bass, L./ Clements, P. et al.: Software Architecture in Practice, 2nd ed. Addison Wesley (2003), 3rd ed. Pearson (2013)

/BL 18/ Bringmann, O./ Lange, W. et al.: Embedded Systems (in German), De Gruyter/ Oldenbourg, 3rd ed. (2018)

/BM 96/ Buschmann, F./ Meunier, R. et al.: Pattern-oriented Software Architecture Vol 1: A System of Patterns, Wiley (1996)

/Bö 94/ Börstler, J.: Programming in the large: Languages, Tools, Reuse (in German), Doct. Diss. RWTH Aachen University, 205 pp. (1994)

/BR 05/ Booch, G./ Rumbaugh, J. et al.: The Unified Modeling Language User Guide, Addison Wesley (2005)

/Bu 84/ Buhr, R.: System Design with Ada, Prentice Hall (1984)

/CB 02/ Clements, P./ Bachmann, F. et al.: Documenting Software Architectures, Views and Beyond, Addison Wesley/ Pearson Education, 485 pp. (2003)

/CN 07/ Clements, P./ Northrop, L.M.: Software Product Lines: Practices and Patterns, 563 pp., 6th ed., Addison Wesley (2007)

/Co 98/ Coulange, B.: Software Reuse, 293 pp., Springer (1998)

/COR 20/ https://www.omg.org/spec/CORBA/About-CORBA/

/Cr 00/ Cremer, K.: Graph-based Tools for Reverse and Reengineering (in German), Doct. Diss., RWTH Aachen University, 220 pp. (2000)

/De 74/ Dennis, J. B.: First version of a data flow procedure language, Symposium on Programming, U. of Paris, April 1974, 241-271

/DK 76/ DeRemer, F./ Kron, H.H.: Programming in the Large versus Programming in the Small, IEEE Transactions on Software Engineering, SE-2, 2, 80-86 (1976)

/DM 78/ DeMarco, T.: Structured Analysis and System Specification. Yourdon, New York, (1978)

/EM 89/ Ehrig, H./ Mahr, M.: Bernd: Algebraic Specification. Academic Press. (1989)

/EN 93/ ECMA/NIST: Reference model for frameworks of software engineering environments, ECMA TR/55, ECMA, 1993. URL: http://www.ecma-international.org/publications/files/ECMA-TR/TR-055.pdf

/Ev 04/ Evans, E.: Domain-driven Design, Addison Wesley, 529 pp. (2004)

/GH 95/ Gamma, E./ Helm, R./ Johnson, R./Vlissides, J.: Design Patterns: Elements of Reusable Object-Oriented Software, 395 pp. Addison Wesley (1995)

/GS 94/ Garlan, D./ Shaw, M.: An Introduction to Software Architectures, TR CMU-CS-94-166, 39 pp., Carnegie Mellon University (1994)

/Gu 76/ Guttag, J.: Abstract Data Types and the Development of Data Structures, Comm. ACM 20, 6, 396-404 (1977)

/HK 07/ Hofmeister, C./ Kruchten, P. et al: A general model of software architectural design derived from five industrial approaches, Journal of Systems and Software 80, 106-126 (2007)

/HP 80/ Habermann. H.N./ Perry, D.: Well-formed System Compositions, TR CMU-CS-80-117, Carnegie-Mellon University (1980)

/ICSR/ International Conference on Software Reuse: Proc. from 1990 to 2017, see also Wikipedia ICSR

/Ja 00/ Jazayeri, M. et al. (eds.): Software Architecture for Product Families, Addison Wesley (2000)

/JC 92/ Jacobsen, I./ Magnus, C. et al.: Object Oriented Software Engineering. 77-79, Addison-Wesley ACM (1992)

/Kl 00/ Klein, P.: Architecture Modeling of Distributed and Concurrent Software Systems Doct. Diss. RWTH Aachen University, 237pp. (2000)

/KM 04/ Kruger, I./ Mathew, R.: Systematic development and exploration of service-oriented software architectures, 4th Working IEEE/IFIP Conference on Software Architecture (WICSA), 177-187 (2004)

/KN 07/ Kraft, B./ Nagl, M.: Visual Knowledge Specification for Conceptual Design: Definition and Tool Support, Journ. Advanced Engineering Informatics 21, 1, 67-83 (2007)

/Ko 96/ Kohring, Ch.: Ausführung von Anforderungsdefinitionen zum Rapid Prototyping, Doct. Diss. RWTH Aachen University, 293 pp. (1996)

/Le 88/ Lewerentz, C.: Concepts and tools for the interactive design of large software systems (in German), Doct. Diss., 179 pp. RWTH Aachen University, Informatik-Fachberichte 194, Springer (1988)

/LS 09/ Land, R./ Sundmark, D. et al.: Reuse with Software Components – A Survey of Industrial State of Practice, in Edwards/ Kulczycke (Eds.): ICSR 2009, LNCS 5791, 150-159 (2009)

/LZ 74/ Liskow, B./ Zilles, S.: Specification Techniques for Data Abstractions, Int. Conf. on Reliable Software, 72-87, IEEE (1975)

/Ma 05/ Marburger, A.: Reverse Engineering of Complex Legacy Telecommunication Systems, Doct. Diss., RWTH Aachen University, 418 pp. (2005)

/Ma 21/ Marwedel, P.: Embedded System Design, 4th ed., Springer (2021)

/Me 91/ Meyer, B.: Eiffel: The Language, 300 pp. 1st ed. Prentice Hall (1991), 3rd ed. 2005

/Me 97/ Meyer, B.: Object-oriented Software Construction, 2nd ed., 1254 pp., Prentice Hall (1997)

/Me 12/ Mengi, C.: Automotive Software – Processes, Models, and Variability (in German), Doct. Dissertation, RWTH Aachen University, 350 pp. (2012)

/MM 87/ Marca, D./ McGowan, C.: Structured Analysis and Design Technique, McGraw-Hill, (1987)

/MP 10/ Meyer, B./ Pedroni, M.: Software Architecture: Architectural Styles, lecture manuscript, 48 pp. (2010

/Mo 09/ Mosler, Ch.: Graph-based Reengineering of Telecommunication Systems (in German), Doct. Diss. RWTH Aachen University, 268 pp., RWTH Aachen University (2009)

/MS BD/ Microsoft: Blackboard Design Pattern, accessed 23

/Na 82-03/ Nagl, M.: Introduction to Ada (in German), 348 pp., Vieweg (1982), 6th ed. Software Engineering and Ada (in German), 504 pp., Vieweg (2003)

/Na 90-20/ Nagl, M.: Software Engineering- Methodological Programming in the Large (in German), 387 pp., Springer (1990), plus further extensions for lectures from 1990 to 2020

/Na 96/ Nagl, M. (Ed.): Building Tightly Integrated Software Development Environments - The IP-SEN Approach, LNCS 1170, 709 pp., Springer (1996)

/Na 19/ Nagl, M.: Gothic Churches and Informatics (in German), 304 pp, Springer Vieweg (2019), see pp. 179-187

/NM 08/ Nagl, M./ Marquardt, W.: Collaborative and Distributed Chemical Engineering – From Understanding to Substantial Design Process Support, IMPROVE, LNCS 4970, 851 pp., Springer (2008)

/No 07/ Norbisrath, U.: Configuring eHome Systems (in German), Doct. Dissertation, 286 pp. (2007)

/NW 99/ Nagl, M./ Westfechtel, B. (Eds.): Integration of Development Systems in Engineering Applications – Substantial Improvement of Development Processes (in German), 440 pp., Springer (1999)

/NW 03/ Nagl, M./ Westfechtel, B. (eds.): Models, Tools, and Infrastructures for the Support of Development Processes (in German), 392 pp., Wiley VCH (2003)

/Pa 72/ Parnas, D.: On the Criteria to be Used in Decomposing Systems into Modules, Comm. ACM 15, 12, 1053-1058 (1972)

/PB 05/ Pohl, K./ Böckle, G. et al.: Software Product Line Engineering, 467 pp., Springer (2005)

/PB 16/ Pohl, K./ Broy, M. et al. (eds.): Adavanced Model-based Engineering of Embedded Systems – Extensions to the SPES 2020 Methodology, Springer, 303 pp. (2016)

/PH 12/ Pohl, K./ Hönninger, K. et al. (eds.): Model-based Engineering of Embedded Systems – The SPES 2020 Methodology, Springer, 304 pp. (2012)

/PW 92/ Perry, D.E. / Wolf, A.L.: Foundations for the Study of Software Architecture. ACM SIGSOFT Software Engineering Notes, 17:4 (1992).

/Re 10/ Retkowitz, D.: Software Support for Adaptive eHome Systems (in German), Doct. Diss. RWTH Aachen University, 354 pp. (2010)

/RJB 10/ Rumbaugh, J./ Jacobson, I./ Booch, G.: The Unified Modling Language Reference Manual, 721 pp., Addison-Wesley (2010)

/Ru 12/ Rumpe, B.: Agile Modeling with UML (in German), 2nd ed., 372 pp., Springer (2012)

/SAD/ Software Architecture and Design Tutorial, TutorialRide.com, https://www.tutorial-ride.com/software-architecture-and-design/software-architecture-and-design-tutorial.htm

/SC 06/ Shaw, M./ Clements, P.: The Golden Age of Software Architecture: A Comprehensive Survey, Techn. Report CMU-ISRI-06-101, 14 pp., Carnegie Mellon University (2006)

/Sc 13/ Schmidt, R.F.: Software Engineering – Architecture-driven Software Development, 376 pp. Elsevier (2013)

/SG 96/ Shaw, M./ Garlan, D.: Software architecture: perspectives on an emerging discipline, 242 pp., Prentice Hall (1996)

/So 18/ Sommerville, I.: Software Engineering, 10th edition in German, Pearson (2018)

/SS 00/ Schmidt, D./ Stal, M. et al.: Pattern-oriented Software Architectures, vol 2 Patterns for Concurrent and Networked Objects, Wiley (2000)

/ST 12/ Sannella, D./ Tarlecki, A.:. Foundations of Algebraic Specification and Formal Software Development. EATCS Monographs on Theoretical Computer Science. Springer (2012)

/TP 16/ Tutorials Point: Software Architecture & Design Tutorial, 74 pp. (2016)

/vB 95/ v. d. Beeck, M.: Ein Kontrollmodell für die Strukturierte Analyse, Doct. Diss. RWTH Aachen University, 282 pp. (1995)

/Wi DFP/ Wkipedia: Data Flow Pogramming, access 2023

/Wi EDA/ Wikipedia: Event-driven Architecture, access 2023

/Wi Ma/ Wikipedia: Multitier architectures, access 2023

/Wi SA/ Wikipedia: Software Architecture, https://en.wikipedia.org/wiki/Software_architecture, access 2021

/Wi SDP/ Wikipedia: Software Design Pattern, access 2023

6 Process Interaction Diagrams are more than Chains or Transport Networks

Manfred Nagl

Software Engineering, RWTH Aachen University, nagl@cs.rwth-aachen.de

Abstract

Process modeling is a broad field of research in different application areas, especially in informatics. Corresponding notations (transport networks, etc.) usually contain sequences, splits and joins of processes. Between processes there are dependencies, which can have quite different semantics. These semantical relations are usually not explicitly expressed.

In this chapter, we focus on a notation for a process, which has different aspects influencing the process, not only the input. This allows to connect different processes in specific ways, making clear what purpose the connection has and, thereby, characterizing different kinds of dependencies between processes. This extended notation we call process interaction diagrams (PIDs). We can express standard interactions of processes more precisely and are also able to express nonstandard forms of interaction.

These diagrams can be applied in different domains, as mechanical engineering, informatics, etc. Interesting and complex interactions can be studied. The notation can be used for different levels of processes, as lifecycle level, project management of development teams, etc. The usual process notations are extended to express interactions like "a process creates a tool to be used in another process".

Keywords: process modeling, dependency relations between subprocesses, different aspects of a process, interaction of different processes, applications in engineering

6.1 Introduction

There is a variety of *notations for processes*, which can be used for quite different kinds and levels of processes, as /AL 16, JB 96, We 99/ to name only a few. They can be *classified* (i) along their main *application* (logistics, business processes, cooperative work in offices, mechanical production, building/ maintaining software, etc.), (ii) *where* processes are *used* (knowledge acquisition, pre-development, development, preparation for production, production, maintenance, customer relationship, etc.), (iii) according to their *granularity* (from lifecycle or ERP to fine-grained tasks), or (iv) whether they are *static* or allow *dynamic* changes.

Process *research* can be *classified* into mining, analysis, formalization, classification, application, or evolution. The latter can happen on single process level, on knowledge for processes, their change, on process type level, on knowledge level for specific processes, and so on.

In most cases, processes connect mostly along output to input (the output of one process is the input of the next) and, therefore, corresponding to *chain dependen-*

cies: The second process is dependent on the first and can only start, when the first process has delivered a necessary result. Such notations are widely used.

All these notations can be used to structure processes by composing them from simpler ones (subprocesses) and thereby building nets of these subprocesses by dependency relations. In graph theoretic terminology these nets are *transport networks* /De 74/, which usually have a starting node (source) and an ending node (target). The networks are built up from chains, splits, and joins. For organizational aspects of one specific process this may suffice.

In this chapter, we look more carefully on the way, how connections can be organized and denoted. Especially, we look at what aspects influence a process, and take these aspects as targets of process dependent edges. Thereby, we *differentiate dependency relations*. We call the corresponding notation *process interaction diagrams*, in short PIDs, thereby adding another meaning to the abbreviation "PID" /PID 21/. Roughly speaking, these diagrams distinguish incoming edges according to their purpose and, thereby make these networks more semantical, corresponding to the different ways, how processes are connected.

Predecessors of PIDs in *simpler forms* are SADT-diagrams /MM 88/, T-diagrams of N. Wirth /Wi 77/ for explaining compiler bootstrapping, or component / connector notations, as /IC 04/.

The *chapter* is *structured* as follows: After having introduced the different aspects of a process, which influence the way processes can be connected in PIDs in sect. 6.2, we discuss different examples of process interactions in PIDs in sect. 6.3. We present interesting and nontrivial examples of PIDs in sect. 6.4. A summary / characterization of the results and the list of references closes this chapter.

In this chapter we concentrate only on *process* interaction, although – as it was discussed in /HJ 08, NW 94/ – a process is also tightly connected to its resulting *product*, and both also to the *resources* needed (active as actors or passive as preresults), the latter two in abstract form (as abilities for abstract resources) as well as in actual form (persons with competences).

6.2 Characterizations of Processes

A *process* is influenced by different aspects, see fig. 6.1. The process has an *input*, and produces an *output* of quite different kinds, as we are going to learn. The process has a *goal*, has to regard different *constraints*, and follows a certain *way to proceed*, expressed from rather vague to precisely determined. The process has an *actor*, usually a human or a group of humans for a complicated task. The process uses *tools* or available *partial results/ solutions* to be a part of the result of the process. Processes apply *knowledge* and/ or *experience*. In /MJW 08, NF 03/ other aspects of a process are discussed. We omit this to keep the discussion simple.

The upper part of fig. 6.1 corresponds to the *planning part* of the process (goal, constraints, way to proceed), the lower part determines the path in *direction* to the *solution* (partial solutions, tools, actor, and experience/ knowledge). To be more precise, one should distinguish between a task and the process to solve the task. By reasons of simplicity, in this chapter a process stands for both. Altogether, we have seven 'input' aspects and only one for the output.

The *actor* of a development process is usually a *human*. In automatic processes, the actor can be a *machine* executing a program. In this case, the goal, constraints, and way to proceed are incorporated in the automatic program. The same is true for knowledge and experience. The machine (actor) determines the level of the program (preciseness, degree of formality).

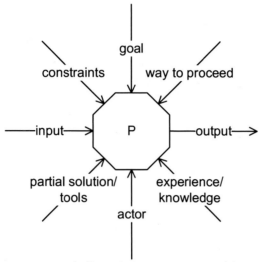

Fig. 6.1: Different aspects influencing a process P and its output

A process corresponds to the solution of a task, which solves an underlying problem. The task may (a) demand for *creativity*, like acquisition or extension of knowledge, pre-development of a product, development of a novel and nontrivial product, extending a solution to a solution for a family, detecting deep reuse for a class of solutions by remarkably changing the process, etc. In all these cases, the process is not determined, it demands creativity and new ideas. The task may (b) be rather *determined*, like often executed processes in business administration or production within mechanical engineering. Finally, a process may (c) run *automatically*, as found in process automation & control. There, everything is running automatically, determined by software, eventually including interactions of the operator.

Processes can be found on different *granularity levels*: We find (i) *coarse-grained* processes, e.g. on lifecycle level, where we only distinguish subprocesses without looking into their structure, as AR for architecture modeling in fig. 1.1 of ch. 1. It can be (ii) *medium-grained*, where we go down to identify actions of single developers in order to manage these developers, without regarding how they do their job, like the implementation of a certain component assigned to a developer, or how a subsystem is decomposed and the parts are assigned to developers. Finally, processes can be (iii) *fine-grained*, as how a designer is doing the task assigned to him/her in detail. One further level down, (iv) we find the *actions* of a *tool* used by a developer to facilitate his/her job. Tools can be used on any granularity level.

Furthermore, development processes may be (1) *local* to a certain department, (2) happen inside a company but involving *different departments*, or it may (3) spread over *different companies* (local, integrated, inter-company processes).

What we have said up to now is mostly *independent* from the *level* and *nature* of a *process*. It also applies to any kind of processes, from research, knowledge acquisition, pre-development, development, realization, preparation, production, to after sales and maintenance. In the last sentence we had mechanical engineering in mind. It could also be process engineering, material production, or anything else.

Development *processes* of teams of developers have a certain *structure*; this can be found in every engineering discipline /NM 08, We 99/, determining or changing the requirements, the design, and the realization. The latter in engineering is called detail engineering. The *product* of a process is a complex *configuration* of different and mutually dependent artifacts.

6.3 Process Interactions

Process Chains for Different Purposes

In fig. 6.2 we regard usual chains of processes in the sense that one process produces a result which, in the next step, is handled by the following process. However, the *purpose of handling* is *different*. The examples are from the development level. In the first case a), the second process P_2 makes the next step of a process, decomposed into steps. In the second example b), it produces a result consistent to the result of P_1. In the third case c), it formalizes a given non-formal result or it makes a formal result operational. Further examples are possible. The specific purpose of the output/ input relation can be given by an annotation to the relation.

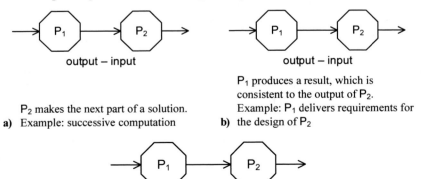

output – input

output – input

P_1 produces a result, which is consistent to the output of P_2.

P_2 makes the next part of a solution.

Example: P_1 delivers requirements for
a) Example: successive computation   **b)** the design of P_2

P_1 produces a result which is made
c) formal or precise by P_2

Fig. 6.2: Process chain relations for different purposes

The purpose of these examples is to demonstrate that *chain dependency relation* between P_1 and P_2 can have *different semantics*. The examples are on the same logical level and they are typical situations occurring in development processes carried out by humans. The examples could also be from other development and application domains (informatics, production engineering, process engineering, etc.).

Processes for Creating Components or Tools

Fig. 6.3 shows that the process P_1 can deliver a *result*, which makes the *process P_2 easier*, as (a) P_1 delivers a partial product, which is helpful for P_2 (fig. 6.3.a), or (b) P_1 delivers a *tool*, which *helps* for the process P_2 (fig 6.3.b). Please note that these supports (a) and (b) are possibly not restricted to P_2. If this were the case, the process P_1 would deliver a part of the solution according to the scheme of fig. 6.2.a, which is then completed by P_2.

In fig. 6.3.c, P_1 delivers a result, which supports the process P_2 by delivering explicit knowledge or experience, helpful for P_2. This can be e.g. a checklist of items, which helps not to forget an aspect important for the actor of process P_2. Again, annotations can clarify.

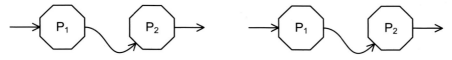

a) P_1 creates a result which helps for P_2, e.g. a needed component

b) P_1 delivers a tool which facilitates the process P_2

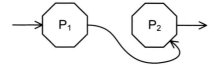

c) P_1 improves P_2, e.g. by delivering experience/ knowledge in explicit form

Fig. 6.3: Actor support: facilitating solution, tool, experience/ knowledge

Clarifications for other Processes

The process P_1 can define/ make precise the goals of P_2 (fig. 6.4.a), or the constraints for P_2 (fig. 6.4.b), or the way to proceed in P_2 (fig. 6.4.c). The latter can be from vague and exemplary to formal and complete.

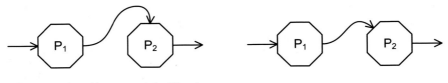

P_1 determines/ improves/ clarifies the
a) goal of P_2

b) P_1 determines the constraints for P_2

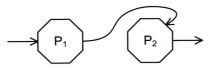

P_1 determines/ improves how P_2
should proceed by giving the steps, a
c) plan how to proceed, or a methodology

Fig. 6.4: Clarifications: P_1 delivers results for different aspects of P_2

We see: The process P_1 can deliver a *helpful result* for *any* of the *'input'* aspects explained in fig. 6.1, see figs. 6.3 and 6.4. The composition of both processes P_1 and P_2 is different from those discussed in fig. 6.2. In all cases, we have a dependency of process P_2 on process P_1. However, we recognize that the semantics of the dependency is different for all cases. Annotations may clarify these distinctions.

Actors and Machines

In all examples of above, we had *human actors*. A human actor is *intelligent* and *creative*. The actor can interpret constraints, evaluate a goal, compare a process result with the goal, can follow advices to proceed, can build/ evaluate and apply partial results, or apply tools to facilitate or improve a solution. The person can use/ apply experience or knowledge. This all is also true for a scientist who is extending knowledge, as well as for a worker, who carries out a fabrication process.

What is to recognize, if the *process* is *automatic* and what to obey, if we switch from a human to an automatic process? In informatics terms, an automatic process is a *program* executed by a *machine*. The program may be an executable specification, or a program formulated by an interpreter language together with an interpreter. It can also be a program Pr of a programming language L, together with a machine for this language (compiler, runtime system, and target machine).

Looking on fig. 6.4 and P_2, we now discuss that P_2 is an *automatic process*. Does this change the situation? P_1 can create the program, P_1' the machine. Both are human processes. The program with the machine is the automatic process, fig. 6.5.a.

A different *explanation in our notation* is that P_1 creates the program, i.e. the way to proceed, and P_1' the actor of P_2. The program has been written to follow a goal, to regard a restriction, to use partial solutions or tools, or to adopt knowledge and experience. This, altogether, is incorporated and fixed in the program Pr. So, all the other aspects of P₂ (fig. 6.1) are determined by the properties of the program. They are no more important for P₂. Fig. 6.5.b shows this situation.

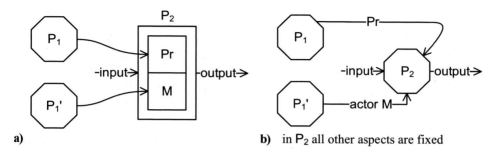

a)   b)   in P₂ all other aspects are fixed

Fig. 6.5: Automatic actor P₂ by program Pr and machine M

6.4 Examples of Process Interaction Diagrams

Production Engineering

We now switch to the field of *mechanical engineering*. That differs from software development in two ways. (a) The products are produced after their development in a more or less complicated production process, which needs a corresponding preparation after product development. Furthermore, (b) also the facilities for production have to be regarded. Usually, this production machinery is used for different products. In the case of a novel product, it might even be that the machinery has to be developed specifically.

This all is usually not the case for *software*. In *rare cases*, there is something like a *production* of software. This production is mostly just configuration and delivery.

We now discuss the *interaction* of the three *processes* (i) development and production preparation, (ii) production and tool use, and (iii) production facility development /NF 03/. The production of the facility is usually done by other companies, and the production machines in most cases serve for different production processes. The three processes are in *different dimensions*, see fig. 6.6.

The example is on the level of *coarse processes* (lifecycle level), which means that the processes are not structured internally. For example, the *product development* is usually done in steps belonging to *different levels* (requirements, conceptual and detailed design, detail engineering), which is not done in fig. 6.6. These levels are structured internally to express that different people do different things, which have to be consistent to each other. This we call middle-grained or *organizational level*, because it structures, how the cooperation of different developers is organized.

In fig. 6.6 we see three process *chains*, which are *orthogonal* to each other: (a) In the middle and drawn horizontally, there is the *physical product lifecycle*. A product is produced, later it is used and maintained (physical maintenance), and even later we see the recycling. The production process uses parts, which are manufactured by suppliers. The chain has the usual output/ input dependency relation.

(b) On top and drawn down, we find the *development lifecycle*, again presented in a coarse form with the usual output/ input relation. We start with pre-development, to show that the development is possible and can result in a reasonable product (we build a prototype and decide to go further or to stop). Then, we develop the product, using different internal steps. If that was successful, we start with the production preparation, also consisting of different internal steps. The results deliver know-how, which either is useful and necessary for the manufacturing process, or which corresponds to experience/ knowledge. Production preparation also delivers constraints and ways to proceed (e.g. NC programs).

(c) At the bottom and drawn upwards in fig. 6.6, we find the process to *provide* the *platform for manufacturing*. The platform is developed in two parallel steps: (i) How the production platform is built up (determination of corresponding tool machines and how they are configured), and (ii) developing the corresponding automation and control programs. They are both combined in the manufacturing *plant*. Typically, the manufacturing tool machines are not specifically developed and built up (that can happen in specific contexts, where no corresponding machines are available on the market). However, the tool machines may need some adaptation. Also, the automation and control infrastructure is available, but specific programs have to be written, adapted, or generated. The production plant together with the corresponding personnel is the actor of the manufacturing process.

Summing up, we see that fig. 6.6 consists of three coarse *processes* in *three dimensions*: physical production, development of the product to be later produced, and making the production infrastructure (plant) available. The processes are connected to the *business administration process* (ERP) for sales, production of a number of products, logistics, maintenance of products in a repair center, after sales relations, etc. This ERP process is not shown in fig. 6.6.

Any of these four processes is a cross-company process. The used intermediate products of all these processes also have a development and need a manufacturing infrastructure. All processes *interact* in *different ways*. This is the main argument to sketch the situation here.

Now, we make the process interaction even more complex by introducing further new tools, which come up in the above three dimensions, see again fig. 6.6: (i) A new software *tool* is introduced which makes the *product development* more efficient and helps to avoid mistakes/ errors. Secondly, (ii) a new mechanical tool is needed for the *specific production* process. (iii) A new software tool helps in the *design* of the *automation and control* part, again for efficiency and quality improvement. These tools introduce further interaction dimensions.

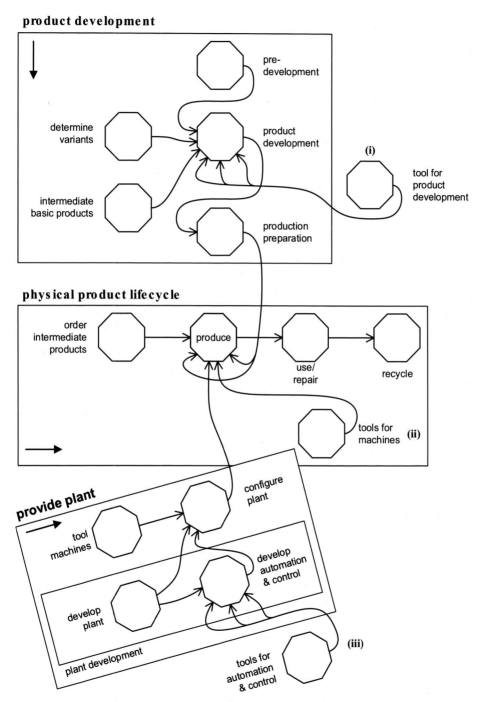

Fig. 6.6: Interleaved and orthogonal processes in production engineering

The new tool for development (i) influences and changes the development process. Especially, it also *changes* the *experience / knowledge* of this process and it also changes the *actors* of this process. The change might be gradual or dramatic. The same is true (iii) for the new tool helping to develop the automation and control part. A tool helping for configuring the production plant (not shown in fig. 6.6) would influence the configuration process in the same way. Another role has (ii) the tool for a tool machine in the production process. It is produced (usually without a development or a complicated production process), and it has to be replaced after some time, due to wear and tear.

Mostly production tool development is *not done in parallel* to product, or facility development, or production. Mostly it is used for the next product cycle. However, it can be that it is needed *in the running process*. The development of a new production tool for the machine is usually done in parallel.

The 'Analogous' Situation in Software Engineering

Now we switch to a similar situation in the field of *software development*. The figure changes noticeably. This change characterizes the difference to a field, which produces mainly physical products (machines, chemical plants, etc.) from a field, where mainly nonphysical products (software) are created. Thus, not only the *characterization* of the *change* but also the *difference* of the *fields* are interesting.

As in software development immaterial products are created, there is usually *no production process* (horizontal chain of fig. 6.6). Software is usually only copied and distributed. I only saw once something like a production process for software products. That was in the company DATEV, which provides and delivers software and IT services for tax consultants /DA 21/. As there are 40,000 consultants being supported by DATEV, who have quite different profiles and also various and different IT infrastructures, delivering an update, extension, or porting of software is a rather complex configuration but also delivering process. Here we find something like a 'production' process. That is not typical in the case of software.

As there is usually no production process, *production preparation* - the last big step of product development in mechanical engineering - does *not appear*, or it appears only in a primitive form. The same is true for the infrastructure to produce the products in production. The production is immaterial, so does *not need* a complex *production infrastructure*.

Therefore, mainly the *product development* process of fig. 6.6 *remains*. This process can include all the relations between subprocesses, we have sketched in this chapter. Furthermore, software as an immaterial product is more flexible w.r.t. changes and also transformations, as in direction of applying reuse strategies.

Hierarchies in and Management of Software Development

We show some further process interactions, which are possible within software development, by sketching some of various situations in this subsection.

Firstly, we look on the dependency relations between *requirements engineering*, where the requirements for a future software system or the requirements for a change of an existing software system are made precise, and the following *realization* of the system, see fig. 6.7.a. In this activity area RE (requirements engineering, modeling and changing requirements), quite different results are produced.

One result of the requirements specification, which determines what the following system is going to do, is often called *functional requirements specification*. This part is (i) the *input* of the realization process. It is used to build up a system in several steps, which is consistent with the functional specification, see fig. 6.2.b. The requirements deliver *further determinations*: (ii) the goal of the system to be built/changed, (iii) the constraints the future system has to follow, e.g. efficiency parameters, or (iv) they determine the ways to produce the result, e.g. the process shares similarities with other development processes already finished, or is in parallel (as ways to structure the interactive input, such that it is uniform to existing systems). Furthermore, it can (v) determine (v.a) some external components to be used, (v.b) tools to be applied. Furthermore, we (vi) predetermine the development process, e.g. by fixing the corresponding quality assurance procedures. Finally, the spec may (vii) state which experiences or which knowledge are to be applied.

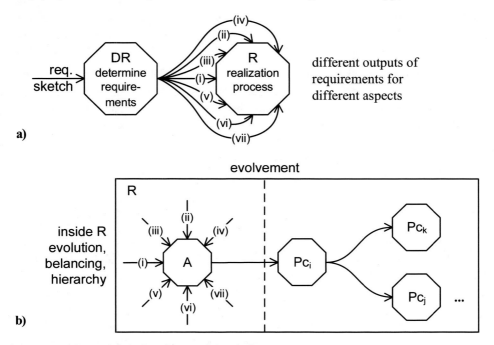

Fig. 6.7: Hierarchy, balancing, and evolution

We see that the requirements area produces quite *different results important* for the following development process which specify what to do (i, ii), the constraints for the future product and process (iii, iv), determining properties of the product (iv, v), and of the process (v, vi, vii). This can be separated and expressed by the *different facets* of a process (see figs. 6.1 and 6.7.a). This example is one of the rare cases, where *all forms of the dependency relations* occur between two processes, here DR and R of fig. 6.7.a.

The following process R (for realization) is *structured internally*, see fig. 6.7.b. It starts with the process A for *architecture modeling*. Most of the incoming edges to R have to be directed towards this process (by so-called balancing). This is easy to see, as requirements determinations mostly deal with or influence the architectural structure of the system. Only some of the incoming relations may also influence the following component realization processes.

We assume that the architecture process is simple; it can be carried out by one designer and, therefore, need not be decomposed. For the following realization processes for components of the system we can only say that they appear. We do not know how many such processes will come up, as we do not know which components have to be realized. This is fixed not before the architectural process A has delivered its result, namely a part of/ the complete architecture of the system. In the *running process* R, by the results of the process A it is determined, how the *following processes look like*, see again fig. 6.7.b. Furthermore, the dependency relations between these processes are also determined (e.g. the process for the component P_{Cj} is dependent on that for P_{Ci}). Thus, a subnet of the process net is determined by the results of A, see again fig. 6.7.b. This we called *evolution dynamics* /Kr 98, Sc 02/.

It should be noted that the extension of the process net of R to get the processes for the components is done by another process, which does not appear in fig. 6.7.b. This *process* is usually done by a human, the *process manager* (or chief designer), who looks at the architecture (the product of A), then makes the extension, possibly supported by a tool. The extension in fig. 6.7.b - a net of subprocesses with dependencies - is the result of this activity. There are *further* and more complex *dynamic situations* possible, some of which we sketch in the summary.

Bootstrapping and Compilers

We come back to the discussion of automatic processes of sect. 6.3. We discuss combinations of such automatic processes and *bootstrapping* of compilers /Wi 77/. With this example, we show that our notation allows to smoothly *connect human and automatic* processes.

Bootstrapping uses so-called T-diagrams /Wi 77/, see fig. 6.8.a. A T-diagram denotes a specific automated process, namely the *translation* of programs written in a programming language. The left part of fig. 6.8.a shows a T-diagram translating programs of a language So (for source) to programs of Ta (for target), written in the implementation language I. Such a T form $^{So}_M{}^{Ta}$ is *executable*, if a corresponding machine M for the language is available (right part of fig. 6.8.a). This M-program can be executed and translates a So to a Ta program. The program M and the corresponding machine M form a process, see explanation of sect. 6.3.

Such T-diagrams can be connected, see lower part of fig. 6.8.a. If a form $^I_M M$ is available - it is a M program translating I to M - the form $^S_I T$ can be used as input, which is an I program. The result is $^S_M T$, a M program translating S to T. Such combinations are used for bootstrapping, i.e. compiling compilers with a reduced effort.

Bootstrapping can be used for different tasks. We discuss here the *extension* of a *programming language* and developing the *compiler* for the extended language, see fig. 6.8.b. For that we need a compiler for S written in S (e.g. a Pascal compiler written in Pascal /Wi 77/) and one S compiler producing M and written in M, both in green. In two development steps and two automatic steps, we get the compiler for the extended language S′ as result.

We take the given $^S_S M$ compiler and *modify* it (1) to become an $^{S'}_S M$ compiler (human process). We *translate* this compiler with the available $^S_M M$ compiler and get an $^{S'}_M M$ compiler (automatic task (2)). This compiler is used for the last and automatic step. For that, we (3) *modify* the $^{S'}_S M$ compiler to a $^{S'}_{S'} M$ compiler (again a human task), i.e. by using the extended features of S′ in the compiler. Finally, we *translate* this compiler, using the $^{S'}_M M$ compiler of step (2), and get the result (automatic process (4)).

Altogether, we have extended the $^S_M M$ compiler to a $^{S'}_M M$ compiler. Step (2) and step (4) produced an $^{S'}_M M$ compiler. The advantage of the last compiler of step (4) is that it *makes use of the advanced features of* S′ in its implementation. These steps for extension (1) to (4) can be used repeatedly to extend the language and the compiler step by step. Therefore, we can start with a simple language and, by repetition, finally end with a complex one. The advantage of bootstrapping is not only simpler development. The compiler quality also has an advantage.

The notation of fig. 6.8.b has *automatic steps* (2), (4), made precise by combinations of T-diagrams, but also informal *human tasks* (1), (3), characterized by dash-dotted lines. What does this say? We explain this in two steps.

T-diagrams represent automated and specific processes. They make a translation of two formal and executable languages. In addition, they are formulated in a formal and executable language. Thus, the input and output of fig. 6.1 is now formal and fixed and the program, how to do, is formal and fixed, too. Restrictions, goals, support, knowledge and experience (see again fig. 6.1) are now not relevant, they all are expressed in the translating program. For this *special case*, we can use a *special notation*, namely T-diagrams of Wirth. We can say the T-diagram part of fig. 6.8.a is only an abbreviation for a part usually expressed by PIDs. The expressiveness of PIDs is not needed for this special case. Furthermore, these T-diagrams have the properties of combination and automatic translation.

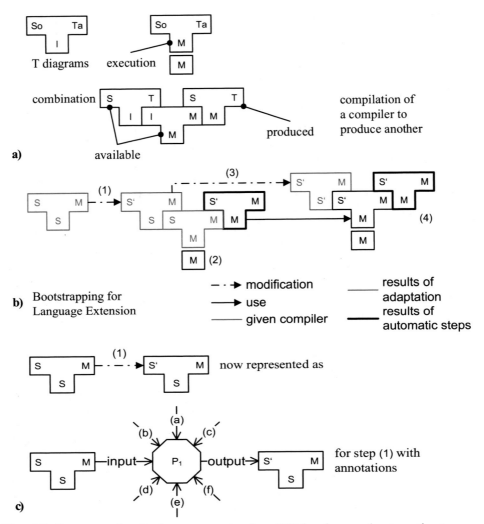

Fig. 6.8: Bootstrapping for language extension, PID has human / automatic steps

It remains to show, that the *human steps* are *better explained* by our PID notation. We look at step (1) of figs. 6.8.b and c, regard the version in our notation for process P_1, see fig. 6.8.c lower part. We discuss the different aspects of the process P_1:

(a) The goal is to extend the compiler such that it translates the extended language S'. So, the difference S'-S has to be translated as the new task.

(b) The restriction is to take the ^S_SM compiler and add the compilation of S'-S.

(c) The way to proceed is to add the missing source code for the difference, written in the language S.

(d) The support is to start with the given ^S_SM compiler. The missing part can be directly coded. Available and more efficient techniques from compiler construction can be used to facilitate coding.

(e) The actor is a person familiar with compiler writing.

(f) Necessary knowledge and experience is bootstrapping, compiler writing (some advanced techniques), and experience with the programming languages S and S'.

The explanations (a) to (f) may appear as *annotations* in the diagram. You get the corresponding text, if you click an annotation.

The second human step can be described similarly. Thus, altogether we have a notation consisting of T-diagrams, which we can regard as shortcut abbreviations of the PIDs of this chapter. They denote special cases. The human processes can be expressed by PIDs with annotations. Therefore, the complete diagram is a PID.

All examples of this section (see figs. 6.6, 6.7, and 6.8) were *nontrivial* and unconventional for usual process diagrams of the literature. Therefore, they demanded for a *suitable notation*. Usual process notations do not offer the necessary concepts.

Another interesting example for showing interaction of processes would have been to show, how a *software development process* and *product* is changed, if we use applications of more or less deep *reuse mechanisms*. Here, the different interactions of subprocesses are interesting for any level of reuse. Especially, it is interesting to look on the change of the development process when the next level of reuse is applied and how the interaction of subprocesses changes correspondingly. We leave this discussion for chapter 7 on reuse.

6.5 Summary

What we have achieved

We have generalized process notations to explicitly express different *influencing parameters* for a process, not only input and output, but also goal, restrictions, how to proceed, actor, helpful means (used components or tools), and experience or knowledge, see fig. 6.1. The purpose was to make *dependency relations* between processes - one needs the 'results' of another - more specific.

That allows to express the *interactions of processes more precisely*, especially the dependency relations. That is why we named that notation process interaction diagrams (PIDs). We see that the output of one process can have quite different semantical influences on another process, not only input, but also to define the goals, the restrictions, the planned proceeding to go, the actor, components or tools, or experience and knowledge, see figures of sect. 6.2. These semantical dependency relations make the diagrams more *meaningful*.

In sect. 6.4, we discussed some *nontrivial examples*, as *interleaving processes* (design of the product and planning its production, life cycle of the product, design and configuration of the producing infrastructure). A similar example of simpler complexity was discussed for software engineering. Further examples are the relation between requirements determination and realization, changes due to process evolution, or showing that management and technical processes are intertwined. Finally, the bootstrapping example showed that processes by humans and automatic ones also interact. All examples were nontrivial and, therefore, have profited from the extended notation introduced in this chapter. Sect. 6.4 also shows that the ideas presented in this chapter are applicable to any engineering domain.

Example processes can be on different levels: coarse (figs. 6.6, 6.7.a), middle (6.7.b, 6.8), or even fine-grained (not used in this chapter). We saw human and automatic processes, different situations of mechanical engineering, application to software engineering, and also software engineering in the systems development domain, as compiler compilers. So, the notation can be used in quite *different situations* w.r.t. granularity, domains, character of subprocesses, etc.

As in above discussions, the output of a process is connected to one of the aspects of another process by a dependency. We could also have combined *processes by gluing* them at the right side of the octagon of fig.6.1. The upside side is given in bold. Fig. 6.9 shows the results for the figures 6.2, 3, 4, and 5 in that glue notation.

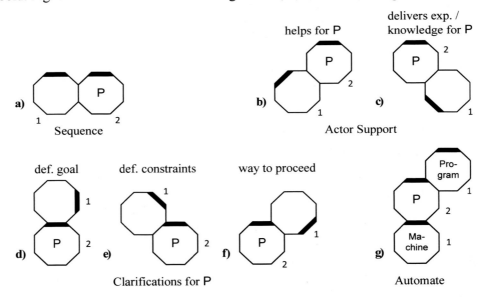

Fig. 6.9: Gluing process elements, a notation only for simple cases

This notation can be used only in more *simple cases*, as in complex situations one looses track of which side is connected to which side. Furthermore, the order of connections and executions cannot be seen easily. This is why we gave numbers.

As we have seen above, the T-diagrams are a *specific notation for a special case*. The same is true for SADT-, SA- and similar diagrams. They are only able to express *some of the aspects* of PID diagrams of this chapter.

Activities in Process Research

Some words on our *activities in process modeling*: We have been active for quite some time in that area and mostly there on the middle-grained level, namely how to organize processes, where their parts are carried out by different persons and also mostly in the development field /We 99, NW 94/. There, we mostly specialized on models and tools. Especially, we focused on *dynamics* problems, i.e. changes that occur in a process in execution. The different aspects are (i) changes due to *evolution* (only in the running process we see by a result, how to proceed further /Kr 98/, see fig. 6.7.). (ii) *Backtracking* (a mistake in the development implies that we have to go back in the process; however, we want to preserve useful results and minimize the modifications of others). (iii) *Extending process knowledge* (new experience and knowledge in form of new process type definitions or workflow pieces) can happen in the running process /He 11, Sc 02/. Finally, there are (iv) *cross-company processes* (where all the above problems occur and a grey-box model is needed, which allows cooperation (both sides know of each other) but also protection (of the knowledge of subcontractors) is necessary /He 08, Jä 03/). Thus, a central challenge in all these cases was to guarantee *changeability* at *process runtime*.

There were many applications and studies. The most influential were in the IPSEN project dealing with new and tightly integrated tools for *software* development /Na 96/, in the SUKITS project on a posteriori extensions of tools in *mechanical engineering* /NW 99/, and in the IMPROVE project on new tools and a posteriori extensions of given tools in *chemical engineering* /NM 08/. Most of our studies developed novel tools, but we also studied extensions of given tools /He 11, Wö 10/.

As indicated above, we concentrated in our research on the middle-grained processes (and on the coarse-grained processes, fig. 6.6, 6.7.a). Furthermore, we concentrated on the product part (the outcome) of processes, by building tools to make the product of a process easier or of a better quality to get, thereby supporting the process as well. We did not regard *fine-grained processes*, i.e. how a single developer is planning or doing his work. This was studied in /MJW 08/, where activity patterns were retrieved and used to build corresponding fine-grained *tool actions*.

We specialized in this chapter only on the process part of process modeling and ignored the product, human actor, the support part, all on abstract and detailed level. The research we carried out (see citations of above) included these parts. The results, presented above in this chapter, can be used to reformulate and *extend* the *process* part of the literature cited above. Therefore, this chapter remains in the tradition of having a clear *focus* in this broad domain of process investigations.

6.6 References

/Al 16/ van der Aalst, W.: Process Mining - Data Science in Action, Springer(2016)

/DA 21/ DATEV. https://www.datev.de/web/de/m/ueber-datev/dasunternehmen/?stat_Mparam=int_footer_azg_das-unternehmen, access Jan. 2021

/De 74/ Deo, N.: Graph Theory with Applications to Engineering and Computer Science, 467 pp., Dover Publications (1974)

/He 08/ Heller, M.: Dezentralisiertes, sichtenbasiertes Management übergreifender Entwicklungsprozesse, Doct. Diss., 501 pp., RWTH Aachen (2008)

/He 11/ Heer, Th.: Controlling Development Processes, Doct. Diss. RWTH Aachen, 430 pp., Aachener Informatik-Berichte SE 10 (2011)

/HJ 08/ Heller, M./ Jäger, D. et al.: An Adaptive and Reactive Management System for Project Coordination, Lecture Notes in Computer Science 4970, 300-366 (2008)

/IC 04/ Ivers, J./ Clements, P./ Garlan, D. et al.: Documenting Component and Connector Views with UML 2.0, Techn. Rep. CMU-SEI-2004-TR-008

/Jä 03/ Jäger, D.: Unterstützung übergreifender Kooperation in komplexen Entwicklungsprozessen, Doct. Diss. RWTH Aachen, 260 pp., ABI 34 (2003)

/JB 96/ Jablonski, S./ Bussler, C.: Workflow Management Modeling Concepts, Architecture and Implementation, International Thomson Computer Press (1996)

/Kr 98/ Krapp, K.A.: An Adaptable Environment for Management of Development Processes, Doct. Diss. RWTH Aachen, 196 pp., ABI 22 (1998)

/MJW 08/ Miatidis, M./ Jarke, M. et al. K.: Using Developers's Experience in Cooperative Design Processes, Lecture Notes in Computer Science 4970, 185-223 (2008)

/MM 88/ Marca, D.A./ McGowan, C.L.: SADT: structured analysis and design technique, McGraw-Hill (1988)

/Na 96/ Nagl, M. (ed.): Building Tightly Integrated Software Development Environments - The IPSEN Project, Lecture Notes in Computer Science 1170, 709 pp., Springer (1996)

/NF 03/ Nagl, M./ Faneye, O.B.: Gemeinsamkeiten und Unterschiede von Entwicklungsprozessen in verschiedenen Ingenieurdisziplinen, in /NW 94/, 311-324, Wiley-VCH (2003)

/NM 08/ Nagl, M./Marquardt, W. (eds.): Collaborative and Distributed Chemical Engineering: From Understanding to Substantial Design Process Support – Results of the IMPROVE Project, Lecture Notes in Computer Science 4970, 851 pp., Springer (2008)

/NW 94/ Nagl, M./ Westfechtel, B.: A Universal Component for the Administration in Distributed and Integrated Development Environments, TR AIB 94-8, 70 pp., Aachen (1994)

/NW 99/ Nagl, M./ Westfechtel, B. (Hrsg.): Integration von Entwicklungssystemen in Ingenieuranwendungen - Substantielle Verbesserung der Entwicklungsprozesse, 440 pp., Springer (1999)

/PID 21/ https://en.wikipedia.org/wiki/PID, access Jan. 2021

/Sc 02/ Schleicher, A.: Roundtrip Process Evolution Support in a Wide Spectrum Process Management System, Doct. Diss. RWTH Aachen, 310 pp., DUV (2002)

/We 99/ Westfechtel, B.: Models and Tools for Managing Development Processes, Habilitation Thesis, RWTH Aachen, 418 pp., Lect. Notes in Computer Science 1646 (1999)

/Wi 77/ Wirth, N.: Compilerbau, Teubner Studienbücher Informatik (1977), 79 – 84

/Wö 10/ Wörzberger, R.: Management dynamischer Geschäftsprozesse auf Basis statischer Prozessmanagementsysteme, Doct. Diss., RWTH Aachen, 304 pp., ABI SE 2 (2010)

7 Characterization of Shallow and Deep Reuse

Manfred Nagl

Software Engineering, RWTH Aachen University, nagl@cs.rwth-aachen.de

Abstract

Reuse in software development avoids to carry out the same processes again and again, thereby being more efficient, i.e. faster and producing less errors. We call such forms *shallow* reuse, as reuse is mostly in the mind of developers. *Deep reuse* means to change the development process remarkably, because upcoming knowledge makes more or less big parts of the development superfluous. Examples are that components and frameworks from former developments are used, steps are automated, etc.

In this chapter, we try to clarify the difference of shallow and deep reuse. Furthermore, we *characterize the changes* due to reuse on three levels: the new product with improved reuse, the change of the development process, and the new parts to be reused in the future. The notation for processes makes the changes and the dependencies of subprocesses more evident.

We take the *multiphase compiler* as running example. It is one of the best studied software products, a good example for the combination of theory and practice, and also of deep reuse.

Key words: shallow (implicit, simple) and deep (explicit, elaborated) reuse, deep reuse forms as table driven or generation software approach, intelligent architectures, global architecture patterns, multiphase compilers and compiler compiler approach, reuse steps: changes of product and process

7.1 Introduction

Shallow reuse means to repeat the development, thereby shortening the time of development and increasing its quality. Corresponding steps of improvement are characterized by models like Capability Maturity Model (abbr. CMM) /PC 95/, namely to use documentation, to manage, and to optimize the process. Doing a similar software development task again can speed up the productivity. Many other factors also influence productivity and quality /SZ 19/. A development process with these characterizations does not change the process structure radically.

Thus, in shallow reuse, *reuse* is mostly *implicit*. The corresponding reuse knowledge is in the minds of developers, as the way to proceed, the form of the result, the experience from former development processes of a similar system, etc. Reuse is mostly *simple* and makes use of copy, paste, and further changes. There is usually no explicit (written, formalized) and important result left for influencing the following development processes. Especially, there is no clear improvement of development knowledge.

This shallow reuse is the *classical* and still *mostly applied* approach in companies and *industry*, even if developers are working for a long time in one specific domain, thereby producing many similar and possibly sophisticated systems.

In this chapter, we go further. *Deep reuse* means to learn from one development for the next by facilitating and automating the development process. Thus, reuse results are made *explicit*. Furthermore, reuse is mostly *elaborated*. This can be easily seen from the changes of the result and the corresponding process. The aim of this chapter is to clarify these changes and transformations from step to step, and to show the tight relations between product and process modifications.

Reuse can be called *historical*, as to be seen from a characterization of the design of Gothic cathedrals (12th to 15th century) and the classification of thereby applied reuse forms /Na 19/. There, we already find *deep reuse* but in *implicit forms*, as there was no easy to use and mechanical way for copy, paste, or change, or even support for deep reuse steps available at that time.

For the clarifications of this chapter, we use one of the best examples of intelligent development and reuse, the *construction of a multiphase compiler*. Other examples for *intelligent development with deep reuse* are: (i) communication protocols by specification and code generation /GG 07/, (ii) control and automation software by making use of predefined partial solutions, which then are graphically composed /WK 16/, or (iii) novel tools for software construction in the academic context (e.g. /Na 96/), and also for other engineering domains.

In the following chapter, we use a *compact product description*. As the architecture of a software system is the master document for the whole development process (/Na 90-20, Na 03/ and ch. 1), we use a compact architectural notation, which is influenced by different programming languages and paradigms /Wi 21b/ and also ch. 2. For the development processes, we use a notation, which specifies the dependency relations (output of a process and purpose of its use in the second process), called *Process Interaction Diagrams* (PIDs, see ch. 6).

The examples in this chapter start with *shallow reuse*. Later, reuse knowledge is explicitly extracted and applied to form new reuse steps. The product changes, due to found invariant components and frameworks, and the process is partially automated (generation of software, table-driven approach, or even generation of tables). All these steps are called *deep reuse*.

The reuse steps explained here are not new. However, the chapter delivers a *new characterization of reuse*. It makes clear that deep reuse is what we should look for when building similar systems for a long time. The chapter is also a plea for deep reuse in industry, as it is mostly applied in academic ecosystems.

This chapter is *not a survey* on the broad field of *software reuse*, or of the different aspects of reuse, or of the vast amount of literature on software reuse. For a first view see /Co 98, LS 09, ICSR/. Instead, this chapter takes just one interesting example and characterizes two forms of reuse (what is usually done vs. what could have been done), by giving interesting characterizations of the product and the process. For deep reuse, this is done by different steps of process and product.

7.2 The Example: A Multiphase Compiler

We assume that the programming language to be compiled belongs to the class of clearly-defined, strongly-typed languages, with many forms of syntactical checks at compile time. *Compilation* by a multiphase compiler (see e.g. /AL 06, Sc 75, WG 84/) is *done in* steps (*phases*), see fig. 7.1.a for a corresponding sketch of an architecture diagram: scanning, parsing, context sensitive analysis (also called static semantics), intermediate code generation, optimization, addressing / target code generation, and post optimization.

All these steps are represented as *functional components*, more likely as composed subsystems than atomic modules. The underlying structure is *functional composition*: splitting a complex functional component into simpler functional components executed one after the other, using intermediate data structures, see again fig. 7.1.

Scanning is analysis on the lowest level of syntax, reading text input and building up lexical units (tokens), as identifiers, word symbols, delimiters, or literals. *Parsing* means to analyze token sequences, whether they reflect the context-free syntax. E.g. an assignment consists of a name on the left-hand side, an assignment symbol, an expression on the right hand side, and a semicolon at the end. *Context sensitive analysis* checks for consistency of parts, which may be far away from each other, as a declaration and its application. Further components are necessary, not shown in fig. 7.1.a. The left part of the compiler including intermediate code generation is called the *front-end* (being programming language dependent), the right part is called the *back-end* (being target machine dependent).

Fig. 7.1.a reflects the *structure* of the compiler after *several* development *iterations*. From version to version the compiler structure became clearer, the compiler development was more efficient in development time and quality (less errors/ mistakes), and the compiler runtime as well as the runtime of compiled code was improved. Possibly, the compiler appears in two versions, as a students' compiler for fast compilation and an optimized compiler for delivering runtime-efficient code. The compiler structure was possibly applied for compilers of different languages, for different versions of the same language, or for different target machines in a software house specialized on compilers.

Compilation of a programming language is a clearly describable problem, to a big part formal. It was studied for a long time in the 60ies to 80ies /Wi 21a/ by some of the brightest persons of computer science. Underlying there is a *specific problem*: *precise description* of input (language), output (machine), and of every internal part. There are no vague parts like "the system must have a nice user interface", "the system must use that and that given big component or technology", "the systems must run in the following specialized target environment", "the system must fulfill that hard efficiency parameters", etc. The knowledge how to write a compiler grew over time, from well-understood handwriting /Sc 75, Wi 77/ to refined forms using automatisms, see below.

That is why we find clear solutions and a theory, on which solutions are based /AL 06, WG 84/. Compiler writing is one of the best examples we have in informatics for *combining theory and practice*. Of course, not every problem to be solved by software, has the above nice features. However, when building similar systems for a certain application domain and for a long time, you will always detect different forms of reuse, of shallow and of deep reuse, the latter if you have time, money, and good people. Quite probably, not the whole program system makes use of intelligent reuse forms. But you find them at least in parts of the system.

The *underlying data structures* of fig. 7.1.a are (i) the stream of lexical units for the input text streams by Scan, (ii) the abstract syntax tree, produced by Parse, the program graph (syntax tree plus symbol list, or attributed syntax tree), etc.

Fig. 7.1.b contains the *process to develop the compiler* according to fig. 7.1.a. We assume that the language L and the target machine M are determined.

In the requirements part we collect information for the language, the target machine, and corresponding compiler techniques. This information is passed forward.

Then, the Realization process starts. All of the output info of Collect_Info goes to Build Arch. There, we design the compiler, see again fig. 7.1.a: the control component, the different functional parts and the data structure components at the bottom, and the corresponding processes, for design and realization. The corresponding information of the language (grammars) is forwarded as constraints to the corresponding phases of the front-end. The lexical syntax goes to Scan, the context-free syntax to Parse, etc. The information corresponding to compiler techniques is forwarded to all phases and, especially, to basic Layer. The information corresponding to the target machine is forwarded to the back-end components.

We do not regard the internal structure of the subsystem components, by reasons of simplicity. All the components identified in the architecture, have to be *implemented*. Afterwards, the component Int *integrates* the results.

Fig. 7.1.c delivers the *captions* for fig. 7.1. We denote the different aspects of the processes, which allows to make the dependency relations between processes to be more precise. The left side explains the architecture notation.

To explain the *notational elements* of the architecture in fig. 7.1.a: fo stands for an object component of functional nature, ado for an abstract data object, or adt (abstract data type) in case of separate compilation, i.e. more than one compilation unit can be compiled in one compilation run. Local (thin) and general (double lines) usability indicate planned local specific or general use. The components of the front-end are language-specific, those of the back-end are machine-specific.

We *denote* elementary *processes* of fig. 7.1.b by an octagon, hierarchical processes by a net inside an octagon. The dependency of subprocesses is specific, see the following explanations and ch. 6.

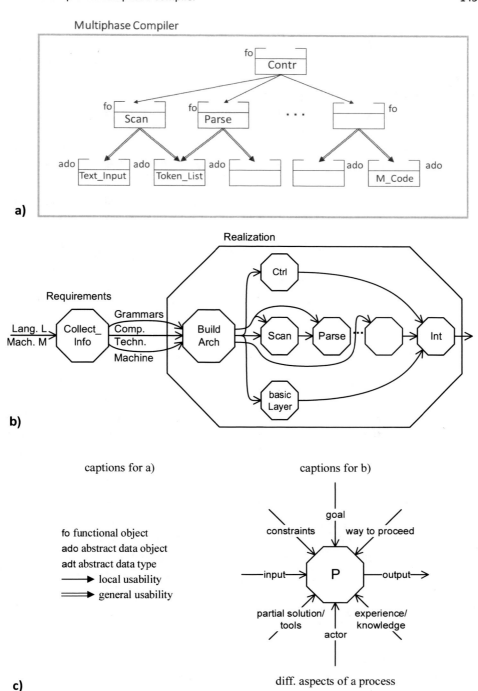

Fig. 7.1: a) The architectural structure of a multiphase compiler, b) its development process after several iterations, c) captions for a) and b)

7.3 The Compiler after Detection of Standard Structures

Fig. 7.1 is the last form of implicit (shallow) reuse, having the corresponding knowledge only in mind. However, it is also the *beginning of explicit* (deep) *reuse*, as indicated in fig. 7.2.a by different colors.

The global structure of the compiler (in blue) is invariant, it is a blueprint or a *global design pattern*, going here down only to the level of subsystems. The control component Contr (green) is invariant and can be used in every multiphase compiler, the functional components (black) are always present, but they are internally different, from language to language.

Even more, at the bottom of the architecture diagram, we see data exchange components (again green), which form a *reusable basic layer of data structures*. This layer can be reused in the next compiler project, as long as the functional structure of the compiler remains the same (multiphase). For the basic layer, we have a series of implemented and ready to reuse components. Internally, they should be *adaptable,* for to be connected to the specific file systems of the development environments and to the programming language. Again, the components are more subsystems than modules (so-called entry-collection subsystems, ch. 2).

Putting together: The diagram of fig. 7.2.a contains a *standard structure* for compilers of the above language class, a framework as a *global pattern* (in blue), where we find reusable components (in green). For the components of the phases we have to deliver specific components (design and implementation, in black). Their connection upwards (how they are invoked) and downwards (how they connect to the underlying and basic layer) is fixed, The components in green for control and for the basic layer of data structures can *be used* for the next compiler, they are already implemented. So, we have a plan to reuse the framework and also different components, which are prepared to be reused. The *basic data structures* for *data exchange* have a universal form for multiphase compilers, and they are easily adaptable.

Now, we start the development of the next compiler and reuse what we have identified, see fig. 7.2.b. The remaining parts to be developed are shown in black, the parts already carried out in green. Only the phase components must be designed and implemented, the rest is already done (components Ctrl and basic layer for data structures after some adaptation). The global build plan is the same.

The development process, shown in fig. 7.2.b, has significantly changed, compare to fig. 7.1.b. The process is much simpler now. If the language is new, the Collect_Info part has to be done again, mainly to pass the corresponding knowledge. If the language is the same (we only want to restructure the compiler), the components' results can just be taken. Only the processes for developing the phases remain, presented in black, the other parts already available are drawn in green. Furthermore, the integration component Int has to be done again.

The upper parts of figs. 7.1 and 2 show the *change* of the development *product*, the lower parts b of both figures show the change of the development *process*. The green parts say what we get from the last and previous developments, either *as product or as process*.

For reasons of simplicity, we concentrate on a part of the front-end in the following explanation. We take *parsing as example*. A similar argumentation holds, if we had taken scanning, context sensitive syntax analysis etc., assuming the same degree of knowledge. Parsing is best studied in literature.

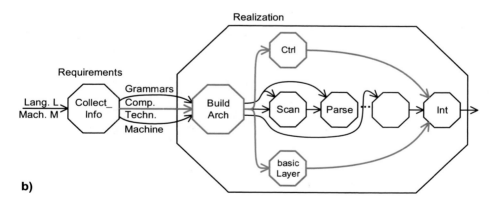

Fig. 7.2: The next iteration: a) standard for the product as framework, reusable Contr, basic and bottom-layer for data structures after some adaptation, b) realization of the next compiler: corresponding process

7.4 Deep Reuse: Table-driven Approach

Typical *deep reuse steps* are explained in the next sections. For the next two sections, we use the parser as running example. Thus, we regard only a part of the architecture. Corresponding reuse steps can be taken for all phases of the front-end.

As example, we look at the hardwired functional component for parsing of above. In the table-driven approach, the *table* now describes the *behavior* of the parser. We need an additional component, called *driver* or interpreter for handling parsing by use of the table. Table and driver depend on the parsing method. Both together have the same functional behavior as the hardwired program component.

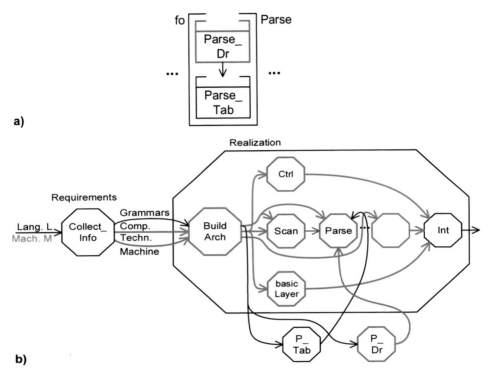

Fig. 7.3: a) Parse is now different, see cutout of the architecture, b) Table-driven architecture, process: driver (only once) and table to be exchanged

So, the *necessary steps* are: (a) The *driver component* development, which is only implemented once for the regarded parsing method (e.g. LL(1), LALR(1)). They can be reused immediately afterwards. We show the component of the architecture as well as the corresponding subprocess in light brown, as it is a preparation for deep reuse. Now, (b) we build up the *table* according to the deterministic context-free grammar. The component Parse_Tab and its subprocess are drawn in black, as they are the product/ description of a human task.

The *steps in direction of reuse and development efficiency* are: (i) Driver only once, then arbitrarily reused. (ii) To build up the table is easier than programming the parser, see fig. 7.3. The remaining *development step* is to build up the table. The same approach can be applied for the scanner. There, we take a regular grammar or a finite automaton as formal description.

7.5 Deep Reuse: Generation of Solutions

In fig. 7.2.a, the *code* for Parse was *developed by a human*. This person looked on the grammar and transformed this grammar into a component, being an analyzer for this grammar. Analogously, in fig. 7.3 the *table*, describing the behavior of the analyzer, was produced by a human.

The tasks to transform the grammar either to code or to a table are *precise* and can be *formalized.* We can solve this *transformation by a program.* The corresponding approach is called to generate the result, or automation by *generation.* The program, which is necessary, is universal for the type of grammar. Thus, it has to be developed only once, and it can be used repeatedly.

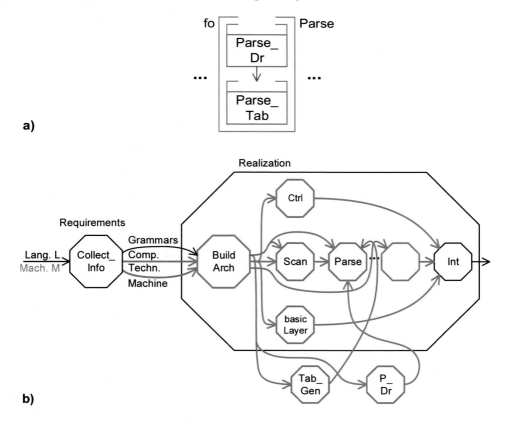

Fig. 7.4: Automation: Generate code or table, here table for the example Parsing

In fig. 7.4.a we see the *resulting cutout of the architecture*. The Parse_Dr is available and reused (green), the table Parse_Tab is generated now, also green. In both cases, there is no development process. The generator development has to be done once and is a step in direction of deep reuse. It is painted light brown in fig. 7.4.b.

Fig. 7.4.b shows the situation generating the *parser table*. The part already done is shown in green. The corresponding driver is available, as having been developed, see fig. 7.3. The corresponding table is produced automatically by the generator. The generator is already available. If a corresponding grammar is available, nothing has to be done by a human. Parse needs no longer a development process, it is now an automatic process.

If the *parser code is generated*, fig. 7.4.b would be simpler. No driver component is necessary. Again, if a corresponding grammar is available, nothing has to be done by a developer, as the parser code is generated. The generator (grammar to code) is developed only once (would be light brown in fig. 7.3.b).

What we have discussed for the parser can also be done for the scanner, here a regular grammar or a corresponding finite automaton is necessary. More generally, it can be done for any part of the compiler, which can precisely be described. Such parts of *automatable transformations* are more in the compiler front-end than in its back-end. We find such problems also *outside of compilers*. If a generator is available, we only have to look for a corresponding formal input description.

Summing up sects. 7.4 and 7.5, we have done another *big step in direction of reuse*. In the table case, (i) the driver is reusable, after having been developed. In both cases, generated table or generated analyzer program, (ii) the generators are reusable, after having been developed. Furthermore, *automation* not only reduces the *effort*, it (iii) even *eliminates* the corresponding development by a human.

In the discussion above, we denoted *processes* or *components* in a green color, where nothing is to do, as a previous process delivered a product which can be taken. The green color shows what has already been done, and what is not necessary to be done again. A green process is *trivial*: The program (component) is available, e.g. a driver with a table is available, the program or the table has been generated, etc. Therefore, the process just means to take something out of a library and use it. As an example, look on process Parse of fig. 7.4.b. We did not introduce trivial processes as distinction to usual processes, for characterizing this situation.

Above, we saw *sequences of architectures*, the transitions from architecture to architecture being defined by a deep reuse step. All the architectures are abstract, i.e. they do not refer to technical details of the system to be developed or its environment. Specifically interesting, but also nontrivial, is reuse for embedded systems, as these systems are connected to technical details. There, we also have sequences of architectures, but there to transform an architecture from an abstract to a concrete form, reflecting the many details of the system or its environment, cf. chs. 3 and 4.

7.6 Deep Reuse: Global Reuse Schemes

The summary of all from above (framework, basic layer, table-driven components, generation of components) is called the *compiler compiler* approach. It is one of the best examples of deep reuse, and a close connection of theory and practice.

It is *deep reuse*, as in every step of figs. 7.2, 3, and 4 the development product as well as its process were *drastically changed*. This reorganization demanded deep understanding (extracting the global build plan, extracting reusable control and basic layer, avoiding to program by using a table with a driver, avoiding to program or to develop the table by automation, using a generator). Deep reuse does not mean to do it only better again, but to learn and to *reorganize* the product and its process essentially.

The discussion of above also gives rise to study global reuse patterns. The first is *front-end reuse*. Here, we use the compiler front-end and care only about different back-ends for various target machines. I.e. the same front-end (for the same language) is used for different back-ends (*different target machines*). The different back-ends have to be developed.

Analogously *back-end reuse* means to have different front-ends to be developed (languages, here compiler-oriented). Here, the back-end is stable (we have the same target machine).

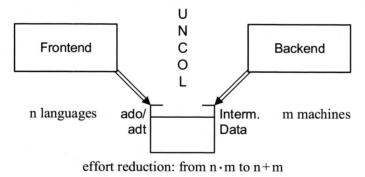

effort reduction: from n ∗ m to n+m

Fig. 7.5: The UNCOL approach as a famous reuse approach: scheme and effort reduction

A combination of both reuse approaches requires a uniform intermediate language (e.g. a graph intermediate language), see fig. 7.5. This combination is called the *UNCOL* (Universal Computer Oriented (Intermediate) Language) *approach* /Co 58/, an old and still very important idea, which can be used for any translation problem.

Using UNCOL *reduces* the *effort* tremendously and thus is an important and global *reuse method*: If we directly translate n languages and want to have the compiler on m machines, we have a development effort for n*m compilers. Using a uniform intermediate code reduces the effort to n+m, a dramatic reduction. Of course, the idea only works for similar translations, in our case compiling typed, compiler-oriented languages with a fixed multiphase scheme, and an agreement for a universal intermediate code.

Above, we mostly studied *product reuse*: global pattern, basic layer, table and driver, altogether products of subprocesses, which are used and which reduce the development process and effort. Only the generator for code or tables belongs to *process reuse*, here in an automatic form.

Recursive descent compilers /Wi 77/ work differently, compared to multiphase compilers. Whereas in multiphase compilers the total task of translation is expressed by a sequence of subprocesses, in a recursive descent compiler we have only one pass working top-down (one pass compiler). In this pass, *all subtasks of above are solved for a language construct* (a declaration, an assignment, a control structure, or a program structuring construct as a procedure). The book /Wi 77/ nicely describes this rather easy way of compilation, such that a student can write a compiler for a simple language according to that scheme after a short time.

In this case, we have *process reuse*: A methodology is introduced, which says what to do and in which order, such that you can *apply the methodology* for a compiler task without getting into hard problems. No intermediate product is reused, everything is done again (for a language, for a machine). But the methodology is reused, which says what and how to do. Therefore, we call this 'process reuse' within the development process.

For languages and one pass compilers there is a method for getting a compiler called *bootstrapping*, which is a mixture of well-defined development subprocesses by a human and automatic subprocesses, This *stepwise compiler development* approach is also described in /Wi 77/. Nearly all Pascal compilers have been developed via this method. It can be used for extending a programming language, for porting a compiler, for improving a compiler, etc.

The starting point is a *compiler for a language written in the same language* (e.g. Pascal compiler written in Pascal) and an *available compiler* written in M for a machine M. Then, after a sequence of human development steps and automatic compilation steps, we get the result. We give no explanation here and refer to the literature. The explanation for 'extension of a programming language' in the notation used in this chapter is given in ch. 6.

7.7 Further Examples of Deep Reuse

Further Examples

Above, we have used the multiphase compiler for classical programming languages as the example to demonstrate deep reuse and changes of the corresponding process and product. We could also have taken *tools* for the *software development process*. In the academic area, we find novel tools on different levels and their *in-*

tegration in a tool environment (e.g. /Na 96, NM 08/), which have been realized with deep reuse, quite similar to the compiler example.

There are further examples for such deep reuse. We find it in the area *automation and control* /HS 19, Po 94/, especially around the IEC 61131 and 61499 norms. There exist libraries of *predefined functions* for controllers and graphical tools to *arrange networks* of such controllers. Building a solution is often just a graphical task, no programming is necessary anymore.

Another area for advanced software reuse is *protocol* development for *telephone and computer networks* /Ho 91, Sc 96/. There are solutions generated from a protocol specification. Here again, no usual programming takes place.

Further Problems for Reuse

There is a branch of software engineering, dealing with *families of systems* /CN 07, Ja 00, PB 05, PK 09/, not with single systems. Necessary for that is to detect the commonalities and the differences between members of the family. Both have to be carefully studied and both are used for the implementation of the members. That is a big structural reuse advantage compared to programming one family member after the other. A similar argumentation holds for *product lines*.

In this chapter, we solely regarded *reuse starting* on the level of architectures. Having similarity of different systems belonging to families or lines usually begins already in *requirements engineering* /EB 06/. There are similarities we can exploit. Even more, these similarities also appear in the *mapping* from requirements specs to the upper layers of the architecture, what we discuss in ch. 11.

Another branch is *domain-driven development* /Ev 04/ which means to firstly develop solutions for the domain (knowledge, components, tools) and reuse them for the construction of examples of the domain. This intersects with *model-driven development* /PB 16, PH 12/, where the solution is described by models, from which a solution can be derived or, in the best case, generated automatically by a generator.

In all the approaches mentioned in this section, the early solutions started with hardwired programming for examples. Then, in these examples or in the corresponding approaches, thinking began to avoid doing programming over and over again. The *process for* getting a *solution changed dramatically*, and intelligent reuse approaches came up.

We could have taken one of the *above examples* or of the above *approaches* to demonstrate, what we have shown in this chapter for compiler construction: There are different reuse steps, which change the product, the process, and which introduce further components, basic layers, or generators step by step, ending with an *intelligent and deep reuse process*.

7.8 Summary, Importance, and Open Problems

Summary and Lessons Learned

Above we have seen: Thinking in structures and reuse needs the right level, namely a *carefully designed software architecture*, which on one hand is precise and clear. On the other hand, it is adaptable, i.e. prepared for extensions and changes of functionality, but also for technical modifications, like exchange of basic components as e.g. basic data structures. Functional and data abstraction – together detail abstraction – are used. Careful discussions, design experience, and new ideas change the way of development.

Reuse is longtime learning: At the beginning we build several times, get experience, get more efficiency – in time and costs – from development to development. This was called in this chapter classical or *shallow reuse*. Then, we make steps in direction of standardization and patterns, as frameworks and basic layers, so into deep reuse.

After further experiences and careful discussions *deep reuse* can continue. This demands for intelligent people and especially for time. The result is a long-term advantage, which does not come for free, as shown in this chapter for multiphase compilers of classical programming languages. These arguments explain that deep reuse is rather seldom in industry, as it costs, needs time, and intelligent developers. The advantage, however, is a *long-term profit*.

Deep reuse in our compiler example *means*: detailed requirements, a careful architecture (fig. 7.1), using the right abstractions, furthermore looking for adaptability, for a framework, and a basic data exchange layer (again fig. 7.1). Afterwards, only the functional layer needs to be developed (fig. 7.2), the other parts remain from the last for future development. The *next steps* are tables for functions and corresponding drivers (fig. 7.3), generation of code or tables (fig. 7.4). Altogether, this is called the compiler-compiler approach. Global reuse patterns, like the UNCOL approach, finalize the main sections. Bootstrapping is another global pattern.

That all doesn't come for free: Hard work is necessary, knowledge, and foresight to see the long-term advantages. Therefore, *deep reuse* methodology is only realistic for *stable domains and stable problems,* from the economy point of view.

If you look on the product (architecture) and the process, you can easily *distinguish between shallow and deep reuse*: As long as the product and the process remain similar, we have shallow reuse (fig. 7.1). If the product and the process change noticeably and in direction of reuse, we have deep reuse (figs. 7.2, 3, 4, 5).

Compilers are Important for Informatics Education

The compiler is a special case in a specific class of systems, named *batch* systems. In this chapter, the specific batch system is the *multiphase compiler* for classical languages. It has nice properties, as no vague and fuzzy aspects occur. The specific class uses functional decomposition and data abstraction structures for coupling the phases.

Why are *compilers* so *important for CS education*? Here is a series of answers:

- We do not *understand a programming language* if we do not see what happens in the compilation process and what at runtime. The interesting thing of compilers is that they introduce the corresponding administration at compile time for the code executed at runtime.
- To say it in other words, we do not *understand to program*, if we do not have a basic knowledge of compilation and runtime systems.
- It is not likely that CS students are later busy in a compiler company. This argument was misused for *erasing* compiler construction from many CS curricula. This is *not appropriate*.
- Furthermore, we quite often find *translation problems* in *practice*, where it is useful to have a corresponding background for solving such problems, namely in compilers.
- Compiler construction is the *parade discipline* for a close *connection* of *theory* and *practice*.
- *Deep reuse* demands for a careful discussion how to solve a problem. If you want to educate your students not only to hack, rather to argue and learn, they should learn compiler construction. It would be nice and important in informatics to have more such areas.
- *Tools* need precise and formal languages. That demands for syntax, semantics, and pragmatics knowledge. Although tools work iteratively and incrementally, the tool development process is rather similar to compiler construction. Compiler knowledge prepares for tool construction.
- Nearly all of the *brilliant ideas* to structure *software*, their *architecture*, and *reuse forms* were found in compiler construction: frameworks and global patterns, universal structures for data exchange, table-driven, generation, bootstrapping approaches. Missing compiler construction means to miss learning intelligent principles and examples.

Open Problems: Dissemination of Deep Reuse and Characterization of Changes

We miss to have more intelligence in software construction. As stated above, the *simple reuse* forms (shallow reuse) are dominating in industrial software development. This is acceptable *in an often changing* context: Informatics is developing rapidly, extensions of applications appear often, using new methods and tools happens frequently, starting new application domains is daily practice, etc. This hinders to think in long terms. Time is hectic – there is no time and money for sustainable development, and there is no corresponding understanding and insight at the management level of companies.

If however, you develop software more often in a *stable environment*, you should think about careful development, intelligent and deep reuse. That needs time, money, and excellent developers, but it is worth a *long-term investment*. Therefore, there is always a weighting long-term versus short-term profit. The long-term profit can be enormous, but it does not come for free.

Deep reuse only works for *specific classes* of *software systems*. The more *specialized* and precise the class is, and the more you *know* about this class, the *deeper* are the results. As already stated, you need intelligent developers and log-term thinking.

In this way, deep reuse contributes to the knowledge of software classes, to deep understanding in your company, and to deep understanding in software engineering subdomains. So, try to do and *contribute* to this way of *knowledge acquisition*.

As already argued, *families* of systems, *model-*, and *domain-driven* development are even more ambitious problems than single system development. In all these cases, we stay in a certain domain for some time and we develop different systems for a certain problem. Thus, the plea for *deep reuse* is even more important here.

Above, we have sketched, how reuse changes products and processes for compilers. This could also be done for other fields. The first is (i) *long-term maintenance*. Systems live for a long time, 20 and more years are not seldom. In that time the systems changes dramatically, see ch. 9. The changes of the system as well as of its maintenance processes could be described in the same way as it was done for reuse in this chapter. The same can be done (ii) for *system families* as sketched above. They usually arise from single system development. Here again, the same characterization as used in this chapter can be applied: describing the changes of the product as well as of the process in a suitable way. Both is missing.

7.9 References

/AL 06/ Aho, A.V., Lam, M.S., Sethi, R., J. Ullman, J.D.: Compilers: Principles, Techniques, and Tools, Addison-Wesley, 2nd ed. (2006)

/EB 06/ Ericson, M./ Börstler, J./ Borg, K.: Software Product Line Made Practical, Comm. ACM 49,12, 49-53 (2006)

/CN 07/ Clements, P/ Northrop, L.M.: Software Product Lines: Practices and Patterns, 563 pp., 6th ed., Addison Wesley (2007)

/Co 58/ Conway. M.E.: Proposal for an UNCOL, Communications of the ACM. 1 (10): 5-8 (1958)

/Co 98/ Coulange, B.: Software Reuse, 293 pp., Springer (1998)

/Ev 04/ Evans, E.: Domain-driven Design, Addison Wesley, 529 pp. (2004)

/GG 07/ Grammes, R./ Gotzhein, R.: Fundamental Approaches to Software Engineering. Lecture Notes in Computer Science 4422, 200–214, Springer (2007)

/Ho 91/ Holzmann, G.J.: Design and Validation of Computer Protocols, 539 pp., Prentice Hall (1991)

/HS 19/ Heinrich, B./ Schneider, W.: Grundlagen der Regelungstechnik, 5th ed., Springer Vieweg (2019)

/ICSR/ International Conference on Software Reuse, Proc. from 1990 to 2017, see also Wikipedia ICSR

/Ja 00/ Jazayeri, M. et al. (eds.): Software Architecture for Product Families, Addison Wesley (2000)

/LS 09/ Land, L./ Sundmark, D. et al.: Reuse with Software Components – A Survey of Industrial State of Practice, in Edwards/ Kulczycke (eds.): ICSR 2009, LNCS 5791, 150-159 (2009)

/Na 90-20/ Nagl, M.: Software Engineering- Methodological Programming in the Large (in German), 387 pp., Springer (1990), plus further extensions for a lecture on Software Architectures from 1990 to 2020

/Na 96/ Nagl, M. (ed.): Building Tightly Integrated Software Development Environments - The IP-SEN Approach, LNCS 1170, 709 pp., Springer, Berlin Heidelberg (1996)

/Na 03/ Nagl, M.: Introduction to Ada (in German), 348 pp., Vieweg (1982), /Na 03/ 6th ed. Software Engineering and Ada (in German), 504 pp., Vieweg (2003)

/Na 19/ Nagl, M.: Gothic Churches and Informatics (in German), 304 pp, Springer Vieweg, 179-187 (2019)

/NM 08/ Nagl, M./ Marquardt, W.: (eds.) Collaborative and Distributed Chemical Engineering – From Understanding to Substantial Design Process Support, IMPROVE, LNCS 4970, 851 pp., Springer (2008)

/PB 05/ Pohl, K./ Böckle, G. et al.: Software Product Line Engineering, 467 pp., Springer (2005)

/PB 16/ K. Pohl, K./ M. Broy, M. et al. (eds.): Advanced Model-based Engineering of Embedded Systems – Extensions to the SPES 2020 Methodology, Springer, 303 pp. (2016)

/PC 95/ Paulk, M.C./ Weber, V.V. et al.: The Capability Maturity Model: Guidelines for Improving the Software Process. SEI series in software engineering. Addison-Wesley (1995)

/PH 12/ Pohl, K./ Hönninge, K. et al. (eds.): Model-based Engineering of Embedded Systems – The SPES 2020 Methodology, Springer, 304 pp. (2012)

/PK 09/ Polzer, A./ Kowalewski, S. et al.: Applying Software Product Line Techniques in Model-based Embedded Software Engineering, Proc. MOMPES'09, 2-10 (2009)

/Po 94/ Pohlke, M.: Prozessleittechnik, 2nd edition, Oldenbourg (1994)

/Sc 75/ Schneider, H.J.: Compiler, Aufbau und Arbeitsweise, de Gruyter (1975)

/Sc 96/ Schwartz, M.: Broadband Integrated Networks, Prentice Hall (1996)

/SZ 19/ Sadowski, C./ Zimmermann, T. (eds.): Rethinking Productivity in Software Engineering, Springer Science + Business Media (2019)

/WG 84/ Waite, W.M./ Goos, G.: Compiler Construction, Springer (1984)

/Wi 77/ Wirth, N.: Compilerbau, Grundlagen und Techniken des Compilerbaus, Oldenbourg (1997), first ed. 1977

/Wi 21a/ Wikipedia: History of compiler construction, access Jan 2021

/Wi 21b/ Wikipedia: History of programming languages, access Jan. 2021

/WK 16/ Wagner, C./ Kampert, D. et al.: Model based synthesis of automation functionality, at – Automatisierungstechnik 64(3), 168–185 (2016)

8 The Software Architecture is the Glue to Deal with Variety and Integration

Manfred Nagl

Software Engineering, RWTH Aachen University, nagl@cs.rwth-aachen.de

Abstract

Whenever a software system consists of different parts – either how they are internally developed and structured, where they are located, when they were developed, which methodology or underlying concepts are used – the problem of integration of these different parts comes up. This chapter shows that the architecture of a software system is the right level to organize the integration and the architecture provides the essence of the glue for the integration.

We give different examples, which show the glue for different situations either in development or in maintenance, in different application domains, using higher or low-level infrastructures, for integration within a system or between a system and its environment, or for a framework applying reuse for its major application components. The ideas are applicable also in other domains outside software development and in the context of model-driven development.

Key words: software development/ maintenance/ integration, forward development/ reverse and reengineering, distributed software systems, improvement for efficiency or clarity, state of technology, integration of different (parts of) systems, bordering systems, of different components, within a framework, or with main application components

8.1 Introduction

Many software systems reflect *technical details*, about the very specific way they were implemented, about the environment in which they act for a certain business process, about the details of their connections to other systems inside the same or between different companies, about the technical infrastructure by which components communicate, in which way reuse was achieved, or in which way aspects from abstract to concrete are regarded.

This is specifically *true* for *embedded systems*, as we have learned in chs. 4 and 3. In this chapter, two of four examples are from the domain automotive. There, we find many details. The development process of a system should give the answer, why, how, and when the details are handled. This is important for maintenance or evolution. Details make differences, varieties, and multiple structures, which have to be bridged in development or maintenance.

The *clearness* and intelligibility of a solution is to a big part bound to the *architecture* of the system, as the architecture determines the internal essential structure of the system. This also applies for integration solutions, which connect different systems or which inherently apply reuse ideas.

M. Nagl, B. Westfechtel, *Software Architectures*, https://doi.org/10.1007/978-3-031-51335-0_8

The statements and messages of this chapter also apply to systems outside the embedded systems' domain. Furthermore, they apply not only to maintenance or evolution, but also to a new development, where there was nothing to be used. The chapter deals with different *forms* of *integration*. Loose integration is easier to handle compared to tight integration. In the same way, integration with similar models is easier than with different underlying models or parts developed with a different methodology, from handcrafted to a model-driven or a generation approach. How to achieve tight integration? In any case, there is no clean and clear integration, if no provisions are made on architecture level before coding the solutions.

The following *chapter is structured as follows*: Variety and integration are described in more detail by the following section. Then, we give two sections dealing with integration, the first (sect. 8.3) for integration of two systems which have not been built by already thinking about integration. This applies often to integration within a company. The second example (sect. 8.4) deals with integration of systems of different organizations. Both examples belong to different domains, the first is from the business administration, the second from the embedded domain. The next two sections deal with new development. Sect. 8.5 first discusses new development from the automotive domain, having specific code on different control units and using a rather simple and low-level infrastructure. As a contrast, more complex software units are discussed, which are connected by a service-oriented infrastructure. Sect. 8.6 deals with deep reuse for an interactive tools environment, using a uniform framework and specific components which are generated. There, we find on one hand integration between the components of the framework, and between the components of the data-driven part and the framework on the other. We conclude with a summary, messages, and open problems section.

8.2 Software Systems are Different

Software *systems*, as well as their parts, can be very *different*. We distinguish different *dimensions*: (a) The underlying theoretical models, (b) the connection to the underlying process/ environment the system is interacting with, (c) the form of the system, like distributed, concurrent, efficient, and (d) the level of operation. They are briefly discussed now.

(a) The software *system* or parts of it may *follow* different *theoretical models*: This can be a discrete model, like a finite automaton, statechart /Ha 87/, or Petri net /PR 08/. It might be a control loop formalism, which we find in automation and control applications /Tr 06/, or a communication model /He 03, Do 08, Ho 91/, if the communication part is dominant or important for the system's structure. Finally, it may be a general computation model, if the system or the part regarded does not follow a more restricted theoretical model. In any of these cases, there is a model the final program has to follow. The model is not the program. It can be a spec for the program, developed according to this model. In rare cases, code has been generated from the model using another program, which "understands" the model.

(b) The *system* is in connection to an *upper-level process* and the system supports this process. This process can be a business process in the domain business administration, a technical process/ environment the system is supporting, or alike. The business/technical processes are different in nature and structure. In any case, the system is part of another process.

(c) The system might be *distributed*, i.e. parts of it are executed on different hardware. The system may act inherently *concurrently*, or concurrency might be the consequence of technical decisions, like distribution. Or, the system might have undergone *efficiency* transformations.

(d) The system might have different *levels of operation*. It represents the application process, the system has to be explicitly started and later stopped, or if it runs, there might be emergency situations, which demand for fast reactions.

Embedded systems (see chs. 3 and 4) share some of these characterizations (a) to (d). We make this clear by taking an *automotive* system as example: The system within a car has parts, which follow a finite automaton, like opening or closing the car. It has other parts following automation and control models like controlling acceleration, speed, or car movement. Some parts act inherently concurrent. The software system acts within a technical system, which offers sensors and actuators to get information or to influence the technical system. The system is distributed over different control units in the car, which are connected by a subnet, subnets again via gateways. The system is explicitly started within the car, when the driver starts the car, and shut down, when the car is locked. Some components of the system demand for high efficiency, any component is expected to react within a certain time. A big problem of the domain automotive is to handle the variety of cars, w.r.t. functionalities, hard-, and software.

Due to the close connection of this chapter to embedded systems, the chapter could have "embedded systems" in its title. However, the *main message* of this chapter also *holds for systems outside* of this domain.

There are *connections* to other *chapters of this book*: The role of the software architectures (ch. 1), different aspects of architecture modeling (ch. 2), different architectures in a sequence (ch. 3), embedded systems and adaptability (ch. 4), reuse (ch. 7), and reverse and reengineering (ch. 9). These aspects are mentioned, but not explained again.

The ideas described in this chapter are important, irrespective which *realization strategy was chosen* for the development of a software system, from "handcrafted" realization to generation of (parts of) the system. The usual way is (a) that the software system is *written along a careful requirements spec*. The way this is done is characterized as (a1) methodologically safe handcrafting, using the method set of software engineering. This can range from doing the development the first time, where we have more steps going back, or doing parts more than once. If (a2) the same or a similar problem is solved several times, we sum up experience and practice to be used in the development process. This might include that (a3) experience is condensed such that components are used from a previous development or the method is getting sophisticated. Handcrafting is improved by components (product reuse), or by a good way how to do (process reuse). These classical ways of development were called shallow reuse in ch. 7. They are not further discussed in this chapter. Also, distribution, improvement of efficiency, or different architectures, are not discussed again, see chs. 2 and 3.

The corresponding arguments for such somewhat *"closed system development"* were given in all the chapters of this book: The architecture is the essence of the development, the architecture drives the development process, its division into parts, the details of these parts and their results, but also their integration to a complete solution.

The same is true for *development changes inside a system* as, (i) from pure hand-crafting to forms of shallow reuse, (ii) integration applied, (iii) distributed system and low-level integration, or (iv) higher-level integration of systems developed with deep reuse, see ch. 7.

In this chapter, we look at three more *"unusual" cases* of software development, see fig. 8.1 for a sketch. Fig. 8.1.a shows a *typical integration* task, where systems Sys1 and Sys2 are given and later connected by new software (a posteriori integration). Before that, integration was realized e.g. by a data transfer with human interpretation and input into the second system. The architectures of both systems have been developed in their realization process. The second example (fig. 8.1.b) connects an automotive system to other systems (as a parking garage) by a high-level and standard interface. The third example (fig. 8.1.c) comes from the development of *a distributed solution*, again automotive. The different parts of the system are developed rather independently, mostly not by the OEM but by suppliers. The overall system is later integrated by a rather low-level architecture based on signal transfer through a network. The last example (fig. 8.1.d) shows integration within a tool, being a part of an integrated tool environment. Here integration is on two levels, in the tool (shown here) and between the tools, both explained later. All figures are rather graphical sketches than architectures.

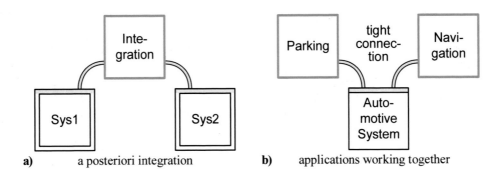

a)   a posteriori integration   b)   applications working together

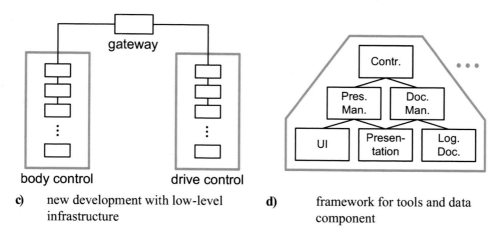

c) new development with low-level infrastructure

d) framework for tools and data component

Fig. 8.1: a) to d) Graphical characterization of the examples of this chapter

8.3 A posteriori Integration of Systems

Two *systems* Sys1 and Sys2 are *available*, which have been developed by a "hand-crafting" development process, or by shallow reuse, or even by deep reuse. They are separate, but have been used together in a connection using low-level mechanisms, as file transfer. The glue was done by humans, i.e. transfer, interpretation, and change of data. Now the question comes up, how to integrate these systems. Of course, the problem can be extended to have more than two systems. Such an integration often appears inside a company.

The two software *solutions* are now *connected* and *integrated.* The human integration is substituted by a system integration component I, see fig. 8.2. There (a) might still be a human *interaction*, but on a higher level: Checking is done automatically, possibly also error detection, correction before data are transferred, and also activation of functionality of the second system Sys2, possibly driven by interactive decisions on a higher level. Or, (b) it may be that the integrating component I is coupling the two systems Sys1 and Sys2 *automatically*, now by reading application items from the first, changing them, and by transferring them to the second system. This kind of a posteriori integration is a *typical task* of *maintenance* and *extension.*

The two given systems remain mainly untouched, their development is not started again (a posteriori integration). Instead, *changes* on both sides are made only to *facilitate* the *coupling*, reading of system Sys1 by the integration part and writing to system Sys2. In between, we find the *integrating* system *part* I with new functionality for the cases (a) or (b) of above.

The possible *modifications* on both sides Sys1 and Sys2 intend to *facilitate* the *coupling*, i.e. by introducing *interfaces* IF1 and IF2, higher level than that previously used, to handle data portions. IF1 and IF2 abstract from details (how data are stored, put together, or transported).

The new *integration functionality* I is needed for coupling. It can be *interactive,* see (a) of above. In this case, the system part I in between has to organize the command input, read a source entry from Sys1, change it (modify or take other data , etc.), form a new target entry, store it in Sys2, and show a result.

Or, I may offer the functionality for *automatic* coupling, see (b) of above. In this case, the system I in between reads portions from the new interface IF1 of Sys1, does something (modification based on algorithmic decision, building up a new entry), gives it to the other Interface IF2 of Sys2, and continues with the next input. The coupling can be loose by complete file transfer, by item after item of the source file and target file, or by having a buffer in between and two processes for Sys1 and Sys2.

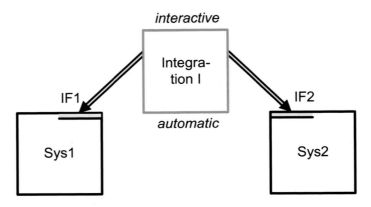

Fig. 8.2: Coupling two unchanged systems: integration software and new interfaces

Summing up: Both systems Sys1 and Sys2 are essentially untouched. There is only preparation for integration by the new Interfaces IF_1 and IF_2, integration functionality I is put on top. The preparation and the coupling is the glue to combine the two systems. The essence of this *glue* is determined *on architecture level*. This architecture, either for the interactive or for the automatic form of I is rather simple.

8.4 Glue for External Connections

Now high-level *systems* are *connected* to form a system with new and *additional functionality*. We regard examples from *automotive*. Three *possible scenarios* are sketched: (a) car and parking garage, (b) car and security infrastructure of the road, (c) car and close connection to the navigation system for a safe drive. All these examples share similarities. Therefore, we only discuss the case (a) here and give some comments for the other examples. The integration of this section often bridges the products of different companies.

Car and Parking Garage

The *scenario is as follows*: The driver is *handing* his *car* over to the organization of the *parking garage*. The car is driving automatically without a driver to a parking place with moderate speed. The user leaves the garage for some further activities outside of the garage. When he/ she comes back, the wish to get the car back is sent to the garage earlier via mobile phone. The car comes automatically to the entrance, the fee is paid, and the driver leaves the garage with the car.

In order to solve the integration problem between car and garage the *car system* has to *cooperate tightly with* the *garage* (fig. 8.3). Either (i), the *garage* system has *access* to the car guiding it through the garage. Or (ii), *vice versa*, the car gets access to the necessary data of the garage, the allowance, and uses them in the automatic drive mode. Possibility (i) is more probable, as there are different cases, where the car is accessed from outside, e.g. in an auto repair shop, in a test station, etc. Furthermore, (ii) legal reasons speak for the responsibility of the garage, and also other processes of the garage are involved, as paying and getting fees, or granting discounts for permanent users, and so on. Of course, opening the car interface from outside has to be done carefully to avoid misuse. Therefore, corresponding strict security mechanisms have to be installed. We see, the solution is between (i) and (ii). Both are active, but the initial action comes from one side.

Whatever solution is preferred: In case (i), we need a *standardized interface* to the car. In case (ii) we need it from the car to the parking garage. A standardized interface not only is precise, it also must be generally available, either for all cars of all producers, or for all garages. Thus, one problem for solutions of the kind discussed in this section is standardization.

Here, subsystems for *different models work together*: In case (i) the automatic navigation system of the garage to navigate the car (left, right, etc.) at time of entrance until exit. Or, (ii) the automatic drive system of the car to find the geometric details of the navigation (find walls, find proper curves). The business administration system of the garage to determine a free place, to determine the fee, possibly using user data for a discount price, for reserving a slot at a future time, and so on. Here, the *responsibility* of the structural navigation is on the side of the garage, the detailed and geometrical navigation on the side of the car.

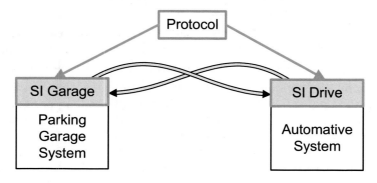

Fig. 8.3: Car and parking garage connection, analogous for other of connections

The solution for (ii) demands for a standardized interface of the garage for the car. Here, the car is the master. The car gets structural data from the garage, as place free is in the 3rd floor, the way to this place is structurally so and so, park in left or right, etc. Then it drives. In case (i) the garage starts the car and gives structural commands. The car drives automatically using the directives of the garage. So, in both cases (i) and (ii) we have a *shared responsibility* between car and garage. *Coarse navigation* is made from the garage, *micro navigation* by the car. The parting line is mainly determined by what is available or likely to be available on this or the other side.

The integration system *in between* determines mainly, what higher functionality is used from the other side and how the part looks like, which determines the cooperation of the other side, either car or garage. It is the drive part of the automotive system (micro navigation), which interacts with the coarse structural navigation of the garage, the master is on the one or the other side. Furthermore, there is a protocol component in between, which initiates the exchange of data and commands, thereby checking the other partner for seriousness and later organizing the exchange.

The protocol part can be a standard, as it is also necessary in other contexts. The extensions of functionality are a standard template. They have to be adapted for each application. The same holds true for the exchange part. The *architecture* of this *interaction* (protocol part, functional extensions on both sides, and exchange) is the essence, the *architecture* of it is the *glue*.

Car and Security or Navigation

Some short remarks to the other examples. Let us start with cooperation between *car* and *security infrastructure* of the road. Quite often, it is suggested to handle this problem by using peer-to-peer connections of cars. This demands for a certain density of traffic, which is not guaranteed at certain times (in the night) and in certain regions (extreme cases Alaska, Siberia). Therefore, we also need an infrastructure, which is available for the roads. In addition, there may be peer to peer connections for the short distance problems in populated regions. In general, a combination of infrastructure of the road and peer-to-peer of driving cars is best. In sparse regions, even the mobile phone connections might have problems.

Again, we find *standard interfaces* which are necessary, here to *infrastructure* and also for *peer-to-peer*. Interfaces to the infrastructure, peer-to-peer system, or even mobile phone specific interfaces have to be available and standardized.

There are useful *applications* in the area *traffic control*. One is *prospective navigation*: You get a warning in time, even in the case of little traffic, for example in the night. The driver gets a warning, the car is automatically slowed or stopped, if there is an accident or a traffic jam behind the next curve. This scenario needs a connection to the road infrastructure for the approaching car, for the cars in the accident/ traffic jam, and one for the peer to peer communications about traffic situations.

Usually, a driver gets *data from* the *infrastructure*, or from peer-to-peer communication, or from the mobile phone, and reacts correspondingly. It is seldom the other way around: Infrastructure *determines car*. This other way is useful in the case of medical emergency and if the car can drive automatically, e.g. after a heart attack or stroke of the driver. The car then drives to a suitable point, for the patient to be taken by another rescue car, or for to be taken up by a helicopter.

The next example is *car and extended navigation system*, i.e. functionality more than usual navigation systems, where the system offers navigation data, taken or denied by the driver. Now the navigation system can work closer together with the automatic drive system, especially in the sense of prospective navigation, as in the case to find a free loading station for the electric car and to drive automatically to this station, or in the case of a medical problem to get to the next meeting point / hospital.

All examples of this section have to do with *complex and standard interfaces* of systems, which have to be integrated to available *components* on both sides of a communication. The central topic is that the interfaces have to be standardized and the standard has to be generally available. Furthermore, a protocol component is necessary, and also extensions of the systems to be closely connected together with extended interfaces. The architecture of that all determines the *glue*.

8.5 Internal Low- or Higher-level Glue

We now look on embedded systems in *automotive* and on their *new development*. In chapter 4, we mentioned the main and rather independent functional parts of such a system, namely body control, motor control, drive control, infotainment, etc.

The subsystems' development for these parts and their components can be *conventional*, with *shallow reuse*, or even with *deep reuse*. The subsystems and their components are integrated to form an integrated overall solution. Please remember that underlying formalisms might be different (finite state systems for opening and closing; automation and control concepts for speed or for drive control, etc.). The subsystems with different underlying conceptual models have to be integrated. The integrated solution is then taken up by the OEM.

There are two *cases*: (I) conventionally developed components which are connected by a *conventional* and *low-level* architecture for the infrastructure on the basis of signals. This is the standard of many automotive solutions today. (II) Nonstandard *higher-level* development of *subsystems* placed on bigger hardware components connected by a *service-oriented architecture*. We now briefly discuss these cases.

We start the discussion of (I): We find different levels. (Ia) The above functional parts (subsystems) are internally structured. For the body control, we might distinguish two levels between opening/ closing a single door as elementary function on one side and opening/ closing the whole car. The code for these *elementary functions* or portions of functional parts are located on *control units*, which are connected to others via a *subnetwork*. Thereby, the functionality of a subsystem is realized. Signals between the units in that subnetwork connect the units at runtime. The same is done for the development of code for the other functional parts, e.g. for control of driving, which is also implemented by components of a subnetwork.

(Ib) The *subnetworks* are statically *connected* by *gateways*. Components of different subnets can also be connected by signals, which leave a subnet and enter another one. This is the case, if the car is closed above a certain speed, or the car is opened in case of an accident to allow rescue people to help from outside. Summing up: The integration within a subsystem for a functional part is realized via a subnetwork with signals at runtime. Furthermore, the integration of different functional parts is organized via gateways and signals, e.g. for summing up different actions, as start software and open car. Even the integration between different functional parts is realized with signals across different subnets (see body and speed of above). So, the subsystems are realized as software on control units of a subnet, as body control in fig. 8.4.a. Integrated functionality needs signals between different subnets.

The above discussion includes the case, that the *components* for elementary functions are *generated* using, for example, a specification. The automatic code generation of big functional parts or even for the complete automotive system is not reasonable, the models are complex as they may have many parts, inter model relations (opening/closing at a certain speed), different underlying concepts, etc. This complex overall model is changing all the time, the generator has to be adapted, new model parts need another basic model for which the generator would have to be extended. It is easier to make the integration via the architecture by integrating different parts of the system. The requirements are easier to fulfil following this way.

Altogether, we have a *low-level architecture* of software components on control units being connected by a local network and signals on that network, or signals crossing such networks via gateways. Furthermore, a component is needed for routing signals. This architecture is the *glue* between different functions of base functionalities or between different base functionalities.

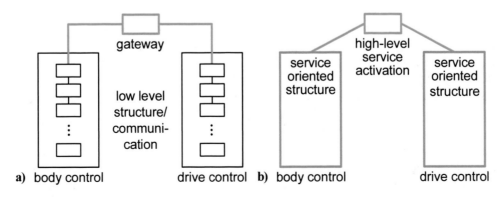

Fig. 8.4: Integration and different formalisms: (a) low, (b) high-level integration

Now we discuss case (II). We develop *subsystems* related to the standard functional parts of above (as body control), which are now placed each on a *big control unit* and not on a subnet. This leads to a dramatic change. Instead of software on 50 to 100 small control units and a big network with connections and gateways, we now have about 5 to 10 control units with corresponding bigger software components on a small network of services, see fig. 8.4.b.

We have a *service-oriented software* development in mind. Whenever formal models play a role, if only for elementary functions, or inside of functional parts, we speak of *model-driven* development. Activation between components on one big control unit is now internally realized by *service activation* and not by a signal transmission to a corresponding subunit. Code generation is simpler now as we rely on a higher connection mechanism. The development of functionality crossing the big software and hardware units is also simpler. We have less functionalities crossing units. In the extreme and improbable case - all the software is on one big control unit - all the connections between parts can be realized by inside service mechanisms.

Now *all* or *most connections* between elementary functions are inside of bigger control units, or by connections between bigger control units, or - in the extreme case - the connections inside of one magic big control unit define the integration. That are the portions of components sending out requests for other services and the way these service requests are handled. The corresponding architecture is the glue.

Summing up: The architecture can be *low-level* as in (I), or *higher level* as in case (II), or in the extreme case *high-level*, the latter all within one magic control unit. In case (I) we usually have *conventional* development of code for many control units and the corresponding complex integration. As there might be available experience, we can find *shallow reuse*. For elementary functions, we might have deep reuse by generating the code out of specs. This is difficult for big parts, especially if they use different elementary functions. No chance at the current state to build a huge and combined model from which the complete realization can be generated.

8.6 Framework and Generation

Again, we discuss *new development*, now having long-lasting experiences, and now with *deep reuse*. As example, we (A) take an environment of tightly integrated tools for development of software, see IPSEN project /Na 96/. A similar problem and a corresponding similar solution can (B) be found for design in engineering, e.g. in chemical engineering in the IMPROVE project /NM 08/. However, there is a difference: Whereas IPSEN was a project in the *a priori* sense (we built new tools for tight integration), the task of IMPROVE was to use existing tools and try to gain tight integration as much as possible by new and additional components (*a posteriori* approach). The discussion in the following concentrates on (A).

Framework for Tools

Such integrated environments show *four levels of integration*. The first is working on (i) one document or on documents of the same class of the corresponding working area, as architectures for software systems. We speak of *specific environments*, as there are different and integrated tools for one working area /Kl 96/. The second level is (ii) to provide the corresponding support for all activities in the development process, see again /Kl 96/. Here, we speak of integrated or overall *environments*. They contain all specific environments. Furthermore, (iii) we need also tools for all transitions, as e.g. from requirements engineering to architecture modeling, from architecture modeling to code etc. This is not discussed here, see chs. 10 to 14. We call such tools for transformations *integrator* tools. Finally, (iv) the *coordination* of work of different developers with different roles in the development process has to be supported. Again, this is not discussed here, see ch. 13. In all cases, from (i) to (iv), we use a model-driven way to get the tools.

We start by restricting us to the level (i) and the example of *tools* for the *architecture* of *software systems*. Corresponding tools help to build up or maintain an architecture, which may contain several documents (overall system architecture, subsystems, both containing further subsystems and modules). We also have tools to check for syntactic consistency, methodological clearness, to evaluate the architecture for completeness, etc. The explanation here is simplified, as this chapter is not on tools but on glue of architectures.

The architecture tools are realized by using a *framework* for model-driven development and a *specific* reuse *approach* (graph rewriting approach for specifications and code generation from these specifications, see below). The approach uses a framework for tools working on one document (specific environment). A simplified version of this framework is given in fig. 8.5.a. The framework handles (a) the input and output for the tools in text or diagram form, (b) storing the results in a graph-like data base, (c) keeping the presentation of results to improve their graphical layout interactively (for diagrams), (d) transforming from input to logical data and vice versa (parsing and unparsing), and (e) the command and update cycle. All standard components for these purposes are integrated in this framework, together with their corresponding code. There are some parameterizations to adapt the framework to a specific situation, which we do not discuss here.

Specific components for the data are *plugged* into the framework, see the logical document in fig. 8.5.a. They are deep reuse components, e.g. generated from specifications /Na 79, Sc 91, Zü 96/, here in the form of graph rewriting specs, which describe how certain commands change the graph-like internal logical document, here the architecture graph. The generated code is plugged into the framework, representing internal data handling, the software architectures are internally handled as architecture graphs. The framework for specific environments offers tools for editing, for immediately analyzing (syntax check), for analyzing documents in certain situations (e.g. completeness), for executing documents (in the case of executable documents as code), all working on one type of documents.

The *framework abstracts* from the *specifics o*f the command-change-show cycle, specifically how parsing (from input to internal change) and unparsing (how a changed situation is presented and shown outside) is done, free from the details of input (style and UI-system used), from the details how presentation and interaction on presentations is realized, and how the internal graph data are stored. The architecture of fig. 8.5.a is simplified, see part 4 of /Na 96/.

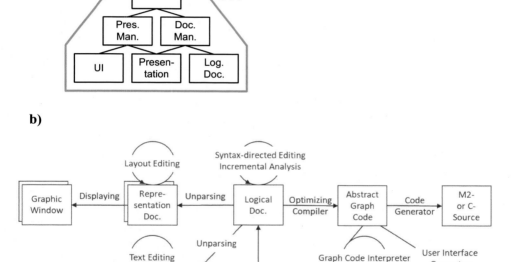

Fig. 8.5: a) Framework as architectural glue for a specific environment, b) data approach for main application components generated from specs /SWZ 96, SWZ 99/

This idea of building specific environments can be extended to all working areas, from requirements engineering to management of workload. The workload organization tool is described in ch. 13. Integrator tools can also be built with a framework and generation (not discussed here, for their functionality see chs. 10 - 14). This was called the second level of integration by an integrated environment above. This level is not shown in fig. 8.5.

The *framework* for *specific environments* is a part of the *glue*. Its architecture contains the essential decisions. It sums up all necessary components and their code. It abstracts from their details, as sketched above. The framework and its standard components are product reuse, the specification and generation mechanisms are process reuse.

Model-driven Generation for Main Application Components of Environments

Now we concentrate on the *data component*, which is called Logical Document in fig. 8.5.a. This component is not programmed but *specified* by graph rewriting and corresponding code is *generated*. A machinery is necessary for this approach.

We first need an *environment for* editing, analyzing, and executing *specs*, here in the form of graph rewriting, see fig. 8.5.b from /SWZ 96, SWZ 99/. For any command, which can be applied on an architecture document, the specification defines the effect of that command on the underlying architecture graph. A specification environment supports to edit, to analyze, or to execute such graph rewriting specs. If the spec is approved, corresponding efficient code can be generated.

Several of such specification *environments* based on graph rewriting are *available*, namely Progres /Sc 91, SWZ 99/, Moflon /LAS 14/ and Fujaba /NNZ 00/. The sketch of fig. 8.5.b describes the different parts of such an environment. The specification can be worked out using the spec environment. There are different executable forms, from direct interpretation of the graph rewriting spec (abstract but inefficient) to the code equivalent to spec (efficient). This way of getting from a graph rewriting spec to efficient and equivalent code, was called *graph grammar engineering* /SWZ 96/.

The *specification* and *generation system* allows a uniform way of specifying and generating the data components of a specific environment in a data-driven way. It also contains a framework, which is quite similar to the framework of the specific interactive final system, see again fig. 8.5.a. The generated code is plugged into the framework for the specific environment. Therefore, the code need not be developed in the usual and "manual" way.

Different *parts* make *the overall glue*: (a) the framework (internal components glue), (b) model-driven and generated application components to be inserted into the framework (model-driven code glue), and (c) the system for spec development, interpretation and code generation (model development glue). All the architectures and their code components interact smoothly. The interaction of these architectures describes a big part of the glue of this section. By the way, we have a similar interaction also within the spec environment.

In most cases of software development, there is *no way* of a *pure model-driven method*, see the remarks about automotive solutions in ch. 4. The argument also hold for this chapter. There is no model available, by which we can describe all standard components of the framework and their interaction, as well as the central data component. Such a model would cover the form and execution of programmed components, graph rewriting, and details of taste how to organize user interfaces. And even if this were possible: Whenever we extend the functionality, the transformation of the model to an extended form, the form of the user interface and so on, this would be a problem, as we had to modify the whole model, especially if these parts come from different development sites.

But the *model-driven method* is possible for the specific and *data-driven central part* within the specific environment, as shown above by process reuse. The rest of development is product reuse, given by the standardized framework.

Integrated Overall Environments and their Development

For all documents occurring in any working area (from RE (requirements engineering) to PO (project organization), see fig. 1.1 of chapter 1) there is a specific environment for the documents of that working area, see fig. 1.5 of ch. 1. Above we used the architecture environment as the running example. The reader should remember that in working areas different documents are produced, which can have different forms (text or diagram) and can represent different hierarchies. Integrator tools support the transformation between different notations, see chs. 10 and following. A specific environment helps to coordinate the developers' work, the results, and the resources needed, which is in close connection to the architecture environment, see ch. 13. Furthermore, there is a framework for integrating specific environments to build up the *integrated overall environment*.

That all is necessary to support the software development process. We did discuss here only, how the specific environments have been realized by a mixed realization process of product reuse (standardized framework) and model-driven approach for central data components to be put into the framework (process reuse). The other specific environments are realized similarly. The realizations of all the other parts (the integrator tools, and the overall environment framework) were not described here, see /Na 96, Kl 96/. For the integrators we need a new way of formalism and specification, called triple graph rewriting /SK 08/, as they couple documents of different working areas.

There is *not an overall spec* for all working areas, their transitions, and further topics such that the corresponding code can be *generated* completely. One argument is that we need different formal mechanisms, namely usual graph rewriting for describing changes of specific documents, triple graph rewriting for the transformations, and so on. Even more important is that there are different aspects, as user interface handling, efficiency of code, etc., which cannot be formally specified. Usual code is more flexible. But code is not the right level, it is too detailed. That is why in practice most of the *glue* comes *from architectures* of specific systems, their new interfaces, their parts of integration and coupling, and so on.

Above, we have discussed (A) the a priori approach of IPSEN, which demonstrated tight integration of novel tools for software development. A similar approach applies (B) to *a posteriori integration*, having been studied to improve and integrate given tools in the field of chemical engineering in the IMPROVE project /NM 08/. Here again, we worked with four levels of integration, with frameworks for single documents and the overall environment, and with a model-driven approach, using specifications from which code for core components can be generated.

The difference between (A) and (B) is that in case (B) the given tools come with different user interfaces and with different internal document structures. Wrappers for given tools have to be built to equalize the different forms of user interfaces and to hide the differences of internal logical data models. These wrappers can also be constructed in a model-driven way. The integration is handled on four levels as above in the a priori case.

What and where is the Architecture Glue?

We start with the *a priori case*. The *architectural glue* for *specific environments* is found in their framework architecture. There we have general components, which can be used for any specific environment (UI handling, change/ show result loop, connecting to basic infrastructure as to data base, etc.). We also find application specific components as architecture graph, which we get by *models* and *code* generation. Fig. 8.5.b indicates the architecture of the model environment and code generation. The same applies to integrator tools, not shown here, for their functionalities see chs. 11-14. The same applies for the management environment, see ch. 13 without implementation details. And, finally, the same applies to the overall environment.

In the *a posteriori case*, new components are necessary for integrating the existing specific tools and for collecting and smoothing their different logical interface levels (/HKN 08/, not discussed here). They are called *wrappers*. The wrapped tools are extended to improve their functionality and prepare them for a higher level of integration. That also makes integrator tools more complicated, as they now make transitions for wrapped and extended tools. The workflow organization environment is similar as above, see /HJK 08/ and ch. 13. Overall environments now collect wrapped and extended tools. Reuse and code generation are restricted as we rely on given tools. Models can be used for building wrappers, for building integrator tools, the management tools, and for combining wrapped tools to an overall environment. They deliver a glue for how to do. In the a posteriori case, there is more variety and even more interplay of different parts. Architectures deliver the glue for wrappers and for integration of wrapped and extended tools.

8.7 Summary and Open Problems

Summary: Integration and Characteristics

We discussed *integration* of *different software systems*. These systems are different corresponding to the dimensions variety, implementation structure, time of development, concepts used, degree of reuse applied, range of functionality, etc. We regarded examples from the domains business administration, embedded systems, and tool development & integration. The examples also covered different statuses, namely new development, maintenance/ evolution, and reuse. The examples are also representative for other domains outside of software development and engineering.

The integration examples have *different characteristics*: (a) Coupling of two existing and different software systems by an integration part, based on two new interfaces and integration software in between, (b) coupling bigger systems to other ones by different new standard interfaces, extensions of the applications and corresponding protocol components, (c) new development for many embedded components with a low-level connection/ or with high level components and service-oriented coupling, and (d) reuse of a framework of standard components, within which the application specific part is generated, using a spec environment and the framework for overall integration.

Messages

The main message of this chapter is: In any case of integration, we need new *software/* interfaces for *integration*, or standard solutions for coupling and generation. That is the glue of the integration. The essentials of it are determined on *architecture level*, as shown by this chapter.

The glue is mainly *independent* from the *state and level* of software development. We need the architecture glue even in the case of model-driven development to integrate the generated components. The reason is that an overall model, specifying all necessary aspects from which the whole system can be generated, is too complicated or not possible. Therefore, the model-driven approach is mostly usable for precise and well-understood parts of the system for which corresponding long lasting experience is available. The generated components are placed within the framework.

Integration is understood here as integrating clean logical working areas and corresponding documents. This is a *general principle*, namely to separate on one side and to integrate separate parts, see ch. 1. This can be seen from working areas and their relations, from specific tools and integrators, from the arguments of this chapter, and from the big projects IPSEN und IMPROVE /Na 96, NM 08/. Integration is not putting everything of different nature into one bag.

Uniform approach: Understanding integration is not restricted to software engineering or engineering in different domains. It is also applicable to find out, how cooperation between different organizations (as companies) should be organized, or science and its disciplines should go forward. An example is knowledge development. Integration also applies to the architecture of buildings and their cultural history /Na 19/. It even applies to sociological and political structures.

In this general setting a third *dimension* comes up: Whenever you have separated and integrated there should be time to *factorize out common parts*, as they influence separation and integration and put both on a more general level to start again with the integration task. In this setting, architectures get a further and new importance. *Reengineering* – see next chapter – has to do with making components and structures cleaner (separation), which then have to be integrated again.

Open Problems

In this chapter, we mostly dealt with new development, or maintenance/ evolution, reuse, and families, when looking on single systems to be integrated. All these terms, from new *development* to *families*, can be understood as a *development in longer time*: What are the steps of development, maintenance, reuse, and preparation for families over the time and how do the results of these steps change. Families of systems are not the focus of this book. *Families* are found after trials and experience, looking for general parts, using the similarity, and starting again on a more general level having the specifics in mind. Thus, families are also the result of long-lasting efforts. Deep reuse in general, see ch. 7, means to make radical steps and not only incremental improvements.

Therefore, we can look from new development, to families now under this aspect of *change* over time, and from *incremental to radical*. Compared to the problems and solutions of single systems in this chapter, the questions and solutions are similar but much more difficult, as we are going from one example system to a series, set, or class of systems and solutions. The goals are definitely more ambitious. In special cases, there might be solutions. Are there results according to this more general view in literature?

All these long-lasting efforts demand for architectural investigations in order to plan, to carry out, to improve, and to start again on an improved level. The *architectural changes drive the long-lasting efforts*: They help to organize, to control, and to deeply understand it. Can there in the future be a "theory" or at least a clear argumentation in direction of architectural changes in connection to the goals of long-lasting maintenance, deep reuse, development of families, and the corresponding ways to get advanced solutions, as reusable architectural frameworks, modeling environments, and generating code for specific components of the framework?

We have shown here that the problems, results, and solutions of this chapter can be used in different domains. We have argued using different examples from different domains and we have cited corresponding references, for examples of big projects and further trendsetting technical results. Is that already a proof of domain independence, at least within engineering disciplines? Can one "prove" this in the literature? What is available for this proof, what still has to be done?

8.8 References

/Do 08/ Donsbach, W. (ed.). The International Encyclopedia of Communication, 12 Volume Set, Wiley-Blackwell. 6038 pp. (2008)

/Ha 87/ Harel, D.: Statecharts: A visual formalism for complex systems, in Science of Computer Programming 8, 3 231-274 (1987)

/He 03/ Herzberg, D.: Modeling Telecommunication Systems: From Standard to System Architectures, Doct. Dissertation, 305 pp. RWTH Aachen University, Shaker (2003)

/HJK 08/ Heller, M./ Jäger, D/ Krapp, C.-A. et al.: An Adaptive and Reactive Management System for Project Cooordination. Ion /NM 08/, 300-366 (2008/

/HKN 08/ Haase, Th./ Klein, P./ Nagl, M.: Software Integration and Framework Development, in /NM 08/, 555-590/ (2008)

/Ho 91/ Holzmann, G.J.: Design and Validation of Computer Protocols, 539 pp., Prentice Hall (1991)

/Kl 96/ Klein, P.: The Framework Revisited: A More Detailed View on the IPSEN Architecture, in /Na 96/, 380-396 and 426-439 (1996)

/LAS 14/ Leblebici, A/ Anjorin, A/ Schürr, A.: Developing eMoflon with eMoflon, in Ruscio/ Varro (eds): Proc. 7th Int. Conf. Theory & Practice of Model Transformations LNCS 8568, 1328-145 (2014)

/Na 79/ Nagl, M.: Graph Grammars: Theory, Applications, Implementation (in German), 375pp., Vieweg Verlag (1979)

/Na 96/ M. Nagl (ed.): Building Tightly Integrated Software Development Environments - The IP-SEN Approach, LNCS 1170, 709 pp., Springer, Berlin Heidelberg (1999)

/Na 19/ Nagl, M.: Gothic Style and Informatics – Intelligent Design then and now (in German), 304 pp., Springer Vieweg (2019)

/NM 08/ Nagl, M./ Marquardt, W. (eds.): Collaborative and Distributed Chemical Engineering – From Understanding to Substantial Design Process Support, LNCS 4970, 851 pp., Springer (2008)

/NNZ 00/ Nickel, U./Niere, J./Zündorf, A.: Tool demonstration: The FUJABA environment. In: Proc. of the 22nd Intern. Conf. on Softw. Engg. (ICSE), Limerick, Ireland, 742-745, ACM Press (2000)

/PR 08/ Petri, C. A./ Reisig, W.: Petri net, Scholarpedia 3 (4): 6477. Bibcode:2008SchpJ...3.6477P. doi:10.4249/scholarpedia.6477 (2008)

/Sc 91/ Schürr, A. Operational Specification with Programmed Graph Rewriting Systems (in German), Doct. Dissertation RWTH Aachen University, 461 pp., Deutscher Universitätsverlag (1991)

/Sc 96/ Schürr, A.: Introduction to the Specification Language PROGRES, In /Na 96/, 248-279

/SK 08/ Schürr, A./ Klar, F.: 15 Years of Triple Graph Grammars, ICGT 2008, LNCS 5214, 411-425, Springer (2008)

/SWZ 96/ Schürr, A./ Winter, A./ Zündorf, A.: Developing Tools with the PROGRES Environment, in /Na 96/ 356-369

/SWZ 99/ Schürr, A./ Winter, A./ Zündorf, A.: The PROGRES Approach: Language and Environment, in Ehrig/ Engels/ Kreowski/ Rozenberg (Eds): Handbook of Graph Grammars and Computing by Graph Transformation: Volume 2, World Scientific (1999)

/Tr 06/ Trevathan, V. L. (ed.): A Guide to the Automation Body of Knowledge (2nd ed.), Research Triangle Park, NC, USA: International Society of Automation (2006)

/Zü 96/ Zündorf, A.: A Development Environment for Programmed Graph Rewriting Systems (in German), Doct. Dissertation RWTH Aachen University, 374 pp., Deutscher Universitätsverlag (1996)

9 Reverse and Reengineering for Old Systems is Seldom Complete

Bernhard Westfechtel

Software Engineering, University of Bayreuth, bernhard.westfechtel@uni-bayreuth.de

Manfred Nagl

Software Engineering, RWTH Aachen University, nagl@cs.rwth-aachen.de

Abstract

The chapter describes two different and practical reengineering projects – one for business administration and the other for mobile phone control software – on a textbook level. Underlying are three doctoral dissertations /Cr 00, Ma 05, Mo 09/. As the example projects are completely different, from the application domain on one side and from the structure of the systems to be reengineered on the other, we believe that the experiences we acquired are more than just two examples.

The chapter emphasizes that a complete reengineering of a system is rather rare due to pragmatic reasons. Therefore, we have to handle changes, which preserve the value of a big part of the system and at the same time offer the necessary and wanted extensions for improved functionality and quality.

Key words: software maintenance/ evolution, reverse and reengineering, distributing software systems, improvement of efficiency, clarity, state of technology

9.1 Introduction

Maintenance is tedious

The normal case is that software systems change over the time. Thereby software gets older /Pa 94/, i.e. less performant, reliable, and understandable, see /BK 21/, sect. 9.2. O*ngoing maintenance* or evolution activities /IE 98, BR 00/ induce permanent *internal* system changes over the time. However, there are also *external* influences, like changed platforms, or computers, or basic components, or changed requirements, or further restrictions the system has to conform to, which demand for modifications. Preventive measures - for example to start with a clear and adaptable architecture and constantly trying to update this architecture - can delay this trend for software aging but cannot completely stop it.

Typical problems of software engineering are so-called *replacement projects*. An old system has to be reshaped, it cannot remain as it is. Nobody can understand the old system or is able to modify it. The first and obvious idea might be to rebuild it from scratch again, to improve its structure, but also to use new structuring principles and methods, to eliminate obvious weaknesses, and to extend its functionality.

There were *urgent reasons* to act in this direction in the past. The reader might remember the year 2000 problem or the Euro problem. Or, he or she might be aware that old mainframe systems had to be reshaped due to urgent distribution necessities, or distribution or a bad shape of the old system caused severe efficiency problems, and so on.

There are only *few cases*, that the completely *new construction* was *successful*. The reasons are: (a) The knowledge about the old system has left the company, when the developers retired or went to another company. (b) The old system was developed in an old-fashioned programming language, uses components or an infrastructure, which were no longer available. (c) Nearly nobody was able to infer the functionality of the old system. (d) The plan for the complete replacement came from young developers, charged with new development method knowledge, looking down on the old guys. The old hands just watch what happens. We have seen several of these complete replacement projects, which failed drastically. A lot of workload and money was wasted.

So, what to do? Try to prevent the useful part of the old system. Try to change what is indispensable. Try to make the architecture at least partially adaptable. Try to avoid the problems (a) to (d) of above as far as possible. This chapter is a *plea* for a course of action, which *accepts reality* and tries to *get forward*, knowing that a desired goal cannot be achieved.

Definitions

The purpose of *reverse engineering* /HM 04, CD 07, EK 02, FT 96, KC 99, KS 02, MO 93, MW 94, Wi RE/ is to find the essential structure of an old software system. This structure is often some "kind of an architecture" of the software system. If the architecture level is regarded to be the dominant aspect, some authors speak of design recovery /CC 90, LW 90/ or architecture recovery /PG 02/. Often, there was no explicit architecture when the system was developed, as programming languages of former times had no concepts to express architectural structures. Even more, the system was changed many times. We know that even in the case, where the system had a reasonable structure, this structure was destroyed by maintenance activities over the time.

The *aims* of reverse engineering can be *different*: Better understanding and comprehension of program systems by visualization of internal relations /BN 04/, preparing for future activities, as to improve quality, prepare for future changes, finding or later using good patterns, applying metrics /BD 05, LS 02/, finding weak points which can be used for attacks, finding malware. This is the reason why reverse engineering /Wi RE/ also appears with other titles, like program analysis /LS 01/ or comprehension, program understanding or visualization. The community has been active since 1990. The goal and the techniques are not clearly distinguished.

Reengineering aims at reshaping existing (legacy) software for making it better, i.e. more efficient, better extensible, less redundant, using new technology, etc. /BB 96, Ko 10, LL 23, Wi ReE/. For that, usually reverse engineering is necessary /BM 96, CC 01/, as either no architecture is available at all, or the architecture is not up to date. Parts of the old system are discarded, the architecture of the new system has to be elaborated by replacement of parts or by extensions of the system to cover the new requirements.

For the way by which we tackle the problem, we coin the term *rough (or coarse) reverse and reengineering*. This specific procedure has two facets: (i) to make reverse and reengineering both in the large, i.e. to concentrate on *architectural design level* and not to care immediately about the details of code modification, which might come afterwards. Furthermore, (ii) changes are not planned for the whole program system. Instead, we care about *essential parts*, which we would like to preserve, due to the reasons mentioned above, and concentrate on modifications in the dual parts.

Refactoring is another term in this context /Fo18, Wi Ref/. It usually means modifications on code level preserving the semantics of the code. The term appears often in connection to agile methods as activity of every iteration circle, and is usually pattern and tool supported. As dealing on source text level, the range of refactoring is not only the architecture and not only a static description. In this chapter, therefore, refactoring is not the focus.

Surprisingly, the above *terms* exist in *all engineering disciplines*, for hardware or software, dealing with informatics, mechanical engineering, electrical engineering, or civil engineering topics. So, we can contribute to a progress in different disciplines. Also surprisingly, a big part of the reverse and reengineering literature does not deal with programs of outdated languages as Fortran or COBOL, but with OO programs /BN 04/.

Two Practical Examples

In this chapter, we regard two practical examples, which span the *variety* of reverse and reengineering projects. Furthermore, in both examples the approach we take is a selective one: We look on specific parts of the system, modify them with care to avoid the abovementioned problems, wrap them and add new parts to the system. We call this approach *reengineering in the coarse*.

The first example deals with modernizing an old and big COBOL program system on a mainframe to *prepare* the system *for improvement* and for *distribution*. The example will show that only a smaller part of the old system remains completely unchanged.

The second example deals with the central part of a telecommunication system for mobile phones, making this part *better to understand* and *more efficient*. Here again, the changes are carefully chosen and precautions are taken in order to preserve the development knowledge of the original system.

The two *examples* are *sufficiently different*. On the one hand, they come from different application domains. The first example is from business administration, more specifically from an insurance company's back office. The second comes from a telecommunication company. The systems are also different: The first is an interactive system, the second an embedded system. The languages in which both systems were written are also different, namely COBOL or Plex. This diversity assures us that the experiences we describe are generally valid and the explanations are transferrable.

This *chapter* is structured *as follows*: First, we present a common basis of both reengineering projects. In the following sections, the business administration and the telecom project are addressed in turn. We are sure that the conclusions and the explanation of these sample projects also hold for further examples. Then, we sum up and sketch open problems.

9.2 Reengineering Approach

Reengineering is composed of three activities that are illustrated in fig. 9.1. In *reverse engineering*, abstractions above the level of source code are reconstructed. *Restructuring* improves the structure of artifacts with the help of horizontal transformations. *Forward engineering* propagates changes from high level abstractions down to the source code.

This conceptual framework was coined in /CC 90/. It may be populated in different ways, depending on the target level of reverse engineering, which may reconstruct the requirements (via the architecture), only the architecture (steps 1-3, see below), or may be omitted altogether. Which target level is strived for, depends on the goals of the particular reengineering project.

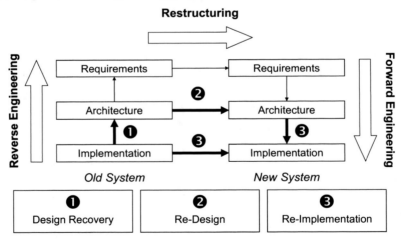

Fig. 9.1: Reengineering approach

Both the business administration and the telecom project require an understanding of the underlying software architecture. Therefore, we followed an *architecture-based reengineering* approach, known as *horseshoe model* /KW98/. It consists of three steps (fig. 9.1): (1) *Design recovery* reconstructs the architecture from the source code (and potentially other data sources). (2) *Re-design* improves the structure of the architecture. (3) *Re-implementation* changes the existing source code in response to the previously performed modifications of the architecture.

By applying an architecture-based reengineering process, we may avoid to rewrite the software system under study from scratch. Still, architecture-based reengineering involves a significant effort for the following reasons: (1) Design recovery is far from trivial. In particular, this applies to old legacy systems written in programming languages that do not support abstractions. (2) Re-design requires informed design decisions ensuring that the software architecture is improved such that maintenance is made considerably easier. (3) In re-implementation, the source code has to be reorganized such that the reengineered system may safely replace the old system that is still being used.

Tool support for reengineering is urgently required and was developed in both reengineering projects to be described below. However, while architecture-based reengineering may be supported by tools, there is no hope that this process can be fully automated. In contrast, reengineering demands for human expertise and continues to be an expensive and risky endeavour.

The problems sketched above are inherent ones. In particular, design recovery and re-design involve creative steps that require human expertise. Furthermore, in re-implementation program transformations are executed that are not guaranteed to be semantics-preserving and even may not ensure syntactic correctness. Thus, the re-implemented system has to be checked for correctness, errors have to be fixed, regression testing has to be performed, and the program code may have to be improved in response to failing test cases.

For these reasons, it has to be investigated carefully when architecture-based reengineering should be performed, which goals should be pursued, and to which parts of the system under study it should be applied. Furthermore, the effects of changes should be confined by *wrapping*: The changes in the reengineered part should be hidden behind an interface ensuring that other parts of the overall system are not affected by the changes.

9.3 *Restructuring a Business Administration System for Distribution*

Overview

The starting point of the BA example was a huge *COBOL mainframe program* dealing with the preparation of an insurance contract in the back office of the company. This program had *severe weaknesses* to be eliminated by restructuring the system:

(a) The program was built for many simple terminals being connected to the mainframe program. The details of UI handling were spread over the whole program. At the time the project started, clients were used, which allowed a better *user interface* and also *preprocessing* on the client side. So, the UI part was newly built.

(b) The data handling was overloaded by many details of the underlying data base storage. The data access was made abstract via data abstraction. This interface was used in the main *business functions*. Doing so, a lot of redundancy in the business functions was detected.

(c) The business function part was *wrapped* to get a clear functional interface of it.

(d) The *control part* as the instance to mediate between input and business functions was freed of UI details and business functions. It became clear and *compact*.

(e) As now, the main components (see fig. 9.2) are loosely coupled, they can be deployed on different machines (clients, mediation, business server, data server) due to different reasons, as improving security, redundancy, balance, etc. This allowed a *distributed solution*.

The steps of *restructuring* were *motivated* (i) by using new technology (UI part now on clients, distribution on clients and servers), (ii) applying software engineering principles (data abstraction in the UI part's interface, data abstraction in the data part's interface, clear functional abstraction for business functions' interface), (iii) wrapping existing parts (business functions and data), (iv) modifying (forgetting details) and preserving the know how of the main components via wrapping, namely the data part and, especially the business functions' part, and (v) building new components (the UI part and the control part, as here reengineering causes more effort than building anew). This, altogether, explains what we mean by reengineering in the coarse.

The new structure is given in fig. 9.2, a remake of fig. 3 of ch. 3. This new structure and the methodology was worked out together with AachenMünchener Insurance. The results were the outcome of the dissertation project of Katja Cremer at RWTH Aachen University /Cr 00, CM 02/.

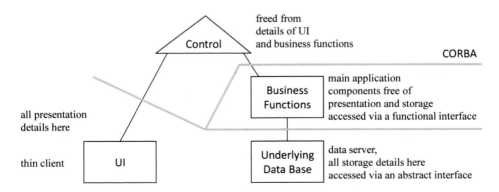

Fig. 9.2: A sketch of the reengineered BA system

In ch. 3, we furthermore explain that the reengineering steps mentioned above make the program system *more adaptable*, especially against expectable changes of the functionality as well as of the realization of the program. We do not repeat this discussion here. Just to take one example: Whatever user interface you chose, other UI style, a different UI management system, other commands of similar functionality, other client (e.g. thick client and extensively checking data), this should not (or only little) affect the main part of the application.

Fig. 9.3 sums up the *reengineering* steps in form of a *process diagram*. In the first step – a simple reverse engineering step – we only identify those parts of the program system, which we would like to preserve, according to the arguments (a) to (d) of above. In our case, these parts are the business function and the data part. Then, we apply the modification steps (freeing from details of UI and data on one hand and wrapping on the other) in order to connect these parts to new parts. The two parts at the beginning are the activities, which we associate with the term reengineering in the coarse. Then, we add new parts (for control and UI). Finally, we deploy the system, using the potential distribution lines together with a corresponding infrastructure (e.g. CORBA /OM 21/). If all parts of fig. 9.2 are deployed differently, we have three deployment steps.

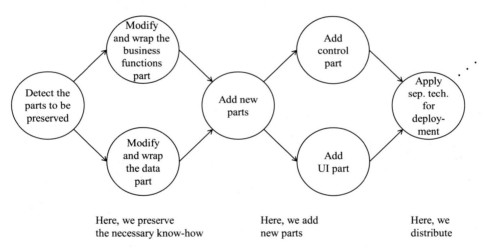

Fig. 9.3: The reengineering process for the BA system

The new architecture of the BA example was worked out in a cooperation with AachenMünchener Insurance (now Generali), especially those parts which have been described above. The example is an *interactive system*, preparing and completing an insurance contract in the back office of the company.

Reengineering Approach

In the following, we focus on the steps "Modify and wrap the business functions/data part" from fig. 9.3. The steps are used to prepare the business application for distribution, as illustrated in fig. 9.2. The subsequent distribution step is not described here, the reader is referred to a companion Ph.D. thesis /Ra 00/.

To prepare distribution, the data part and the business functions part are *migrated* from *COBOL 85* /SW 93/ to *Object COBOL* /DH 97/. Due to its object-oriented language constructs, Object COBOL facilitates *wrapping* of the application: Data are encapsulated by classes and may be read and modified via methods, which provide for data abstraction. After having migrated to Object COBOL, object distribution technologies such as CORBA may be used to provide object-oriented interfaces, behind which Object COBOL classes are hidden.

In the following, we describe the steps of reengineering. By and large, we follow the conceptual framework illustrated in fig. 9.1. However, the cut between design recovery and re-design was performed in a different way, as we will explain below.

Design Recovery

In COBOL 85, an application is composed of a set of *programs*, each of which is structured into multiple *divisions*. A program includes a *data* and a *procedure division*. Data are separated from procedures, according to procedural programming.

The *data division* consists of three sections: a *data linkage section* for storing parameters of program calls, a *file section* for data stored in files, and a *working storage section* for data stored in main memory. Data in all sections are structured into *records*, which may be nested. Altogether, the data division constitutes a space of global data that may be used in the procedure division.

Like a natural language text, the procedure division is structured into *sections*, *paragraphs*, and *sentences*. Both sections and paragraphs are named. A program is called by executing a *call statement*; parameters may be passed via the linkage section. When a program call is executed, its procedure division is executed from its beginning. Control may be transferred to another location by a global program call, by a local procedure call, and by a *goto statement*. A procedure is called by a *perform statement* without any parameters. The target of a perform statement is a section or a paragraph; control returns to the call site when the respective section or paragraph has been executed to completion.

Design recovery receives the source code as input and converts it into a structured representation. The resulting *system structure graph* resembles an abstract syntax graph and is constructed by parsing the source code. The nodes of the system structure graph contain references to the respective source code fragments, which are used in re-implementation to construct the source code of the migrated application. The system structure graph represents the application on different levels of granularity, ranging from the whole system down to the level of individual statements.

In the context of this reengineering project, the notion "design recovery" may be considered a misnomer: The system structure graph faithfully represents the application as it stands, and is obtained through a deterministic parsing process. No attempts are made at this stage to recover design abstractions such as classes; this task is deferred to re-design.

Re-Design

In the re-design step, elements of the system structure graph are mapped onto an *object-based architecture*. The architecture description language employed to this end resembles the language introduced in ch. 2 of this book; see /Cr 00/ and /Ra 00/ for a detailed explanation. Inheritance is not exploited in the mapping; the resulting classes are not organized into an inheritance hierarchy. Furthermore, classes are singletons, i.e., for each class only a single instance exists (corresponding to *abstract data objects*, see ch. 2). Singleton classes are obtained from the mapping because COBOL 85 does not support dynamic instantiation of data from types.

In contrast to the conceptual frameworks introduced in /CC 90/ and /KW 98/, re-design is not a horizontal transformation; rather, it raises the level of abstraction. All design decisions are performed in re-design; design recovery merely converts the source code into a structured representation that provides the information required for re-design.

Mapping a COBOL 85 application to an object-based architecture is far from trivial. The source code is not structured accordingly, and may have to be reorganized considerably. Reorganization is hampered by several language features that may result in monolithic programs that are hard to decompose. For example, the procedure division may be executed sequentially (section by section, and paragraph by paragraph), which is called *fall-through execution*. Simultaneously, a section or paragraph may serve as target of a local procedure call. In that case, the control flow would return to the calling site when the respective unit has been executed to completion – unless it is left before via a goto statement. After all, there is no language construct for defining procedures; whether sections or paragraphs may be considered procedures, depends on the way they are used.

Performing re-design manually is out of question; the implied effort is not acceptable. Therefore, several *re-design algorithms* are proposed in /Cr 00/ that should be applied under different premises and yield different object-based architectures:

(1) In the case of a monolithic program with goto statements and fall-through execution, the respective program may be mapped to a single class exporting a single method.

(2) If the procedure division is structured weakly, but may be decomposed into multiple procedures, the respective program may be mapped to a single class with multiple methods (one method for the externally callable program and one method for each procedure).

(3) If the procedure division may be decomposed into multiple procedures and these procedures may be grouped into clusters operating on disjoint data, the respective program may be mapped onto multiple classes, each of which exports a group of methods. This mapping is realized by adapting an algorithm contributed by Liu and Wilde /LW 90/.

(4) If the procedure division may be composed into multiple top-level procedures, each of which may call further local procedures, a functional decomposition is

obtained by creating multiple classes, each of which exports a public method corresponding to a top-level procedure and further private methods corresponding to local procedures. This mapping is realized by adapting an algorithm proposed by Cimitile and Visaggio /CV 95/.

All of these algorithms should be considered as heuristics, by means of which a proposal for an object-based architecture may be created. The resulting architecture has to be inspected and potentially revised by a reengineering expert. This results in a *semi-automatic re-design* process.

Re-Implementation

Like re-design, re-implementation is not a horizontal transformation: The source code written in COBOL 85 has to be lifted to Object COBOL, which provides for object-oriented language constructs. Re-implementation is a program transformation that is based on multiple inputs: the source code, the system structure graph, the object-based architecture (which is represented as a graph, as well), and the mapping between the source code and the system structure graph as well as between the system structure graph and the architecture graph.

Re-implementation is realized with the help of a *code-merging generator* that works as follows: From the object-based architecture, the *skeleton* of an Object COBOL application is created. The skeleton code is filled with source code fragments that are retrieved from the original source code with the help of the mappings mentioned above.

While the code merging generator operates automatically, the resulting code may still contain syntactic and semantic errors that need to be fixed. Altogether, re-implementation is a semi-automatic process that may require significant work to be invested by reengineering experts.

9.4 Restructuring a Telecom System and Improving Efficiency

The *E-CARES* project (*E*ricsson *C*ommunication *AR*chitecture for *E*mbedded *S*ystems) was carried out in cooperation with Ericsson Eurolab Deutschland (EED). E-CARES addressed the reengineering of AXE10, the software for *Mobile Service Switching Centers* (MSC). AXE10 comprises about 10 million lines of code, distributed over 1,000 units.

Under the umbrella of the E-CARES project, 3 Ph.D. theses were completed /He 03, Ma 05, Mo 09/. Furthermore, a number of conference papers about E-CARES were published /MH 01, MW 02, MW 03, MW 04, MW 10/.

Problem Statement

The E-CARES project differed from the reengineering project described in the previous section in multiple ways. First, it targeted a *process-centered* rather than a data-centered *application*. Thus, it did not focus primarily on the recovery of data abstraction modules; instead, domain-specific abstractions had to be developed that are adequate for this kind of application. Second, E-CARES strived for *perfective* rather than adaptive *maintenance*. It was not intended to migrate AXE10 to a new platform (or migrate it to a different programming language). Rather, the structure of the application should be optimized in order to improve efficiency and to facilitate maintenance.

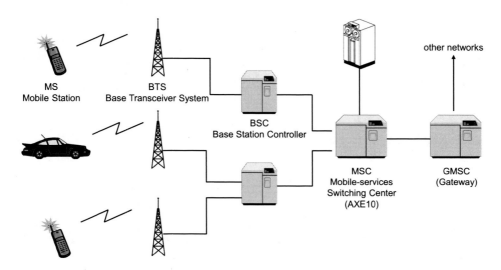

Fig. 9.4: GSM network

An MSC serves as a core part of a GSM network (see fig. 9.4). Service requests originating e.g. from mobile phones are transmitted through Base Transceiver Systems (BTS) and Base Station Controllers (BSC) to the MSC, which is connected through gateways (GMSC) to other networks (e.g., a landline network).

Fig. 9.5 illustrates the steps that are performed to establish a connection between two mobile phones. From the MSC of the A side, the B side is located via the GMSC, a home location register (HRL), and the MSC of the B side (steps 1-3). A roaming number is sent back via the HLR to the GMSC (4-5), which sends a call request to the MSC of the B side (6). The MSC responds with an Address Complete Message (ACM) that is forwarded to the MSC of the A side (7-8). Now, user data may be transferred, as illustrated by the dashed line.

AXE10 is programmed in a proprietary language called *PLEX* (*Programming Language for EXchanges*). PLEX is a domain-specific, concurrent, asynchronous real-time language that is based on a signaling paradigm. A program consists of *blocks* which serve as units of compilation. Blocks encapsulate their data, which cannot be accessed from other blocks. Blocks interact by sending and receiving different types of *signals*, which support both asynchronous and synchronous communication. In response to an incoming signal, a sequence of statements is executed, which includes sending of signals to other blocks. For serving calls, *instances* of blocks are created dynamically, which are arranged into *link chains*.

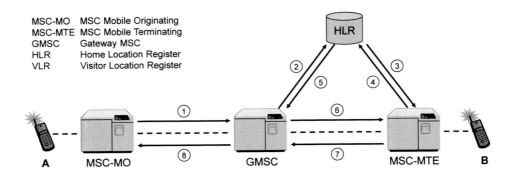

Fig. 9.5: Mobile originating call

Reengineering Approach

In E-CARES, the conceptual framework illustrated in fig. 9.1 was populated in a way that differs from the reengineering approach adopted in the business application project. Since it was not intended to migrate the AXE10 system to a new platform, both *re-design* and *re-implementation* are *horizontal transformations*. Thus, both the original and the reengineered source code are programmed in PLEX; at the architectural level, programs are represented by system structure graphs. Furthermore, *design recovery* and *re-design* are *separated* in different ways: In the business application project, recovery of design abstractions is performed exclusively in re-design. In E-CARES, design abstractions are reconstructed in design recovery; the resulting architecture is improved in re-design.

Design Recovery

The first step of *design recovery* involves the construction of a *system structure graph*. Fig. 9.6 presents a simplified example. The system structure graph is located at a higher level of abstraction than an abstract syntax graph. For example, statements are aggregated into statement sequences. In particular, the system structure graph reflects the signaling paradigm underlying the PLEX language: A signal is received through an entry point, and is processed by a labeled statement sequence that in turn sends signals to other blocks. The system structure graph also includes subroutines and their calls, participations in link chains, and data accesses (the latter of which are not shown in fig. 9.6).

The system structure graph is created by parsing the source code (and other types of documentation, which we will not consider here). Still, it is a *representation* of the underlying *PLEX program* and does not incorporate any design decisions. Thus, the first step of design recovery is performed completely automatically and operates deterministically.

In a second step, *functions* and *modules* are recovered from the system structure graph. Both functions and modules are conceptual units that are not materialized as language constructs in PLEX. Design recovery extends the system structure graph with functions and modules. This recovery step enhances program understanding and constitutes an added value on its own. In addition, it may be used to prepare re-design.

The *external interface* of a block is composed of *functions* that process incoming signals. A function is retrieved from the system structure graph by following the control flow starting from a signal entry. By a transitive closure from a single entry point, we obtain a set of elements including statement sequences, subroutines, and variables. From this set, we remove all elements that are reachable from different signal entry points. In this way, mutually disjoint sets of elements are constructed. For each function, a corresponding node is inserted into the system structure graph and is connected to all elements of the respective set.

A *module* is a group of logically related functions. In AXE10, blocks are large code units that may comprise multiple modules. One of the algorithms that have been developed for recovery of modules is based on clustering as proposed by Liu and Wilde /LW 90/. Functions are grouped into modules based on common data accesses. Thus, if two functions f and g access a common data element d, they are grouped into the same module. Clustering is performed recursively until the data accessed by different modules are mutually disjoint. Since this approach may yield modules that are too large, the original algorithm had to be adapted by constraining the considered data accesses. To this end, a coding convention is exploited: A module stores its own data in a record that includes a field for representing its state. For each module recovered in this way, the system structure graph is extended with a node that is connected to all of its functions and its encapsulated data.

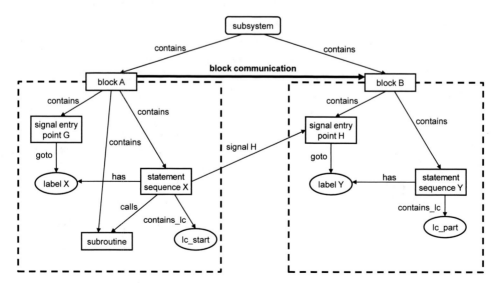

Fig. 9.6: System structure graph

Recovery of functions and modules constitutes the second step of design recovery. It differs considerably from the first step: *Heuristics* are applied that are based on coding conventions. In general, many algorithms have been proposed for design recovery; see /Ko 09/ for an overview. Thus, by running different algorithms, we may obtain different proposals for functions and modules (see also /Mo 09/). Whatever proposal is created: The software developer should inspect the result carefully and adapt it manually, if required.

All steps that we considered so far aid in program understanding, but merely generate *views* of the underlying software system. In the following, we move on to *re-design* and *re-implementation*, which aim at changing the subject system to improve its structure.

Re-Design

In E-CARES, only reengineering scenarios were studied which involved *local restructuring*. A pervasive global reengineering effort was not intended. More specifically, reengineering addressed reorganizations at the block level: *Merging* of *blocks* is considered to improve efficiency; communication across blocks is more expensive than local communication. Conversely, *splitting* of *blocks* strives for improving software maintenance; splitting is performed to reduce the size of the code units to be maintained. In the following, we discuss the latter scenario, following /Mo 09/.

Splitting of blocks involves *restructuring transformations* on the system structure graph: Each module is moved to one block. For example, let us assume that two modules M1 and M2 were recovered in some block B (fig. 9.7, part a). After restructuring, these modules are located in blocks B1 and B2, respectively. This restructuring transformation raises a couple of problems to be discussed below.

First, block B may contain elements that do not belong to either of the two modules (shared subroutines and data elements). *Shared elements* may be allocated either to B1 or to B2, or they may be placed elsewhere (e.g., a block-local variable may be moved to a communication buffer stored in a file).

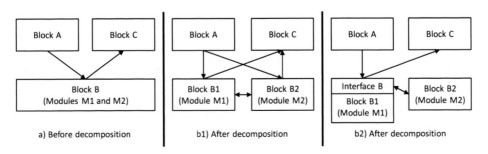

Fig. 9.7: Block splitting

Second, the *local communication* between M1 and M2 has to be converted into global communication between B1 and B2. For example, a local signal has to be replaced with a global signal, and a subroutine call that now targets a different block must be replaced with a combined signal for synchronous communication.

Third, the *impact* on the *context* of B has to be considered. Without further provisions (fig. 9.7, b1), signals sent by block A have to be distributed to B1 and B2. Likewise, block C now receives signals from B1 and B2. Thus, blocks in the context of B would be affected by the restructuring, as well. To avoid this propagation of changes, the architecture is changed such that one of the new blocks may play the role of the old block, providing the same interface as the old block (fig. 9.7, b2).

Note that providing an interface to the restructured part is an example of the *wrapping* approach mentioned in the previous section dealing with the BA application: The reengineered part is encapsulated by a wrapper, the other parts of the application remain unaffected.

Altogether, re-design is far from trivial. While it may be supported by tools offering re-design transformations, the overall process is *interactive* and requires manual steps to be performed by developers, exploiting their knowledge of the system.

Re-Implementation

After re-design, *re-implementation* propagates the changes to the source code level. This is achieved with the help of a *code merging generator* that traverses the system structure graph and assembles code fragments that are referenced by its nodes. For example, a node for a statement sequence carries attributes for the start line and the end line of the corresponding source code fragment. However, the old code fragments cannot be reused as they stand; they may be affected by the re-design transformations. For example, if a local signal has been replaced with a global signal, the affected source code fragment has to be updated accordingly.

After having executed the code merging generator, further *manual changes* may have to be performed on the generated source code. This is necessary if new elements were added to the system structure graph for which no code is available yet. This results in generated code containing empty parts that have to be filled in by the programmer. The new code may replace the old code only after it has been compiled and has passed all regression tests successfully.

9.5 Summary and Open Problems

Summary

The essence of the business administration example is the following: In the *business functionality part* and *the data access part* we find the value of the system, which should be preserved. Therefore, we reengineer with care (eliminating only UI and data details, and care about new interfaces). We do *not essentially touch* the code fixing the business functionality.

The UI part and the control part can be *structured* in a *new* way. The clean wrapping of the old parts and the methodological structure of the new parts induce *loose coupling* of the different parts of the system. This is necessary for distributing the system. A corresponding infrastructure minimizes the required effort.

The new form of the system improves *adaptability*: Hiding of details of style and layout on the UI part, details of data handling through a clear new interface, clear separation of dialog control and executing the corresponding business functionality.

While the business administration project was concerned with software migration (from mainframe application to client-server), the *telecom project* aimed at *perfective maintenance*: The overall system is reengineered in a minimally invasive way in order to improve its structure and performance. The reengineering scenarios addressed restructurings such as splitting and merging blocks; thus, a global reengineering effort was not intended. Migration to a new platform was not considered.

From a bird eye's view, a similar tool chain was developed and applied for reengineering, supporting *design recovery, re-design*, and *re-implementation* (see fig. 9.1). While the tool chain is useful to support software developers in reengineering, the overall process still requires significant manual work in order to deliver an efficient, maintainable, and stable reengineered system. Design recovery is driven by heuristic algorithms that generate proposals, which have to be reviewed and revised by software developers. Likewise, re-design requires a number of judicious design decisions, and re-implementation creates reorganized source code that has to be inspected, adapted, and tested carefully.

Tool support for reengineering is useful and urgently required, but the analysis of its limitations reveals the reasons why *reengineering* is *seldom complete*. Thus, reengineering should focus on carefully selected parts of the overall system.

Wrappers may support reengineering in different ways. First, old code that is not intended to be modified may be hidden behind a wrapper that enables access from a more recent platform (e.g., by providing object-oriented wrappers to procedural code). Second, reengineered code may be wrapped in order to prevent or confine the propagation of changes into its context.

Both example projects are rather different: Application domain, class of systems, functionality and support, very different implementation languages (COBOL und PLEX), etc. So, to a certain degree we demonstrated the independence and *broad applicability* of the ideas of this chapter.

Let us come back to the *a posteriori approach* of IMPROVE /NM 08/, which we have discussed in ch. 8. It is a third example, which we could have discussed here. The approach uses given tools, which are indispensable, they still have their value and the users are familiar with them. *Wrappers* are used, for equalizing their logically different levels of interfaces and to prepare for further integration and extension. This is the *reengineering* part.

New functionality was added in IMPROVE. It was provided by integrator tools, bridging the gaps between different working areas, see chs. 10, 11, 12, and 14. Furthermore, the adaptive management system, able to react on dynamic changes in the development process, offered novel management functionality, see ch. 13. (There are further aspects, as tools for defining detailed process knowledge, and tools for different ways for developers' communication /NM 08/.) This all was put together to a new integrated overall support environment, with partially new functionality. This is the *integration or extension part*, see ch. 8.

The Message of this Chapter

Reengineering of legacy systems has proved challenging. Redeveloping them from scratch may turn out to be economically infeasible. This statement also applies to pervasive modifications, which are costly to perform and validate. For this reason, we suggest to decide carefully which parts of an application should be discarded and redeveloped on a new platform, which parts should be reengineered, and which parts should stay untouched.

For solving the reengineering problems considered in this chapter, architectural knowledge is indispensable. Therefore, we follow the conceptual framework of fig. 9.1, which distinguishes between design recovery, re-design, and reimplementation. As argued above, re-design and re-implementation should focus on selected parts of the overall system.

The methods and tools contributed by both sample projects provide valuable support for reengineering processes. Without such support, reengineering would have to be performed more or less manually, implying a high development effort. But we also have to acknowledge inherent limitations of this support: Applications that were not built with functional and data abstraction in mind may prove to be hard to restructure. Furthermore, design recovery may be supported by algorithms, which, however, constitute heuristics: The resulting proposals need to be inspected carefully – and in general require further adaptations.

Open Problems

Many *further examples* in different domains are possible for applying this moderate and practical approach.

The above problems come from modernizing *one specific* system. We get a *new quality* of problems, if we regard a *series of systems* which share some similarity:

(a) Make a *family of systems* or a product line /CN 07/ out of similar systems /SP 12/. This means that inherent similarities and differences have to be found, worked out, and made explicit.
(b) The *complexity* of *systems* and their *similarity* in relation to structure and complexity should be made clear. For both software metrics should be applied to formalize reasoning.
(c) Extract *domain knowledge* from different programs of a domain. Again, this makes something explicit.

(d) If, in a certain and specific context programs are developed, then reuse is usually applied. Deep reuse in the sense of ch. 7 is rarely found. *Reuse steps* might be regarded as specific reengineering modifications. Can the finding of deep reuse steps be supported? Can the reuse knowledge be extracted? There are further problems of this kind.

Compared to the above problems of single systems, the questions are similar but much more difficult, as we are going from one example system to a *series*, *set*, or *class* of systems. The goals are definitively more ambitious. In special cases, there might be solutions.

9.6 References

/BB 96/ Baumöl, U./Borchers, J. et al.: Einordnung und Terminologie des Software Reengineering, Informatik Spektrum 19, 191-195 (1996)

/BD 05/ Balzer, M./ Deussen, O./ Lewerentz, C.: Voronoi Treemaps for the Visualization of Software Metrics, ACM Symp. On Software Visualization, 165-172, ACM Press (2005)

/BK 21/ Broy, M./ Kuhrmann, M.: Einführung in die Softwaretechnik, 665 pp., Springer Vieweg (2021)

/BM 96/ Burd, E./ Munro, M./ Wezeman, C.: Analysing Large COBOL Programs: The extraction of reusable modules, Proc. Intern. Conf. on Software Maintenance (ICSM '96), 238-243, IEEE Comp. Soc. Press (1996)

/BN 04/ Balzer, M./ Noack, A./ Deussen, O./ Lewerentz, C.: Software Landscapes: Visualizing the Structure of Large Software systems, Joint Eurographics IEEE TCVG Symp. On Visualization (VisSym) (2004)

/BR 00/ Bennett, K./ Rajlich, V.: Software Maintenance and Evolution: A Roadmap, Proc. ICSE '00, 73-87, ACM Press (2000)

/CC 90/ Chikofsky, L. C./ Cross II, J. H.: Reverse Engineering and Design Recovery: A Taxonomy, IEEE Software 7(1), 13-17 (1990)

/CC 01/ Canfora, G./ Cimitile, A./ De Luca, A./ Di Lucca, G. A.: Decomposing Legacy Systems into Objects: An eclectic approach, Information and Software Technology 43 (6), 401-412 (2001)

/CD 07/ Canfora, G./ Di Penta, M.: New Frontiers of Reverse Engineering, in Proc. Future of Software Engineering (FOSE '07), 326-341 (2007)

/CM 02/ Cremer, K./ Marburger, A./ Westfechtel, B.: Graph-based tools for reengineering, Journ. of Software Maintenance and Evolution, Research and Practice 14, 257-292 (2002)

/CN 07/ Clements, P./ Northrop, L. M.: Software Product Lines: Practices and Patterns, 563 pp., 6th ed., Addison Wesley (2007)

/Cr 00/ Cremer, K.: Graphbasierte Werkzeuge zum Reverse Engineering und Reengineering, Doct. Diss., RWTH Aachen University, 220 pp., Deutscher Universitätsverlag (2000)

/CV 95/ Cimitele, J./ Visaggio, G.: Software Salvaging and the Dominance Tree, Journ. of Systems and Software 22, 117-127 (1995)

/DH 97/ Doke, E.R./ Hardgrave, B.C.: An Introduction to Object COBOL, 204 pp., Wiley (1997)

/EK 02/ Ebert, J./ Kullbach, B./ Riediger, V./ Winter, A.: GUPRO – Generic Understanding of Programs: An Overview, El. Notes in Theor. Comp. Science 72(2), 10 pp. (2002)

/Fo 18/ Fowler, M.: Refactoring: Improving the Design of Existing Code, 2nd ed., 418 pp., Addison Wesley (2018)

/FT 96/ Fiutem, R./ Tonella, P./ Antoniol. G./ Merlo, E.: A Cliché-based Environment to Support Architectural Reverse Engineering, in Proc. Intern. Conf. on Software Maintenance (ICSM '96), 319-328, IEEE Comp. Soc. Press (1996)

/He 03/ Herzberg, D.: Modelling Telecommunication Systems: From Standard to System Architectures, Doct. Diss., RWTH Aachen University, 305 pp., Shaker (2003)

/HM 04/ Hoglund, G./ McGraw, G.: Exploiting Software: How to Break Code, 512 pp., Addison-Wesley Professional (2004)

/IE 98/ IEEE Std. 1219: Standard for Software Maintenance, IEEE Computer Society (1998)

/KC 99/ Kazman, R./ Carrière, S. J.: Playing Detective: Reconstructing Software Architecture from Available Evidence, Journ. Aut. Software Engineering 6(2), 107-138 (1999)

/Ko 09/ Koschke, R.: Architecture Reconstruction – Tutorial on Reverse Engineering to the Architectural Level, in: De Lucia, A./ Ferruci, F. (eds.): International Summer Schools on Software Engineering 2006-2008, LNCS 5413, 140-173, Springer (2009)

/Ko 10/ R. Koschke: Lecture on Software Reengineering, U. of Bremen (2010)

/KS 02/ Kollmann, R./ Selonen, P./ Stroulia, E. et al.: A study on the current state of the art in tool-supported UML-based static reverse engineering, in van Deursen/ Burd (eds.): Proc. 9th Working Conf. on Reverse Engineering (WCRE '02), 22-32, IEEE Comp. Soc. Press (2002)

/KW 98/ Kazman, R./ Woods, S. G./ Carrière, J.: Requirements for Integrating Software Architecture and Reengineering Models: CORUM II, Proc. 5th Working Conf. on Reverse Engineering (WCRE '02), 154-163, IEEE Comp. Soc. Press (1998)

/LL 23/ Ludewig J./ Lichter, H.: Software Engineering: Grundlagen, Menschen, Prozesse, Techniken, 4th ed., 692 pp., dpunkt.verlag (2023)

/LS 01/ Lange, C./ Sneed, H. M./ Winter, A.: Applying the graph-oriented GUPRO approach in comparison to a relational data base approach, in Proc. 9th Intern. Workshop on Program Comprehension IWPC '01, 209-218, IEEE Comp. Soc. Press (2001)

/LS 02/ Lewerentz, C./ Simon, F.: Metrics Based Refactoring, Proc. 1st Intern. Workshop on Visualization for Understanding and Analysis VISSOFT, 70-80, IEEE Comp. Soc. Press, 70-80 (2002)

/LW 90/ Liu, S. S./ Wilde, N.: Identifying Objects in a Conventional Procedural Language: An Example of Data Design Recovery, in Proc. Conf. Software Maintenance (CSM '90), 266-271, IEEE Comp. Soc. Press (1990)

/Ma 05/ Marburger, A.: Reverse Engineering of Complex Legacy Telecommunication Systems, Doct. Diss., RWTH Aachen University, 418 pp., Shaker (2005)

/MH 01/ Marburger, A./ Herzberg, D.: E-Cares Research Project: Understanding complex legacy telecommunication systems, in Sousa/ Ebert (eds.): Proc. 5th Eur. Conf. on Software Maintenance and Reengineering (CSMR '01), 139-147, IEEE Comp. Soc. Press (2001)

/MO 93/ Müller, H, A./ Orgun, M. A./ Tilley, S. R./ Uhl, J. S.: A Reverse Engineering Approach To Subsystem Structure Identification, Journ. Software Maintenance: Research and Practice 5(4), 181-204 (1993)

/Mo 09/ Mosler, C.: Graphbasiertes Reengineering von Telekommunikationssystemen, Doct. Diss., RWTH Aachen University, 268 pp., Shaker (2009)

/MW 94/ Müller, H. A./ Wong, K./ Tilley, S. R.: Understanding Software Systems Using Reverse Engineering Technology, 62nd Congress of L' Association Canadienne Francaise pour L' Avancement des Sciences (ACFAS '94), 41-48 (1994)

/MW 02/ Marburger, A./ Westfechtel, B.: Graph-based reengineering of telecommunication systems, in Corradini/ Ehrig et al. (eds.): ICGT '02, LNCS 2505, 270-285, Springer (2002)

/MW 03/ Marburger, A./ Westfechtel, B.: Tools for understanding the behavior of telecommunication systems, Proc. 25th Conf. on Software Engineering (ICSE '03), 430-441, IEEE Comp. Soc. Press (2003)

/MW 04/ Marburger, A./ Westfechtel, B.: Behavioral analysis of telecommunication systems by graph transformations , in Pfaltz/ Nagl /Böhlen (eds.): AGTIVE '03, LNCS 3062, 202-219, Springer (2004)

/MW 10/ Marburger, A./ Westfechtel, B.: Graph-Based Structural Analysis for Telecommunication Systems, in Engels et al.: Graph Transformations and Model-Driven Engineering – Essays Dedicated to Manfred Nagl on the Occasion of this 65th Birthday, LNCS 5765 Festschrift, 363-392, Springer (2010)

/NM 08/ Nagl, M./ Marquardt, W. (eds.): Collaborative and Distributed Chemical Engineering – From Understanding to Substantial Design Process Support, LNCS 4970, 851 pp., Springer (2008)

/OM 21/ Object Management Group: Common Object Request Broker Architecture, Version 3.4 (2021)

/Pa 94/ Parnas, D. L.: Software Aging, Proc. 16th Intern. Conf. on Software Engineering (ICSE 1994), 279-287, IEEE Comp. Soc. Press 1994)

/PG 02/ Pinzger, M./ Gall. H.: Pattern-supported Architecture Recovery, in Proc. 10th intern. Workshop on Program Comprehension (IWPC 2002), 53-61 (2002)

/Ra 00/ Radermacher, A.: Tool Support for the Distribution of Object-Based Applications, Doct. Diss., RWTH Aachen University, 191 pp. (2000)

/SP 12/ Schubanz, M./ Pleuss, A./ Botterweck, G./ Lewerentz, C.: Modeling Rationale over Time to Support Product Line Evolution Planning, Proc. 6th Int. Workshop Variability Modeling of Software-Intensive Systems (VAMOS '12), 193-199, ACM Press (2012)

/SW 93/ Schwickert, A./ Wilhelm, A./ Schiweck, C.: Strukturierte Programmierung in COBOL, 316 pp., Oldenbourg (1993)

/Wi Ref/ Wikipedia: Refactoring, accessed April 2023

/Wi RE/ Wikipedia: Reverse Engineering, accessed April 2023

/Wi ReE/ Wikipedia: Reengineering, accessed April 2023

10 Processes and Model Transformations on Different Levels

Manfred Nagl

Software Engineering, RWTH Aachen University, nagl@cs.rwth-aachen.de

Abstract

This chapter consists of three parts. The first is on lifecycle processes and their relation to the working area graph model WAM. The second gives principal remarks on abstraction levels of processes, their products as partial results, and their integration to the overall configuration. The third part discusses, what development and changes mean on that configuration, and why transformations between results of different working areas are specifically important. In this chapter, we discuss those transformations, where the architecture of the system to be developed or changed is involved.

Altogether, the purpose of this chapter is the preparation for the following chapters 11 to 14. Finally, we shortly characterize these transitions/ transformations, which are discussed in these chapters.

Key words: lifecycle process models, their relation to the working area model, levels of processes/ their products, and their connecting relations (interaction, integration, and reactivity), characterizing the properties of transformations between different working areas

10.1 Introduction

(1) The *working area model* (WAM) of ch. 1 /Na 90/ defines logical levels and their mutual relations. It does not differentiate between building up a model, e.g. for design, or later maintaining this model. The reason is that modifications occur more often than straightforward development. The model clearly distinguishes between different logical levels of activities and also of their cooperation. This facilitates the discussion of transformations between models and of their integration.

The working area model does *not define how* the development processes - using these levels and relations - look like. In sect. 2 of this chapter, we show that the *working area model* can be *used for quite different forms of processes*.

These *processes* can be of a *classical* form, like the waterfall process model /PC 86/ or the V model /VM 92/. They can also be of *other forms*, as incremental, iterative, spiral, or whatsoever. We give a *new characterization* of these different lifecycle models by *relating* them to the WAM. In essence, we simulate them in the working area model and, at the same time, make them more precise. Doing so, we detect that the expressiveness of these process models can be improved and that their preciseness can be extended.

(2) After this discussion we make clear: *Processes* exist on *three levels of granularity*: (i) coarse-grained as lifecycle models, (ii) middle-grained, where we can

specify who is doing what and which results exist/ have to be integrated, but not how this is done. Finally, (iii) on the fine-grained or detailed level, we look how a single developer is working, into his results, and how they are built up / changed.

These three *levels* we also find *on* the *product* side, i.e. between the results of the processes. The corresponding detail or last level also covers the many *relations* in documents or between parts of different documents, being built up or modified in the development process.

(3) This discussion prepares for the last part of this chapter, where we look on *products* on the *fine-grained* or detail level. This level describes how the documents are finally built up from increments, thus their internal structure and internal relations. It also describes the many increment to increment relations between different documents of the same working area and between different working areas.

These fine-grained, *increment to increment relations* between different documents are discussed in chs. 11 to 14 of this book. According to the title of the book, we concentrate on those relations, where the *source or the target* of the relations are increments of an *architectural design* document.

These different fine-grained relations between different documents - where the architecture is specifically regarded - are discussed in the following next four chapters. As an introduction to these chapters we give a *global characterization* of these relations: how and why the relations are inserted, that their insertions/ modifications are interactive and incremental, must regard the target model, connect related syntactical units, and so on.

10.2 Working Area Model and Lifecycle Processes

We revisit the working area model WAM of ch. 1, see fig. 10.1. The graph represents the development process on a *coarse-grained level* (also called lifecycle level), i.e. complex activities, like architecture modeling, are represented as atomic nodes without regarding their inner structure. Some relations are double-sided, the one-sided relations can be interpreted in both directions.

Inside of the nodes of the coarse-grained level, we find subprocesses, which might be carried out by different developers, as inside the node of AR for architecture modeling. If we describe, how these processes look like, i.e. how these developers interact, we speak of the *medium-grained level*. For example, architecture modeling might be done by a group of designers, headed by a chief architect, every designer has a specific design task. If we now determine how these group members are interacting, who is doing what, how the activities are integrated, we speak of a medium-grained process description. We come back in detail to this level in ch. 13.

Finally, a process description, saying how a single developer is planning and organizing his work, is called the *fine-grained process level*. Rather seldom, a developer is planning and structuring his or her subprocess in a formal way and in advance. But he/ she is happy, if there is substantial support by intelligent tools.

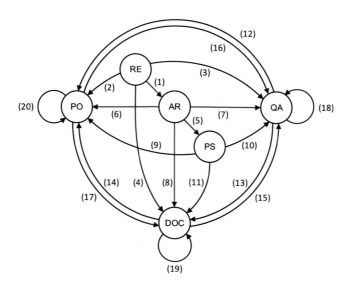

Fig. 10.1: Working (WAM) area model revisited

In this section we only regard the lifecycle level. We take different *lifecycle models* as examples and we discuss, what they *mean* in our *working area model*. In a later section we go down to the medium-grained level. The fine-grained level for working out single documents is not addressed in detail in this book. The corresponding processes are usually carried out by single developers without making a process plan beforehand. However, more or less big chunks of these processes can be offered by tools, a developer is using /Po 96, MJW 08/, especially if they incorporate the knowledge of the tool user. The fine-grained links between documents, where one of them is an architectural document, are discussed in the next four chapters.

Traditional Lifecycle Models

We now start the discussion with traditional life cycle processes and later continue with process forms which still are in the current process discussion.

The *waterfall model,* in short WM /PC 86, Ro 70/, see fig. 10.2.a, is a *simplification/* or abstraction of the development process, as *no real-world process is linear*. In real-world-processes, we find backtracking, changes to look for alternatives, or iterations, until we have reached a status with which we would like to go further. We also find thinking about the future, in order to minimize later backtracking. One example is, when we make a review for a part of the architecture to check whether it can be implemented, before starting the implementation. Nevertheless, the waterfall model is still of value, although we know that no process in practice follows this scheme.

The WM is a linear model, *ordering* activities according to *time*, one after the other. *Activities* of the WM are *not clearly related to logical levels*, e.g. in architectural design we look at the requirements spec, we model the architecture piece by piece, and we look forward to check to get confidence for the later implementation. The same is true for the other nodes of the WM. Furthermore, we find no clear distinction between technical activities like architecture modeling on one hand, and management, documentation, and quality assurance activities on the other.

The *simulation in the working area model* is as follows, see again figs. 10.1 and 10.2.a: The technical activities RE, AR, and PS correspond to Requirements Analysis, Systems Design, and Implementation. The next two phases System Testing and System Deployment we discuss in connection to the V model coming next. In the WAM, there is no maintenance working area, as maintenance corresponds to taking up the other working areas again. Which ones are taken and in which order is not expressed in the waterfall model. Furthermore, quality assurance, project organization and documentation are not explicitly contained in the waterfall model. They are connected in some unclear way to the technical working areas. We come back to these activities of QA, PO, and DOC in chs. 13 and 14, especially in connection to architectures, which are the main topic of this book.

Let us explain how *backtracking* steps, which are missing in the waterfall model, are expressed in the *working area model*. Assume that in the coding activities we find out, that some requirements are not fulfilled, or some requirements are missing. Then we go back to RE and correct or extend the requirements spec, if necessary. We go forward to AR and make the corresponding architectural changes/ extensions for the new requirements, and then to PS to make the corresponding changes or extensions on code level. The corresponding changes on RE, AR, and PS level can be difficult. Therefore, *creative* ideas may have to be taken.

QA, PO, and DOC activities are connected to RE, AR, and PS activities in the WAM, which are also *not expressed* in the waterfall model. Let us *discuss QA* as example. Whenever we have worked out the requirements specification or the requirements definition as an early and more sketchy form of it, we can make a review by independent people to find out, whether it makes sense to proceed further. If the requirements spec is executable, we can execute it and get some approximate information about the future system behavior. Analogously, after having worked out the architecture, we can make a review to find out weaknesses. In an analogous way, we could have argued for PS, and for PO and DOC activities. Summing up, we see that the working area model is more expressive to cover constructive steps corresponding to quality assurance, project organization, and documentation.

The *V model* is to be discussed next, see /VM 92, VM 10/ and fig. 10.2.b. It is also a linear model. It differs between *development* on one hand (left branch) and *integration* of results on the other (right branch). It can be regarded as a linear model, which is folded. We go down left (planning and structuring) and we go up right (testing and integrating). It also *binds* the *integration* and *quality assurance* activities of the right side to the corresponding *planning, design, and implementation* activities of the left side by horizontal edges saying what to check and what to integrate. Furthermore. it explicitly distinguishes between requirements gathering and system analysis on the left branch and software design and module design. In the right branch it distinguishes between integration test in the developing company and the integration and acceptance test on the customer's site.

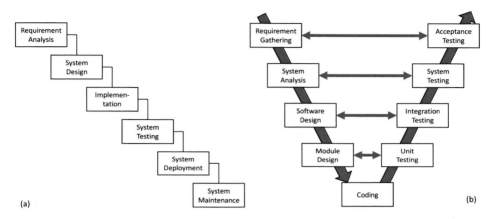

(a)

(b)

Fig. 10.2: (a) Waterfall and (b) V model

We see that the *order* of activities is *similar*. We also see that the activities are *more specific* compared to the waterfall model. The arguments, how the V-model is to be compared with the graph model, is *similar* to the discussion above. We do not repeat the arguments, although they are slightly different.

The right side of fig. 10.2.b consists of testing and integration. (a) *Unit testing* is expressed by the horizontal edge 10 between PS and QA in fig. 10.1. It can even be differentiated by unit testing of the developer (e.g. by white-box tests) and unit testing by a member of the QA department (e.g. by black-box tests), (b) *Integration testing* needs the architecture on one side and the already tested components on the other and, in addition test drivers and test stubs. This corresponds to edges 7 and 10 of the WAM. Again, we may distinguish between the test of the developers on one hand and the independent tests of the quality assurance department. (c) *System testing* is similar, but also needs edge 3 of the graph model in order to compare the integrated solution with the requirements spec. (d) The same is true for the *acceptance test*, which needs relations 10, 7, 3. Again, the acceptance test may be done by a mixed team of developers and customer specialists, or first by the developer team and then by the customer team.

Summing up, we see that the *activities* of the V model (right side of fig. 10.2.b) and the *horizontal edges* of this model can be expressed more specifically and more precisely by the working area model. Especially the preciseness comes from distinguishing strictly between activities corresponding to their logical level, not to distinguish between building and modification, and by looking more carefully of which different parts of subtasks an integration test consists of, and who is responsible for it (see e.g. the acceptance test).

Reactive Lifecycle Models

There are various *further lifecycle models* /BK 21, chapter 3/, which take into account that development includes iterations, incremental changes, agile methods of behavior /Bo 88, BT 05, Me 14/, and so on. We call all of these models here *reactive models*, as *change* and the reason why it happens is what they propagate. They (i) *welcome changes*, as changes will exist in any case. Furthermore, (ii) they propagate that we should *react* on changes as soon as possible in the overall development process (iii) in order to *avoid* huge *backtracking* steps, which cost a lot. We only discuss the spiral model, the incremental and iterative, and the agile model here. The discussion of other models in relation to the WAM is similar.

The essential idea of the *spiral model* (/Bo 88/ and fig. 10.3) is that development needs *iterations*. It is not only one straight-line development but there are several developments as cycles, by which we approach the wanted solution. Every cycle has four parts (a) define the objectives, (b) identify and resolve risks, (c) start a development and approve it, and (d) plan the next iteration.

We now look on an *example*, which is a blueprint for a new development, where we evidently *have the risk to fail*. (1) The first cycle could be to build a prototype, the only purpose of which is to reduce the overall risk of a failure. Thus, the first cycle delivers a dirty-hack prototype to demonstrate some behavior to the customer to get his approval. The functionality is neither complete, nor efficient. The prototype only shows some of the functionality in an inefficient way. It may have used available components, which will never be a part of a final solution. (2) After acceptance by the customer, we plan the second cycle. As the planned system is also new for the contractor, the purpose of the second prototype is to implement a part of the core functionality of the planned system. Now, we concentrate on a solution – again not complete and possibly not efficient – the purpose of which is, to convince the customer that the contractor can be successful with this nontrivial task. (3) After having got the prolongation to continue, we now get into a development cycle, which is more of a classical form: design, code, integration, together with tests. The aim is to get a rough and unpolished, not fully complete and also efficient form. If this is again successful, we (4) enter the last cycle, where we complete and polish the solution and make it more efficient. The advantage of this lifecycle model is that we expect to fail at the beginning. Furthermore, we get the confidence after a shorter time to fail or to be successful.

In *terms of the graph model* a cycle is a development from RE to PS, possibly with backtracking steps, and where technical activities are accompanied by quality assurance, management, and documentation activities, especially in the later cycles. The first three cycles of our example deliver a solution, which is neither complete nor efficient, they more probe than contribute to the final solution. Every cycle has a new starting point with different requirements compared to the last one and delivers some form of a product. This avoids that we continue, although a self-critical analysis already signals a final failure. The milestone of the next available version is shorter in the spiral approach, so the customer earlier asks for the next version to have a look at and does not wait for an eventual final failure.

There are many *iterative* and *incremental* process models on lifecycle level, see /BK 21, Wi IID, LB 03, Wi IBM/, or many others. Mostly, incremental probing is combined with iterations. The approach is typically bottom-up, the solution in the final result consists of a kernel, which is successively completed by the main parts of the system. The first iteration looks for the kernel, the following ones add the different parts. Iterations are for different purposes, kernel development and development of the additional parts as above. The basic requirement is that the system is modular. Step by step (or iteration by iteration), we get closer to the final solution. The discussion of the simulation in the graph **WAM** is similar to that of above. Therefore, we omit the discussion here. The reader is encouraged to define a possible path through the working area model himself or herself.

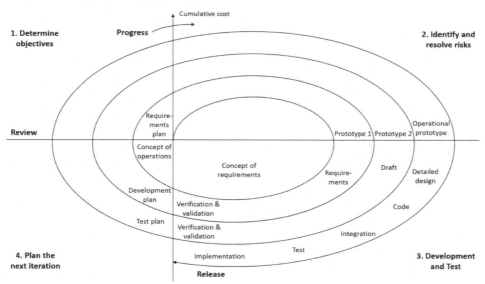

Fig. 10.3: The spiral process model

There are various definitions of *agility* in development processes, see for example /BB 10, AA 13/. Agile methods criticize bureaucracy in development processes and *emphasize* the *role of person and cooperation/ communication quality* within the development team. They can be regarded as the long overdue swing of the pendulum in the core direction of software development, away from regarding software discipline as a mainly organizational, bureaucratic, and methodological task. They work out that software development is the main goal and not an overhead, which "guarantees" some kind of quality. In this way, the agile approach is not comparable to the above process lifecycle models, as it is mainly on a level to make it differently. If it comes to rules for the process definition, agile methods emphasize repetitive processes, where an iteration only takes weeks or months. The arguments are as above. Another characterization is that there is a *product owner* (responsible on the customer side) and a product *manager* (responsible on the side of the realizing company). This was already the case 700 years ago for the planning and building process of a gothic cathedral, see /Na 19, there section 19.1/ and /Va 10/.

Model-driven Development

Model-driven software development /Wi MDD/ follows a different scheme. It is less oriented towards processes but to the way, activities and their results are internally characterized. The central idea is to work with formal models from which software can be generated, preferably in an automatic way. Thereby, modeling languages, domain-specific languages, and generators/ interpreters are used. That works well for specific systems, special parts of a system, and in domains, where detailed and long-term experience and formal models are available. The approach has limits for complete systems, where not formalizable topics, as taste, efficiency, or connections to details of the real world, play an important role.

Summary of this Section

The WAM is a *basic model*, which defines logical levels for looking on a system to be developed or changed (outside, essential structure, details) together with accompanying views (management, quality assurance, and documentation), necessary for a development project. The model is free of time/ ordering in modeling activities, defining intermediate or final results, forward modeling or correction. That allows to precisely define the relations between working areas and how they are used.

The working area model is a *generic model*, which allows to simulate different lifecycle models as instantiations. It also allows to introduce different notations and methods to be used for specific area activities and their results and also for the transformations from area to area or from cycle to cycle.

The WAM can be *extended* and *tailored*, thereby defining specific lifecycle models, either conventional or reactive. Extensions are time of activities, availability of partial products, decisions to be made (see /We 20/, for the V model / HH 08/), and also notations and methods to be used for activities and transformations.

10.3 Levels of Processes, Products, and their Relations

Levels of Processes and Products

This is a section *necessary* for *understanding* the following chapters and, especially, to properly assess them. We regard different levels of processes with respect to their role in the overall development process. As a first example, we look for the design of a very small software system.

We start on *lifecycle level*, see fig. 10.4, left side. There is *no structure* in the *process* node AR design: What are the subprocesses of the node and the structure of their mutual relations, i.e. how is the process of this node decomposed into subprocesses? How do these subprocesses interact and compose the node AR design? The same applies to the product AR spec. How the different parts are to be integrated, is not shown on lifecycle level, or how the relations are inside refined to more detailed ones. Thus, the unstructured design process has an unstructured *result*, both process and product are *connected by an unstructured relation*.

Organizational (or management) *process* descriptions aim at *coordinating* different developers in a working area, here for design of the small system, see fig. 10.4, middle and upper part. We decompose the design process, identifying corresponding design tasks, the overall design diagram task ODp, which contains a subsystem design SSDp, and also the detailed design DD of export and import specs of all components M_1, M_2, M_3, and SS.

The corresponding *results* (middle and lower part) are the overview design diagram OD, the subsystem design diagram SSD, and the detailed design exports and imports of these components, altogether as *organizational* results for later detailed design tasks or results. Correspondingly, the *relations* are only from organizational nodes for processes to organizational nodes as results. Often, we have a 1:1 relation between process nodes and product nodes. This, however, need not always be the case: A person documenting design results, for example, might have different processes or products being regarded by one documentation process or result, summarizing the similarities or differences of them.

Working out the diagram for OD and for the textual descriptions of export and import interfaces of the components and their mutual relations corresponds to the *detail engineering process level* of the design process. In general, the detail engineering level corresponds to the detailed work of single developers and also their interaction, see fig. 10.4, upper right part. Usually, the structure of detailed processes is not planned and structured beforehand (the process is not structured explicitly on that level). The designer as developer is working using creative ideas, being supported by more or less intelligent tools. Planning all these steps beforehand in detail would be an overhead. Tools can support this detailed and creative process level, by offering help for so-called process chunks /MJW 08, Po 96/. Processes on this detailed level are usually only regarded when analyzing or mining already given processes. Methods may give rough recommendations as, for example, in bottom up design first regard the lower design levels of the system.

Fig. 10.4 lower right part contains the *detailed structure* of the *design result* for the overview diagram OD. The other results, e.g. the subsystem design diagram result SS_4, or the detailed textual export or import specs of the components M_1 ... M_3 and SS_4 are not shown in fig. 10.4. Furthermore, we do not show the relations within and between these design results.

On *detailed level* we see the *internal result structure*, here only of the overview diagram OD. We call the parts of this detailed product description increments. The internals of a document are a part of this fine-grained level, which is usually structured and worked out by one developer, e.g. the detailed design spec of a component by text for export and import interfaces. The document has *increments* and also *internal relations* between the increments. It also has *external* relations to increments in other documents, worked out by another designer. This is the case between the export interface of a component on one hand, and the import clause for this component in another document (not shown in fig. 10.4).

These *interdocument relations* can be within the *same level* of development (e.g. design between a subsystem definition in a design document and the subsystem's internal body decomposition in another document). Of course, these interdocument relations between increments can also span relations between documents of *different levels*, e.g. the relation between an interface increment of a module (design) and the corresponding code (implementation).

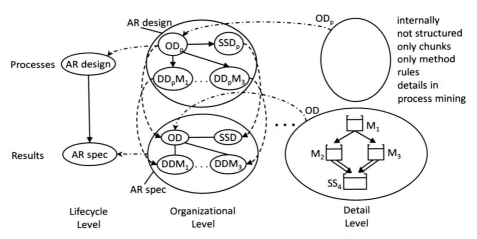

Fig.10.4: AR design processes & results on lifecycle, managerial, and detailed level

Summing up, we look at the development *process* on *three levels*: (i) the lifecycle level, where we have the whole process in mind without looking into the subprocesses (as of AR design), (ii) on organizational or managerial level, where we describe how different actors interact without going into details how they do their jobs, and (iii) on detailed level, where the process results approach the final degree.

If we go *from the right* side *to* the *left* in the lower *product* part, we see that the overview diagram OD shrinks to one organizational node in the product description of fig.10.4 middle. The corresponding organizational product information shrinks to one node on lifecycle level in fig. 10.4 left. The same applies to the *processes* in the upper part or to the *relations* in between.

The Development Configuration as the Overall Result and its Parts

Now we look on *all results* of a process, wherever they belong to, and also how they are hierarchically structured, cf. fig. 10.5. We see the overall result of a development process with various structures. The picture is tremendously simplified w.r.t. quantity and quality, as the development result here only regards a trivial architecture of four components.

The whole picture represents what we called the overall *configuration* in ch. 1, i.e. all parts of the development's result are put together. If we go to the topmost level (outmost nodes with rounded corners), we find the *coarse-grained* structure, if we do not look inside the nodes. That is, the results are just nodes for RE, AR, PS (technical configuration), and the accompanying areas PO, DOC and QA. The relations between these nodes have no inner structure. They are not given in fig.10.5. They would only sum up the other more detailed relations given in the figure.

One level down on *middle-grained* level, we see the constituents of the nodes, given in rectangular nodes: The RE node has four parts, the AR node five, namely one simple architecture diagram with four components together with the four export and import descriptions of these components. The PS node has four parts for the bodies, and so on. The PO has three parts, for processes, products, and resources. This is the *middle-grained configuration* level consisting of documents, being built-up and modified often by single members of the development team.

One further level down, we see the inner structure of documents, e.g, for the AR part the structure of the architecture diagram and also for the four textual export/ import descriptions. The structures of all these documents form the *fine-grained* overall *configuration*. The inside relations are set-use, context-sensitive syntax, or consistency relations due to methods. These relations are installed by developers or by tools supporting developers. As already mentioned, tool construction is not the focus of this book.

An essential part of the overall configuration on fine-grained level are the *fine-grained relations between different documents*, as the relation from module M_3 to its corresponding export/ import description, or from that to the corresponding body. Again, they belong to syntax, consistency, and method rules, which connect different documents. Such relations were in the focus of our research projects /Na 96, NM 08/, see the following chs. 11 to 14. They are usually not regarded and supported in industrial tools. They have a tremendous importance for the success of a development project, as they represent the dependencies between the activities, their results, corresponding views, and methods of different developers, although they belong to different levels, views, or disciplines.

The *relations* (coarse-, middle-, and fine-grained) in the overall configuration have rather *different semantics*: (a) between RE, RE documents, or internal structure of these documents on one hand and AR, AR documents and their detail structure on the other: The constraints of RE have to be fulfilled in AR. Conversely, these are the requirements belonging to architectural parts. Thereby methods can be important, as OO /Me 98, Ru 04, UM 17/. (b) Between AR and PS: These are the code details of components, which are already fixed on architecture level, (c) AR and DOC: This is the explanation for the why and how decisions of AR described in DOC. (d) Between AR and QA: These are the different quality assurance measures for architectural units we have taken and their results. (e) AR to PO: These are the mappings done for organization. Analogously we argue for the other relations between results of fig. 10.1. These different semantic relations and how they are installed or maintained are discussed in chs. 11 to 14.

Thus, we have three levels in the overall configuration of fig. 10.5, namely *coarse-*, *middle-*, and *fine-grained* (for processes, products, and relations), which correspond to *lifecycle*, *organizational*, and *detail* level of above, where we regarded levels according to their role in the development process.

However, they are *not the same*. Have a look on the management documents, which have a fine-grained inner structure, which, however, belongs to management information, corresponding to the managerial level (character middle grained). The same is true for the architecture diagram. The export/ import descriptions - although also belonging to architecture information, which is middle-grained from nature - are fine-grained and belong to detailed information.

The overall configuration has different parts. We speak of the *RE subconfiguration*, if we regard the documents corresponding to the outside and requirements level. This includes all levels (coarse, middle and detail) corresponding to nodes and contents as well as relations and their detailed structure. Analogously, we speak of the *architectural subconfiguration,* or the *programming subconfiguration* (in engineering called detailed design). Please note that the subconfigurations for RE, AR, PS, also refer to corresponding parts in subconfigurations for QA, DOC, and PO.

The overall configuration contains *different hierarchical relations*, (a) between processes/ products and internals (and also for products) on three levels as explained above, (b) between the description levels of a process (outside requirements/ architecture as essential structure/ code details), (c) inside an architectural document due to different semantic relations: hierarchies in locality, general realization layers, OO structures, etc. see ch, 2. The architectural configuration - and also the requirements and the programming configuration - is a graph complex, the overall configuration is a complex of complexes. This all can be seen from fig. 10.5.

A *similar* situation as discussed above in fig. 10.5, we find in *engineering* projects, e.g. in mechanical engineering /NW 99/ or for chemical engineering /NM 08/.

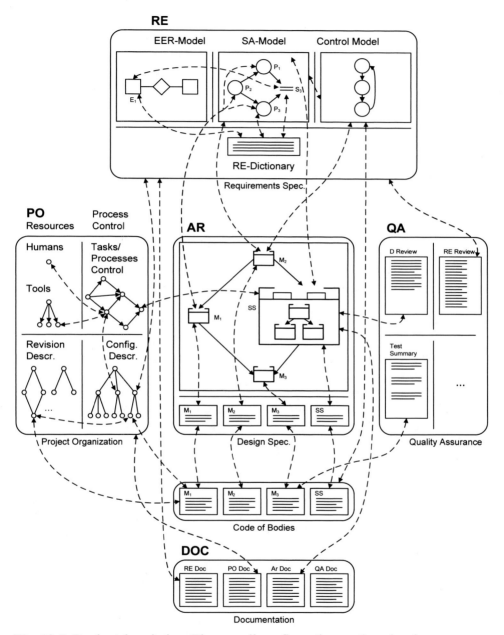

Fig. 10.5: Product description: The overall configuration on three levels

Now we get back to the discussion about shrinking models from the last subsection around fig. 10.4. We give some additional remarks. The overall configuration of fig. 10.5 is a product model on the fine-grained level. If we forget the *inner structures* of rectangular nodes (as the diagram of AR), then graphs merge to nodes (one node for the diagram). We end up on the level of middle-grained structures (5 nodes remain). The fine-grained *relations* of fig. 10.5 merge to middle-grained relations. This structure corresponds to the level of the inner structure of PO in fig. 10.5. Now, if we shrink graphs again and melt relations, then we get the working *area model* of fig. 10.1. So, by *two shrink and melt steps* the *overall configuration* ends up in the WAM; the WAM can also be interpreted as a product model.

Development means to *transform models*, on different levels according to the process, the granularity inside or outside, different views, different disciplines, or whatsoever. The most interesting transformations are those between the technical working areas, or between the technical working areas and the surrounding ones PO, QA, DOC. The interesting model transformations with a tight relation to architecture modeling are discussed in chs. 11-14.

Reactivity

Above, we have introduced the term reactivity as early reaction on changes. Let us make this term *more precise* now. In fig. 10.6.a, we see two subprocesses sp_i and sp_j, which interact in some way; see ch. 6, which describes different forms of *interaction*. The standard form is that the result of the first process is the input for the second, but also different nonstandard forms exist. Both subprocesses of fig. 10.6.a produce a result, namely res_i and res_j. These results are parts of the overall result of the development process. Thus, they must be *integrated* in the overall result.

This figure contains *examples* of *reactivity* in the sense of eager reaction on changes. It may be that the result res_i influences the next process sp_j in a way that the process sp_j is mainly determined by res_i. As example, please look on the overall design, where the big chunks are identified. The subprocess sp_i identifies the chunks, they are designed in more detail in sp_j and others. We call this *forward* reactivity or evolution, as the result of a process determines what the following process has to do, so the relation stands for determination and not for input.

We had an *example* of *forward reactivity* above in the last subsection on the overall configuration. The activity to produce the overview diagram in fig. 10.5 produces the details of the diagram. This diagram contained the components SS and the modules M_1, M_2, and M_3, the interfaces of which are then worked out. Thus, all the corresponding processes and results are reactively influenced by the result of this first process. This is true on organizational level as well as on code level. More precisely, from the organizational level we go to the detail level process, then to its result, which reactively influences the organizational process by introducing corresponding processes. These are carried out and might introduce further reactivity steps.

Another example of fig. 10.6.a is that sp_j has identified a design error in the past and has sketched where in res_i the design has to be changed. The subprocess sp_i is changing the design in res_i. This is called *backward reactivity*. There, we can have different situations, (a) only local changes in a component, the rest is untouched,

(b) changes which change what we have already done after the error in some cases and the rest remains, (c) that everything after the error has to be done again.

We can give *another explanation* of reactivity, according to the *PID notation* introduced in ch. 6. Fig. 10.6.b repeats the octagon notation of a PID process and the corresponding influences on a process. The forward reactivity is defined by constraints for the second process. The PID notation was introduced in ch. 6 to handle unusual process interactions as, for example, that a tool is developed in a development process and is used in the same process. By this PID notation we can also define different other forms of reactivity.

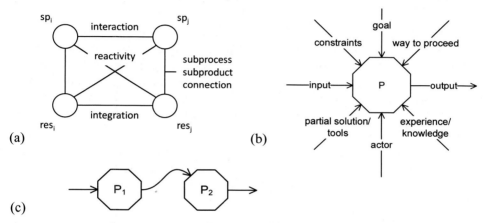

(a)

(b)

(c)

Fig. 10.6: Interaction of processes, integration of results, reactivity: (a) their interplay, (b) influences of a process as PID, (c) process defines constraints for next

There are *further levels of processes and products*, if we look on the development of tool support for processes and products /MN 08/, as (d) outside functionality level for tools, (e) internal tool modeling level, (f) programming level for tools and, finally, (g) the level of a distributed infrastructure for tools, which contains data as well as program code. These internal levels (d) to (g) are not further discussed in this chapter and the book, as tools are not the focus here.

Direct (or informal) *communication* /SST 08/ to discuss problems, sketch possible solutions, evaluate the range of changes etc. take place between developers. They are important for the success of the development process. The results of these discussions are the base for organized cooperation (formal communication) by project organization afterwards. Although being important from a practical view for software architectures, this direct communication /SST 08/ is not discussed here.

Transformations on Different Levels

Let us now have a look on transformations between the three levels of granularity. As example, we look on the transformations between Requirements Engineering (RE) and Architectural Design (AR), as we need such transformations in chs. 11-14.

On the *coarse-grained level* we have *no structure inside*, neither for the processes nor their results, and not for the transformation between both, see fig. 10.1.

One level down on the *middle-grained level*, we see that both have internal information of bookkeeping/ organization nature. For example, the RE process works out the requirements specification, which has different internal parts, like structuring the business process, the data to be defined and used, the times when the business processes start, work, or end, and some detailed descriptions of these parts, see fig. 10.5. Therefore, the result of this RE process also has *some structure results* (rectangular form), i.e. it contains the parts just mentioned. However, we cannot see, how these parts are built up internally. Therefore, we only see how the transformation between RE and AR connects these parts.

On the *fine-grained level*, we see the corresponding detailed results inside the rectangular parts, worked out by different developers, see again fig. 10.5. We see the internal *structure* of the *requirements* specification, not only the parts it consists of, but also how these parts are internally looking like. We also see the fine-grained *links* between increments of these documents. So, the RE spec is complete to go further.

In the course of further development, the *design documents* are *worked out* using the RE documents. This means (1) internally structuring all design documents and (2) the fine-grained links internal to these documents, but also (3) between these documents.

Even more, we have (4) to define all *fine-grained links between these two levels/ stages* RE and AR. This is done by interactive tools for the mapping, see ch. 11.

These *fine-grained links* from/ to *architectural design* from or to the *surrounding working areas* are discussed in the following chs. 11 to 14. These links have to be inserted in the development process, but also modified in the case of changes, either on the source or target side. They are either implicit (only existing in the heads of developers) or explicit (realized in some underlying database). Their insertion/ modification can even be supported by tools, see the following chapters. How this support is realized within tools is not discussed in this book.

But we *characterize* what we have to look at, if and when the corresponding *links between subconfigurations* (as RE and AR) on detail level are installed. This applies to the manual case – the designer installs them himself –, or the 'automatic' case – a tool installs them, or the interactive case, the designer decides and the tool helps.

10.4 Development Steps, Changes, Process Chains and Product Traces

Changes within Overall Configurations

In this section, we try to make clear, how *modifications* are handled *by developers* /MN 08, Na 96/. Every developer does only see a specific part of the overall configuration, i.e. of the overall product of the development process in a certain stage of completeness. This is the part to be built up/ modified which, however, also contains further necessary information. It consists of the corresponding document to be changed, but also contains the context, usually produced by other developers.

That *context consists* of other documents necessary to understand the construction or modification task, but also of rules to obey, hints to follow, explanations of the task to be written/ obeyed, etc. These specific parts of the configuration are produced, changed, and stored in a distributed manner, by persons having different roles, on possibly different computers, and using different tools.

The elimination of errors and mistakes, the modification of a design, the extension of a design and development product, the adaptation according to new requirements, or the reuse of nontrivial parts of existing developments induce *significant structural changes* within and of the overall configuration. To support those changes, the subproducts of different developers have to be integrated.

Modifications of the overall configuration are (i) *changes* of and within documents, e.g. in a subsystem's design and the modifications implied by these changes (*I change, others* have to *react*). Even more, (ii) there are changes due to modifications of other persons in other documents, e.g. according to modified requirements (*others change, I* have to *react*). Or (iii) someone found a serious *problem*, I have to *change*, the change has serious *effects* on my work and that of others.

Between documents there are consistency *relations*, either only *in the heads* of the corresponding developers. Or, they are *explicit* in the form of fine-grained relations connecting increments saying e.g., the target is the design decision related to the source, source and target increments are bound together for navigation, the target explains the structure of the source, and so on. Both, changes in one document and induced modifications in the other, have to be regarded transitively. For changes, code, documentation, and others have to be changed consistently.

Hence, we get *change chains* in the product or *change traces* of the process. These changes are coordinated using organizational information about roles, persons, availability, effort, and so on, see ch. 13. Thus, any change of the overall configuration is a *cooperative and logically distributed process*. Interaction and integration can have different forms.

Construction or change steps and their parts are mostly creative, as there are many different ways to solve a subtask, to change or extend a solution, to apply a nontrivial reuse step, and so on. A developer can give different answers how to modify a document, and another developer can have different answers how to react on this change in order to modify a dependent document. Thus, as explained above, in cooperative development processes we have *creative interaction* of subprocesses and *integration* of their results.

The detailed *structure of a development process* and its *product* is in most cases only *determined in the process itself*, as design decisions of whatever form predetermine following processes and products. In the same way, made modifications or specific repairs imply what and how to do. We call this the dynamics within the process, see the short discussion on reactivity of above.

The ore some results of a completed development process can be used in a following one. They are just used and need not be developed. This drastically changes the overall structure of the next process, see ch. 7. Furthermore, knowledge about processes and products can be introduced in form of patterns and templates. Their use within a process, evidently changes the following development process. Also, a predetermination of the process evidently influences further products. So, we also have dynamic situations here.

So, changes within an overall configuration in a project as well as changes of the configuration from project to the next project are group activities with persons of different roles and competences, needing managerial control, as well as detailed experience of the project members in different areas. We build up models, modify these models, consider the consequences on different levels of the process and the product. Thereby the architecture plays a specific role. That is explained in the following chapters of part 3 of this book.

Characterization of Model Transformations on Detailed Level

Here we make only some introductory remarks, most of these transformations are discussed by examples in chs 11 to 14. We characterize these model transformations /BNW 08, Le 96/ here to introduce some direction to the following chapters.

Transformations are interactive, incremental, and regard the structure

(1) Transformations are *rarely automatic*, i.e. can be performed by a program. Exceptions: (a) Generating the module frame (programming level) for an architectural unit, which is later worked out by a programmer. Another example is the (b) the generation of a documentation frame for every architectural unit, which is later filled by a documenting person. In these examples, the generation only corresponds to create an envelope, which is later filled by a creative person.

(2) Transitions are *mostly interactive*: There are different possibilities how to transform. A developer has to decide, which kind of transformation he/ she wants and has to input the right data in order to perform the transformation. The way how to transform is a creative decision.

(3) Transformations have to be *incremental*: Unchanged parts should not be transformed again. Transformation in this case should be restricted to changed parts. The transformation of these changed parts is again interactive.

(4) Transformations also have to take into consideration that the *target model* has been *elaborated* in the meantime. So, for example, if we transform a change of an architectural unit into code, we have to take into account that this unit already has been further structured or even changed code level. Also, the *source* side can have been changed. Thus, we usually have relations between the pre-

viously elaborated and related parts. The new parts on source and on target side have to be transformed. The transformation is again interactive and creative.

(5) Transformations regard the *structure* of documents: *Syntactical* units of the source documents are transformed to syntactical units of the target document. Nevertheless the transformation can allow *different semantics*.

Interdocument Links

(6) Transformations might touch *different roles*: If an architect is changing a unit description, then the programmer follows this change and makes the corresponding code modifications.

(7) Any transformation installs logical "bindings" between increments of the document to be transformed and the target document.

(8) These *bindings* are later *used* for navigation purposes in forward or backward direction, for looking what is tied together and alike, see below.

(9) These bindings are materialized by *cross document links* between increments (syntactical units) of different documents.

(10) To install all these *links manually* does *not pay off*. A lot of interactive work is necessary, the profit is limited, if we regard the necessary work.

(11) Instead, the *links* should be *installed by the tool*, which is necessary for the transformation, see /BNW 08, Le 96/.

(12) These *interdocument links* can appear *within* one subconfiguration, for example in the RE subconfguration of fig, 10.5 from SA to EER model. Or it can appear *between subconfigurations*, as from an increment of the RE model to an increment of the AR model, as from P_2 to M_1 in fig. 10.5.

The Use of Links

(13) Forward transformation by a tool: The installation is done, according to a designer's decision.

(14) Backward look-up: We look for the corresponding increment, which is the source item to a target item.

(15) Link insertion: An existing source and an existing target increment are automatically or interactively bound together.

(16) Parallel insertion of increments with corresponding links: This is possible if the relation between two increments is fixed or has been determined interactively.

10.5 Summary and Conclusions

Summary

The first part of the chapter introduced different lifecycle process models (waterfall model, V model, spiral, iterative or incremental model) and traced these models back to the graph working area model WAM. The WAM is a *generic model*, allowing to *instantiate* quite *different process models*.

The second part showed that *processes, products*, and *relations* exist on *three levels*, namely on coarse-, medium-, and fine-grained level. This is necessary to understand, to structure, to carry out, and to monitor a project. The overall configuration is a fine-grained product model. There exist contractions to the middle- and coarse-grained level.

There are more changes than straightforward development steps in a project, which must be handled on the complex overall configuration. Changes happen within documents, but they have implications to others. This yields chains of changes or process traces.

Messages

The working area model **WAM** has advantages, as it better *differentiates* logical levels by *nodes*, and the *relations* between nodes are more precise. Finally, we can use it to instantiate different lifecycle models and make them all more precise by looking on the connections to **PO**, **QA**, and **DOC**.

Processes, products, and *relations* exist on *three levels*: lifecycle, organization, and detail from the role in the development process, coarse-, medium-, and fine-grained from their inner granularity. This also applies to the parts of the overall configuration, which describe the complete result of the development process. We can regard interaction of processes, integration of results, and reactivity between processes and results.

The *fine-grained links* between documents, from increments of one document to increments to the other have a specific and *important role*. They connect the results of different developers, and they install consistency relations. If they are not available, the developers must be aware of them in their mind.

They *connect* different *views* as, for example, the architectural description of a subsystem as bigger component on one side, and the explanation of this component in the documentation. These relations are important to understand, to explain, and to modify the architecture in later stages of the development and, consequently, are important for the whole system to be developed or maintained.

According to the aim of this book we only discuss those *transformations* of documents, where the *architecture* is *involved*, either on the source or target side.

Open Problems

All the problems described in this chapter get much more complicated, if we regard *long-term changes*, which demand for more complex structural modifications. This is the case for *long-term maintenance*, which appears for some software systems within decades. This is also the case for changing a system by applying reuse, especially by using *deep reuse forms* /Co 98, ICSR/ and ch. 7. Finally, this also happens, if we go from a specific system to the family of similar systems, called *system families* or product *lines* /CN 07, Ja 00/. How to structure these changes and to support them by specific tools is widely unknown.

10.6 References

/AA 13/ Agile Alliance: What is Agile Software Development?, accessed July 23

/BB 10/ Beck, K., Beedle, M., et al.: Manifesto for Agile Software Development, Agile Alliance (2010)

/BK 21/ Broy, M./ Kuhrmann, M.: Einführung in die Softwaretechnik, eBook, 665 pp., Springer Vieweg (2021)

/Bo 88/ Boehm, B. W.: A Spiral Model of Software Development and Enhancement, IEEE Computer, 21, 5, 61-72 (1988)

/BNW 08/ Becker, S./ Nagl, M./ Westfechtel, B.: Incremental and Interactive Integrator Tools for Design Product Consistency, in /NM 08/, 224-267

/BT 05/ Boehm, B., Turner, R.: Balancing Agility and Discipline – A Guide for the Perplexed, 304 pp., Addison Wesley (2005)

/CN 07/ Clements, P./ Northrop, L.M.: Software Product Lines: Practices and Patterns, 563 pp., 6th ed., Addison Wesley (2007)

/Co 98/ Coulange, B.: Software Reuse, 293 pp., Springer (1998)

/HH 08/ Höhn, R./ Höppner, St.: The V Model XT (in German), 612 pp., Springer(2008)

/ICSR/ International Conference on Software Reuse, Proc. from 1990 to 2017, see also Wikipedia ICSR

/Ja 00/ Jazayeri, M. et al. (Eds.): Software Architecture for Product Families, Addison Wesley (2000)

/LB 03/ Larman, C./ Basili, V.: Iterative and Incremental Development: A Brief History, IEEE Computer, 2-11 (2003)

/Le 96/ Lefering, M.: Realization of Incremental Integration Tools, in /Na 96/, 469-481

/Me 14/ Meyer, B.: Agile! The Good, the Hype, and the Ugly, 170 pp., Springer (2014)

/Me 98/ Meyer, B.: Object-oriented Software Construction, Prentice Hall 2nd ed. (1998)

/MJW 08/ Miatidis, M./ Jarke, M., Weidenhaupt, K.: Using Developers' Experience in Cooperative Design Processes, LNCS 4970, 185-223 (2008)

/MN 08/ Marquardt, W./ Nagl, M.: A Model-driven Approach for A-posteriori Tool Integration, LNCS 4970, 3-38 (2008)

/Na 90-20/ Nagl, M.: Software Engineering - Methodological Programming in the Large (in German), 387 pp., Springer (1990), plus extensions for a lecture on Software Architectures 1990 to 2020

/Na 96/ Nagl, M. (Ed.): Building Tightly Integrated Software Development Environments - The IPSEN Approach, LNCS 1170, 709 pp., Springer (1996)

/Na 19/ Nagl, M.: Gothic Churches and Informatics (in German), 304 pp., Springer Vieweg (2019), see pp. 179-187

/NM 08/ Nagl, M. / Marquardt, W. (eds.): Collaborative and Distributed Chemical Engineering – From Understanding to Substantial Design Process Support, IMPROVE, LNCS 4970, 851 pp., Springer (2008)

/NW 99/ Nagl, M./ Westfechtel, B. (eds.): Integration of Development Systems in Engineering Applications - Substantial Improvement of the Development Processes (in German), 440 pp., Springer (1999)

/Po 96/ Pohl. K.: Process-centered Requirements Engineering, 342 pp., Research Studies Press (1996)

/PC 86/ Parnas, D.L./ P. Clements, P.C.: A rational design process: How and why to fake it, IEEE Transactions on Software Engineering 2, 251-257 (1986).

/Ro 70/ Royce, W.: Management of the development of large systems, IEEE Wescon (1970)

/Ru 04/ Rumpe, B.: Modeling with UML – Language, Concepts, Methods, 281 pp., Springer (2004)

/UM 17/ OMG, Unified Modeling Language (UML) Specification, Version 2.5.1, Techn. Report OMG (2017)

/SST 08/ Schüppen, A./ Spaniol, O./ Thißen, D.: Multimedia and VR Support for Direct Communication for Designers, in /NM 08/, 268-299 (2008)

/Va 10/ Vallon. T.: Ist die Informatik ein Handwerk?, Vortrag zum 60. Geburtstag von R. Dürre, Blog Dürre und Freunde (2010)

/VM 92/ German Directive 250, Software Development Standard for the German Federal Armed Forces, V-Model, Software Lifecycle Process Model (1992)

/VM 10/ Deutsches Bundesministerium des Innern: V-Modell XT Online Portal (2010)

/We 20/ Westfechtel, B.: Software Processes, Lecture manuscript (in German), U. of Bayreuth, 165 pp. (2020)

/Wi IID/ Wikipedia: Iterative and Incremental Development, accessed Febr. 2022

/Wi IBM/ Wikipedia: Incremental Build Model, accessed Febr. 2022

/Wi MDD/ Wikipedia: Modellgetriebene Softwareentwicklung. Accessed June 23

11 Transformation from Requirements to Architectures is not Automatic

Manfred Nagl
Software Engineering, RWTH Aachen University, nagl@cs.rwth-aachen.de

Bernhard Westfechtel
Software Engineering, University of Bayreuth, bernhard.westfechtel@uni-bayreuth.de

Abstract

After we have discussed the relation of architecture modelling to all surrounding working areas, from requirements engineering to management in chapter 10, we go deeper now by investigating the specifics of the transformation from requirements engineering to architecture modelling. This is the most interesting transformation.

In section 1 of this chapter, we summarize again the central role of the architecture and which problems still remain. Section 2 discusses, that the upper part of the architecture „can be derived" from the requirements specification by the architect making interactive decisions. The lower parts more correspond to technical decisions. Section 3 addresses the transformation RE to AR for a classical requirements spec. In section 4, we study this transformation for an OO requirements spec; the ideas are rather similar. In both cases, we see that there are various possibilities for the mapping, such that the architect has to map interactively. Section 5 sketches the transformation for an embedded system, where even more technical details have to be regarded. Section 6 discusses the rare case that the transformation can be automated, which demands for a long period of gaining experience. This altogether explains the title of the chapter. Section 7 gives a summary and open problems.

Key words: transformation RE to Arch, no automatism, intelligent interactive decisions are necessary, integrator tools, fine-grained relation between increments of different documents

11.1 Introduction

In this book, we have concentrated on classifying workload by introducing clear working areas and corresponding notations for these areas. Especially, we have focused on the *development process*, in order to gain a result with high quality and reasonable effort, starting with the requirements specification and ending with the shipped system. The *architecture* plays an *important role* in the process in the sense of flexibility, quality, and getting experience.

What and how to think and argue on the level of *architectures*, we discussed in chs. 1 to 10. The underlying base is the architecture paradigm, see ch. 1. For what to do on *detail level* (programming, quality assurance of code, detailed documentation, integration of code etc.), see chs. 11-14.

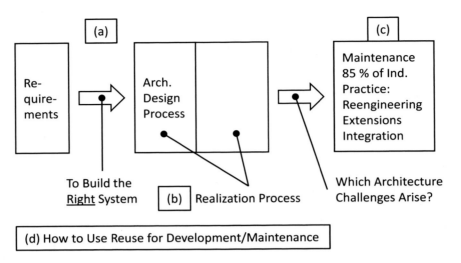

Fig. 11.1: The main topics of software development

There are four *essential problems*, which need specific attention, see fig. 11.1: (a) The requirements specification has to be worked out carefully in order to (a1) specify the *right system*. Otherwise, we might get a good product, but not the expected one. Even more, the transition to get the architecture has to be done with care to (a2) guarantee the properties of the requirements specification. (b) The main part of the development process starting with the abstract architecture and ending with the running system has to be carried out accurately, in order to *get the system right*. (c) *Maintenance* (correction, reengineering, extensions, and integration) should not get stuck in a jumble of technical details. This mainly means that the architecture and the realization process are based on a clear architecture and clear realization steps. Finally, (d) *long-term properties* and *reuse* play an important role, if a system lives for a long time and the development experience is used to get a long-term profit, see ch. 7.

All of these essential problems (a) to (d) depend *specifically on the architecture* and the *mapping from the requirements spec to the architecture*, i.e. on the problem (a) of above: This is trivial for (b) to (d), as without (a) there is the danger that a system is built, which is not the wanted one. For maintenance, it is important to handle the change of requirements, and also how to change the architecture accordingly. For reuse – as argued in ch. 7 – we have this change cycle (changed requirements and changed realization) several times. Especially in the case of deep reuse we furthermore draw conclusions and build the system differently using new abstractions and also new mechanical realization steps as e.g. using big infrastructures or generation out of a specification.

Modelling on architecture level starts with an *abstract form*. Later we add technical *details* (like for distribution) and *extensions* (like semantics of components and component interaction), see chs. 2 and 3. The whole architectural modelling process is driven by the *architecture paradigm*, i.e. to look on essential structures and to assume the idealization, that the architecture can be built up/ modified before implementation (see ch. 1).

Another important topic is the discussion about '*What can change?*' Brainstorming is the right format for such discussions. There are *two points of time*, which are specifically appropriate. (i) The first is after *finishing the requirements specification* or a main part of it. Then we get answers corresponding to changes of the outside behaviour. That leads us to think about these modifications when building up the architecture. To say it in other words, we build the architecture not only for the existing requirements spec but also for probable modifications. (ii) The other time is after *finishing the architecture* or a big part of it. Then, on the one hand, we get delayed answers to question (i). The essential answers now are to changes of the realization. These answers are helpful to think about abstractions in the architecture, which make such changes easily manageable. In most cases, we get the locations in the architecture where data abstractions were not used, but should have been used.

An idea, discussed in literature /Kr 03, MP 06/ is that (1) architecture modelling starts with the requirements spec and *extends* that spec with *further information* belonging to the architecture level. Is that right and is that reasonable? Or, has the requirements and outside level to be separated strictly from the architecture level, which is the starting point of the realization? Furthermore, (2) how is this *transformation* from the requirements to the architecture *handled*, automatically or interactively? The discussion of these questions is a key of this chapter.

In this chapter we *pick up the above problems* (a) to (d), (i), (ii), (1), (2), and give answers.

11.2 Sketch of what to Map and its Range

We start with looking on the *requirements specification* and discuss, which different aspects are covered. We see that this spec contains rather *different and heterogeneous* information, see fig. 11.2. Essentially, it is split into the so-called functional and the non-functional part.

The *functional part* models the outside functionality. Functional here does not mean to be driven by functions, like functional parts on architecture level. Instead, it means the part which can more precisely be described by formal or semiformal models. In literature of the eighties or nineties - the time of 'structured approaches' /dM 78, Yo 89/ - we found a combination of models like SA for the business processes, EER for data description, and CTR for specifying when processes are started or triggered. Later in this chapter, we also discuss the OO approach /OMG 11, OMG 17/ for writing requirements and architectures. This is done in order to show that the approach and notation are not important for the arguments of this chapter.

The *non-functional part* covers quite different topics: We find (a) *efficiency parameters*, the later system has to fulfil, like runtime for a user operation or reaction time for an interactive command. (b) We also find *limitations* for the *system*, like the hard-ware on which the system has to run on, the components from outside, which have to be used and, therefore, are not developed in the project, the minimum storage and runtime of components, or further hardware which has to be available. Finally, (c) we find *determinations* of the following *development process*, like the following de-velopment approach or method to be applied, the tool to be used, the quality assur-ance method to be followed, the programming language to be taken for the realiza-tion, the corresponding compilers to be used, and so on.

Therefore, the *functional* part of the requirements spec determines the *behaviour* of the system to be constructed, changed, or extended. The *non-functional* part of the spec defines *restrictions* to be guaranteed by the later system, or by parts to be in-corporated, or how the development is looking like.

We now discuss the *mapping* from the requirements spec to the architecture, see figs. 11.2 and 11.3. The functional part of the requirements spec describes the outside behaviour of the system to be developed or maintained. It must be understandable for the people of the client (who are more interested in business processes or user functions) as well as for the development team, which is realizing the system with this behaviour. They, therefore, introduce a lot of technical details in order to achieve the final goal. So, we conclude: The relation between the *functional part* of the re-quirements spec and the architecture can only be relevant for the *upper part of the architecture*, which deals with the outside behaviour, i.e. the business functions, the business data entities, the control of activation, the style/ form of user interface, etc.

Below of this upper part we find the *results of technical decisions* (components, lay-ers, data storage, communication mechanisms, basic infrastructure, distribution, etc.), necessary and responsible that the upper part can work. These parts *cannot be derived* from the requirements spec, they rely on technical decisions of the architects, programmers, quality people, etc.

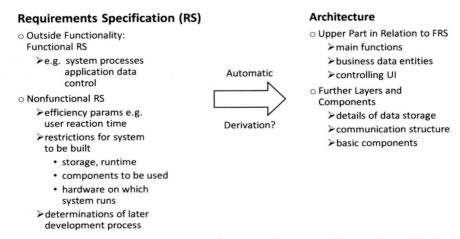

Fig. 11.2: The requirements specification contains quite different determinations

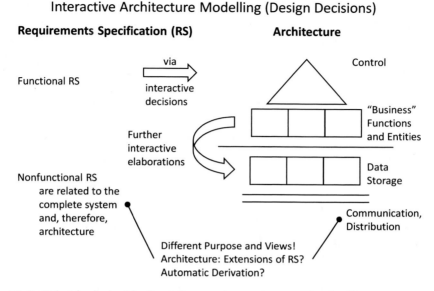

Fig. 11.3: What is derivable from the requirements specification?

However, the various *restrictions* defined in the *non-functional part* of the require-ments spec define limitations, the technical team has to follow. For example, it might be that a certain big component from outside has to be used (because specific knowledge is necessary which is not available, the component is used in other sys-tems of the client company, etc.). Then, this restriction must be followed by the de-velopment team, beginning in the architecture.

In sects. 3 and 5 of this chapter, we discuss the *transformation* for a simple business *admin* system as well as for a simple *embedded* system, respectively. There, we con-centrate on the *upper parts* of the system. The corresponding decisions correspond to the question what elements of the architecture belong to regarded elements of the functional requirements specification. We shall see that the corresponding elements on RE and AR level can look quite differently. This difference is necessary to achieve changeability of the system to be developed or maintained. So, *interactive transfor-mations* are necessary to get the upper part of the architecture.

This is also true for the *middle* and *lower parts* of the architecture, where we do not find corresponding elements in the requirements specification. There, we have usual design activities, which cannot be done automatically, but need intelligent decisions of the architect. Therefore, we also need *interactive decisions* to model the architec-ture, but here for other reasons.

If there were an *automatic correspondence* between requirements spec and architec-ture – by an automatic tool or by the architect following a method, which suggests an automatic correspondence – then we would have a 1:1 correspondence between elements of the requirements spec and the architecture. There are more arguments that this is not reasonable. Let us give one striking argument at the beginning and immediately here. The requirements spec is often changed in development, but especially in maintenance. Any *requirements change* would lead 1:1 to a *changed architecture*. Therefore, many architectural changes and following realization changes would happen. Instead, as already argued above, we should design the architecture such that not only the given requirements spec is mapped, but also probable and slight changes of it. This is only possible, if the architect regards these probable changes and introduces an architecture, which remains stable if the changes occur. As a consequence, interactive and intelligent transformation steps are necessary.

11.3 The Transformation for a Business Administration System

Classical SA, EER, CTR Requirements

We start with an 'old-fashioned' approach to define the requirements, which was heavily used in the 80ies and 90ies. The requirements definition consists of *SA diagrams* /dM 78/, *EER diagrams* /Ch 76/, and a *control model* /Yo89/. It took us some time to integrate these languages to a coherent RE language /Be 95, Ja 92, Ko 96, Le 95, Sc 94/, although our main goal at that time was to build tools. In this section, we study a business administration example, namely the management of a small, scientific department library. The library model is not the focus. Therefore, it is only sketched in order to discuss the transformation to an architecture.

The RE model consists of *three submodels*:

(a) The SA model consists of *process diagrams* (also called data flow diagrams) describing the functional part, i.e. the business subprocesses and their internal structure by further subprocesses on object (not type) level, but also by data stores as containers for data. Processes (nodes) are connected by data flows (arcs). Processes can also be connected to data stores, either to read from them or to update them.

(b) The *EER* (for Extended Entity Relationship) *model* structures the more complex data on type level, the objects of which appear as data flows or inside of data stores. Simple data are contained in the data dictionary.

(c) The *control model* (CTR) describes when the system, its data flow diagram and its refinement start or end, how they synchronize, are interrupted, triggered, etc. This is specifically used for embedded systems. The control model is not further discussed in this chapter.

The topmost diagram is the *context diagram*, see fig. 11.4. It describes the system to be developed (*system node* LibOrg) in its environment, and thereby the outside connections to be considered. The outside nodes are called *terminators*, they can be processes or data stores. Here, the terminators stand for person roles (as Borrower of the library, etc.). In this way, the context diagram describes *what* must be *considered* (as e.g. asking for or getting a book in our example) and also *what* is *not* considered (e.g. the strategy for procurement, the delivery or payment of new books, the process to transport the books from the magazine to the front desk, etc.). Another question we should address is what the aspects are, of which the library model is *independent* of, for example the types of books, or – in a certain range – the size of the library, the character of the library as scientific, company, or open library. The terminators should be logically different; never put logically different things into one terminator.

Just a *sketchy part* of the *explanation*: A potential user asks for the permission for using the library. This allows the next two roles to borrow or to get info. The last two terminators describe roles within the organization of the library, namely to update the book magazine and to procure new books from a bookseller.

The Borrower (middle left node) requests a book or gives it back. He/ she gets the book or a message that it is not available, either borrowed, or not existing in the library. If it does not exist, he gets an answer and the info goes to an internal list. The Informer wants to know, whether a book is available. If yes, he gets a message. If no, he can post a corresponding wish. A library employee can give an UpdateDemand to the library, either demand for a new book or deletion of a book, which is lost. Finally, Procure gets a request for a book status and can give the corresponding answer InfoBookStatus (already ordered, already in a list of books to be later considered, expected to be delivered, or already delivered and ready for borrowing after internal registration). This info is the contents of the message to the Borrower. This might be enough for the context diagram. The example shows that a data flow can be physical (a book) or virtual (a message).

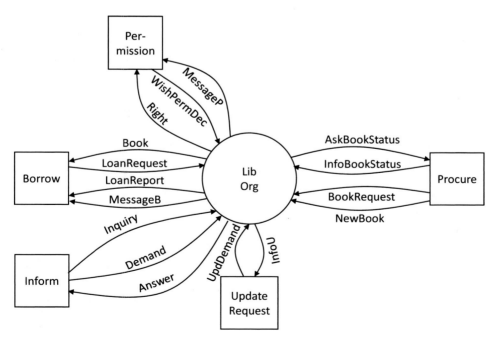

Fig. 11.4: The context diagram for the library example

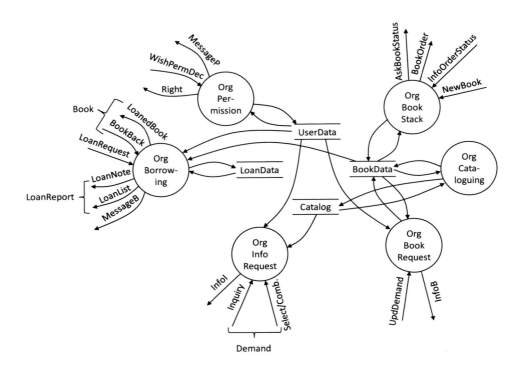

Fig. 11.5: The next level data flow diagram

One level down, we find the *structure inside* the system node LibOrg. It is a data flow diagram containing further processes and here also data stores. The diagram describes the internal structure of the node. The book order request is going to the Org-Borrowing process, where it is checked whether the user has the right to order (UserData) and not all copies of the book have been borrowed (LoanData). The book is taken from the magazine, transported to the front desk, and delivered. Please remember that this part organizing the physical book from magazine to desk or vice versa is not modelled in the example.

Fig. 11.5 is called a refinement of the node LibOrg of fig. 11.4. Looking on figs. 11.4 and 11.5, we see that for a *bundle of data flows* in the context diagram one level deeper there is a *process handling* this bundle. The data flows can be passed 1:1 to the next level. This is the case for the lower three data flows to Borrow. It can be that a data flow is split, as for the book to express getting or handing back a book. It can even be the case that a data flow is split to indicate that the info of the split flows together is "equivalent" to the non-split flow. There are *balancing rules* for data flow diagrams for splitting. By *EER* (for extended entity relation) *diagrams* we describe, how the more *complex data* are structured. This corresponds to the data found in data stores and in data flows. Simple data flows are given in a data lexicon/ repository, more complex ones have a corresponding EER diagram. We see the EER diagram for our library system in fig. 11.6. It consists of logically *different parts* marked by dashed rectangles. These parts are separated and should be assigned to logically different data stores.

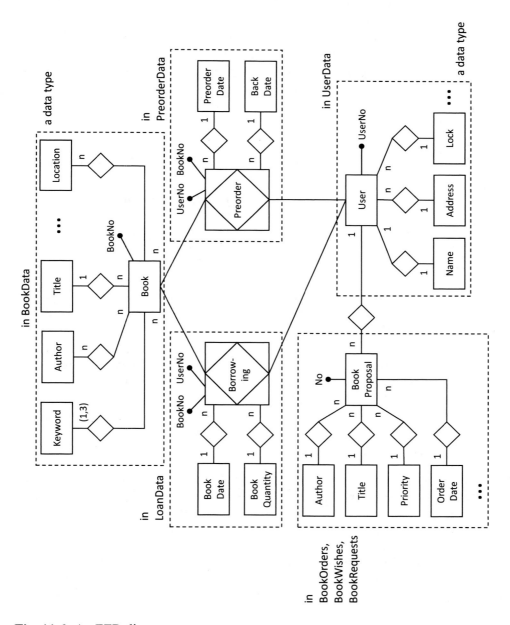

Fig. 11.6: An EER diagram

The diagram consists of *components* (or attributes) marked as rectangles and *relations* marked as diamonds. Relations can have cardinalities. For example, the relation of Title to Book says that a book has one title, but a title can appear in different books. Relations also can have attributes. In this case, a relation has an enclosing rectangle, like Preorder. Relations can connect different parts like Preorder and can have cardinalities, like that between User and BookProposal. An EER diagram represents a *set* of *type definitions* of programming languages and their connection. Thus, they are more on the level of detail programming.

The data types belong to the data stores BookData, LoanData, and UserData of fig. 11.5, or they belong to data stores PreorderData, BookOrders, BookWishes, and BookRequests defined in lower levels of the dataflow diagrams and, therefore, not shown in figs. 11.4 and 11.5. This can be regarded that BookData is internally split.

Models for CTR are informal minispecs, finite automata, control processes, state transition diagrams, etc. /BJ 88, HP 87, WM 85/. As mentioned, the control model is not regarded here.

M*odels* are *dependent* on each other. The different data flow diagrams are defining the internal structures of processes of one level up. Thereby methodological restrictions should be obeyed, as already explained above that 'a process one level deeper is handling bundles of data flows one level above', or 'the flows deeper have to reflect the balancing rules'. Furthermore, the different *models* do *interact*. The EER diagram defines the structure of data to be found in data stores, or of data flows between processes. It can be or it should be that an EER diagram defines data, the parts of which are found in different data stores, see fig. 11.6. In this case, the different parts of the EER diagram should be separated clearly.

A rather big number of diagrams results for this rather simple example. The dataflow model consists of three levels altogether having about hundred nodes (processes and data stores), and even more data flows. There is no room to explain it here. The reader should only get an impression of how to model with these diagrams. The purpose of this section is to transform these diagrams to an architecture. Especially, we show the variety of transformation possibilities in the next subsection.

How to Interpret the SA and EER Diagrams

Fig. 11.7.a shows the *refinement* of a *process* P' within a data flow diagram P and the corresponding refinement diagram for P'. Here, a node within a diagram is refined by a diagram. This refinement has to obey the balancing rules we spoke above. Refinement is refinement *on implementation level*: There is no distinction between a definition on one hand and an applied occurrence of this definition on the other, what we usually have on architecture level. We *miss* here the *interface*. If there were an interface on the lower level, we would see the P' in the upper level as an applied occurrence of this interface. Then, the balancing rules would get a different and more precise meaning.

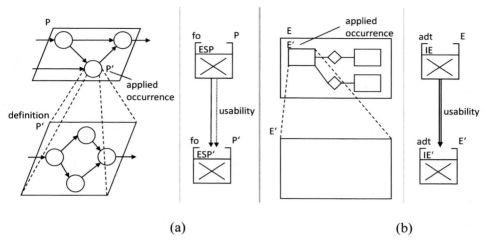

(a)   (b)

Fig. 11.7: Refinement and its interpretation by defined and applied occurrences

Fig. 11.7.b shows the counterpart of *refinement* on the *data side*. Here, we have an EER diagram E which contains an E' and the corresponding EER for E'. Again, E' is only detailing the E of one level above. Again, there is no interface of E' such that we could interpret the E' of the first level as an applied occurrence of this interface. Thus, refinement of EER diagrams is just detailing a given structure.

We have a *different view* on *architecture level*, see right parts of figs. 11.7.a and 7.b: We define interfaces of components and usability rules between components, see ch. 2. The bodies are hidden, so not regarded on architecture level, see 'architecture paradigm' of ch. 1.

Many *aspects cannot be expressed* in data flow diagrams or EER diagrams: For example, in dataflow diagrams, we only have objects and no types. In EER diagrams, we only have types and no single objects. In both we have no common processes or entity types. Also, there are many method rules, which are not identified on diagram level. And so on.

Transformation to Architectures

As already mentioned, we have another view on architecture level: Components with clear interfaces, not looking on bodies, the components have different types (functional object, functional type, data object, data type), and are connected by different usability relations (local, general, and inheritance). We have this in mind, when we discuss the transformation of the abovementioned diagrams to architectural units and their combination. So, the transformation includes the method abstraction shortly discussed here. We can see this in the first transformation of tab. 11.8: A process definition, which really exists in SA, is mapped having different alternatives. So, we make transformations of RE concepts to architectures, which do not exist.

The *transformation possibilities* can be seen in tab. 11.8, see fig. 11.9 for a graphical explanation.

(1a) We can map a SA *process definition* to an interface part of a function object of the AR language. Alternatively, (1b) we can map it to a functional object, i.e. to a complete fo module. We can map it (1c) to a functional interface part of a functional subsystem. Finally, (1d) we can map it to a local functional component in the body of a subsystem.

(2a) A *data store* with an interface (not formally and detailed) is mapped to an ado with a precise data abstraction interface. (2b) Different data stores which are similar are mapped to an ado subsystem with different interfaces belonging to the data stores. (2c) A data store and surrounding processes, which can be seen as the operations on that store, are mapped to one ado component.

(2d) The definition of an *EER diagram* is mapped to an adt with an interface, which now is detailed. (2e) Different EER definitions which share similarities are mapped to an adt subsystem, different interfaces composing the interface of the subsystem.

(3a) The *relations* between two *SA diagrams* can be mapped to local usability, if the refinement has only a local importance. (3b) It can be mapped to general usability, if the lower component is used from different upper components. (3c) In SA diagrams there is no refinement of data stores. It appears only implicitly, see example above for books. This can be mapped on local usability, if the lower component is only of a local importance. Otherwise, (3d) it is mapped on general usability. The relation between *entity types* (3e) is usually mapped to general usability. If similarity is modelled, inheritance can be used (see (2f) and (3e)).

Table 11.8: Parts of requirements spec diagrams and their transformation

Summary

(A) There are many possibilities for the *transformation* of single *RE components* or groups of components. Therefore, there cannot be an automatic transformation. (B) So, we need an intelligent designer to do the transformation. (C) Furthermore, as argued above, the architecture is not an extension of the requirements specification. (D) The RE spec describes the outside functionality for the client, the architecture the essence of the realization for developers.

(E) The *lower levels* of the architecture in most cases have no counterpart on requirements spec level. They are purely developed by the architect. (F) Restrictions of the requirements spec get their technical realization in an abstract way on architecture level. This, specifically, applies for the *non-functional part* of the requirements spec. (G) Due to the architecture being the master structure of the whole development, *long-term properties* of the system, as reuse and the corresponding experience, we mostly find only on architecture level.

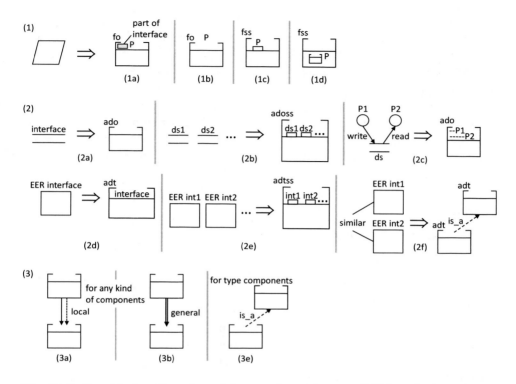

Fig. 11.9: Graphical explanation of the transformation possibilities of tab. 11.8

11.4 The OO Approach: Requirements and their Transformation

In the previous section, we examined the transition from requirements to software architecture in the context of *structured methods*. We demonstrated that the transition involves a bunch of design decisions that are hard to automate. It has been argued frequently that the problems encountered in this transition are due to the fact that structured methods employ heterogeneous modelling languages for requirements engineering and architectural design, respectively. The heterogeneity of the respective modelling concepts would make it difficult to map requirements to the software architecture.

In contrast, *object-oriented methods* promise a seamless transition among technical working areas such as requirements engineering, architectural design, and programming in the small. In particular, the concept of a class would be employed consistently at the levels of requirements engineering (analysis classes), architectural design (design classes), and programming in the small (implementation classes). In this way, an analysis class would be mapped in a natural way to a design class, which would in turn be mapped to an implementation class. The purpose of this section is to investigate to what extent this statement holds.

In the context of this chapter, we are interested only in the transition from requirements engineering to architectural design; see ch. 12 for the transition from architectural design to programming in the small. We focus on object-oriented methods based on the *Unified Modeling Language (UML)* /BR 17, JB 99, OMG17/.

This focus still leaves us with a *number of choices* of processes that may differ with respect to the selection of UML-based languages, and the way how these languages are used in analysis and design, respectively. To illustrate our arguments, we roughly follow the presentation given in /BD 13/, which differs from other approaches viewing object-oriented analysis and design as one integrated discipline /Kr 03, MP 06/. To support our arguments, we will present a small and simple running example (a banking application).

Overview

Tab. 11.10 provides an overview of the relevant disciplines introduced in /BD 13/, their mapping to the working area model, and their artefacts. We discuss them in the order of the table.

Working area	*Discipline*	*Artefacts*	*Artefact types*
Requirements engineering	Requirements elicitation	Requirements specification	Natural language text
	Analysis	Functional model	Use case diagrams
		Behavioural model	Activity, state, sequence and communication diagrams
		Structural model	Package and class diagrams
Architectural design	System design	Structural model	Package, component and deployment diagrams
	Object design	Structural model	Class diagrams
		Behavioural model	Activity, state, sequence and communication diagrams

Table 11.10: Overview of object-oriented disciplines and their artefacts

Requirements Elicitation

The working area of requirements engineering is decomposed into two disciplines: requirements elicitation and analysis, see next subsection. *Requirements elicitation* is concerned with understanding and documenting the requirements to the system to be built from the perspective of the client. Both functional and non-functional requirements need to be addressed. In scenario-based requirements elicitation, concrete examples of using the system are constructed cooperatively. From these *scenarios*, *use cases* are abstracted that describe the functionality of the system in more general terms. The overall result of requirements elicitation is a *requirements specification* that serves as a contract between client and contractor.

Use case name	Withdraw
Participating actors	Client, ATM (Automatic Teller Machine)
Flow of events	1. The client inserts the card.
	2. The ATM validates the card.
	3. If validation fails, the ATM ejects the card and aborts the use case.
	4. Otherwise, the ATM displays the menu for entering the PIN.
	5. The client enters the PIN.
	6. The ATM validates the PIN.
	7. If validation fails, the ATM ejects the card and aborts the use case.
	8. Otherwise, the ATM displays the menu of selectable amounts.
	9. The user selects the requested amount.
	10. The ATM charges the selected amount to the account of the card.
	11. If charging fails, the ATM ejects the card and aborts the use case.
	12. Otherwise, the ATM returns the card.
	13. The client seizes the card.
	14. The ATM outputs the cash.
	15. The client seizes the cash.
Entry condition	-
Exit condition	1. The use case was executed successfully, resulting in a withdraw transaction on the account of the card and delivery of cash.
	2. The use case was aborted by the ATM for one of the following reasons:
	a. The card was not valid.
	b. The entered PIN was not valid.
	c. The amount could not be charged to the card's account.

Fig. 11.11: Use case Withdraw

According to /JB 99/, p. 41, "a use case specifies a sequence of actions, including variants, that the system can perform and that yields an observable result of value to a particular actor". As an example, fig. 11.11 presents the description of the use case

Withdraw to be supported by our banking application. The use case is described in a tabular form.

The use cases are documented in a requirements specification, which is written in natural language, as well. Thus, UML models are not employed here. The main focus of requirements elicitation lies on specifying the requirements in a way that the client understands. Natural language serves as a universally applicable medium that serves this need.

Analysis

In *analysis*, the requirements are elaborated into a form that may be interpreted uniquely by developers. Natural language is well known for impreciseness and ambiguity; models are considered more appropriate to document requirements in a more formal way. The overall *analysis model* needs to be understandable by developers, not (necessarily) by the client. Therefore, the UML comes into play at this stage of development, a notation that the client may not be familiar with.

The analysis model is composed of three parts: a functional, a behavioural and a structural model. The *functional model* describes the functions to be supported without specifying their behaviour; it constitutes the heart of the analysis model. It is derived from the use cases documented in the requirements specification. In analysis, use cases are captured in *use case diagrams*, which are composed of use cases, actors (of all kinds), and their mutual relations. An example is given in fig. 11.12, which shows actors such as Client, Clerk, and ATM, use cases (e.g., Withdraw) and relations among actors and use cases.

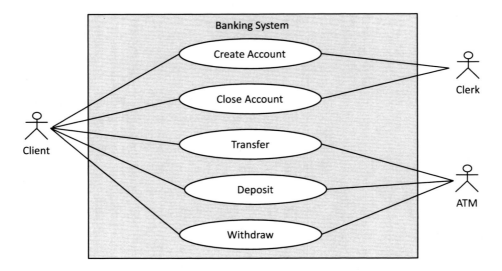

Fig. 11.12: A use case diagram

The *behavioural model* supplements the functional model by specifying the behaviour of use cases. To this end, the UML offers multiple types of diagrams (sequence, state, activity, and communication diagrams). Any of these types may be employed for analysis. Here, we present an example based on *activity diagrams*, which bear similarities to notations for business processes such as BPMN (Business Process Model and Notation /OMG 11/). The activity diagram of fig. 11.13 translates the natural language description of the use case in fig. 11.11 into UML syntax. The diagram is organized into vertical partitions, each of which corresponds to an actor.

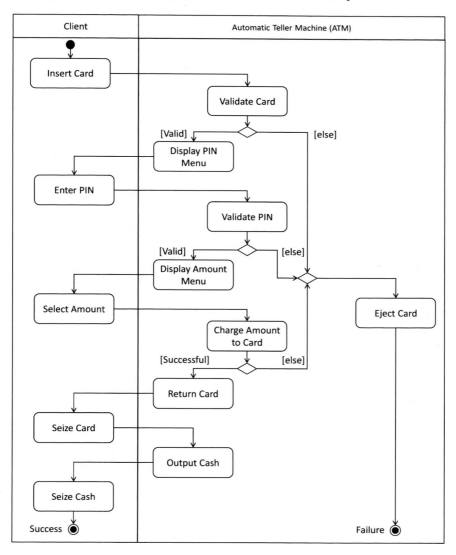

Fig. 11.13: An activity diagram for the use case Withdraw

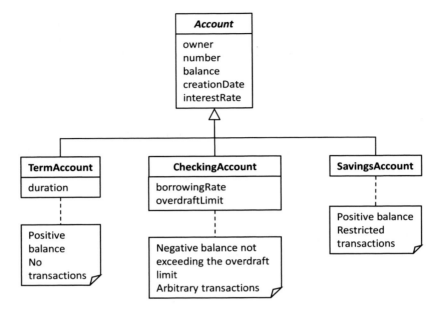

Fig. 11.14: An analysis class diagram

Finally, the *structural model* serves to define the data the system has to deal with: domain objects, their properties, and their relations. The term *domain model* stresses the fact that only objects from the application domain should be represented here; design details should be addressed later. Using the UML, the domain model may be expressed by class and object diagrams. For *class diagrams*, the UML offers a rich modelling language. In analysis, however, only a small part of the available language constructs is used to avoid the discussion of design details. As an example, fig. 11.14 depicts a simple class diagram for our banking application, which defines a set of classes for different types of accounts. For attributes, only their names are specified. Operations are not included; the attachment of operations to classes is considered a design issue. Common attributes are factored into a superclass.

System Design

Analysis is centred around the use case model. It is located in the *problem space* and strives to provide a precise specification of the requirements of the client. Based on the analysis model, *system design* enters the *solution space*. The focus shifts towards the structure of the system that implements the requirements of the client. System design is concerned with the coarse-grained structure, which is refined in object design (see next subsection).

System design addresses fundamental *design decisions* that deeply impact the system architecture. These decisions concern the management of data (in files or databases), control (by transactions or workflows), distribution of data and functional components, infrastructures for communication among processes, security issues, robustness against hardware and software failures, system administration (usage statistics, installation, backups), use of libraries and off-the-shelf-components, etc.

The architecture of the system acts as its blue-print. Therefore, system design focuses on a *coarse-grained structural model* of the system. It contains a lot of technical components that may not be traced directly back to domain objects, such as object request brokers, transaction managers, workflow engines, etc.

For the coarse-grained structural model, the UML offers different types of diagrams. *Package diagrams* are used to define package hierarchies that are populated by classes. *Component diagrams* are employed when a component-based approach is followed: each component encapsulates its internals and provides an external interface to other components. *Deployment diagrams* describe the physical distribution of software components over hardware units.

Object Design

Object design refines the coarse-grained structural model produced by system design. Refinement means that classes and their collaborations are designed in detail, such that the classes' interfaces are specified precisely. In this way, the transition to programming is prepared.

The result of object design is documented in *class diagrams*. In contrast to analysis, the full range of language constructs is employed in object design. Model elements are decorated with visibilities, which are not relevant in analysis. Attributes are specified in detail by defining their types and multiplicities. Similarly, associations are specified with the help of their aggregation kind, and the names and multiplicities of association ends. Furthermore, operations are attached to classes; for each operation, its signature is defined. Static are distinguished from non-static properties, stereotypes indicate different kinds of classifiers, etc.

Class diagrams from analysis serve as one starting point for object design – in addition to package, component or deployment diagrams created in system design. As already mentioned in the previous subsection on system design, many (or even most) design classes have no immediate counterpart in the analysis model. In particular, application of *design patterns* /Ga 94, Bu 96, FR 20/ results in the definition of many classes that support design for change – an issue not relevant in analysis.

Fig. 11.15 gives a simple example of a class diagram produced in object design for the banking application. A command line interface is assumed, provided by the Control class which uses two utility classes for input and output. Even this simple design class diagram is considerably more complex than the corresponding analysis class diagram (fig. 11.14). All details of above have been specified. Furthermore, the classes Control, In, and Out have no counterpart in the analysis class diagram. Finally, the inheritance hierarchy has been re-designed by introducing the abstract intermediate class DisposableAccount, which factors out deposit and withdraw operations.

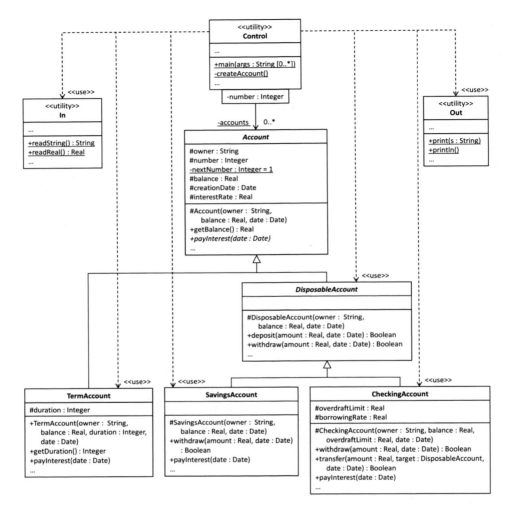

Fig. 11.15: A design class diagram

The structural model may be complemented with a behavioural model. To this end, the same types of diagrams may be employed as in analysis. However, in object design these diagrams refer to design classes and have a formal interpretation. For example, a state diagram may be used to define intra-object behaviour in terms of operations of the respective design class. Inter-object behaviour may be specified by sequence or communication diagrams. For example, the collaboration between model, view, and controller in the MVC design pattern may be defined by sequence diagrams that define how design objects interact dynamically.

Behavioural diagrams prepared in analysis usually are not transferred to and refined in object design. Like the activity diagram from fig. 11.13, they may specify procedural details that become relevant only later in programming in the small. Furthermore, they are composed of informal steps performed by actors rather than operations performed by design objects.

Summary

Object-oriented methods *promise* a *smoother transition* from requirements engineering to architectural design than structured methods. The UML acts as a unified language that may be applied consistently throughout the software lifecycle. In particular, the concept of a class is pervasive and may be applied uniformly to analysis, design, and implementation.

Nevertheless, the transformation from requirements to software architectures is *far from automatic* even in object-oriented methods. This is due to a fundamental shift in perspective: While requirements elicitation and analysis focus on the problem space, system design and object design belong to the solution space.

In requirements elicitation and analysis, the system to be developed is specified from the *perspective of the client*, who is interested primarily in the system's functionality. The analysis model is centred around a functional use case model, which is supplemented with a behavioural model. The domain model defines the objects of the application domain in terms of class diagrams, but many details intentionally remain unspecified. Altogether, the analysis model is composed of UML diagrams, but these diagrams are semi-formal only.

The design model created in system design and object design is *not* merely a *refinement of the analysis model*. Use case diagrams for the functional model are not transferred to the design model at all. Behavioural diagrams may describe procedural details that become relevant for the system's implementation, but do not affect the design model, which is concerned with defining units of abstraction. The term "refinement" applies at most to the domain model, which is transformed into a part of the structural design model. However, many technical decisions have to be performed that cannot be automated. New types of diagrams are created that are not employed in analysis (e.g., component or deployment diagrams). Furthermore, the architect has to decide which architectural and design patterns /Bu 96, FR 20, Ga 94/ should be applied. Altogether, the software architecture consists of numerous classes for user interface elements, controllers, proxies, clients and servers, elements of design patterns, etc. that have no counterpart in the domain model. So, we have the same arguments as around fig. 11.3.

11.5 The Transformation for Embedded Systems

The arguments for *interactive transformations* are the same for *embedded systems* as explained above, see the summary at the end of sect. 11.4. Therefore, there is *no possibility to automate the transformation* (for rare cases see the next section). We need a good architect to make the right decisions regarding details of the system developed or maintained. And, hopefully, there is also a suitable support by interactive, integrated, intelligent, and incremental tools for the transformation.

There is another difficulty appearing in connection to embedded systems. To avoid *technical details*, which hinder intelligibility and abstraction, we have to be careful in modelling. This is difficult anyway, but it is even more difficult in embedded systems compared to those of business administration. The way is to use *abstraction* and to get rid of the details, see chs. 3 and 4, and for a few further remarks see below. This even applies to requirements engineering, where we try to abstract from details of the embedded system in order to open a path for a design allowing an easier future modification of the system developed or maintained.

The data flow diagrams of SA contain *concurrency*. They are hierarchically ordered. The semantics of hierarchy and concurrency are not easy to combine /Be 95/. From this SA notation we can derive an abstract architectural notation. The same is true for the OO method. This is the starting point of other architectures (semantics, distribution, efficiency forms of the architecture, and also concurrency), see the series of architectures in ch. 3. Therefore, concurrency *plays a role both* on *requirements* spec, but especially also on *architectural* spec level.

All these aspects are *specifically important* for embedded systems. They have to do with technical details, see ch. 4. We not only try to avoid unnecessary details in the development, which hinder this development. We even try to abstract from details of the given context.

11.6 Automatic Transformation / Development: The Rare Case and Reuse

In this section we deal with *reuse*. This consists of two parts. The first is on *RE level*. The second deals with reuse in the *transformation* between RE and AR. Both can be combined.

Reuse already on Requirements Specification Level

In chs. 3, 4, 7, and 8 we discussed *reuse* on architecture level, namely by introducing specifics late, by abstracting from specifics, by looking on diverse forms of reuse, and by combining given systems to achieve new functionality. Reuse ideas can already be applied on the RE level. Regarding the information between the outside level and the system level (*topmost diagram* in sect. 11.3 and similarities of business classes in sect. 11.4) we can try to concentrate on the essential parts and abstract from unnecessary details. We specify the exchanged information and neglect the representation and presentation of this information, e.g. what information is necessary from outside or put to outside and neglecting how it is given.

Similarly, we can use *processes*, which relate to abstract functionality and not to concrete one, like grind without fixing the way to do this, i.e. to abstract from the physical effect and the specific device from a company in ch. 4. That makes it easier to change the specification and *reusing the abstracted* part. This is to be formulated by the interface of these processes.

The same applies to *EER diagrams* detailing the specifics of underlying data or *classes* for the *business data*, in sects. 11.3 and 11.4. We use them with interfaces in mind, which correspond to the *data abstraction* purpose. Of course, it not reasonable to expect formal interfaces, as those on architecture level. This was the idea and the level of *classes* in sect. 11.4.

This abstraction is of *specific importance* in the case of *embedded systems* as argued above. There may appear sensors or actuators which reflect physical effects and are delivered by different companies with a company-specific interface. The same arguments hold for processes, relying on physical/ chemical/ technical effects, also with specific interfaces. Both have to be abstracted by further abstract components, see ch. 3.

This altogether means to apply *abstraction* already on *RE level* and not to start with abstraction late and completely on architecture level. That makes requirements specs adaptable and therefore also to prepare them for changes. The abstracted parts can still be reused – at least some parts of it – if changes appear.

Reuse of RE specs is more probable, if abstraction is already used. It is also more probable, if the system to be built or changed is not the first in an application domain. To say it more rigorously: If we have systems out of a class of systems with a strong similarity and there was time to think about this similarity, then reuse on all levels is more probable.

Reuse for the Transformation

If there are *similarities* of different *development processes* in a domain, then there might be similarities between the corresponding *requirements specs*. If these similarities have been made explicit, then there might be similarities between the corresponding *interactive transformations* to architectures. The simplest way now is to use corresponding architecture fragments (product reuse) and to make the rest interactively by using the experiences of preceding transformations (process knowledge reuse).

Bigger *steps in direction of reuse* are possible, if the similarity of the development processes/ results is strong. We call the corresponding systems to belong to a *class of systems*, e.g. motor control software for cars. We also speak of *system families* or *product lines* /CN 07, Ja 00, PB 05/.

In this case, the question comes up, whether it is possible to *automate the transformation*. In general, this is not possible, as explained in this chapter above. However, there are *special cases*, where a *long-lasting period of repetitive developments* exists, the *developers had corresponding ambition* as well as *time* and money. We have discussed these cases of advanced reuse in ch. 7. Let us shortly discuss the domain compiler construction again.

The first example to discuss is the recursive descent compiler, the second example is the frontend of the multi-phase compiler. What are the *specific arguments*, that in these cases we find *big steps* in direction of *automation* in the development?

In both cases we have a special requirements spec: The essential part of it are *formal* descriptions in the form of *grammars* (lexical, deterministic context-free, context-sensitive). There are no informal requirements, like the taste of IO, and there are no restrictions in direction of hardware and software, like weird sensors/ actuators or strange outside components to use.

Now, we sketch the situation of *recursive decent compilers*. They are so-called one-pass compilers /Wi 77/, i.e. they translate the context-free grammar (and inside the lexical grammar) not only to a corresponding architecture. They make the whole *compilation* (lexical scan, top-down parsing, context-sensitive grammar checks, and also the generation of the target code) inside the *one-pass program*. The architecture and the code of this compilation program are human-made, although parts of it can be generated. The method to produce the program is completely clear /Wi 77/. Thus, we have process reuse by taking the written experience. The program is *derived from input and experience*, but not generated by a program.

The situation of the *frontend* of a *multiphase compiler* /AS 06, WG 84/ is different. The phases have a specific task (scanning, parsing, context-sensitive checks, intermediate code generation, etc.) and perform this task for the whole input program. The architecture of the overall program is rather fixed (specific program domain), it need not be translated. The code of the phases is generated by a program (compiler-compiler approach) from the formal input grammar descriptions. The target part of the compiler (addressing, code generation, post optimization) also has reuse potential, but is not in the same and elegant way automated.

These advanced reuse examples are rare in the industrial context. We find the good examples mostly in university projects. A similar potential has the domain software development environments (e.g. /Na 96/), as it is closely related to compilers. Deep reuse with other approaches we find in automation and control and in communication protocols, see ch. 7.

Coming back to *usual industrial practice* of program development for various domains, we can state: The translation of requirements to the architecture fulfilling the requirements needs *intelligence* of an architect and *interaction* of the *architect*. It has to be incremental, in order not to start again from scratch after changes of requirements. Usually there is no automation.

Reuse on Tool Level

A third kind of reuse is the *support* of the development process by *suitable tools*. We can support to build up or modify requirements specs by *interactive, intelligent, and incremental* tools. We can also support the transformation of this spec by tools. And, we can support further extensions/ modifications of this architecture, also by tools. This type of tools can be used for all documents, for their *build/ modification, integration*, and *transformation* in the development process /Na 96/. Transformations should be in both directions, see chs. 10 and 12. The tools should be usable for any form of development process, including loops or cycles.

This is specifically *interesting* for systems with long-term properties as *adaptability, extensibility, reusability*, not doing it again just using the experience of former developments. We work more or less only with specifications and generators. This way of thinking is hundreds of years old, shown for gothic cathedrals around 1300 to 1500 /Na 19/.

This is not a book on tools for the development process, and this chapter is not devoted to this aspect. The transformation between requirements engineering and architecture modelling had a specific importance in our group. We called such tools integrator tools. On the one hand, it is one of the /or even the most *complicated transformation*. On the other hand, after having built such tools, we tried to address the aspect of *mechanization* in tool development.

This is not possible without a *deeper understanding* of such tools in form of precise notations or even formalisms: In /Ja 92/, the RE-AR integrator was built by developing a graph grammar for the requirements specification and of the architecture language, with a common meta model for both languages. The next step was to describe the coupling between both languages by a graph grammar /Le 95/, or a correspondence relation on graphs and graph grammars /Gr 99/. In /Sc 94/, the idea of pair grammars of /Pr 71/ was generalized to graphs with a coupling by another graph grammar (triple graph grammar). These triple grammars have a successful history, /SK 08/ summarizes the first 15 years. So, there is a *theoretical base for integrator tools*. The formalism has also been used for document coupling in chemical engineering development processes, see /NM 08, Be 07, Kö 09/, and also for developing integrators by a reuse approach. Further activities were requirements specs for rapid prototyping /Ko 96/.

11.7 Summary and Open Problems

Summary and Lessons learned

This chapter regarded *requirements specifications* with their functional part and their non-functional part. The functional part was described by two different approaches: a 'structural' one integrating different languages (SA, ER, CTR) and a more current OO one. In both cases, the non-functional part describes restrictions the system and its development have to fulfil.

The form of the requirements spec does not influence the main message of this chapter: The transformation of the spec to an architecture is not automatic, sects. 11.3 and 11.4. And, the requirements spec is not extended to get the architecture. Instead, both requirements spec and architectural description are two views, built up by different persons with different roles.

There are (a) main examples from *business administration* in this chapter and (b) only few remarks on *embedded systems*. The details of the requirements of (a) come from (i) not abstracting from details of the context, (ii) specific ways how to handle the processes or the data, (iii) and not regarding expected changes. In embedded systems, the number of these details is even bigger. The details are responsible for the difficulty of translating to the architecture. The details can be reduced, by already introducing abstraction on requirements level and by already regarding probable changes. Nevertheless, the transformation is interactive.

An *automatic transformation* is only possible in rare and specific cases: (1) having carried out many developments which are similar and having collected corresponding experience, (2) detected strong similarity by regarding a class of problems and class (family, product line) of solutions, (3) giving ambitious developers enough time and money to think about new ways to proceed. (4) If this also includes corresponding tools, in specific domains with formal input or output, and well-understood transition steps, the transformations can be automated. It is taking a long time, money, and long-term strategy to get this mature reuse level.

Open Problems

We have mentioned that long-*term properties* of software systems like adaptability, extensibility, portability, and reuse demand for corresponding activities already on architecture level. *Reuse* has various *levels*, from learning from one development to the next to generation of systems or parts, by developing and using generators. How does a *comprehensive strategy* for reuse and its support by tools look like? How is the transition between different levels?

The questions for this chapter, discussing the *mapping from RE to AR*: How does this *strategy* look like? (A) Different form of support for reuse for building up/ maintaining the requirements spec, supporting the transitions to higher levels of reuse, either by support within a requirements spec or to the requirements spec of the next development. Furthermore, (B) the same questions for the transition to the corresponding architecture. Finally, (C) the same question for the corresponding architecture. Answering these questions could be a blue print for all working areas and their results, as well as for the corresponding transitions to other results.

11.8 References

/AS 06/ Aho, A.V./ Lam, M.S./ Sethi, R./Ullman, J.D.: Compilers: Principles, Techniques, and Tools, 2nd ed., Addison-Wesley (2006)

/BD 13/ Brügge, B./ Dutoit, A.H.: Object-Oriented Software Engineering Using UML, Patterns, and Java, 3rd edition, Pearson International (2013)

/Be 95/ von der Beeck, M.: A Control Model for Structured Analysis (in German), Doct. Diss., RWTH Aachen University, 282 pp. (1995)

/Be 07/ Becker, S.M.: Integrators for Consistency of Documents in Development Processes (in German), Doct. Diss., RWTH Aachen University, 306 pp., Shaker (2007)

/BJ 88/ Bruin, W./Jensen, R. et al.: An Extended Systems Modeling Language Based on the Data Flow Diagram, Software Engineering Notes 13(1) 58-67 (1988)

/BR 17/ Booch, G./ Rumbaugh, J./ Jacobson, I.: The Unified Modeling Language User Guide, 2nd ed., Addison-Wesley, Object Technology Series (2017)

/Bu 96/ Buschmann, F. et al.: Pattern-Oriented Software Architecture, John Wiley & Sons (1996)

/Ch 76/ Chen, P.P.: The Entity Relationship Model: Towards a Unified View of Data, ACM Transactions on Data Base Systems 1(1) 9-36 (1976)

/CN 07/ Clements, P./ Northrop, L.M.: Software Product Lines: Practices and Patterns, 563 pp., 6th ed., Addison Wesley (2007)

/dM 78/ de Marco, T.: Structured Analysis and System Specification, Yourdon (1978)

/FR 20/ Freeman, E./ Robson, E.: Head First Design Patterns, 2nd ed., O'Reilly (2020)

/Ga 94/ Gamma, E. et al.: Design Patterns – Elements of Reusable Object-Oriented Software, Addison-Wesley (1994)

/Gr 99/ Gruner, S.: A Schematic and Grammatical Correspondence Method for the Specification of Consistent and Distributed Data Models (in German), Doct. Diss., RWTH Aachen University, 218 pp., Shaker (1999)

/HP 87/ Hatley, D.J./ Pirbhai, I.A.: Strategies for Real-Time System Specification, Dorset (1987)

/Ja 92/ Janning, Th.: Integration of Languages and Tools of Requirements Engineering and Programming in the Large (in German), Doct. Diss., RWTH Aachen University, 174 pp., DUV (1992)

/Ja 00/ Jazayeri, M. et al. (eds.): Software Architecture for Product Families, Addison Wesley (2000)

/JB 99/ Jacobson, I./ Booch, G./ Rumbaugh, J.: The Unified Software Development Process, Addison-Wesley, Object Technology Series (1999)

/Ko 96/ Kohring, Chr.: Execution of Requirements Specs for Rapid Prototyping – Requirements Engineering and Simulation RESI, Doct. Diss., RWTH Aachen University, 293 pp., Shaker (1996)

/Kö 09/ Körtgen, A.Th.: Modeling and Realizing Tools for Consistency Assurance in Simultaneous Document Development (in German), Doct. Diss., RWTH Aachen University, 279 pp., Shaker (2009)

/Kr 03/ Kruchten, P.: The Rational Unified Process, 3rd ed., Addison-Wesley (2003)

/Le 95/ Lefering, M.: Integration Tools in a Software Development Environment (in German), Doct. Diss., RWTH Aachen University, 253 pp., Shaker (1995)

/MP 06/ McLaughlin, B.D./ Pollice, G./ West, D.: Head First Object-Oriented Analysis & Design, O'Reilly (2006)

/Na 90-20/ Nagl, M.: Software Engineering- Methodological Programming in the Large (in German), 387 pp., Springer (1990), plus extensions for a lecture on Software Architectures from 1990 to 2020

/Na 96/ Nagl, M. (ed.): Building Tightly Integrated Software Development Environments - The IPSEN Approach, LNCS 1170, 709 pp., Springer (1999)

/Na 19/ Nagl, M.: Gothic Churches and Informatics (in German), 304 pp., Springer Vieweg (2019)

/NM 08/ Nagl, M./ Marquardt, W.: Collaborative and Distributed Chemical Engineering – From Understanding to Substantial Design Process Support, IMPROVE, LNCS 4970, 851 pp., Springer (2008)

/OMG 11/ Object Man. Group: Business Process Model and Notation (BPMN), V.2.0 (2011)

/OMG 17/ Object Man. Group: OMG Unified Modeling Language (OMG UML), V.2.5.1 (2017)

/PB 05/ Pohl, K./ Böckle, G. et al.: Software Product Line Engineering, 467 pp., Springer (2005)

/Pr 71/ Pratt, T.W.: Pair Grammars, Graph Languages, and String-to-Graph Translations, Journ. of Computer and System Sciences 5(6) 560-595 (1971)

/Sc 94/ Schürr, A.: Specification of Graph Translators with Triple Graph Grammars. in: Mayr, E.W., Schmidt, G. (eds.): WG 1994, LNCS 903, 151–163, Springer (1995)

/SK 08/ Schürr, A./ Klar, F.: 15 Years of Triple Graph Grammars, in: Ehrig, H. et al. (eds.): Int. Conf. On Graph Transformation (ICGT 08), LNCS 5214, 411-425, Springer (2008)

/WG 84/ Waite, W.M./ Goos, G.: Compiler Construction, Springer (1984)

/Wi 77/ Wirth, N.: Compilerbau, Grundlagen und Techniken des Compilerbaus, Oldenbourg (1997)

/WM 85/ Wards, P.T./ Mellor, S.J.: Structured Development for Real-Time Systems, Yourdon (1985)

/Yo 89/ Yourdon, E.: Modern Structured Analysis, Yourdon (1989)

12 The Architecture is the Blueprint for the Code

Bernhard Westfechtel

Software Engineering, University of Bayreuth, bernhard.westfechtel@uni-bayreuth.de

Abstract

This chapter explores the relationship between architectural design and programming in the small. Compared to relationships to other working areas such as requirements engineering or quality assurance, the architecture and the implementation of a software system are coupled tightly: The architecture serves as a blueprint for the implementation of the software system to be developed. Essentially, the architecture defines the skeleton of the system that is complemented with code written by programmers. Accordingly, the conformance of the implementation with the architecture may be defined by a set of consistency relations. Finally, different variants of processes describing the coupling between activities in the working areas architectural design and programming in the small are elaborated and compared.

Key words: software architecture, programming in the small, architectural conformance, forward engineering, roundtrip engineering, model-driven engineering

12.1 Introduction

Fig. 12.1 displays an excerpt from the working area model used throughout this book. Except for requirements engineering, architectural design acts as the master in each of the dependencies shown in the figure. The current chapter focuses on the dependency between *architectural design* and *programming in the small*.

Among the relations to other working areas, the relation of software architecture to programming in the small has been explored most thoroughly, starting with fundamental research on programming in the large in the 1970's /DK 76, Pa 72/, which recognized the need for a level of modeling above program code. The architecture was perceived as a description of the coarse-grained structure of a software system, which is defined in terms of components and relationships between them. The program code should adhere to this structure and add the necessary algorithmic details required for an executable implementation.

Compared to relationships to other working areas, the architecture and the implementation of a software system are coupled tightly: The architecture serves as a *blueprint* for the implementation of the software system to be developed. Thus, the transition from the architecture to the implementation may be supported by *deterministic model transformations*. This degree of automation may not be achieved in the transition to other working areas. For example, the transformation from requirements to architectures is not automatic (see ch. 11): Many design decisions may have to be performed, resulting in a transformation that is driven by user interactions.

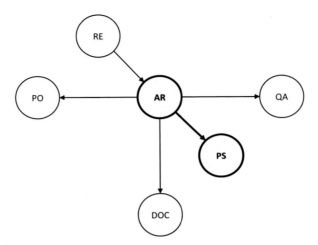

Fig. 12.1: Focus of the current chapter

Since the architecture serves as a blueprint, one may expect that it is easy to ensure *conformance* of the implementation with the architecture. However, this is not necessarily the case. Checking and enforcing conformance requires adequate *tool support* and a *disciplined software process*. Therefore, the current chapter will also discuss different variants of tools und processes and their impact on conformance checking and enforcement.

This chapter is structured as follows: Sect. 12.2 briefly summarizes the notion of software architecture as presented in ch. 2 of this book, and introduces a small running example. Sect. 12.3 explores the relation between the architecture and the implementation of a software system at a conceptual level. Sect. 12.4 describes the mapping of the architecture modeling language to programming languages. Sect. 12.5 refines these considerations by defining the notion of conformance of an implementation with the software architecture. Sect. 12.6 introduces and compares different variants of tool support and software processes. Finally, sect. 12.7 gives a brief summary, including the messages conveyed by this chapter.

12.2 Software Architecture Modeling

As pointed out in ch. 2 of this book, the software architecture may be defined in an integrated way based on a structural description of its components and their relationships. This *structural model* serves as the backbone that may be enriched with behavioral aspects such as semantics, concurrency, or distribution. In the current chapter, we will focus on the core structural model without considering the other aspects. At a coarse-grained level, the structural model is represented by diagrams, while the details of interface specifications are described in a textual notation.

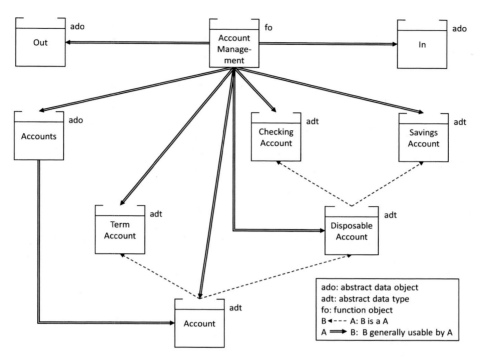

Fig. 12.2: Architecture of a simple banking application

abstract data type module Account **is**
    type AccountType **is private**;
    procedure createAccount(owner : **in string**, number : **in integer**,
        amount : **in rational**, account : **out** AccountType);
    function getOwner(account : **in** AccountType) **return string**;
    function getNumber(account : **in** AccountType) **return integer**;
    function getAmount(account : **in** AccountType) **return rational**;
    procedure payInterest(account : **in out** AccountType);
    ...
end

abstract data object module Accounts **is**
    general import from abstract data type module Account
        using AccountType, ...;
    procedure insert(account : **in** AccountType);
    procedure remove(accountNumber : **in integer**);
    function getAccount(accountNumber : **in integer**) **return** AccountType;
    function isEmpty() **return boolean**;
    ...
end

Fig. 12.3: Examples of interface specifications

Without striving for complete coverage of the provided language constructs, fig. 12.2 shows an *architecture diagram* of a simple banking application, serving as a running example throughout this chapter. The architecture is composed of modules of different types that are connected by different types of relationships (inheritance and general usability). AccountManagement is a *function object* that performs the central control of the application. The *abstract data objects* In and Out are used for the command line interface. Accounts manages a single collection of accounts (abstract data object), with the *abstract data type* Account serving as its entry type. Furthermore, Account acts as the root of a small inheritance tree that introduces different account types (Term, Checking, and Savings Accounts); the commonalities of Checking and Saving Accounts are factored out into the supertype Disposable Account.

Fig. 12.3 displays examples of *interface specifications* that refine the coarse-grained description given by the architecture diagram. The employed notation is inspired to a certain degree by Ada /Na 99/, but it is independent of the programming language to be used for implementation. The interface specifications reside on a syntactic level; they could be enriched with semantic aspects, as demonstrated in ch. 2 of this book. The data type module Account exports a *type* the definition of which is hidden. Exported operations are classified into *functions*, which do not have side effects, and *procedures*, which perform state changes. Parameters are classified into in, out and in out parameters. Since Accounts is a data object module (operating on a single object), it does not export a type.

12.3 Relation between Software Architecture and Implementation

As argued in ch. 1 of this book, the software architecture plays a central role in the software development process. The architecture serves as the *blueprint* for the implementation of the software system to be developed. In particular, the software architecture defines the *static structure* of the software system in terms of components and relationships. As described in ch. 2 of this book, the architectural configuration consists of *subsystems*, *modules* for functional and data abstractions, various kinds of relationships among them (*hierarchy*, *usability*, and *specialization*), and specifications of component interfaces /Na 90/. An illustrating simple example was given above (see fig. 12.2 and fig. 12.3).

Concerning the relation between software architecture and implementation, the *software architecture* acts as the *master*, while the *implementation* is a *dependent* artefact. In particular, the software architecture
(a) defines the components that need to be implemented,
(b) defines the interfaces of these components in terms of provided resources (types and operations),
(c) defines and constrains the required resources (i.e., which other components and which parts of their interfaces may be used for the implementation of a component), and
(d) establishes inheritance hierarchies in the case of object orientation.

The *bodies* of components go beyond the scope of the software architecture. Intentionally, only the interfaces are described. Functional and data abstraction are important concepts for decoupling the implementations of components. The body of a component defines how these abstractions are realized in terms of data structures and algorithms. In general, abstractions may be realized in different ways. Furthermore, the realizations may be changed without affecting client components as long as the interfaces remain untouched.

The transition from the software architecture to the implementation may be supported by a *deterministic model transformation* that generates *implementation frames* to be filled in by programmers (see sect. 12.4). The mapping is not unique; in general, there are multiple ways to map the architecture modeling language to a programming language. However, mapping decisions may be performed either a priori by the transformation developer, or by the user of the transformation with the help of configuration parameters. The resulting model transformation may then be executed without user interaction. Thus, no interactive decisions are required when the transformation is being executed.

Compared to the *relations* to *other working areas*, the relation between *software architecture* and *implementation* is rather *tight*. For example, let us consider the relation between requirements engineering and software architecture (see ch. 11). Proceeding from requirements engineering to architectural design involves the transition from the problem domain to the solution domain. Many design decisions have to be performed in order to fix how the requirements are to be realized. These *interactive decisions* concern the overall architecture as well as many details regarding the application logic, the user interface, the control flow (e.g., by using a workflow management system), the data storage (in the file system, a relational database system, or a NoSQL database system), system security, system administration, etc. Except for constrained domains, it is therefore not feasible to generate (parts of) the software architecture from the requirements in a similar way as implementation frames for code may be generated from the software architecture.

Nevertheless, implementing a software architecture by no means is a trivial task. Ideally, the software architect is capable of pre-planning the implementation completely: The architect knows precisely which components are needed and which interfaces they have to implement, using only the resources fixed in the software architecture. In our simple banking application, this statement may hold. In practice (i.e., when developing large and complex systems), this is the case only rarely. Depending on the level of experience in the respective domain, the architect has a more or less vague idea of the implementation. In particular when the domain is novel and the system to be built is large and complex, the architectural knowledge is built up only gradually. This statement applies e.g. to our own work on the *IPSEN project* (*I*ntegrated *P*roject Support *EN*vironment /En 86, Sc 86, Le 88, We 91, Na 96/), where the architecture modeling approach presented in this book was used to define a novel standard architecture for software development environments (see fig. 12.4, which displays the architecture at the subsystem level).

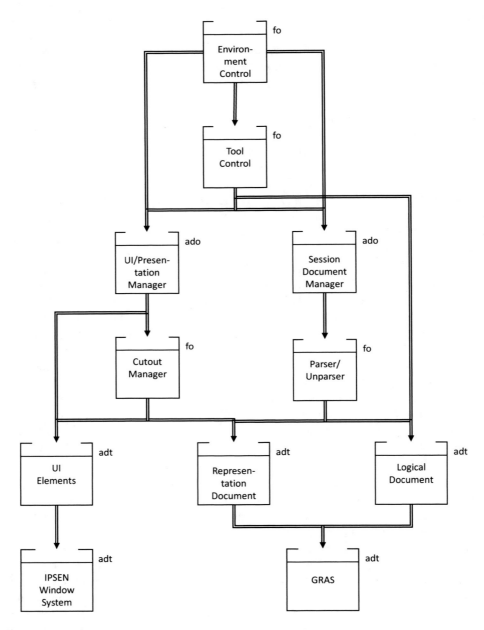

Fig. 12.4: Coarse architecture of an IPSEN environment (/Na 96/, p. 381)

Based on this characterization of the relation between software architecture and implementation, the notion of *blueprint*, which has been transferred from the *architecture* of *buildings*, has to be reconsidered. In that domain /Na 19/, the architecture in fact acts a precise build plan that is composed of diagrams such as floor plans, electricity plans, etc. As explained in ch. 2 of this book, the architecture of a building is described on different levels of granularity, covering different aspects, with a clear integration of different architectural models. A software architecture does not offer the same level of precision. The program code of the system is not determined uniquely by the architecture. In software engineering, the term *building* refers to the automatic derivation and deployment of executable code rather than to the construction of program source code from the software architecture. Altogether, the notion of blueprint should be used with some grain of salt when applied to software architecture (except for domains in which architecture models are fully executable, which requires to fully model the behavior in addition to the structure of the software system). This insight deeply impacts the overall software process, which will be elaborated in sect. 12.6.

12.4 Mapping the Architecture to Different Programming Languages

From the software architecture, *implementation frames* may be generated /Le 88/ to be completed by programmers. The actual complexity of the transformation of the architecture into the implementation depends on the *conceptual distance* between the architecture modeling language and the respective programming language. Below, this is demonstrated by discussing two sample programming languages (Java and C). These examples also serve to illustrate that the architecture modeling language is independent of the selected programming language(s). In particular, it may be used to provide a neutral architectural description when different components of the overall software system are implemented in different languages. For a deeper discussion of the mapping to different programming languages, see /Na 90/, ch. 6.

Fig. 12.5 shows a mapping of the interface specifications from fig. 12.3 to the programming language *Java* /Go 23/. It is assumed that all modules belong to one subsystem, which is mapped to a Java package. Comments mark the fragments of program code that have to be provided by programmers to make the overall program complete.

It should be noted that the interface specifications from fig. 12.3 cannot be mapped 1:1 to Java because of semantic differences between the underlying languages. While the architecture modeling language distinguishes between different module types, Java provides only a single kind of program unit called class (apart from interfaces, which are not used here). The abstract data type module Account is mapped to a class of the same name, which is used also as the type name. Based on conventions to be followed in the interface specification, the procedure createAccount is mapped to a constructor. All other operations are translated into methods, assuming that the first parameter of each operation designates the object on which the respective method is to be called. The abstract data object Accounts is simulated in Java by a class with static methods. Rather than instantiating the Java class, all methods are called by qualifying them with the class name. Finally, while the architecture modeling language distinguishes between different parameter modes (in, out, and in out, respectively), Java supports only a single mode.

Altogether, the mapping from interface specifications to Java is rather straightforward. For example, (single) inheritance between data type modules may be mapped 1:1 to inheritance between classes. Below, the mapping to the programming language *C* /KR 00/ is discussed. Altogether, this mapping is more complex because C supports neither data abstraction nor inheritance.

```
package banking;
public class Account {
    // Implement data structure
    public Account(String owner, int number, double amount) {
        // Implement constructor
    }
    public String getOwner() {
        // Implement method
    }
    // Likewise for getNumber() and getAmount()
    public void payInterest() {
        // Implement method
    }
    ...
}
package banking;
// No import for class Account of the same package needed
public class Accounts {
    // Implement data structure
    public static void insert(Account account) {
        // Implement method
    }
    public static void remove(int accountNumber) {
        // Implement method
    }
    public static Account getAccount(int accountNumber) {
        // Implement method
    }
    public static boolean isEmpty() {
        // Implement method
    }
    ...
}
```

Fig. 12.5: Java implementation frames for the interface specifications in fig. 12.3

```
/* Header file Account.h */
typedef void* AccountType;
AccountType createAccount(char* owner, int number, double amount);
char* getOwner(AccountType account);
int getNumber(AccountType account);
double getAmount(AccountType account);
void payInterest(AccountType account);
...
/* C file Account.c */
#include "Account.h"
typedef struct {
    char* owner;
    int number;
    double amount;
} AccountData;
AccountType createAccount(char* owner, int number, double amount) {
    AccountData* accountData = (AccountData*)malloc(sizeof(AccountData));
    accountData->owner = owner;
    accountData->number = number;
    accountData->amount = amount;
    return accountData;
}
...
/* Header file Accounts.h */
#include "Account.h"
void insert(AccountType account);
void remove(int accountNumber);
AccountType getAccount(int AccountNumber);
int isEmpty();
...
```

Fig. 12.6: Header and C files for the interface specifications in fig. 12.3

In the case of C, interface specifications may be mapped *to header files*, which may be fully generated (fig. 12.6). The mapping of the data object module Accounts is even simpler than for Java: The respective header file (see bottom of fig. 12.6) consists of a set of function definitions. For the C file, function declarations with empty bodies may be generated, in the same style as shown above for Java. Thus, for data object modules data abstraction may be provided in the generated code. Mapping of data type modules is more difficult since C does not support private types. This problem may be solved by defining an untyped pointer type (see top of fig. 12.6), denoted by **void*** in C. This pointer type is used in the header file, and is mapped to a typed pointer in the C file (**AccountData***). Data abstraction is provided because clients of the module **Account** do not know the type of the referenced data. However, the correct use of untyped pointers cannot be checked at compile time.

The mapping to C gets much more convoluted if *inheritance* is considered (which is not the case for the code shown above). In order to simulate *dynamic binding* (runtime polymorphism), function pointers need to be stored in records (called structures in C), providing a level of indirection when function calls are executed at run time. The generated code must ensure that for each called function the correct body is executed, depending on the dynamic type of the respective object. Essentially, the transformation from the architecture modeling language to C has to perform the work that would be carried out by a compiler of an object-oriented programming language with dynamic binding. Since this makes the generated C code complicated and hard to use, it might be considered more appropriate to refrain from using inheritance in the architecture modeling language for systems that are intended to be implemented in C. Alternatively, it might be decided to use C++ instead of C as programming language.

To summarize, the architecture modeling language may be mapped to different programming languages. Above, this was demonstrated for Java and C. Further mappings (to FORTRAN, Pascal and Ada) are described in /Na 90/. In all of these cases, the transition from architectural design to programming in the small may be supported by deterministic model transformations. However, the complexity of the mapping depends on the conceptual distance between the architecture modeling language and the respective programming language. Concepts that are not supported in the programming language have to be simulated, and programmers need to write code conforming to the chosen simulation.

12.5 Conformance Implementation and Software Architecture

In the relation between the software architecture and the implementation, the former and the latter act as the master and the dependent, respectively. Accordingly, the *conformance* of the *implementation* with the *software architecture* has to be assured /CL 15, Pa 10, Te 15/. When conformance cannot be assured, the software architecture gets outdated and may lose its central role in the development process regarding e.g. project planning, determination of test strategies, etc. Furthermore, it may become more and more difficult and costly to maintain the implemented system, due to *architectural erosion*, which results in unintended coupling of components and blurs separation of concerns /SB 12, Li 22/.

Checking and enforcing architectural conformance manually is both laborious and error-prone. Therefore, adequate *tool support* is urgently needed. *Analysis tools* assist in *checking conformance* by reporting conformance violations. *Transformation tools* may be used for *enforcing conformance* by generating implementation frames and by updating existing implementations to re-establish conformance with the software architecture (see also sect. 12.6).

All of these tools need to operate on the basis of a *definition* of *architectural conformance*. This definition is composed of a set of *rules* that may be classified roughly into completeness and consistency rules. *Completeness rules* ensure that all components defined in the software architecture are actually implemented. *Consistency rules* ensure that all constraints imposed by the software architecture are satisfied.

In the following, *conformance rules* are sketched briefly, without striving for completeness. To this end, we use Java as exemplary programming language. Please note that the rules given below depend not only on the programming language, but also on the way in which the architecture language is mapped onto this language.

Completeness rules require an implementation for each element of the architecture:
(1) For each module, there must be a corresponding Java class with the same name.
(2) For each abstract data type module, its Java class must provide
  (a) a public constructor for each create procedure. Apart from the out parameter for the instantiated type, the constructor must have the same parameters as the create procedure (which are assumed to be in parameters).
  (b) a public non-static method for each procedure or function. For a function, the corresponding method must have the same parameters (except for the first one) and return type. For a procedure, all in parameters (except for the first one) are mapped to method parameters. Furthermore, if there is no out parameter, the return type of the method is void; if there is one out parameter, its type serves as return type; if there are multiple out parameters, a nested class needs to be defined for grouping them into the method's return type.
(3) For each abstract data object or function module, its Java class must provide for each procedure or function a static method with similar rules for its signature as described above.

Consistency rules exclude the existence of elements of the implementation, e.g.:
(1) There is no Java class that does not realize a corresponding module.
(2) For each Java class, there is no public element beyond those elements which are required by completeness rules. I.e., the exported interface should not go beyond the corresponding interface specification in the software architecture.
(3) In each Java class, at most those resources are used from other classes which are granted by inheritance or usability relationships in the software architecture.

In particular, the third consistency rule excludes unwanted coupling between components of the implemented system. For example, this is essential in a layered architecture such as displayed in fig. 12.4, where accesses violating layers must be prohibited.

12.6 Software Process

A *software process* is a set of partially ordered process steps intended to reach a goal. The working area model groups logically related activities and defines dependencies. However, it does not determine the order in which activities are executed, and in which ways and directions artefacts are passed among them.

Concerning the relation between technical working areas, we may distinguish among three types of processes, which differ regarding the direction of data flows (fig. 12.7):
(a) In *forward engineering*, data flows are directed in the same ways as in the working area model (from the master to the dependent).
(b) In *reverse engineering*, data flows are oriented in the opposite direction. Reverse engineering is performed to reconstruct the software architecture from the implementation (or the requirements specification from the software architecture).

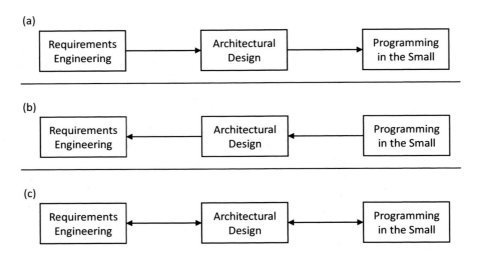

Fig. 12.7: Forward, reverse and roundtrip engineering

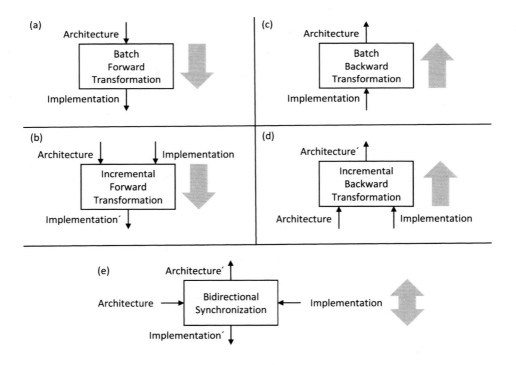

Fig. 12.8: Transformations between software architecture and implementation

(c) In *roundtrip engineering*, changes to artefacts are propagated in both directions. Thus, it is allowed to make changes in a dependent artefact which do not conform to the master artefact and to propagate these changes back to re-establish conformance.

In the following, we focus on the relation between architectural design and programming in the small. With respect to this relation, any of the process types introduced above needs to establish *conformance* of the *implementation* (dependent) with the *software architecture* (master). Conformance may be established manually, or with the help of different kinds of *tools* (see fig. 12.8, which will be explained later). As to be demonstrated, both process and tool types deeply impact the task of establishing conformance.

Forward Engineering

Forward engineering may be supported by a *batch forward transformation* (fig. 12.8.a), which generates an implementation from the software architecture from scratch. Typically, *implementation frames* are created which need to be supplemented by handwritten code (see sect. 12.4). In constrained domains, the implementation may be generated even completely, as exemplified by the vision of *Model-Driven Architecture* (MDA) /Ob 14/. So far, this vision has proved ambitious; thus, we assume in the following that manual programming is still required.

Batch forward transformations assume a *strict forward engineering process* like the *waterfall model* /Ro 70/, where the design phase precedes the implementation phase. This approach requires to define precisely not only the coarse-grained architecture, as documented in architecture diagrams, but also fine-grained interface specifications as given in fig. 12.3. This may be possible for small systems in well-known domains (such as our running example, the banking application), but does not scale to large systems in unfamiliar domains (as illustrated by the IPSEN architecture displayed in fig. 12.4).

Incremental forward engineering is more flexible because it allows to overlap architectural design and programming the small. To this end, *incremental forward transformations* (fig. 12.8.b) are used to propagate changes of the software architecture into the implementation. An incremental forward transformation receives the current versions of the architecture and the implementation and updates the implementation, resulting in a new version that conforms to the architecture. Incremental forward transformation tools were developed e.g. in the IPSEN project /Le 88, We 91, Na 96/ and in the context of model-driven software engineering /Sc 06, St 09/.

Incremental forward engineering covers the following cases, which would be excluded by a waterfall process: (1) Programming may start already when the software architecture is not yet complete or stable. (2) After programming has started, the software architecture may still be updated according to changed requirements. (3) Design decisions may be changed after program code has been written. (4) Errors in the architecture may be fixed in response to problems detected in the implementation. In all of these cases, incremental forward transformations may be used to re-establish conformance of the implementation with the software architecture.

Reverse Engineering

Reverse engineering /CC 90/ aims at recovering high-level abstractions such as software architectures or even requirements from the program source code. Applied to architecture modeling according to the notation introduced in ch. 2 of this book (and employed in the current chapter), this means to recover modules for functional and data abstraction from the source code. Reverse engineering is usually performed as a first step of a *reengineering process*, which, according to the horseshoe model /KW 98/, comprises the phases architecture recovery, architecture transformation, and architecture-based development, such that forward engineering may be applied subsequently.

Reverse engineering may be supported by *backward transformations*, which recover the software architecture from the implementation. Like for forward engineering, we may distinguish between *batch* and *incremental transformations* (fig. 12.8.c and 12.8.d, respectively). Batch transformations assume that architecture recovery is a one-shot activity; incremental transformations are required when the implementation is still changed after architecture recovery has started.

The backward transformation is much more difficult than the forward transformation. The forward transformation maps the concepts of the architecture modeling language in a systematic way to the concepts of the respective programming language. As a result, we obtain well-structured implementation frames that are extended subsequently by programmers with manually written code. In contrast, the source code of a legacy system usually does not conform to these structures and patterns. For the recovery of functional and data abstractions, *heuristics* have to be applied that are based on assumptions that may or may not be satisfied /LW 90, CC 01/. As a result, we may obtain a *virtual architecture* in which modules are scattered over different files and locations in the source code (see also ch. 9 of this book).

Roundtrip Engineering

Roundtrip engineering denotes a process in which two interdependent artefacts are modified in parallel and changes are propagated in both directions /RD 21/. Change propagation may be achieved with *incremental forward* and *backward transformations* (fig. 12.8.b and 12.8.d, respectively), as realized e.g. in /BG 08/ for roundtrip engineering between UML models and Java source code. Alternatively, a *bidirectional synchronization tool* /Xi 13/ may be used that receives current versions of interdependent artefacts and produces updated versions for both of them (fig. 12.8.e).

In roundtrip engineering, interdependent artefacts are considered as *peers*. This view does not match the conceptual relation between the software architecture (*master*) and the implementation (*dependent*): The implementation has to conform to the software architecture and not vice versa. Thus, roundtrip engineering should be applied only in a restricted way: Arbitrary deviations of the implementation from the software architecture should not be permitted, and backward transformations should be applied only to fix errors in the architecture that would have to be fixed manually by editing the architecture in an incremental forward engineering process.

Furthermore, as already discussed above, forward and backward transformations are *not symmetric*. A forward transformation generates source code conforming to certain patterns. Programmers have to conform to these patterns not only when they extend implementation frames – but also when they introduce changes to be propagated back into the software architecture. Otherwise, backward propagation does not work properly.

Summary

Forward engineering offers the best match to the conceptual relation between software architecture and implementation. Batch forward engineering assumes a waterfall-like process, which we consider too restrictive. *Incremental forward engineering* is more flexible and allows to propagate architectural changes due to modified requirements, revised design decisions, refinements and extensions of the architecture, and feedback from the implementation.

Tool support for incremental forward engineering was developed e.g. as part of the IPSEN software development environment, which offered incremental tools enforcing conformance of the implementation with the software architecture /Le 88, We 91, Na 96/. In IPSEN, implementation frames are generated that ensure both consistency and completeness. In the source code, generated implementation frames are marked as protected regions that cannot be modified by programmers. Implementation frames are filled in by programmers, who implement data structures and algorithms. Programmers can modify neither the export nor the import interfaces of modules, and they can neither add, delete, nor rename modules. Incremental changes to the architecture are propagated with the help of fine-grained links; subsequently, the source code has to be adapted according to the changed specifications.

Reverse engineering is required when no architectural description is available or the software architecture got outdated. Recovering the software architecture aids in program understanding; as such, it constitutes a value on its own. In addition, it may serve as a first step of a reengineering process, which eventually aims at applying incremental forward engineering after conformance of the software architecture with the implementation has been established.

Tool support for reverse engineering is more difficult to provide than for forward engineering. Algorithms for reverse engineering attempt to detect patterns in the source code that may be mapped to functional or data abstraction components in the software architecture. These algorithms constitute heuristics creating a preliminary software architecture that usually requires manual rework (see ch. 9).

Roundtrip engineering differs from incremental forward engineering by supporting backward propagation of changes. Roundtrip engineering does not match the conceptual relation between software architecture (master) and implementation (dependent) since both artefacts are considered as peers. To ensure conformance of the implementation, roundtrip engineering should be applied in a restrictive way, allowing for backward propagation only in certain cases (e.g., to fix errors in the software architecture). Tool support for roundtrip engineering is currently provided primarily by research prototypes.

12.7 Summary and Open Problems

Summary

This chapter investigated the relation between architectural design and programming in the small. After having recapitulated the approach to architectural design that is introduced in ch. 2 of this book, the conceptual relation between architectural design and programming in the small was characterized: The software architecture serves as the *blueprint* for the implementation.

The transition from the software architecture to the implementation may be performed with the help of *deterministic model transformations*; the complexity of the mapping depends on the *conceptual distance* between the architecture modeling language and the respective target programming language. *Architectural conformance* of the implementation may be defined with a set of rules that formalize both the *completeness* and the *consistency* of the implementation.

Finally, different *software processes* were discussed, which are classified into *forward*, *reverse*, and *roundtrip engineering*. Five types of model transformations were identified that may be employed to realize these processes (*batch* and *incremental forward* and *backward transformations*, and *bidirectional synchronizations*).

The Message of this Chapter

The core message of this chapter concerns the nature of the relation between architectural design and programming in the small: The software architecture acts as the *blueprint* of the implementation. Large and complex systems can be realized successfully only when the software architecture has been designed carefully and the implementation conforms to the software architecture. However, frequently the central role of software architecture is not recognized.

To ensure conformance of the implementation with the software architecture, *software architects* and *programmers* need to *cooperate closely*. *Conformance* must be *checked* and *re-established frequently*, otherwise the implementation will deviate from the software architecture, resulting in architectural erosion. Since the architecture serves as a specification for the implementation, cooperation between software architects and programmers is *not symmetric*: The software architecture plays the role of the master artefact, on which the implementation depends. Thus, *incremental forward engineering* was identified as the process variant which offers the best match to the conceptual relation between software architecture and implementation and provides the required flexibility to propagate changes into the implementation.

Open Problems

The notion of a blueprint implies an *architecture-centered process*. However, many current process models do not acknowledge the central role of architectural design. In particular, *agile processes* such as Extreme Programming /BA 14/ or Scrum /SS 20/ focus on the delivery of working software and tend to consider other artefacts of the software process as documentation that is expensive to create and maintain. However, the effort of architectural design has to be invested, in particular for the development of large, complex and long-lived software systems.

As stated above, we recommend an *incremental process* that constantly keeps the software architecture and the implementation synchronized. However, *tool support* for such a process still is an open problem (in spite of the work that has been done so far). Powerful tools are required for checking and enforcing conformance. Only when such tools are available, is it possible to perform the incremental architecture-centered process sketched above successfully.

12.8 References

/BA 14/ Beck, K./ Andres, C.: Extreme Programming Explained – Embrace Change, 2nd ed., 216 pp., Addison-Wesley (2014)

/BG 08/ Bork, M./ Geiger, L./ Schneider, Chr./ Zündorf, A.: Towards Roundtrip Engineering – A Template-Based Reverse Engineering Approach, in.: Schieferdecker, I./Hartman, A. (eds): Model Driven Architecture – Foundations and Applications, Proc. 4th European Conf., 33-47, LNCS 5095, Springer (2008)

/CC 90/ Chikofsky, E.J./ Cross II, J.H.: Reverse Enginering and Design Recovery: A Taxonomy, IEEE Software 7(1) 13-17 (1990)

/CC 01/ Canfora, G./ Cimitile, A./ De Luca, A./ Di Lucca, G. A.: Decomposing Legacy Systems into Objects: An Eclectic Approach, Information and Software Technology 43 (6) 401-412 (2001)

/CL 15/ Caracciolo, A./ Lungu, M.F./ Nierstrasz, O.: A Unified Approach to Architecture Conformance Checking, Proc. 12th Working IEEE/IFIP Conference on Software Architecture, 41-50 (2015)

/DK 76/ DeRemer, F./ Kron, H.H.: Programming in the Large versus Programming in the Small, IEEE Transactions on Software Engineering SE-2(2) 80-86 (1976)

/En 86/ Engels, G.: Graphs as Central Data Structures in a Software Development Environment (in German), Doct. Diss., University of Osnabrück, Germany, 190 pp. (1986)

/Go 23/ Gosling, J. et al.: The Java Language Specification – Java SE 20 Edition, 837 pp., Oracle (2023)

/KR 00/ Kernighan, B.W./ Ritchie, D.: The C Programming Language, 2nd ed., 288 pp., Prentice Hall (2000)

/KW 98/ Kazman, R./ Woods, S.G./ Carriere, S.J.: Requirements for Integrating Software Architecture and Reengineering Models: CORUM II, Proc. 5th Working Conference on Reverse Engineering, 154-163 (1998)

/Le 88/ Lewerentz, C.: Interactive Design of Large Program Systems (in German), Doct. Diss., RWTH Aachen University, 179 pp., Informatik-Fachberichte 194, Springer (1988)

/Li 22/ Li, R. et al.: Understanding Software Architecture Erosion – A Systematic Mapping Study, Journal of Software Evolution and Process 34(3), 45 pp. (2022)

/LW 90/ Liu, S. S./ Wilde, N.: Identifying Objects in a Conventional Procedural Language: An Example of Data Design Recovery, in Proc. Conf. on Software Maintenance (CSM '90), 266-271, IEEE Comp. Soc. Press (1990)

/Na 19/ Nagl, M.: Gothic Churches and Informatics (in German), 304 pp., Springer Vieweg (2019)

/Na 90/ Nagl, M.: Software Engineering – Methodological Programming in the Large (in German), 387 pp., Springer (1990), plus further extensions for lectures on Software Architectures 1990 to 2020

/Na 96/ Nagl, M. (ed.): Building Tightly Integrated Software Development Environments: The IPSEN Approach, 728 pp., LNCS 1170, Springer (1996)

/Na 99/ Nagl, M.: Software Engineering with Ada 95 (in German), 496 pp., Vieweg (1999)

/Ob 14/ Object Management Group: Model Driven Architecture (MDA) – MDA Guide rev. 2.0, 15 pp., OMG Document ormsc/2014-06-01 (2014)

/Pa 72/ Parnas, D.: On the Criteria to be Used in Decomposing Systems into Modules, Comm. ACM 15(12) 1053-58 (1972)

/Pa 10/ Passos, L. et al.: Static Architecture-Conformance Checking: An Illustrative Overview, IEEE Software 27(5) 82-89 (2010)

/RD 21/ Rosca, D./ Domingues, L.: A Systematic Comparison of Roundtrip Software Engineering Approaches Applied to UML Class Diagram, Procedia Computer Science 181, 861-868 (2021)

/Ro 70/ Royce, W.R.: Management of the Development of Large Systems, Proc. IEEE WESCON, pp. 1-9 (1970)

/SB 12/ de Silva, L./ Balasubramaniam, D.: Controlling Software Architecture Erosion: A Survey, Journal of Systems and Software 85(1) 132-151 (2012)

/Sc 86/ Schäfer, W.: An Integrated Software Development Environment: Concepts, Design and Implementation (in German), Doct. Diss., University of Osnabrück, Germany, 259 pp., VDI Verlag (1986)

/Sc 06/ Schmidt, D.C.: Model-Driven Engineering, IEEE Computer 39(2) 25-31 (2006)

/SS 20/ Schwaber, K./ Sutherland, J.: The Scrum Guide – The Definitive Guide to Scrum: The Rules of the Game, https://scrumguides.org/docs/scrumguide/v2020/2020-Scrum-Guide-US.pdf, 14 pp. (2020)

/St 09/ Steinberg, D./ Budinsky, F./ Paternostro, M./ Merks, E.: EMF Eclipse Modeling Framework, 2nd ed., 704 pp., the eclipse series, Addison-Wesley (2009)

/Te 15/ Terra, R./ Valente, T.M./ Czarnecki, K./ Bighona, R.S.: A Recommendation System for Repairing Violations Detected by Static Architecture Conformance Checking, Software Practice and Experience 45, 315-342 (2015)

/We 91/ Westfechtel, B.: Revision and Consistency Control in an Integrated Software Development Environment (in German), Doct. Diss., RWTH Aachen University, 321 pp., Informatik-Fachberichte 280, Springer (1991)

/Xi 13/ Xiong, Y. et al.: Synchronizing Concurrent Model Updates Based on Bidirectional Transformation, Software and Systems Modeling 12, 89-104 (2013)

13 Architecture-Centered Project Organization

Bernhard Westfechtel

Software Engineering, University of Bayreuth, bernhard.westfechtel@uni-bayreuth.de

Abstract

Project organization is a working area that is concerned with the management of products, activities, and resources in software projects. Project organization is the only managerial working area in the lifecycle model used throughout this book, and is addressed by disciplines known as project management, software configuration management, or process management.

In contrast, architectural design belongs to the class of technical working areas. Like all other technical working areas, architectural design is controlled by project organization. Conversely, architectural design strongly impacts project organization, particularly with respect to implementation and quality assurance. Accordingly, we present a management approach that acknowledges the central role of architectural design, but also takes the importance of other working areas into account.

Key words: Project organization, software architecture, project management, software configuration management, process management

13.1 Introduction

According to the working area model introduced in ch. 1, *project organization* (PO) is concerned with the management of software projects, while *architectural design* (AR) is in charge of creating a blueprint of the software system to be implemented. As illustrated in fig. 13.1 (a simplified version of the working area model from ch. 1), this chapter primarily focuses on the relations between project organization and architectural design. Before delving deeper into the study of these relations, a more general view on the software process is required: As emphasized in the figure, project organization is a *managerial working area* that controls all *technical working areas*. This is illustrated by double-headed arrows between project organization and the other working areas. Technical working areas are in charge of creating artefacts that describe the software system from different perspectives. In contrast, project organization needs to coordinate activities performed in technical working areas. Thus, the managerial working area and the technical working areas are arranged in *control-feedback loops*: An arrowhead pointing to a technical working area stands for *control*, its opposite represents *feedback* that influences management.

Due to its central role in the software process, architectural design strongly influences project organization. Since the software architecture defines the modules and subsystems to be implemented, it may be used to define work packages (tasks) assigned to programmers. Similarly, testing tasks may be defined based on the software architecture. Milestones may be defined for project planning, referring to the components of the software architecture. Finally, the project team may be organized according to the structure of the software architecture.

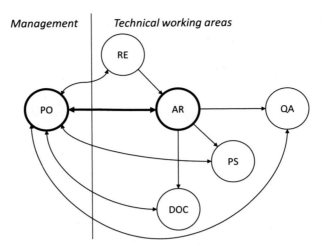

Fig. 13.1: Focus of the current chapter

This chapter is structured as follows: Sect. 13.2 introduces basic notions and clarifies what we understand by management. Sect. 13.3 briefly summarizes several well-known approaches to management known from the literature. Sect. 13.4 proposes an architecture-centered approach to project organization, and sect. 13.5 concludes.

13.2 Management: Basic Notions and Understanding

This section introduces our understanding and use of the term management, roughly following /We 99/, sect. 1.2. In general, *management* can be defined as "all activities and tasks undertaken by one or more persons for the purpose of planning and controlling the activities of others in order to achieve an objective or complete an activity that could not be achieved by the others acting alone" /Th 88/. This definition stresses *coordination* as the essential function of management /MC 94/. More specifically, we are concerned here with the management of software processes. In this context, management coordinates the work of software engineers who cooperate to develop or maintain a complex software system.

For the purpose of management, the software process has to be considered and represented at an adequate level of abstraction. At a *coarse-grained level*, software processes are represented at the level of phases or milestones. At a *medium-grained level*, software processes are decomposed into tasks that are assigned to software engineers. At a *fine-grained level*, the detailed steps are considered that software engineers perform to complete their assignments.

While *senior management* is usually concerned only with the coarse-grained level of phases and milestones, *project managers* also need to address the medium-grained level in order to coordinate the daily work of software engineers effectively. However, they need to abstract from the fine-grained level because it is neither desirable nor feasible to exercise too detailed control over the work of software engineers.

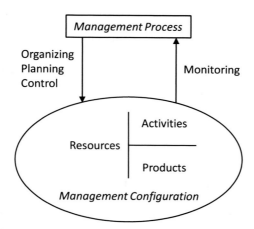

Fig. 13.2: Management configuration (/We 99/, p. 10)

To support both senior and project managers, the *managerial level*, which defines how management views software processes, comprises both coarse-grained and medium-grained representations of the software process. The *technical level* refines the managerial level down to the details of fine-grained process steps, which are not controlled by managers.

The elements to be managed may be classified into three categories. *Products* record the results of the work performed by software engineers throughout the whole lifecycle, including e.g. requirements specifications, analysis models, software architectures, module implementations, test plans, test code, test results, build plans, technical and user documentations, etc. *Activities* are work units that create these products, such as design of a software architecture or implementation of some module. *Resources* are the assets that are required to perform activities, including both human resources (software engineers) and technical resources (hardware and software).

For the purpose of management, an abstract representation of the elements to be managed is required. As argued above, project managers require a representation that is refined up to the medium-grained level. This representation is called *management configuration* and includes products, activities, and resources, as well as their mutual relations (lower part of fig. 13.2).

A management configuration represents products, activities, and resources from the technical working areas (right-hand side of fig. 13.1). From the perspective of a manager, a management configuration constitutes a *product* on which the manager operates (including e.g. a project plan, a representation of the project team, and a configuration of artefacts). The *management process* shown at the top of fig. 13.2 employs the management configuration to plan, organize, and control technical activities. Furthermore, the management configuration is used to provide feedback to the management process. Thus, managerial and technical activities are arranged in a *control-feedback loop*.

13.3 Other Approaches to Management

Numerous approaches to managing software processes have been developed. Below, these approaches are classified into three categories: project, software configuration and software process management. With respect to these approaches, we focus on the following issues: coverage (of products, activities, and resources), granularity, and the role of software architectures.

Project Management

Project management /Ke 22/ is a generic discipline that is concerned with the management of projects in different domains. Typically, project management is decomposed into functions such as planning, organizing, staffing, leading, and monitoring. Planning is based on activity networks such as *Gantt diagrams* or *CPM networks*. Often, these plans are fairly coarse-grained, focusing on milestones to be achieved by the project team. However, project plans may be refined down to the level of tasks assigned to individual members of the project team. Different forms of organizing the project team have been proposed, including e.g. functional, matrix, and role-based organization. Organizational structures are represented by *organization charts*. Since products are domain-specific, they are not considered in generic approaches to project management; in particular, this applies to software architectures.

Generic approaches to project management have been transferred and applied to software projects, see e.g. /Th 88/. Specific approaches to managing software projects do exist, and will be discussed below (see software process management). See /Pa 01/ for an approach to software project management that acknowledges the central role of architectural design for planning, cost estimation, and task assignment.

Software Configuration Management

Software configuration management is the discipline of controlling the evolution of complex software systems /Ti 88/. In an IEEE standard on systems and software engineering, configuration management is defined as a "discipline applying technical and administrative direction and surveillance to: identify and document the functional and physical characteristics of a configuration item, control changes to those characteristics, record and report change processing and implementation status, and verify compliance with specified requirements" /IEEE 12/.

Software configuration management primarily focuses on *product integrity*. However, products are usually considered as files organized into directories, abstracting from the actual contents of the artefacts stored in these files and their mutual non-hierarchical relations. Architectural design does not play a major role in software configuration management, even though both disciplines are interrelated and even overlap /WC 03/.

To ensure product integrity, software configuration management applies strict procedures for *change control*. Essentially, the software process is considered as a set of independent changes, resulting in corresponding tasks assigned to software engineers. In this way, minor changes performed in software maintenance such as bug fixes and small isolated modifications may be handled. However, planning and control of more pervasive changes, as they are performed in software development or in software reengineering, are not addressed.

Software Process Management

Numerous process models have been proposed, a few of which are discussed below. We distinguish between *plan-driven processes*, which are inspired by mainstream engineering fields and are based on a well-structured plan-design-build paradigm, and *agile processes*, which favor a lightweight management approach and are executed in short iterative cycles /BT 05/.

The *Rational Unified Process* (RUP) /KK 03/ is a plan-driven process for object-oriented software engineering that is based on the Unified Software Development Process /JB 99/. The Rational Unified Process makes a distinction between two dimensions: *disciplines*, which roughly correspond to working areas in the lifecycle model used throughout this book, and *phases*, which constitute consecutive time spans in a software project being dedicated to different goals. The software architecture plays a central role in all phases. In *inception*, a coarse architecture is designed for an initial feasibility study. In *elaboration*, this architecture is refined such that all crucial design decisions have been performed and all technical risks have been eliminated. In *construction*, the initial implementation of the architecture is refined and completed. In *transition*, the implemented system is delivered to the customer.

The *V Model* (official name: V-Modell XT /An 20/) is a standard for software processes that are executed by or on behalf of governmental organizations in Germany. Similar to the Rational Unified Process, the V Model defines a set of *disciplines*, including system design for both hardware and software components. Accordingly, (software) architectural design is a part of system design. *Process building blocks* aggregate activities from different disciplines, and *project strategies* compose process building blocks in turn. In contrast to the Rational Unified process, the V Model does not assign a central role to architectural design.

Extreme Programming (XP) /BA 14/ is an agile process that focuses primarily on implementation and testing. Extreme Programming is designed for small teams whose members cooperate closely e.g. through *pair programming*. The primary artefact of interest is working software, including both program and test code that are created in a *test-driven development* process. Extreme Programming relies on lightweight management practices. The long-term work is planned in quarterly cycles. More emphasis is put on weekly cycles, organizing the daily work of the team. A short meeting at the beginning of the week is used to define work units in terms of story cards, each of which requires a few hours of work to be completed.

Scrum /SS 20/ is another agile process which differs from Extreme Programming by focusing exclusively on management. The requirements to a product to be developed are recorded in a *product backlog*. Development is organized into *sprints*, which should not exceed one calendar month. The *sprint backlog* is extracted from the product backlog and defines the tasks to be completed in the current sprint. Entries from the sprint backlog are assigned to the development team in daily meetings. Scrum defines three roles: The *product owner* defines the requirements. The *development team* is responsible for product development. The team is self-organizing rather than being directed by a project manager. The *Scrum master* merely ensures that the rules of the Scrum process are followed.

Table 13.3 summarizes the main characteristics of the management approaches described above with respect to three criteria: coverage (of products, activities, and resources), granularity, and role of architecture.

(a) Generic approaches to *project management* cover activities through project plans and resources through organizations of the project team. Project plans may be coarse- or medium-grained. However, generic approaches to project management fail to take the central role of the software architecture as a blueprint of the system to be built into account; the software architecture is not exploited for project planning.

(b) *Software configuration management* mainly focuses on product integrity and pays little attention to the organization of the project team. Only change control activities are considered; a coarse-grained level above change requests is missing. Software configuration management covers all artefacts of the software lifecycle. However, the software architecture is treated as a black box and is handled like any other artefact.

(c) The *Rational Unified Process* provides a comprehensive process model covering products, activities and resources. This process model includes all levels of granularity, down to detailed instructions for object-oriented design. Furthermore, it acknowledges the central role of the software architecture (but also of other artefacts such as the use case model).

(d) Like the Rational Unified Process, the *V Model* defines in a detailed way different types of products, activities, and resources. With respect to granularity, it does not go as far as the Unified Process. In particular, the V Model does not prescribe specific modeling notations like object-oriented modeling. Architectural design is covered by the V Model, but the software architecture essentially is just an ordinary artefact.

(e) While *Extreme Programming* does cover products, activities, and resources, as well, it mainly focuses on programming and testing. Long-term project planning is hardly addressed at all. Medium-grained planning is performed in terms of story cards, defining small work units assigned to developers. The software architecture does not play any role in Extreme Programming.

(f) *Scrum* constitutes an agile management approach which defines a simple role model for project participants and organizes activities with the help of product and sprint backlogs, which constitute the only artefacts considered by Scrum. Thus, Scrum is as architecture-agnostic as Extreme Programming. Scrum merely addresses management practices, not programming or testing practices.

Approach		Coverage	Granularity	Role of Architecture
Project Management		Activities Resources	Coarse-grained Medium-grained	Architecture-agnostic
Software Configuration Management		Products Activities	Medium-grained	Architecture-agnostic
Software Process Management	Rational Unified Process	Products Activities Resources	Coarse-grained Medium-grained Fine-grained	Architecture-centered
	V Model	Products Activities Resources	Coarse-grained Medium-grained	Architecture-aware
	Extreme Programming	Products Activities Resources	Medium-grained Fine-grained	Architecture-agnostic
	Scrum	Activities Resources	Coarse-grained Medium-grained	Architecture-agnostic

Table 13.3: Classification of management approaches

13.4 An Architecture-Centered Approach

Most of the approaches discussed above do not recognize the central role of the software architecture. As a blueprint of the system to be built, the software architecture strongly impacts project organization in various ways:

(a) *Project planning*: The architecture may be used to assign development tasks to the members of the project team, and to determine the order in which these tasks may be executed. Furthermore, the project plan may contain milestones referring to the completion of modules or subsystems.

(b) *Cost estimation*: As part of project planning, cost estimation may be based on the software architecture. For example, the post-architecture model variant of CO-COMO II /Bo 00/ employs the software architecture to derive a cost estimate.

(c) *Team organization*: The project team may be organized according to the software architecture, e.g., by assigning a group within the team to each of its subsystems.

(d) *Impact analysis*: In a reengineering effort that deeply impacts the software system to be improved or adapted, the impact of changes to the system may be determined with the help of dependencies among components of the software architecture. Based on such an impact analysis, the reengineering project may be planned and organized.

In the following, we demonstrate the impact of the software architecture on project organization with the help of an *integrated approach* to managing *products*, *activities* and *resources* that was proposed and described in /We 99, He 08a, Kr 98, Jä 03, Sc 02, He 08/. To illustrate this approach, we refer to an example drawn from a research project on integrated software engineering environments /Na 96/.

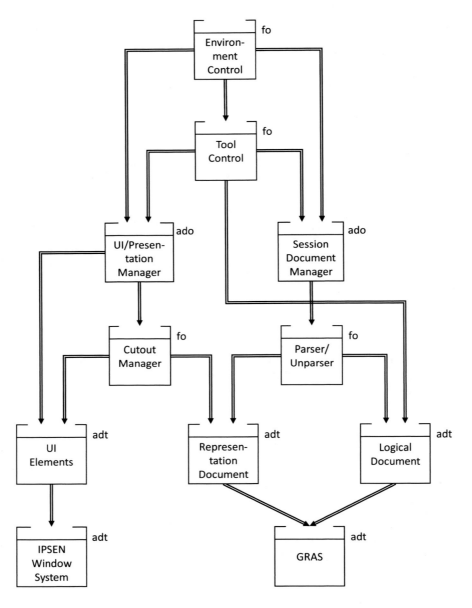

Fig. 13.4: Coarse architecture of the IPSEN environment (/Na 96/, p. 381)

Example

In the *IPSEN* project /Na 96/, an *I*ntegrated *P*roject *S*upport *EN*vironment was developed. Since IPSEN was an innovative research project, the software architecture of the software engineering environment to be built was not known beforehand, but was designed and evolved in the course of this project.

The diagram of fig. 13.4 employs the modeling notation introduced in ch. 2 of this book. Each box represents a component (*module* or *subsystem*). Components are classified into *abstract data types* (adt), *abstract data objects* (ado), and *function objects* (fo). Double arrows represent *usability relationships*.

At the bottom layer, IPSEN Window System provides an interface to the window system, and GRAS constitutes a graph-based database system for structured documents. UI Elements abstracts from the low-level services of the window system. Logical Document is used to store and manipulate abstract syntax graphs. Representation Document offers a data structure for text and diagram representations of logical documents. Parser/Unparser offers transformations between logical and representation documents; Cutout Manager is responsible for the mapping of representations to UI elements. These components are controlled through the Session Document Manager and the UI/Presentation Manager, respectively. Tool Control is used to control single tools, while Environment Control controls the whole environment.

Management of Activities

Due to the dynamics of software processes, project plans evolve continuously while a project is being executed. This is considered by *dynamic task nets* /HJ 96/. A task net may be considered as an extension of a project plan such as e.g. a Gantt diagram. It consists of *tasks*, their *inputs* and *outputs*, and various kinds of *task relations*. From the perspective of a project manager, a task net is a product employed for project planning and monitoring, and belongs to the activities part of the management configuration (fig. 13.2). During the lifetime of a project, a task net may change not only with respect to the execution status of tasks, but also with respect to its structure: Elements of task nets may be added, deleted, and modified as required.

Fig. 13.5 displays a coarse-grained task net that is composed of tasks that need to be refined further. Each *task* is represented by a labeled box with attached *input* and *output ports* (white and black circles, respectively). Tasks are assigned to (groups of) engineers, ports refer to artefacts. Tasks are ordered by *control flows* (thick solid arrows), which resemble precedence relationships in project plans. Control flows are refined by *data flows* (thin solid arrows) that connect output to input ports. Finally, *feedback flows* (dashed arrows) represent feedback in the software process, implying that preceding tasks have to be improve their outputs.

The task net of fig. 13.5 seems to represent a sequential, phase-oriented process where each successor task is executed only after its predecessors have completed. However, this is not necessarily the case. The execution behavior depends on the type of control flow (which is not visualized in the diagram). In the case of a *sequential control flow*, the successor may start only after its predecessor has terminated. In the case of a *simultaneous control flow*, the successor may start after its predecessor has started; thus, execution of predecessor and successor task may overlap. For example, requirements engineering and architectural design may overlap when their connecting control flow is defined as simultaneous rather than sequential.

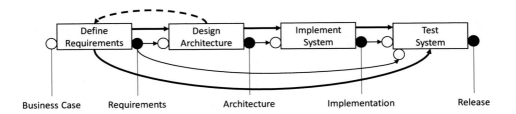

Fig. 13.5: Coarse-grained dynamic task net

Traditional project plans are acyclic graphs that may not represent feedback in the software process. In dynamic task nets, feedback may be expressed by *feedback flows* that are oriented oppositely to control flows. Usually, feedback flows are inserted into task nets on demand only. As an example, fig. 13.5 shows a feedback flow from architectural design back to requirements engineering, which may be caused by inadequate, incomplete, or inconsistent requirements. A feedback flow may be refined by a data flow, along which the problem which occurred is communicated (not shown in fig. 13.5).

Apart from the feedback flow, the task net of fig. 13.5 is *static* and invariant to the project to be executed. While the task net does contain an architectural design task, the impact of the architecture on project organization is not visible yet. As soon as the software architecture is available, planning may proceed further. Only then is it possible to assign development tasks for the components of the software architecture. To this end, the coarse-grained task net is refined further down to a level where we may assign development tasks to the members of the team.

In the following, we consider the refinement of the task Implement System. The software architecture defines the components to be implemented and tested, but it does not fix a development strategy. Here, we assume a simple *bottom-up development strategy*: Each component is implemented and tested after all components on which it depends. How strictly this order is enforced, depends on the types of control flows: Sequential control flows enforce a strict order. Simultaneous control flows allow for overlapping development tasks; in this case, preliminary results are released to successors before the predecessor has terminated.

Fig. 13.6 shows the resulting *task net*. The topology of the task net is independent of the selected control flow types. To emphasize the correspondence to the software architecture from fig. 13.4, the task net is drawn vertically rather than horizontally. The task net is derived from the software architecture as follows: For each component, a corresponding task is created. For each usability relationship, a control flow is created that is oriented in the opposite direction. This demonstrates the close correspondence between the software architecture and the project plan. Please note that the components at the bottom of the software architecture are developed first, and thus appear at the top of the task net.

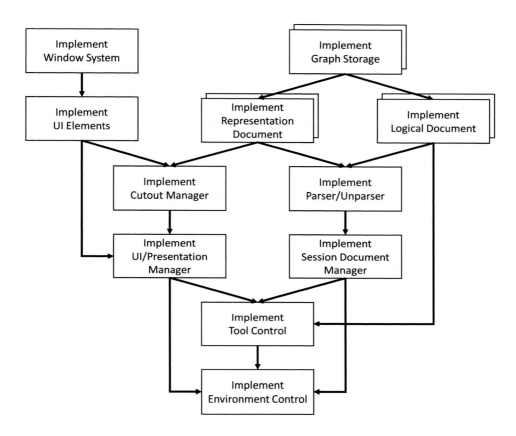

Fig. 13.6: Refining task net for Implement System (only control flows)

So far, we have assumed a *software development* scenario where all components of the software architecture have to be implemented from scratch. In software maintenance, many changes are minor ones (e.g., small bug fixes), but *architecturally significant changes* may need to be addressed, as well. In such a case, an *impact analysis* may be carried out with the help of the software architecture in order to determine which components are affected and in which order the changes should be addressed. Subsequently, either a new task net may be constructed which contains only a subset of the tasks in the development task net from fig. 13.6. This task net would contain *change tasks* which receive the current versions of the artefacts to be updated as inputs and deliver the new versions as outputs.

Alternatively, the already existing task net may be reused. For example, let us assume that the graph storage should be re-implemented on top of a relational database management system. If this change affects its export interface, then the implementations of Logical Document and Representation Document may have to be updated, as well. If these updates do not affect the export interfaces of these components, change propagation may stop by reusing the already existing implementations of Cutout Manager and Parser/Unparser. Thus, new *task versions* (represented by double-framed rectangles) are created only for affected tasks.

Management of Resources

The software architecture may also affect team organization. In particular, this applies to large and complex software systems as the IPSEN software engineering environment. In such a case, it is difficult to implement the (secondary) shared code practice as suggested in Extreme Programming: Each developer should have the right (and competence) to modify each part of the system at any time. Rather, dedicated product expertise is required to change complex components such as e.g. the underlying graph storage. Therefore, a *component-based team organization* may be preferred where each developer acquires technical expertise in a certain component and is responsible only for this component.

Fig. 13.7 illustrates management of resources. As it is commonplace in project management /Ke 22/, we distinguish between *organizing* (defining the organizational structure of the project) and *staffing* (selecting the employees to fill the positions in the project team). In addition to general positions such as Manager and Chief Designer, the organization chart for the IPSEN project defines positions for developing the components of the software architecture such as Database Expert and UI Expert. Tasks are assigned to positions rather than directly to employees. Thus, an employee receives assignments according to the roles (s)he plays in the team. When the employee is replaced, the successor will inherit his (her) task assignments.

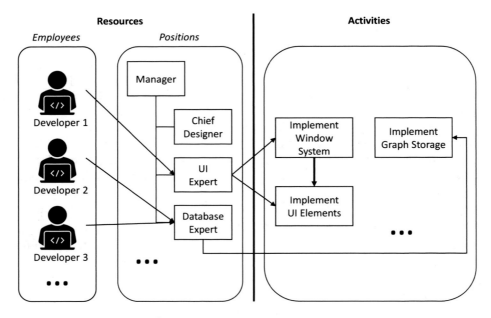

Fig. 13.7: Management of resources

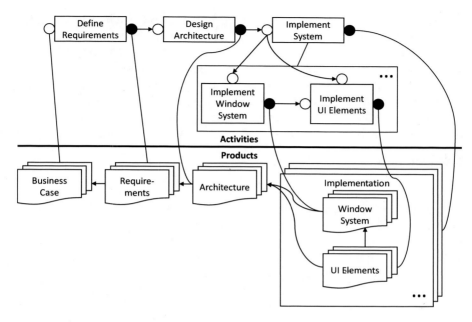

Fig. 13.8: Management of products

Both the mappings of employees to positions and the assignments of positions to tasks need not be 1:1, but may be *m:n* in general. For example, in fig. 13.7 two developers share the Database Expert position due to the complexity of this component. In contrast, only a single developer is assigned to the UI Expert position because the user interface components are simpler than the database component. For the same reason, the UI expert is assigned to two tightly related components (Window System and UI Elements).

Management of Products

Fig. 13.8 illustrates the management of products and the integration between products and activities. *Software configuration management* is in charge of managing the products of software engineering activities. All artefacts created throughout the software lifecycle are aggregated into *product configurations*. The symbols used for these artefacts indicate that they are submitted to *version control*. A version represents a state of an evolving artefact. Versioned artefacts are organized *hierarchically*, as shown for the implementation artefacts. Furthermore, they are connected by non-hierarchical *dependencies*. For example, the architecture depends on the requirements, which in turn depend on the initial business case.

The upper part of fig. 13.8 shows some activities and their connecting data flows; control and feedback flows were omitted from the figure. As illustrated by the lines crossing the border between activities and products, ports are connected to versioned artefacts.

The software architecture deeply impacts parts of the overall product configuration. As the figure sketches, implementation artefacts (program source code) are derived from the software architecture (see also ch. 12 on the relation between architectural design and implementation). Ideally, the source code artefacts should be mapped 1:1 to modules of the software architecture, and their implementation dependencies (e.g. import relations) should be traced back 1:1 to usability and inheritance relationships in the software architecture. Altogether, we may conclude that the *software architecture* has a *deep impact* on the *management* of products, activities, and resources.

13.5 Summary and Open Problems

Summary

In this chapter, we explored the relationships between architectural design and project organization. To this end, we defined basic notions and clarified our understanding of the term "management". Subsequently, other approaches to management were discussed, including project, software configuration and software process management. The discussion revealed that many existing approaches do not consider the role of software architectures in an adequate way. Finally, an approach to management was introduced that goes beyond other approaches as described below.

The Message of this Chapter

The management approach of this chapter is characterized by the following features:
(a) *Integrated management of products, activities, and resources.* The elements to be managed as well as their mutual relations are represented in an integrated management configuration which plays the role of a product from the perspective of a project manager. The manager employs the management configuration for planning, organizing, staffing, leading, and controlling.
(b) *Medium-grained approach.* The management configuration is not confined to the coarse-grained level of phases or milestones, but is refined to a medium-grained level such that the tasks assigned to software engineers as well as the artefacts produced by them are represented. In this way, software projects may be managed precisely without delving into irrelevant details.
(c) *Tight integration with other working areas.* Since the management configuration provides an abstraction of a technical configuration, management is integrated tightly with other working areas such as requirements engineering, architectural design, programming in the small, quality assurance, and documentation.
(d) *Central role of software architectures.* Since the software architecture serves as a blueprint of the software system to be developed, many artefacts and tasks may be derived from the software architecture. In particular, this applies to implementation and testing tasks, which refer to the components of the architecture. Thus, project plans may be derived from the software architecture, artefacts such as module implementations occur as parts of software configurations, and the project team may be organized according to the software architecture.

(e) *Dynamics of software processes.* Software processes evolve continuously, due to a number of reasons: (1) The knowledge about the software system to be developed evolves, in particular with respect to its software architecture. Thus, many tasks to be performed are not known beforehand. (2) Requirements may evolve continuously, requiring changes to dependent artefacts such as software architectures and implementations. (3) Feedback may occur in the software process, implying modifications of design decisions or fixing of errors. Furthermore, the consequences of these changes need to be propagated to dependent tasks and artefacts. The presented management approach considers all of these kinds of dynamics.

Open Problems

So far, a number of open problems have not been addressed:

(a) *Long-term software maintenance.* Primarily, software development processes following an incremental forward engineering approach were considered. Long-term software maintenance of existing systems was not studied in depth.

(b) *Long-term process evolution.* Software processes evolve with increasing experience gained in the respective domains. In order to obtain significant advances in software process performance, non-incremental process improvements may be required, as exemplified e.g. by compiler construction, which proceeded from systematically handwritten to generated compilers (*deep reuse*, see ch. 7).

(c) *Software product lines.* Families of software systems managed in a software product line /Po 05/ imply additional challenges for the management approach.

13.6 References

/An 20/ Angermeier, D. et al: V-Modell XT – Das deutsche Referenzmodell für Systementwicklungsprojekte, Version 2.3, Verein zur Weiterentwicklung des V-Modell XT e.V. (Weit e.V.), https://ftp.tu-clausthal.de/pub/institute/informatik/v-modell-xt/Releases/2.3/V-Modell-XT-Gesamt.pdf (2020)

/BA 14/ Beck, K./ Andres, C.: Extreme Programming Explained – Embrace Change, 2nd ed., 216 pp., Addison-Wesley (2014)

/Bo 00/ Boehm, B.W. et al.: Software Cost Estimation with COCOMO II, 544 pp., Prentice Hall (2000)

/BT 05/ Boehm, B./ Turner, R.: Balancing Agility and Discipline - A Guide for the Perplexed, 300 pp., Addison-Wesley (2005)

/He 08/ Heller, M.: Decentralized View-Based Management of Interorganizational Development Processes (in German), Doct. Diss., RWTH Aachen University, 501 pp., Shaker (2008)

/He 08a/ Heller, M. et al: An Adaptive and Reactive Management System for Project Coordination, in: Nagl, M./ Marquardt, W. (eds.): Collaborative and Distributed Chemical Engineering – From Understanding to Substantial Design Process Support, IMPROVE, 300-366, LNCS 4970, Springer (2008)

/HJ 96/ Heimann, P./ Joeris, G./ Krapp, C.A./ Westfechtel, B.: DYNAMITE: Dynamic Task Nets for Software Process Management, Proc. 18th International Conference on Software Engineering, 331-341, IEEE (1996)

/IEEE 12/ IEEE Computer Society: IEEE Standard for Configuration Management in Systems and Software Engineering, IEEE Standard 828-2012 (2012)

/JB 99/ Jacobson, I./ Booch, G./ Rumbaugh, J.: The Unified Software Development Process, 494 pp., Addison-Wesley, Object Technology Series (1999)

/Jä 03/ Jäger, D.: Supporting Interorganizational Cooperation in Complex Development Processes (in German), Doct. Diss., RWTH Aachen University, 266 pp., Augustinus, Aachener Beiträge zur Informatik 34 (2003)

/Ke 22/ Kerzner, H.: Project Management – A Systems Approach to Planning, Scheduling, and Controlling, 13th ed., 880 pp., Wiley (2022)

/Kr 98/ Krapp, C.A.: An Adaptable Environment for the Management of Development Processes, Doct. Diss., RWTH Aachen University, 196 pp., Augustinus, Aachener Beiträge zur Informatik 22 (1998)

/KK 03/ Kroll, P./ Kruchten, P.: The Rational Unified Process Made Easy - A Practitioner's Guide to the RUP, 458 pp., Addison-Wesley, Object Technology Series (2003)

/MC 94/ Malone, T.W./ Crowston, K.: The Interdisciplinary Study of Coordination, ACM Computing Surveys 26(1) 87-119 (1994)

/Na 96/ Nagl, M. (ed.): Building Tightly Integrated Software Development Environments: The IPSEN Approach, 728 pp., LNCS 1170, Springer (1996)

/Pa 01/ Paulish, D.J.: Architecture-Centric Software Project Management – A Practical Guide, 320 pp., Pearson Education, SEI Series in Software Engineering (2001)

/Po 05/ Pohl, K./ Böckle, G./van der Linden, F.: Software Product Lines – Foundations, Principles, and Techniques, Springer (2005)

/Sc 02/ Schleicher, A.: Management of Development Processes – An Evolutionary Approach, Doct. Dissert., RWTH Aachen University, 332 pp., Deutscher Universitäts-Verlag (2002)

/SS 20/ Schwaber, K./ Sutherland, J.: The Scrum Guide – The Definitive Guide to Scrum: The Rules of the Game, https://scrumguides.org/docs/scrumguide/v2020/2020-Scrum-Guide-US.pdf, 14 pp. (2020)

/Th 88/ Thayer, R.H.: Software Engineering Project Management: A Top-Down View, in: Thayer, R.H. (ed.): Tutorial Software Engineering Project Management, 15-54, IEEE Computer Society Press (1988)

/Ti 88/ Tichy, W.F.: Tools for Software Configuration Management, in: Winkler, J.F.H. (ed.): Proc. Int. Workshop on Software Version and Configuration Control, 1-20, Teubner (1988)

/WC 03/ Westfechtel, B./ Conradi, R.: Software Architecture and Software Configuration Management, in: Westfechtel, B./ van der Hoek, A. (eds.): SCM 2001/2003, 24-39, LNCS 2649, Springer (2003)

/We 99/ Westfechtel, B.: Models and Tools for Managing Development Processes, 418 pp., LNCS 1646, Springer (1999)

14 Quality Assurance and Documentation Related to Architectures

Manfred Nagl

Software Engineering, RWTH Aachen University, nagl@cs.rwth-aachen.de

Abstract

In this chapter, we regard the connections of architectures to quality assurance and to documentation. Both are different, but the relations to architectures share some similarities. The study can be extended to all technical working areas (RE, AR, PS) and accompanying working areas (QA, DOC and PO). We restrict the discussion here mainly to architectures, according to the title of this book. First we make clear what we understand by quality assurance and by documentation. This is especially necessary for the term documentation, for which different definitions exist.

Different examples for documentation and quality assurance are given, in order to get an overview of how they are related to architectures on one side and on the other, what typical situations between documents, their increments, and subconfigurations exist. The detected similarities give arguments why both are discussed here.

Thus, this chapter is not about documentation and quality assurance in general. It concentrates on architectures and there on the parts of the overall configuration corresponding to documentation and quality assurance.

Key words: software architectures, quality assurance, documentation, links between different artefacts, mutual relations between architectures and quality assurance or documentation

14.1 Introduction

We have discussed the relation RE-AR in sect. 11, AR-PS in sect. 12, AR-PO in sect. 13. Now we deepen AR-QA but also AR-DOC in this chapter, see fig. 14.1. The preceding ch. 10 gave characterizations of all AR-X relations.

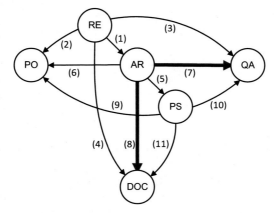

Fig. 14.1: Relations of architectures to quality assurance and documentation

There are arguments (a) on *conceptual* and (b) on *user* side that both relations AR-QA and AR-DOC are given in one chapter. Again, we do *not* discuss *tools* here. The arguments on conceptual level give a frame, how tools should and would behave.

The *chapter* is structured *as follows*: First, we define what we understand by the terms quality assurance and documentation. This is important for the term documentation, which is overloaded in literature and where we have a special meaning in mind. The following two sections discuss the relations of architectures to documentation and quality assurance, respectively, on increment, artifact, and grouping level, thereby refining the coarse relations of fig. 14.1. Finally, we sum up what we have discussed, characterize the similarities/ differences of documentation and quality assurance, argue that both are discussed here, and sketch open problems.

14.2 Fundamental Terms

Quality Assurance

Quality assurance within the software development or maintenance process means to keep or to improve *software quality* /CH 18, EM 12, Ga 03, IS 11, JD 21, Wa 17, Wi SQ/. The different *aspects* of software quality are given in fig. 14.2 according to the ISO/IEC 9126 standard /IS 11/. Their compliance depend on the form of the process, the quality of the team members, the environment of the process, and alike.

Functionality and *usability* depend mainly on how the requirements specification is carefully worked out and afterwards translated, via a reasonable architecture into the systems' code. The same is valid for *reliability*, *efficiency*, *modifiability*, and *portability*. The architecture is even more important here.

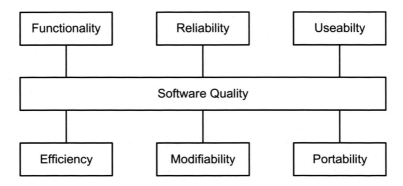

Fig. 14.2: Quality aspects according to /IS 11/, there more detailed

There are quite different *means* at hand to *care for quality,* on management, technical, or organizational side: (a) On project *management side* by carefully selecting team members, demanding for expertise, offering further education, and a reasonable environment, (b) on *technical side* by following reasonable review or test methods, using advanced tools on technical and also quality assurance side, (c) on *organizational side* by defining clear and realistic goals, corresponding tasks and results, suitable project team forms, looking for stable conditions in relation to the customer, etc.

Furthermore, we can *classify* quality assurance from the *way, how to do* it: (i) *human investigations* as human reviews, inspections, walkthroughs, (ii) *experiments* as all forms of tests, (iii) *semiautomatic* support by interactive *tools* or *automatic* support by software algorithms, (iv) *formal* ways, as formal logical Floyd/ Hoare verification /Wi Ho/ or design by contract /Me 86/ in comparison to *informal* procedures, (v) *constructive* steps of quality assurance in the development process to decrease or minimize errors or mistakes, or *analytic* steps to check given results, and so on.

Of *practical value* is the dimension constructive vs. analytic. *Constructive* means to care for quality in the development or maintenance process by applying methods, languages, tools, management or organizational care, etc. *Analytic* quality assurance tries to find errors or mistakes afterwards in the results, either by the developer or by an external person, such that no or less errors remain. The most important methods are (i) human analyses and (ii) experiments by different forms of test.

Quality assurance is always *double-sided*: Any result in the development process is quality assured directly by its developer. We call this *internal* quality assurance. There is no way to delegate quality assurance completely to someone else. However, it is an often-used practice that quality assurance is, in addition and furthermore, done by an external and neutral person from a separate quality assurance department (*external* quality assurance).

The developer has a *double role*: developer in a *constructive* role for any activity of fig. 14.1 and, at the same time, quality assurance engineer for his/ her results. The external person has a *single and destructive role*: He/ she is primarily a quality assurance engineer to find problems. He/ she can read, comment, and criticize, but not correct or improve directly, to keep the two roles and the responsibilities separate.

In this chapter we *concentrate* on the *relation of quality assurance to architectures*, although quality assurance is practiced also for all the other working areas (see again fig. 14.1), namely the other technical working areas requirements engineering and programming-in-the-small, and even more, also for the nontechnical areas as project organization, documentation, and even for quality assurance itself.

Quality assurance forms in connection to *architectures* can be: (a) A review for the whole architecture or reviews for its parts, as (b) a part of the architecture, which is connected, (c) a subsystem of the architecture, (d) the bottom infrastructure, (e) a layer of the architecture, or (f) export interfaces and import relations. Furthermore, as we have learned from chs. 2 and 3, the whole architecture or its parts can have (g) different views, as the abstract and static view, the semantical view, the concurrency view, the distribution view, or the efficiency view.

Even more, we can regard *traceability connections to other areas*, as (h) from RE to AR (see ch. 11), to see whether all requirements are answered on the architecture side or vice versa, whether (i) the architecture contains no parts which are not in relation to requirements, directly or indirectly. Similarly, we can check whether (j) all modules as atomic components have been implemented or, vice versa, (k) all components have an architectural description.

Tests at the developer side can be on component, subsystem, or integration level. The same applies for the acceptance test at the customer's site. All have to do with the *code* level. They also have to do with the *architecture* level, as usually in an incremental manner the code of a component is integrated to an already integrated set of code. The way of integration - which components in which order - is determined by looking at the architecture.

There are *further approaches* and papers combining software *architectures* and *quality* assurance as, for example, metrics-based /CH 10/ or model-based /FG 12/ to name only two. We do not discuss them here.

Documentation

There exist quite *different semantics* of the term *documentation*, in a technical or a more general sense /CS 89, DL 14, GG 15, SA 05, Wi SD, Wi SQ/: (a) One is on *technical writing* about results: In general, all descriptions should be complete, easy to understand, precise, etc. This applies to any kind of results and their documentation, not only to software. (b) The next, demands quality *requests for specific parts* of the software development process results, as for the requirements specification, the architecture description, the code, the user documentation in contrast to the technical documentation /Wi SD/, etc. (c) The third meaning of documentation is that all the results of single developers of a project team are *collected* and *presented* in a *well-organized way*. This applies to documents (also named artifacts) as results, or to their composition. Furthermore, (d) we would like to extend (c) of above by also adding the results of the "nontechnical" working areas as project organization, quality assurance, and documentation itself, and (e) also the transformations between these different technical or nontechnical working areas and the connections between their artifacts. Finally, we (f) find a rather simple definition of documentation as everything, useful for software development or maintenance /Al 23, SA 05/.

Before continuing, we discuss some ideas to *classify documentation* in literature. In fig. 14.3 from /Al 23/ software documentation is split into process and product documentation, the latter into system documentation on one side, and user documentation on the other. System documentation is ordered in the usual way, from requirements to maintenance, process documentation from plans to standards.

Our understanding of the *result* of a development or maintenance process is that it consists of single technical documents (as a description of a module), configurations of such documents (e.g. for a subsystem), ordered collections for a specific purpose, as to compose the requirements specification, the architectural configuration, or the code for the atomic or composed components, or even the whole system configuration description. It also includes documents and composition of documents for project organization, quality assurance, and documentation. Furthermore, it also includes the relations between such artifacts, as, for example the increment-to-increment relations between the requirements specification and the architectural specifications, see fig. 10.5 of ch. 10. More generally, it includes all such relations for all transformations of this part of the book (chs. 10 to 14). All are configurations of configurations of documents. We called the result of the process the *overall configuration*, see fig. 10.5.

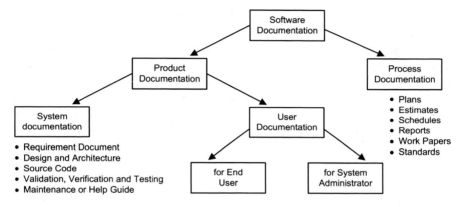

Fig. 14.3: Different kinds of software documentation /Al 23/

Let us now *relate* the above *meanings* (a) to (f) of the term *documentation* in literature to the parts of the *overall configuration*: Definition (a) means to write any part of this configuration in a clear and understandable way. (b) This is especially true for logically "closed" parts, as the requirements specification, the architectural specification, the code, etc., where understandable and clear has a specific importance. (c) The overall configuration collects all results of developers in a well-organized way. (d) This also applies to documents corresponding to organization/ management, quality assurance, and documentation. (e) The increment-to-increment connections between documents are contained in the overall configuration as well. (f) The overall configuration contains everything, needed for development/ maintenance process.

So, all definitions of documentation given in literature are related to parts of the overall configuration. If we do not want to replace a vague definition of documentation by another vague one, as 'any meaningful part of the overall configuration', we need a new definition for the term documentation: The *documentation* of *technical* and *nontechnical documents, collections* of them, relations between these parts, or the *complete system* in our understanding is everything, which helps to understand how and why it looks, works, which decisions have been made, why they have been made, which consequences these decisions have, and so on. In other words, documentation is everything, which explains, helps to understand, characterizes, delimits, illustrates, gives associations, shows similarities or differences to overview or deeply understand the results of development or maintenance. This may be connected to any granularity (atomic component, big component, the whole system) to any form of description (text, graphic, formal, informal, etc.).

Shortly, every *additional* description in text or graphical form or *explanation*, which helps to *elucidate* or *deeply understand* a part or the whole overall configuration is *called documentation* here. Especially, the rationale of underlying decisions is an essential part of the documentation. We are aware that this definition of documentation is not widely used in the software engineering literature. It allows us to *separate documents* as technical and other results *from* their *documentation*, as explanations to understand these results. In this sense, documentation is a very *specific part* of the overall configuration.

A documentation in this sense is *helpful*, and it can *range* from *trivial* to *elaborated*. To give an example for trivial: In my industrial time many years ago, I had to extend a software solution. To do so, I tried to find out how the given solution was built and why it was built this way. This took me some time and I found no easy explanation. It was evident that there were better solutions. The solution of the mystery was that the developers had no time to go deeper. The corresponding sentence of documentation "We know that there are better solutions, but we had no to time to find them" was missing. That would have saved time. An elaborated documentation is that for any essential decision made in the process we find an easy-to-understand rationale.

Documentation in the sense of our definition is *mostly informal*: explaining the essence, giving the rationale for the major decisions, etc. *Formal* and detailed additional descriptions are part of the overall configuration, as for example, a formal description for the interface of an architectural component, or the contract on one hand of the export interface and needed import interface and the code of the component, fulfilling this contract. For further parts of the overall configuration, see again the different views of an architecture, as argued in ch. 3: static, dynamic, concurrency, distribution, efficiency, or part of the system vs. remote in the web and interacting with the system.

Documentation in this sense is *double-sided*, as for quality assurance of above. Every developer is writing it on one side. A further person writing/ extending/ completing the documentation comes from outside. This is mostly true for user documentation.

The developer has again a *double role*, namely as developer in a constructive role and, at the same time, an explaining role for his/ her results. The external person has only a *single and explaining role*: He/ she can explain and argue, but he/ she does not correct or improve the technical documents, to keep the two roles disjoint. However, he/ she can suggest improvements of the developer's result or documentation.

Examples, where the *outside person* has *specific importance* are: The description of the outside behavior of a system in the form of the user handbook or user pocketbook, described by someone specifically familiar with the knowledge, the way of thinking or understanding of the later users. This is more related to requirements engineering and documentation. But a specific user-friendly behavior might also demand for specific architectural solutions. Another example is a documentation of the system for senior and upper-level people of the customer, who are no IT specialists. A third example is the connection knowledge between architecture and code level, which we get in integration tests. The corresponding test persons might deliver this knowledge for documentation.

Different forms of documents and correspondingly *documentations* (similar to that shown above for quality assurance) for architectures are: the static view, semantic view, concurrency view, efficiency view (ch. 3), as extensions or annotations, referring to other documents.

Please be aware that the *documentation* of a part of the overall configuration is something *separate* from the result description of that part by the developers(s). It is mostly written in a natural language, concentrating on the main ideas, decisions, and the rationales for them. It is written by the developer (double role) in a way different from the corresponding results (here the why and not the what). Sometimes it is completely written by an external person (single role), as the user documentation. The documentation is usually *assigned to a part* of the overall configuration.

What we have written above for quality assurance also applies here for documentation: The *documentation* is assigned to a *meaningful part* of the architecture or, more general, of the *overall configuration*. So, parts of a document, documents, configurations of documents up to the complete system can be documented. Also, relations between documents are documented. The parts are results of specific working areas or of transformations between working areas. In this chapter we mainly concentrate on architectures.

Commonalities and Differences

We shortly discuss now similarities and differences between quality assurance and documentation, we have put forward in the above subsections.

Similarities: Both quality assurance and documentation is extra: It has to be done in addition to development: Double-sided by the developer, one-sided by quality engineer or documentation writer on the other. The developer has a double role, the external person a single role.

In this chapter, we specialize on architectures. However, what we explain for architectures, also holds for other working areas, either technical or nontechnical, and their results. Both quality assurance results as well as documentation results belong to the overall configuration. What we discuss here has a broader appearance for all technical and nontechnical working areas and their results, which all belong to the overall configuration.

Differences: Documentation is mostly not formal; quality assurance artifacts can have all forms. In quality assurance, we often find quality assurance measures, which are chosen differently to those selected by the developer, e.g. black box test by external quality engineer, white box test by the developer for components of code. This can also apply to documentation (see user documentation) but need not apply to all documentation: The rationale for a component can be and is often written by the component designer and coder.

14.3 Architecture Relations to Documentation

Documenting Architectures

We argue in the *documentation,* (a) why the architecture consists of the *components* chosen and (b) why their *composition* to bigger units builds up the *architecture.* The first part (a) is the rationale for decomposition, and where to set the borders of components. The second part (b) is the rationale for composition, grouping, and forming the structure from these components.

The rationale for a *component* can be: why (i) this part is put into one component, and the purpose of this component as part of the global architecture w.r.t. services delivered to the outside, or needed services from other components. This is the *static view*. The other (ii) is the purpose of the single component at runtime within the computation of the overall system. This is the *dynamic view*. Both argue for a component. Or, (iii) it can be the *formalization* of the different services in the export interface, e.g. in form of algebraic laws as semantics specification. The latter is the case in fig. 14.4.a. There, we find a graphical form of the component appearing within a diagram, the corresponding detailed description of the export services and the imports both given in an architecture description language (ADL), the corresponding formal semantic description, and for all three descriptions (iv) the rationale for this component in one documentation artifact.

The other part is the rationale for *composition* and *grouping,* see fig. 14.4.b. What is the *rationale* for meaningful *parts* of the architecture *grouping* different *components*, as building up a layer of the system, a closed subsystem of the system, a meaningful part of the architecture as (i) the user interface part, (ii) the data handling part, (iii) the functional part, (iv) the part which is located remote, and so on. Therefore, for any *meaningful part* of the architecture, a documentation in the sense of a *rationale* (why and how decisions for grouping have been taken this way) can be given. In fig. 14.4.b we see as example the bottom layer of a system, containing different components, their ADL description, and the corresponding documentation. Here, every component has a separate documentation. Furthermore, there is a documentation and explanation artifact for the whole layer.

The part of fig. 14.4.b could also contain the similar situation for a *bigger part* of the architecture in form of a *subsystem* instead of a layer. This subsystem has a graphical form, a textual detailed form for the export/ import interface, can have a formal extension of this textual form, as above for a semantic description, or for describing synchronization properties. The documentation of the subsystem explains the interface grouping, the grouping of the internal body architecture, the import grouping, and the role of the subsystem. As stated above, the example could also be an important component from outside, or an essential part of the system, as the data part of an interactive system. The explanations are similar.

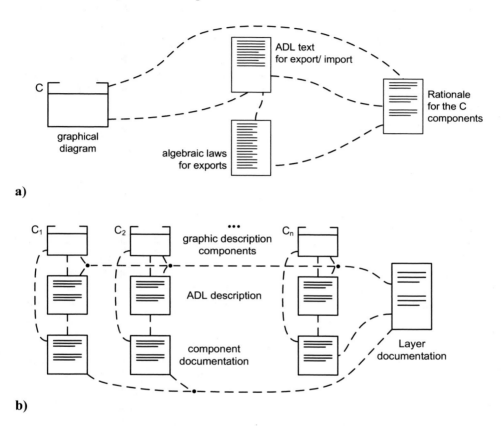

a)

b)

Fig. 14.4: Rationale (a) for a component, (b) a closed logical part of a system (here a layer), and the difference of extensions and documentation

As already mentioned, rationales, ideas, and explanations given in the *documentation* are usually given as plain natural language texts. We argue why this way is followed and not another way. They are usually *separate* from technical artifacts. They do not give sophisticated and *technical extensions* and additions of components or other bigger parts of the architecture. If such extensions occur, we find them as specific extensions or as separate documents which are *referred to*, see fig. 14.4.a for the detailed ADL description, or the semantics description. There, the documentation is a further artifact giving the rationale for different artifacts.

More *formal* or *precise extensions* or *annotations* we find as separate specific descriptions as (i) inline extensions of artifacts, or (ii) as separate descriptions referred to, see fig. 14.4.a. Here we see the graphical form of a component, the separate textual and detailed ADL interface and import description of this component, both belonging to the architecture subconfiguration. There is an additional artifact, for specifying algebraic equations for the relations between different services. This again, either as inline insertion to the textual ADL description, or as a new artifact, which is referred to from the textual description (as shown in the figure), is a part of the architectural subconfiguration. Furthermore, we see a rationale artifact explaining the decisions, related to the graphical and the textual description or even to the formal and separate extension of the textual description. This artifact belongs to the documentation.

Documenting the Transformation from Requirements Specification to Architecture

See chs. 10 and 11 as introductions, especially ch. 11, which deals with that transformation. What was the reason for a certain *choice* how to relate an architectural increment, or component, or composed component to a requirements unit or different units? Why is it done this way and not differently? This is again described in a *documentation artifact*, here belonging to the transformation from RE to AR.

The explanations of this documentation either belong to all transformation decisions or to well-separated parts of the transformation. In fig. 14.5 all transition decisions made are explained in form of one *composed* rationale artifact. Alternatively, *different documentation artifacts* for these transition choices are introduced, which are linked together to see the whole mapping explanation. Furthermore, there exist documentation artifacts for the requirements specification and for the architecture, which are not shown in fig. 14.5.

In fig. 14.5, we see increments of the requirements specification at the top. They may belong to different parts of this specification. We discuss here, which different choices exist for a function increment, see ch. 11. This increment may be mapped to one architectural component in a 1:1 mode (left side). It can also be that different functional RE increments are mapped to one architectural component. Here the mapping is m:1, the different functional increments are mapped on different services of this one component, see fig. 14.5 middle. Finally, we find that one function RE increment is mapped on n components in an 1:n mode (right).

What we have sketched here for functional parts of the requirements specification can also be used for *data* parts, *control* parts, see ch. 11. Each of them may have an own decision documentation, or it may be that the documentation groups 'local' increments (functional, data, etc. which belong together).

Further components and bigger composed *units* of the architecture are found *below of the mapped units* as decisions of the architect. They form the lower parts of the architecture, see ch. 11 and the arguments that only a part of the architecture can interactively be "derived" in some way from the requirements specification. Many further architectural parts come later by decisions of the architect, which are not derivable. They have to be documented as well. For that, see the arguments of above for documenting well-defined parts of the architecture.

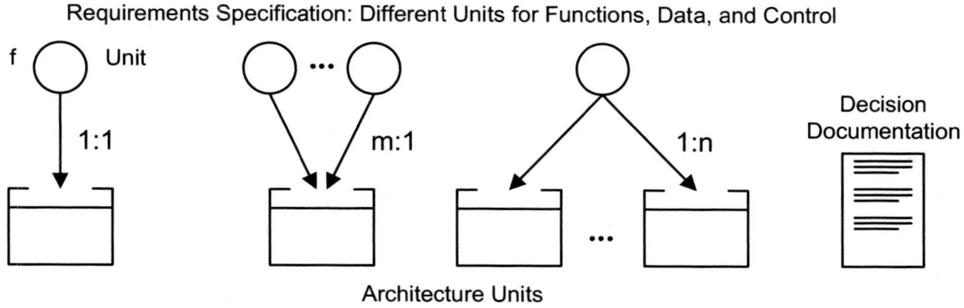

Fig. 14.5: Rationales for architectural parts, interactively assigned to requirements

Documenting the Integration of Code using the Architecture

Above we had merely human activities for documentation of more or less abstract artifacts. We now take another example. The architecture delivers *arguments* for how to put the code for components together to get the whole system by incremental steps, which is called system integration. Now, we are on the detailed or code level. The architecture is the underlying background for this *integration task*, namely what and how to do in the integration process.

For that different *decisions* have to be taken: (a) Determining the integration *strategy* (e.g. bottom up vs. top-down, or else), (b) determining the integration *order* (take probable dangerous or possibly erroneous components first within a chosen strategy), (c) determination of *intermediate results* for integration, e.g. integrate user interface, functional part, or data part of an interactive system separately first. We determine how the integration is carried out, from single components to the complete system. For all the decisions to make, the *architecture* is the *basis for the solution*.

All these decisions have to be explained in form of a rationale. Again, we need *a documentation artifact*, either for all decisions, or *different artifacts* which are related to each other and are combined, to find out the whole story.

Fig. 14.6 shows such an integration task for a rather simple example. We proceed bottom-up and decide to start with component 1 and then integrate 2, as both are possibly the riskiest of the bottom components. Then, we integrate component 3. After that, we integrate 4, then 5, and then 6. The integration order is graphically shown. Alternatively, we give a textual form in the lower part of the figure. Please note that strategy and order do not uniquely determine how the integration happens. The integration documentation determines and explains the decisions and how to integrate. This in fig. 14.6 is done in one documentation artifact.

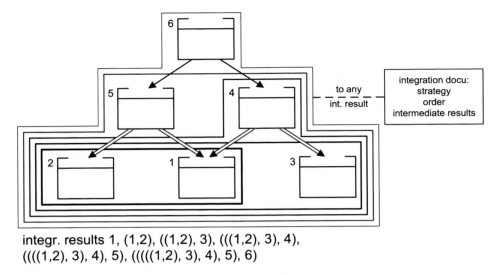

integr. results 1, (1,2), ((1,2), 3), (((1,2), 3), 4),
((((1,2), 3), 4), 5), (((((1,2), 3), 4), 5), 6)

Fig. 14.6: Code integration, the role of the architecture, and documentation

14.4 Architecture Relations to Quality Assurance

We take the same examples of above or similar ones, now for explaining quality assurance documentation: How it is described by artifacts, and how these artifacts are related to an architecture. We argue and explain, how it can work.

Review of an Architecture

We start with the *quality assurance* for designing an abstract *architecture*, which is mostly carried out as a *human activity*, for example by writing a documentation in the form of a rationale of this architecture by the designer (this can be regarded as a constructive QA step) or by writing a review as a critical report (by external quality assurance persons). In the latter case, we assume that the corresponding documentation of this architecture is available too, as it gives valuable input for the review task. We discuss this situation in the following.

We distinguish different cases: (A) The *overview architecture* of a simple system, where the components are not further decomposed. We assume the components' documentation is available.

There is a 1:1 relation of components' technical descriptions and components' documentation. For every *component* there is also a *review report*, again in a 1:1 relation, see fig. 14.7.a. It may be related to the *graphical view* of the component: "This is more a data type component and not a data object component.", or "The import relations are not necessary for all components.", and alike.

(B) For the *ADL description* of a component we could see remarks like (i) "The resources in the export interface are not orthogonal." The remarks are missing in those cases, where there are no critical comments. The organization is mostly 1:1, for every component there can be a review remark. So, many or most of the components or their documentation have a link to a review, containing descriptions as (ii) "Very good description, nothing to improve, is essential for understanding.", "What is the purpose of this component, why different from another component's description? I see strong similarities." (iii) "There are good arguments … for restructuring the component and its context.", and alike.

There can also be remarks (C) not related to a single component but to a *group of components*, see again fig. 14.7.a right side. In this case, there is hopefully also a documentation related to this group. Review remarks can be like "The situation can be generalized.", "There is a well-known pattern for this situation, you did not apply.", etc. In this case, the relations between the group consisting of m components and the review report is m:1 .

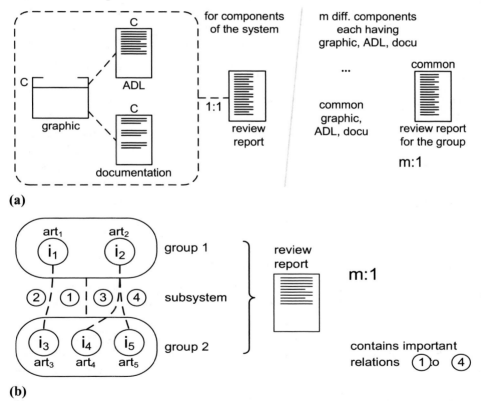

(a)

(b)

Fig. 14.7: Review remarks (a) for one/ more components and (b) for big parts

Now (D) the system is *composed from bigger parts*, which are separately reviewed, as big subsystems, the basic layers of the system, a big component from outside, where the requirements spec has determined that is should be used, etc. Now a more complex organization of the review is necessary, fig. 14.7.b: (i) The parts are checked independently. Furthermore, (ii) there may be relations between these big components, see fig. 14.7.b for the case of a subsystem. Now we get review remarks as "The interface of this subsystem is too complex, it needs to be restructured like …", or "The implementation of the subsystem is questionable …", or "The subsystem is similar to another one in the architecture. Could that be unified?", and so on.

The *schema* now for bigger parts is that k different artifacts get a review report, so *not* 1:1 *but* k:1, see fig. 14.7.b for k is 2. Furthermore, the k big parts may have j relations to each other, which also have to be approved, so in addition j:1. We need that we can connect a component to a review remark or different artifacts to one review remark. In addition, we need the possibility that two different groups of artifacts are related to each other, and these relations are quality assured, thereby producing a further review report. For example, for the case that a big component (group 1) is connected to a basic layer (group 2), as the connection between both is questionable. Even more, the relations can be refined to start or end at l specific internal increments of components. Thus, the schema is m:1, where m depends on k, j, and l. Even more, there might be more than two groups of artifacts. The group can be built by different components or different representations (graphic, text, formal text, etc.). In all above cases, the review remark is natural text, so informal.

Between group 1 and group 2 there exist *relations on three levels*, see fig. 14.7.b: First in a coarse form between group 1 and group 2, see relation (1). These are refined to relations between artifacts, see (2). Finally, these relations are further refined to get relations between increments of artifact i to artifact j., see (3) and (4). Level 3 is what we would like to have; these fine-grained relations are important for development, maintenance, documentation, and also quality assurance. The review report must at least describe the important relations on these three levels.

Traceability QA: Requirements Specification and Architecture

This is a short form of chapter 11 and solely devoted to quality assurance. We now regard the *quality assurance of the mapping* from RE to AR.

We have learned from ch. 11: A *requirements engineering element* can be mapped onto one *architecture unit*, or onto a part of an architecture unit, or onto different architecture units. So, for the correspondence, we can have 1:1, n:1, or even 1:m. Furthermore, we have learned that the decision has to be made by an architect, it cannot be made automatically, as by a tool alone. (Of course, a tool can support the reviewer. The links according to the architect's decisions could and should be inserted by the tool.) These decisions should have been described and explained in the documentation. The above variations exist for functional, data, or other parts of the RE specification. The decisions can be different for different RE elements.

In quality assurance, we *check* these *relations*. This can be done by a *person* having the role of quality engineer, who gives comments. In the case of syntactic or semantic restrictions, the check can be done or *supported by a tool*, if this tool knows about the restrictions. The mapping relations, see fig. 14.5, may be commented, questioned, or criticized in the review.

As also argued in ch. 11, most *parts* of the *architecture* are *not bound* to requirements specification determinations. These parts are found in deeper architecture levels. They belong to technical architecture design steps below of that part of the architecture, which is influenced by the requirements specification. However, these architecture parts may refine the layers below of elements being a consequence of the mapping RE spec to AR spec. In this way, the lower components may be indirectly bound to the decisions of the mapping.

For all the possibilities of the relations of RE to AR elements 1:1, m:1, and 1:n of fig. 14.5, there may be a comment in the review report. We assume that there is one report for quality assuring these relations, or k different reports, if either the number of relations is high, or there is one for each for the different elements (as functional, date, and control elements). Therefore, regarding the artifacts, we have the situation 1:1 or 1:k .

Integration Test after Unit Test

Now, we have a *combination* of program code, architecture, test, test results, and implications, where the *architecture* plays a *driving role*. Tests are experiments, so cannot be complete, due to principal and economic reasons. We take similar examples as above.

We assume that the *unit test* has already taken place. For every component test of the architecture, we need a driver and, in most cases, also a stub. We assume that the unit test has been carried out as white box test by the developer and, additionally, as black box test by the external quality assurance person.

Now, we start the *integration test*, following a *bottom-up* strategy, i.e. we start from lowest components of the architecture and go up, component by component (called incremental integration test). Looking at the architecture, we choose a suitable integration strategy and integration *order* of components, for example by integrating complicated or possibly erroneous components first to check them early and again in the integration test. In this way, we get up until we have reached all components of the system. The integration test is carried out in the development or maintenance environment. A similar proceeding can be taken later in the acceptance test at the customer's site.

Let us regard a *step of incremental integration test*, see fig. 14.8. The part A indicates the part already integrated and tested. Now a new component B of the planned integration order is added. This component has been unit tested before. So, it has a driver and stubs. The driver for A can be used, if the level of B is below the level of A. If B now is the topmost component, its driver may be used. The stub(s) of B might not be necessary, as now there might be corresponding components in A. Now the source code of B is integrated to A, making the integrated code larger.

The *test of A+B* is started, i.e., we get a new QA experiment. We run the test cases of A with B or of B with A. We get test results, or errors at binding time or runtime. The data are analyzed: If the data are as expected, nothing is to be done. If the data are unexpected, we try to find out the cause. If we got error messages at bind or run time we try to get the answer too.

The findings imply *changes* of the *code*, within a component, for relations of different components, or even at the architecture level. The change has to be checked to ensure, that no further problems come up after the change.

For any integration step we may have a problem report, describing what happened, what was done, which implications occurred, what was corrected. After a correction, we may have a modified situation, which, again, has to be checked. So, we have a *series of problem reports*. They are related to code artifacts, the architecture description, the documentation, and also to artifacts describing the integration strategy, the integration order, etc. So, we have a series of n:1 situations.

The above activities are those of the integration tester (internal QA). The external quality assurance people may the review integration steps. Even better is a load sharing: The external quality assurance person checks the integration test plan (strategy, order, intermediate results, constraints, etc.) The approved test plan is afterwards used for integration tests by the internal quality assurance people. In this sense, the QA load sharing gives clear roles: The external quality engineer for the plan, the technical details for the integration testers.

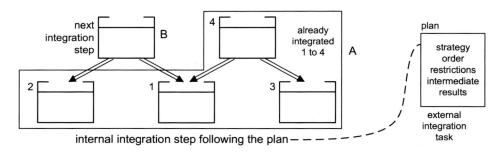

Fig. 14.8: Integration steps following the integration plan

14.5 Summary, Message, and Open Problems

Summary

We have regarded and discussed *documentation* and *quality assurance* for *three situations*: (i) Looking at the architecture level of a system, (ii) looking at the transformation of the requirements specification and its transformation to the upper levels of an architecture, and (iii) looking at the integration test, which means we look at strategy, order etc., mostly determined by the architecture. (ii) is the start of the design process, (i) the kernel, and (iii) the end of the process.

We could have taken many *other examples*. We hope that three examples, which are quite different, convince the reader that the *results* of this chapter also *apply* for other examples.

We have introduced a *strict definition for documentation*, which separates technical *details*, being a part of the technical overall configuration, from their *essence* and *rationale* behind, described in the documentation. Only the latter, is called documentation in this chapter and book. The same separation is applied for QA and PO. The corresponding documentation artifacts can have quite different relations to other artifacts of the configuration, from 1:1 to m:n, and also correspond to very different relations between subprocesses, from coarse between working areas, to medium between artifacts, to fine-grained between increments of different artifacts. This also applies to the results, namely configurations, artifacts, to internal increments of artifacts.

The same is true for *quality assurance*, where we distinguish between technical activities by internal QA persons on one side and the main decisions being approved by external QA persons. Other remarks, as the different forms of relations and the different granularity apply as well. It is surprising that these similarities exist, which we would not expect at the first glance.

Characterization of Commonalities and Differences: QA and DOC, Examples

Commonalities: Internal and external QA or internal and external documentation and asymmetry: Internal documentation or quality assurance is both done by the corresponding developer, the external only for specific tasks by corresponding external people (as for user documentation and for "destructive" quality assurance). The external DOC or QA does *not improve* or change a solution, but might give advice to do so. Therefore, internal documentation and quality assurance are *double-sided*. External DOC and QA is *one-sided*. *Relations*: In both cases we can have the situations from 1:1 to m:n.

Differences: The documentation in the specific sense of this chapter is plain text, explaining and emphasizing the central decisions and their essential ideas. Quality assurance artifacts can have any form, from plain text to formal.

The Message of this Chapter

We gave a *strict* definition of *documentation* in this chapter to separate it from technical activities. This applies to internal as well as external documentation. In this way, documentation is explaining the essence and the decisions of other activities.

There are strong *similarities* between *documentation* (as we understand it) and *quality assurance* corresponding to their relations to technical and nontechnical working areas, their subprocesses, and their fine-grained activities. The same applies to the product side. This also applies to the granularities and the different forms of relations from 1:1 to m:n. This might not be obvious at the first glance. This is a surprise and message at the same time.

Open Problems and Specialization

In ch. 3 we have seen that there is not only one architecture but a *series of architectures*, ranging from the abstract and static architecture (logical architecture) to that having efficiency considerations in mind (distributed and efficient architecture). Intermediate steps are semantic annotations, concurrency, distribution, and technical concurrency, and efficiency transformations. In embedded systems, we have in addition regulated start / stop of the system and emergency handling.

In the examples regarded in this chapter, we only discussed static architectures and semantic annotations. We could have *regarded* the *other aspects* as well. That makes the examples for documentation and quality assurance more complicated. All arguments of this chapter still remain valid.

What we learn from these arguments is that the discussion of the *overall configuration*, as given in chs. 1 and 10, is still too simple. Please think about the architectural configuration now also regarding the different forms of architectures from logical to efficient. This architectural configuration would be even more complex.

In this chapter, we have mainly concentrated on documentation (DOC) and quality assurance (QA) of architectures and the steps before and after modeling architectures. The discussion could be *extended* to the technical *working areas* requirements engineering RE, programming in the small PS, and also to the accompanying area project organization PO. In this way, the other parts of the overall configuration from the requirements to code, and also the parts accompanying the technical parts, *would have to be extended*.

It could even be extended to the areas DOC and QA we have regarded in this chapter. Even the *documentation* and also the *quality assurance* can be *documented* and also *quality assured*. Furthermore, all the *transformations* between different working areas could be handled as well.

This implies an extension of the results of this chapter to further areas and transformations between all these areas. However, we do *not expect* that this extension causes a *principal extension* of the *ideas*, namely what to do and how to do, as presented and described here. Therefore, we should have a quantitative but not a qualitative extension.

We miss investigations and literature for *specific manifestations* of *documentation* and of *quality assurance* in *different projects*. Such manifestations could be: (a) specific *projects* and systems like *long-term maintenance* projects /BR 00, IE 98/, reverse and reengineering projects (/BD 05, BM 96, BN 04, CC 90, CC 01, CD 07, CK 06, CMW 02, Cr 00, EK 02, Fo 18, FT 96, KC 99, KS 02, LS 02, Ma 05, Mo 09, MH 01, MO 93, MW 94, MW 02, MW 03, PG 02, SP 03, Zu 93/ and ch. 9), *reuse projects* (from a component reuse library to generation of code out of specifications into a framework architecture), see /Co 98, ICSR, LS 09/ and ch. 7, product lines or *product families projects* /CN 07, Ja 00, PB 05, SP 12/, (b) for specific *classes of systems* as batch systems, interactive systems, embedded systems, (c) for *specific domains* like automotive, telecommunication systems etc., as specialized examples of embedded systems, (d) for specific ways *how the system is built*, using specific methods /BJ 02, Ev 04, He 03, MW 03, MW 04, PB 16, PH 12/, frameworks, specific big parts from outside as determined in the requirements specification, etc.

There are many of such manifestations. For all of them we might ask for *specific* ways how to develop specific *documentation* or *quality assurance* methods, tools, or experiences. This is specifically important and *useful* for companies, which are working in such environments for a *long time*. As an example, please think of a company having been building aircrafts or telecom systems for 50 years, where more and more software is involved, and where specific rules, knowledge, and experience have to be applied, which have tremendously extended over these many years. These arguments, by the way, apply to any chapter of this part of the book relating AR to any other working area of the development or maintenance process, see next and summary chapter.

14.6 References

/Al 23/ AltexSoft Inc.: Technical Documentation in Software Development; Types, Best Practices, and Tools, Techn. Report (2023)

/BD 05/ Balzer, M./ Deussen, O./ Lewerentz, C.: Voronoi Treemaps for the Visualization of Software Metrics, ACM Symp. On Software Visualization, 165-172, ACM Press (2005)

/BJ 02/ Böhlen, B./ Jäger, D./ Schleicher, A./ Westfechtel, B.: UPGRADE, a framework for building graph-based interactive tools, in Mens, Schürr, Taentzer (eds.): Proc. Workshop on Graph-based Tools (GrBaTs '02), El. Notes on Theor. Comp. Sci. 72(2), 149-159 (2002)

/BM 96/ Burd, E./ Munro, M./ Wezeman, C.: Analysing Large COBOL Programs: The extraction of reusable modules, Proc. Intern. Conf. on Software Maintenance (ICSM '96), 238-243, IEEE Comp. Soc. Press (1996)

/BN 04/ Balzer, M./ Noack, A./ Deussen, O./ Lewerentz,. C.: Software Landscapes: Visualizing the Structure of Large Software systems, Joint Eurographics IEEE TCVG Symp. On Visualization (VisSym) (2004)

/BR 00/ Bennett, B./ Rajlich, V.: Software Maintenance and Evolution: A Roadmap, Proc. ICSE '00, 73-87, ACM Press (2000)

/CC 90/ Chikofsky E.J./ Cross II, J.H.: Reverse Engineering and Design Recovery: A Taxonomy, IEEE Software 7(1), 13-17 (1990)

/CC 01/ Canfora, G./ Cimitile, A./ De Luca, A./ Di Lucca, G.A.: Decomposing Legacy Systems into Objects: An eclectic approach, Information and Software Techn.43 (6), 401-412 (2001)

/CD 07/ Canfora, G./ Di Penta, M.: New Frontiers of Reverse Engineering, in Proc. Future of Software Engineering (FOSE '07), 326-341 (2007)

/CH 10/ Cristensen, H. B/ Hansen, K. M. et al.; Lightweight and Continuous Architectural Software Quality Assurance Using the aSQA Technique, Proc. EC SA, LNCS 6285, 118-132 (2010)

/CH 18/ Chopra, T: Software Quality Assurance: A Self-Teaching Introduction, 660 pp., Mercury Learning and Information (2018)

/CK 06/ Clements, P., Kazman, R., Klein, M.: Evaluating software architectures: methods and case studies, Addison-Wesley (2006)

/CMW 02/ Cremer, K./ Marburger, A./ Westfechtel, B.: Graph-based tools for re-engineering, Journ. of Software Maintenance and Evolution, Research and Practice 14, 257-292 (2002)

/CN 07/ Clements, P./ Northrop, L.M.: Software Product Lines: Practices and Patterns, 563 pp., 6th ed., Addison Wesley (2007)

/Co 98/ Coulange, B.: Software Reuse, 293 pp., Springer (1998)

/Cr 00/ Cremer, K.: Tools for Reverse Engineering and Reengineering (in German), Doct. Diss. RWTH Aachen University, 220 pp., Deutscher Universitätsverlag (2000)

/CS 89/ Curtis, B./ Sheppard, S.B. et al.: Experimental evaluation of software documentation formats, Journal of Systems and Software 9(2), 167-207 (1989)

/DL 14/ Ding, W./ Liang, P. et al.: Knowledge-based approaches in software documentation: A systematic literature review, Information and Software Technology 56(6), 545-567 (2014)

/EK 02/ Ebert, J./ Kullbach, B./ Riediger, V./ Winter, A.: GUPRO – Generic Understanding of Programs: An Overview, El. Notes in Theor. Comp. Science 72(2), 10 pp. (2002)

/EM 12/ Elberzhager, F./ Münch, J. et al.: A Systematic Mapping Study on the Combination of Static and Dynamic Quality Assurance Techniques, Information and Software Technology 54(1), 1-15 (2012)

/Ev 04/ Evans, E.: Domain-driven Design, 529 pp., Addison Wesley (2004)

/FG 12/ Feiler, P. H./ Guch, D. P. et al.: Model-Based Software Quality Assurance with the Architecture Analysis and Design Language, AIAA Conf. and SEI of CMU (2009)

/Fo 18/ Fowler, M.: Refactoring: Improving the Design of Existing Code, 2nd ed., 418 pp., Addison Wesley (2018)

/FT 96/ Fiutem, R./ Tonella, P./ Antoniol, G./ Merlo, E.: A Cliché-based Environment to Support Architectural Reverse Engineering, in Proc. Intern. Conf. on Software Maintenance (ICSM '96), 319-328, IEEE Comp. Soc. Press (1996)

/Ga 03/ Galin, D.: Software Quality Assurance: From Theory to Implementation. 590 pp., Pearson (2004)

/GG 15/ Gatousi, G./ Gaousi-Yusifoglu, V. et al.: Usage and usefulness of technical software documentation: An industrial case study, Information and Software Technology 57(1), 664-683 (2015)

/He 03/ Herzberg, D.: Modeling Telecommunication Systems: From Standard to System Architectures, Doct. Dissertation, 305 pp., RWTH Aachen University, Shaker (2003)

/ICSR/ International Conference on Software Reuse, Proc. from 1990 to 2017, see also Wikipedia ICSR

/IE 98/ IEEE Std 1219: Standard for Software Maintenance, IEEE Computer Society (1998)

/IS 11/ ISO/IEC 9126: Standard for Software Quality (2011)

/Ja 00/ Jazayeri, M. et al. (eds.): Software Architecture for Product Families, Addison Wesley (2000)

/JD 21/ Jorgensen, P.C./ DeVries, B.: Software Testing: A Craftsman's Approach, 5th ed., 552 pp., CRC Press (2021)

/KC 99/ Kazman, R./ Carrière, S.J.: Playing Detective: Reconstructing Software Architecture from Available Evidence, Journ. Aut. Software Engineering 6(2), 107-138 (1999)

/KS 02/ Kollmann, R./ Selonen, P./ Stroulia, E. et al.: A study on the current state of the artin tool-supported UML-based static reverse engineering, in van Deursen, Burd (eds.): Proc. 9th Working Conf. on Reverse Engineering (WCRE '02), 22-32, IEEE Comp. Soc. Press (2002)

/LS 02/ Lewerentz, C./ Simon, F.: Metrics Based Refactoring, Proc. 1st Intern. Workshop on Visualization for Understanding and Analysis VISSOFT, 70-80, IEEE Comp. Soc. Press, 70-80 (2002)

/LS 09/ Land, R./ Sundmark, D. et al.: Reuse with Software Components – A Survey of Industrial State of Practice, in Edwards/ Kulczycke (Eds.): ICSR 2009, LNCS 5791, 150-159 (2009)

/Ma 05/ Marburger, A.: Reverse Engineering of Complex Legacy Telecommunication Systems, Doct. Diss., 418 pp., RWTH Aachen University, Shaker (2005)

/Me 86/ Meyer, B.: Design by Contract, Interactive Software Engineering, 50 pp., TR-El-12/CO (1986)

/MH 01/ Marburger, A./ Herzberg, D.: E-Cares Research Project: Understanding complex legacy telecommunication systems, in Sousa, Ebert (eds.): Proc. 5th Eur. Conf. on Software Maintenance and Reengineering (CSMR 2001), 139-147, IEEE Comp. Soc. Press (2001)

/MO 93/ Müller, H.A./ Orgun, M.A./ Tilley, S.R./ Uhl, J.S.: A Reverse Engineering Approach To Subsystem Stucture Identification, Journ. Softw. Mainten. Research and Practice 5(4), 181-204 (1993)

/Mo 09/ Mosler, C.: Graph-based Reengineering of Telecommunication Systems (in German), Doct. Diss, 268 pp., RWTH Aachen University, Shaker (2009)

/MW 94/ Müller, H.A./ Wong, K./ Tilley, S.R.: Understanding Software Systems Using Reverse Engineering Technology, 62nd Congress of L' Association Canadienne Francaise pour L' Avancement des Sciences (ACFAS '94), 41-48 (1994)

/MW 02/ Marburger, A./ Westfechtel, B.: Graph-based reengineering of telecommunication systems, in Corradini/ Ehrig et al. (eds.): ICGT '02, LNCS 2505, 270-285, Springer (2002)

/MW 03/ Marburger, A./ Westfechtel, B.: Tools for understanding the behavior of telecommunication systems, Proc. 25th Conf. on Softw. Eng. (ICSE 2003), 430-441, IEEE Comp. Soc. Press (2003)

/MW 04/ Marburger, A./ B. Westfechtel, B.: Behavioral analysis of telecommunication systems by graph transformations, in Pfaltz/ Nagl/ Böhlen (eds.): AGTIVE 2003, LNCS 3062, 202-219, Springer (2004)

/PB 05/ Pohl, K./ Böckle, G. et al.: Software Product Line Engineering, 467 pp., Springer (2005)

/PB 16/ Pohl, K./ Broy, M./ Daemkes, M./ Hönninger, H. (Eds.): Advanced Model-based Engineering of Embedded Systems – Extensions to the SPES 2020 Methodology, 303 pp., Springer (2016)

/PG 02/ Pinzger, M./ Gall, H.: Pattern-supported Architecture Recovery, in Proc. 10th Intern. Workshop on Program Comprehension IWPC '02, 53-61 (2002)

/PH 12/ Pohl, K./ Hönninger, K./ Achatz, H./ Broy, R. (eds.): Model-based Engineering of Embedded Systems – The SPES 2020 Methodology, 304 pp., Springer (2012)

/SA 05/ Souza, S.C./ Anquetil, N. et al.: A Study of the Documentation Essential to Software Maintenance, SIGDOC 05, 68-75 (2005)

/SP 03/ Seacord, R.C,/ Plakosh, D./ Lewis, G.A.: Modernizing Legacy Systems, Addison-Wesley (2003)

/SP 12/ Schubanz, M./ Pleuss, A./ Botterweck, G./ Lewerentz, C.: Modeling Rationale over Time to Support Product Line Evolution Planning, VAMOS 12, 193-199, ACM Press (2012)

/Wa 17/ Walkinshaw, N.: Software Quality Assurance, Consistency in the Face of Complexity and Change, 181 pp., Springer (2017)

/Wi Ho/ Wikipedia: Hoare Logic, access July 2023

/Wi SD/ Wikipedia: Software Documentation, access June 2023

/Wi SQ/ Wikipedia; Softwarequalität, access June 2023

/Zu 93/ van Zuylen, H.J. (ed.): The REDO Compendium: Reverse Engineering for Software Maintenance, 405 pp., John Wiley (1993)

15 Summary, Lessons Learned, Messages, Open Problems

Manfred Nagl
Software Engineering, RWTH Aachen University, nagl@cs.rwth-aachen.de

Bernhard Westfechtel
Software Engineering, University of Bayreuth, bernhard.westfechtel@ uni-bayreuth.de

Abstract

In this chapter we sum up in four sections. The first deals with the messages, summaries, and lessons learned. This is done chapter by chapter. The second gives statements/ messages, which are valid for different/ all chapters. The same is applied to open problems: chapter by chapter in sect. 3 and across chapters in sect. 4.

15. 1 Summary and Lessons Learned, Chapter by Chapter

Ch.1 Message: The Architecture is the **Center** of the **Development Process**

The working area model (short **WAM**) is a *coarsest-grained* development process presentation, distinguishing different logical levels (RE, AR, etc.) together with dependencies. Different lifecycle process models can be regarded on top (waterfall to agile). It also describes the coarsest form of the overall configuration (RE, AR etc.).

The WAM is organized along *levels of modeling*, not regarding the time order of activities, or the difference between construction and change. We get clear logical levels, and also clear relations between them. The model is symmetric.

Looking where the main structural decisions are made, regarding the part of work being determined by these decisions, and the amount of work for these parts, we see: *Architecture modeling* is in the *center* of the development process, w.r.t. quantity and quality. Or, the *architecture* is the *center* of all project results in the *overall configuration*, which contains processes, data, and relations on 3 granularity levels.

Development means *permanent changes*; the architecture helps to master the changes. Changes can be determined by brainstorming *requirements* and *architecture*. A good architecture handles realization changes by detail abstraction: Requirements changes are facilitated by looking on changed interfaces and their uses.

A good architecture is *never a 1:1 extension* of the requirements specification, has hidden details, which can change, and is stable for minor requirements changes. There are dynamic changes within a development process and also from project to project (ch. 13). The architecture is the level for changes (evolution, backtracking).

Ch. 2 Message: Different **Aspects** of **Architecture Languages**

We start with *static* or *abstract architectures.* We introduced different *components*, for functional or data abstraction, as objects (fo, ado) or as types (ft, adt). Also different kinds of *relations* were introduced, structure and usability relations. Thus, different kinds of construction *principles* can be applied, as locality, layers, or object orientation. We distinguish different kinds of *consistency* relations (context-sensitive syntax) and good use of the language (*method* rules). *Patterns* are different: as it should be, from wrong to right, specific to general, abstract to detailed/ efficient. The approach unites design and *parametric* design. The presentation is *graphical* (overviews) or *textual* (details).

Further aspects are expressed by *annotations* in design artifacts, with refinements in form of additional details, or by other artifacts referred to: *Semantic* notations for interface specifications, runtime traces, behavioral specifications, *concurrency* annotations to denote processes, synchronization protocols, further parts for system *start/ stop* and *emergency* handling, in embedded systems. For abstract *connectors* (request and supply of services) different *mechanisms* are introduced, as signal, trigger, interrupt, or event handling by broadcast. The *distribution* of a system can be annotated by distribution *lines*, or in detail by additional *components* and *connectors* of an underlying *platform*.

The architecture is the *essential structure* of the development process, used for decisions and arguing about structures, realizations, extensions, maintenance, explaining concepts, and methodology to build the system. It integrates essential activities. The architecture is *composed* of different *views* regarding various aspects, with more or fewer details. The relations between different artifacts and units of artifacts should always be clear. All stakeholders of a system development have to do with the architecture in different degrees of detail, for writing or verifying an artifact, or roughly explaining and coarsely understanding it.

Different Views in one Notation: Books on software architectures present fragments of the above concepts, which vary from book to book. We put them together in one notation. This *integrates* artifacts: (i) We understand, how they relate to each other. (ii) A two-level approach uses abstract annotations within architectural diagrams, and their details mostly presented separately as text. (iii) The integration is easy to understand, and the details can be exchanged.

Ch. 3 Message: There is not only one **Architecture**, but a **Sequence**

The conceptual architecture is the most abstract architecture, ignoring most details. We go step by step to concrete forms of the architecture regarding different further views. Thus, *architectures* appear in *sequences* within a development process.

An example of the *embedded systems domain* was discussed. After (i) having elaborated the conceptual architecture, we determine the components (ii) executed concurrently and their synchronization for cooperation and competition. The next step is (iii) explicit start and explicit shut down, both by further control processes. (iv) Emergency handling is denoted, i.e. the normal execution is abandoned, special code is executed to avoid that the technical infrastructure is destroyed. We accept some (data) damage to avoid serious (hardware) damage. Then we (v) distribute and deploy the system, (vi) introduce technical concurrency due to distribution, and (vii) further improvement of runtime efficiency. Another example discusses the steps for a *business administration* example.

The architectures are ordered by reasons of clearness, probability of changes, and minimizing the total change effort. We give some rules for this order and their transformations from step to step. The number of stages and the order depends on the class of systems, the domain, the infrastructure the system is running on, etc. All *stages* are *handled* on *architecture level*. The stages determine the architecture of the final system after development/ maintenance.

Ch. 4 Message: *Adaptability* is even more important for *Embedded Systems*

Embedded software systems have specific *characteristics*: They run "forever", depend on the technical system they control, and often have emergency handling. They are efficient, react in short time, and mostly address concurrency. They are developed together with engineers. Technical hardware details dominate the solution. Many variations corresponding to functionality, structure, and realization are possible. We studied 3 examples of growing complexity. The findings apply to all of them.

Simple coffee machine. Sensors and actuators should not have a *vendor specific* form: *abstract* from this. Clear *physical* and *logical values* should appear in the interfaces. In the body of a component, you connect to a specific sensor/ actuator. Abstract from *physical hardware realizations.* Separate *usual functions* from *error* handling/ *reacting* on errors/ *start* or *stop.* Make the *user interface* adaptable. The client components of the UI should only know, what has been selected, put in or out, but not how this is done, styled, or with which layout. Altogether, use *data* abstraction and *functional* abstraction wherever possible.

Automotive. Start with a *variability model.* That helps to identify the common parts, the specific parts of architectures, and the family characteristics. Make the conceptual architecture as a *network* of *services* on the right abstraction level, corresponding to that of a software architecture. The *software architecture* in its first form is *abstract. Distinguish* between the architecture and the *implementation* level, and also between conceptual and software architecture. Realization components, as for infrastructure or layers, should appear in the software architecture but not in the conceptual architecture. The *mapping* from conceptual architecture to the software architecture can be 1:1, bundled, or services are split. Do not model behavioral and implementation details, which correspond to the internals of software units. *Formal models*, like Simulink models, correspond to *components* of the conceptual or software architecture. The *integration* of the different components is ensured on *architecture level*, not between formal models. *Forget* in the first steps about the *hardware architecture.* Think about *distribution* of software components, later about the *hardware architecture.* Think about *deployment* of software components or groupings of such components into the hardware architecture. Tight coupling has to be answered.

Layered systems of production/ chemical plants. The *plant design* must be *fixed* before starting the design of automation & control in hard- or software. If a plant is often realized and in different forms, start with a variability model. There should be a *clear structure* of the underlying *technical system*, software cannot repair a bad plant design. A solution might not use processes and synchronization, but fixed schedules. The solution is *organized* in layers (automation pyramid). Make clear that the *functionality* you are realizing, is on the *right layer*. Components needed in higher levels should have *clear interfaces*. Do *not spread lower level knowledge upwards* and *upper level knowledge downwards*. Do *not mix* technical knowledge with quality assurance, strategy, business administration. If embedded systems are *integrated*, be careful which *knowledge* is visible on both sides. Think about *possible changes to happen* and that these changes do not have global consequences. In an *OO design*, separate domain knowledge from the specific solution.

Ch. 5 Message: Architecture *Styles/ Patterns* can be *Traced back*

Architectural styles/ patterns are *abbreviations* of our architectural notation. They can be used in this notation, without leaving its conceptual frame.

Data flow patterns/ data flow styles: We discussed four examples, starting with the simplest and ending with general forms. We used *forward simulation*: We can precisely define the *semantics* of patterns or *variations* thereof. We can use patterns as *abbreviation* for classical architectural solutions. We can *mix* both *notations*, e.g. architecture diagrams containing data flow parts.

Technical architectures, *patterns/* styles: They are heavily dependent on specific mechanisms: We discussed two examples for *event-* or signal-*based architectures*, callback and broadcasting. We discussed one example for an architecture, which is determined by a *distribution infrastructure*, here CORBA. We used "*backward simulation*", we looked for an *abstract notation*, which neglects the technical details. This notation fits better for architectural discussions to start with. *Annotations* then refer to the technical solution. Extending or exchanging technical solutions is simpler, if we start with abstract architectural design.

Global patterns/ solutions: They are patterns on a coarse level. We studied the example N-Tier and Blackboard. We used again forward simulation but now on a coarser level. The results of that simulation are more architectural sketches. The approach delivered a clear demarcation between architectural pictures on one side and *architectural sketches*. We see *advantages* of the latter: We identified a false hierarchy in N-Tier architectures, we expressed the importance of a clear UI and data access part, and we discussed variations of the blackboard pattern.

Ch. 6 Message: PIDs are *Extensions* of Process Diagrams

We introduced a generalized process notation in order to express different *influencing parameters* for a process: Not only input and output, but also goals, restrictions, how to proceed, actor, helpful means (components, tools), and experience or knowledge. The purpose was to make the *dependency relations* between processes more specific and to allow more complex forms of interaction.

That allows to express the *interaction of processes* more *precisely*, especially their dependency relations. That is why we named the notation process interaction diagrams. We see that the output of one process can have different semantic influences on another process, not only input, but also to define the goals, the restrictions, etc. These semantic dependencies make the interaction diagrams more *meaningful* than transport networks.

We discussed some *nontrivial examples*, as interleaving processes (as design of the product/ planning its production; life cycle of the product/ design and configuration of the producing infrastructure). A simpler example was discussed for software engineering. Further examples are the relation between requirements determination/ the realization, changes due to process evolution, and showing that management and technical processes are intertwined. Finally, a bootstrapping example showed that processes of humans and automatic ones do interact. The ideas presented are applicable to any engineering domain.

Example processes can be coarse-, middle-, or fine-grained (not used). We saw human and automatic processes, different situations of mechanical engineering, software engineering, also for compiler development. Thus, the notation can be used in *different situations* w.r.t. granularity, domains, and character of subprocesses.

*Ch. 7 Message: There are Different **Reuse Forms** from Shallow to Deep*

Thinking in structures and reuse needs the right level, namely a *carefully designed software architecture*. It should be adaptable, i.e. prepared for extensions/ changes of functionality, but also for technical modifications, like exchange of basic components/ data structures. Functional and data abstraction are used. Discussions, design experience, and new ideas change the development.

Reuse is longtime learning: We build several times, get experience and more efficiency in time and costs. This was called *shallow reuse*. We step forward in direction of standardization/ patterns, frameworks/ basic layers. *Deep reuse* demands for intelligent people/ time/ and money. The result has a long-term advantage, but it also costs, as shown for multiphase compilers for programming languages. Deep reuse is rather seldom in industry, due to costs, time, and knowledge. But we can get enormous *profit* in the long run.

Deep reuse in our compiler example *means*: precise requirements, a careful architecture, the right abstractions, looking for adaptability, for a framework, and a basic data exchange layer. Then, only the functional layer needs to be developed, the other parts remain. The *next steps* are tables for functions and corresponding drivers, generation of code or tables (compiler-compiler approach). Global reuse patterns, like UNCOL or Bootstrapping, finalize ch. 7.

That all costs: Hard work is necessary, money, knowledge, and foresight to see the long-term advantages. *Deep reuse* is only realistic for *stable domains and stable problems*. The PID notation of ch. 6 was used to show progress by reuse.

If you look on the product (architecture) and the process, you can *distinguish between shallow and deep reuse*: If the product and process remain similar, we have shallow reuse. If the product and process change noticeably, we have deep reuse.

Ch. 8 Message: The **Architecture** is the **Glue** for **Integration** of Systems

The *integration* of *different software systems* was discussed. The systems are different corresponding to variety, implementation structure, time of development, concepts used, degree of reuse applied, or range of functionality. We regarded examples from the domains business administration, mobility/ embedded systems, and tool development & integration. We also covered different statuses, as new development, maintenance/ evolution, and reuse. The examples are also representative for other domains outside of software development.

The integration examples have *different characteristics*: (a) Coupling of two existing and different software systems by an integration part, based on two new interfaces and software in between; (b) coupling a bigger system to other ones by new standard interfaces, extending the applications, and protocol components; (c) new development for embedded components by a low-level connection/ or higher level components and service-oriented coupling; (d) reuse of a framework of standard components, in which specific parts are generated, using a spec environment and an integration framework. In any case, we need *new software/* interfaces for *integration*, and standard solutions for *coupling* and generation. The glue is the *architecture*.

The glue is mainly *independent* from the *state and level* of software development. We need the architecture glue even in the case of model-driven development to integrate the generated components. The reason is that an overall model, specifying all necessary aspects from which the whole system can be generated, is too complicated or not possible. Therefore, the model-driven approach is only usable for precise and well-understood parts of a system for which corresponding long lasting experience is available, see ch. 7 for the compiler-compiler example. The generated components are placed within the integrated solution.

Ch. 9 Message: Reverse and **Reengineering, neither Complete** nor **Rigorous**

Reengineering of legacy systems is challenging. Redeveloping them from scratch is economically infeasible. This also applies to pervasive modifications, which are costly to perform and validate. Thus, decide carefully, which parts of an application should be discarded and redeveloped, which should be reengineered, and which stay untouched (*reengineering in the coarse*).

Methods and tools of two sample projects provide *valuable support* for reengineering. Without them, reengineering is performed manually, implying a high development effort. We also have to acknowledge inherent limitations: Applications built without functional and data abstraction are hard to restructure. Design recovery may be supported by algorithms with heuristics, but the resulting proposals need to be inspected and require further adaptations.

The essence of the *BA example*: In the *business functionality* and the *data access* we find parts of the system to be preserved. Therefore, we *reengineer with care* (eliminating only UI and data details, care about new interfaces). We do not essentially touch the code for the business functionality. The UI and the control part are *newly structured*. Wrapping of the old and the clear structure of the new parts induce loose coupling, necessary for distribution. A corresponding infrastructure minimizes the effort. The new form of the system improves *adaptability*: Details of style/ layout of UI, details of data handling through a clear new interface, clear separation of dialog control and executing the business functionality.

While the BA project was concerned with software migration (from a mainframe application to a client-server system), the *telecom project* aimed at *perfective maintenance*: The system is reengineered in a minimally invasive way to improve its structure and performance. The scenarios addressed are splitting and merging of Plex blocks. Global reengineering and the migration to a new platform was not intended.

A tool chain was developed and applied for reengineering, supporting *design recovery*, *re-design*, and *re-implementation*. While the chain is useful to support software developers in reengineering, the overall process still requires significant manual work to deliver an efficient, maintainable, and stable system. Design recovery is driven by heuristic algorithms that generate proposals, which have to be reviewed and revised. Re-design requires design decisions, and re-implementation creates re-organized source code that has to be inspected, adapted, and tested. Tool support for reengineering is useful and required. The analysis of its limitations reveals that *reengineering* is *seldom complete*.

Wrappers may support reengineering in different ways. (i) Old code not intended to be modified is hidden behind a wrapper that enables access from a more recent platform (e.g., by providing object-oriented wrappers to procedural code). (ii) Reengineered code may be wrapped in order to prevent or confine the propagation of changes. Both example projects are rather different w.r.t. domain, class of systems, functionality and support, different implementation languages (Cobol, PLEX). Thus, we demonstrated the independence and *broad applicability* of the presented ideas.

Ch. 10 Message: *Models* and *Transformations* Exist on *Different Levels*

The chapter is an overview and introduction to the following chs. 11-14. The first part introduces different lifecycle process models (waterfall, V, spiral, iterative and incremental model) and traces them back to the generic WAM, able to *instantiate different process models*. The second part shows that *processes, products*, and *relations* exist on *three levels*, namely coarse-, medium-, and fine-grained, (lifecycle, organization, and code, from the role in the development process), necessary to understand, structure, carry out, and monitor a project. The overall configuration is a fine-grained model, which has contractions to coarser levels.

There are more *changes* than straight development in a project, which have to be handled on the complex overall configuration. Changes happen within documents, but have implications to others, yielding chains of traces. We can regard interaction of processes, integration of results, and reactivity between processes and results.

The *fine-grained links* between documents, from increments of one document to increments to the other, have a specific and *important role*. They connect the results of different developers. If they are not available, the developers must have them in their mind. They connect different views, as the architectural description and its explanation in the documentation. These relations are important to understand, explain, modify and also handle the consequences of changes.

The architecture is a configuration of diagrams, detailing texts, annotations within a description, references to corresponding detailed elaborations. A part of this configuration is directly devoted to architectural views and aspects. Other parts outside of the architectural configuration belong to quality, documentation, and management of the development or are derived from the architecture, as program code. Thus, the architecture *integrates different aspects* and artifacts and is the center for integration.

Ch. 11 Message: **No Automatic Transformation** *Requirements - Architecture*

The chapter regarded *requirements specifications* with their functional part and their nonfunctional part. The functional part was described by two different approaches: a 'structural' one integrating different languages (SA, ER, CTR) and a more modern OO one. In both cases, the nonfunctional part describes restrictions, the system or its development have to fulfil.

The specific approach does not influence the main message of this chapter: The *transformation* of the requirements spec to an architecture is not automatic, and the requirements spec is not extended to get the architecture. Instead both, requirements spec and architectural description, are *two* different *views*, built up by different persons with different roles.

There are two main examples in this chapter (a) for *Business Administration* and (b) (only remarks) for *Embedded Systems*. The details of the requirements of (a) come from (i) not abstracting from details of the context, (ii) of specific ways how to handle processes or the data, (iii) and not regarding expected changes. In embedded systems, the number of these details is much bigger. The details are responsible for the difficulty of translating to the architecture. The details can be reduced, by already introducing abstraction on requirements level and by already regarding probable changes. The *transformation is interactive*.

An *automatic transformation* is only possible in rare and specific cases: (1) having carried out many developments which are similar and having collected corresponding experience, (2) having detected strong similarity by regarding a class of problems and the class (family, line) of solutions, and (3) giving ambitious developers enough time and money to think about new ways to proceed. (4) If this also includes corresponding tools, in specific domains with formal input or output, and well-understood transformation steps, the transformations can be automated. It takes a long time, money, and long-term strategy to get this mature reuse level.

*Ch. 12 Message: Without **Architectures**, one cannot **Master** the **Code***

The chapter examines the *relation* between *architectural* design and *programming* (code). The architecture and the implementation are coupled tightly: The software architecture acts as a *blueprint* for the *code* of the system developed/ maintained.

The concepts underlying the proposed *architecture description language* originate from modular and object-oriented languages. Essentially, the architecture description language aims at enforcing a disciplined use of programming concepts, by defining components of different types, and different types of usability.

Accordingly, *conformance* of the implementation with the software architecture may be defined by *rules* referring to syntactic elements of the respective underlying languages. Rules may be classified into *completeness* or *consistency*.

The metaphor of blueprint may be illustrated by the *generation* of *implementation frames* that have to be filled in by programmers: Since the software architecture defines the static structure of the respective software system, its behavior has to be added at the level of programming. To this end, data abstractions have to be realized, and bodies of functions or procedures have to be implemented.

While the conceptual relation between the software architecture and the implementation is clearly defined, it depends on the underlying software process how conformance of the implementation with the software architecture is achieved. An *incremental forward engineering process* provides the best match: The architecture acts as the master, on which the implementation depends. Furthermore, an incremental process takes into account that the software architecture has to be changed in the process for a variety of reasons and the changes need to be propagated to the implementation.

*Ch. 13 Message: **Architecture**-Centered **Project Organization***

Project organization is the only managerial working area in the WAM. Due to its central role in the software process, architectural design strongly influences project organization. Since the software architecture defines the modules and subsystems to be implemented, it is used to define work packages (tasks) assigned to programmers. Furthermore, the software architecture is used to schedule these tasks in an order that is derived from the dependencies of these components. Similarly, testing tasks are defined based on the software architecture. Milestones are defined for project planning, referring to the components of the software architecture. Finally, the project team may be organized according to the structure of the architecture.

Thus, the architecture should play a central role in project organization. This is achieved by a management approach based on the notion of a *medium-grained management configuration* covering products, activities, and resources. This configuration provides an abstraction of the technical configuration representing all elements of the software process down the fine-grained level. Both the product and activity parts of the management configuration strongly depend on the software architecture.

Task nets may be derived, including implementation and testing tasks for the components of the software architecture. The dependencies among these tasks may be derived according to the selected implementation and test strategies.

As software processes evolve continuously, the management configuration is subject to permanent changes. Thus, the *dynamics* of software processes needs to be considered by management. This includes e.g. modifications to the requirements, revision of design decisions, *feedback* from implementation and testing to requirements engineering and architectural design, as well as both *shallow* and *deep reuse* (ch. 7), implying small and radical process improvements.

Ch. 14 Message: Quality Assurance, Documentation, and Architectures

We have discussed *documentation* and *quality assurance* for *three situations*: (i) Looking at the architecture of a system, (ii) looking at the transformation of the requirements spec to the upper levels of an architecture, and (iii) looking at the code integration test, its regarding plan, strategy, and order of integration, mostly determined by the architecture. Thus, (ii) is the start of the AR design process, (i) the kernel, and (iii) the end of the design process. The examples should convince the reader that the essential *results* of this chapter are valid.

We have introduced a strict definition for *documentation*, which separates *details*, of the *technical* part of the overall configuration, from explaining their *essence* and *rationale*, usually in natural language. Only the latter, was called documentation in this chapter. The corresponding documentation artifacts can have different *relations* to other *artifacts* of the configuration, from 1:1 to m: n. This also corresponds to different relations between subprocesses, from coarse (working areas), to medium (artifacts), to fine-grained (increments of different artifacts). The same is true for *quality assurance*, where we distinguish between technical activities by internal QA persons and checks of external QA persons.

There are strong *similarities* between *documentation* and *quality assurance* corresponding to their relations to technical and nontechnical working areas, their subprocesses, and fine-grained activities. The same applies to the products, their granularities, and forms of relations. Both can be internal (done by the developer) and external (by someone outside). Documentation is plain text, QA artifacts have any form.

15.2 Messages across Chapters

Integration 1: Specific Approach: Separation and Integration (Chs. 1-3, 10-14)

Clear *logical levels* of *processes, products,* and their *relations* are needed, for building up complex processes (by process models) and products (by configuration models). Architecture modeling is the center of the global process and the architectural configuration the center of the overall product. *Integration* needs precise *separation* followed by precise *putting together*.

Thus, we understand *integration* here as integrating clear logical working areas and corresponding results. This is a *general principle*, namely to clearly *separate* on one side and to tightly *integrate* the separate parts on the other, see chs. 1 - 3. This can be seen for working areas, their results, and their relations with all refinements, and from the mappings and relations of chs. 10 to 14. We see it also from area-specific tools and integrators, and from the big projects as IPSEN und IMPROVE. So, integration is *not putting anything of different nature into one bag.*

We find different *occurrences* of this *principle* in the book: WAM or parts of the overall configuration in ch.1. Different conceptual parts of the architecture language in ch. 2. Different architectures over the time in ch. 3. Adaptability rules by separation and integration in ch. 4. Putting styles/ patterns and modular architectures together in ch. 5. Clear process separation and integration by PIDs in ch. 6. Different forms of reuse and their integration in ch. 7. Different systems and their integration by glue in ch. 8. Old systems and their new form by reverse and reengineering in ch. 9. Processes interaction, products integration along different granularities/ mapping of models in ch. 10. Integrating RE and AR in ch. 11, AR and PS in ch. 12, integrating AR and PO in ch. 13, integrating AR with QA/ DOC in ch. 14. Finally putting messages/ open problems together in ch. 15.

Uniform approach: Understanding integration is *not restricted* to software engineering or engineering in different domains. It also applies to find out, how cooperation between different organizations can be organized, or science and its disciplines should go forward in knowledge development. Integration also applies to the architecture of buildings and their history. It even applies to social and political structures.

In this general setting a third *dimension* comes up: After separation and integration there should be time to *factorize out common parts*, as they influence separation and integration, and put both on a more general level. Thereby, architectures get a further and new importance. *Reengineering,* see ch. 9, has to do with making components and structures cleaner (separation), which then can be integrated easier.

Integration 2: Different **Methodological Aspects** in **Architectures** *(Chs. 1,2,3)*

The *architecture* of a software system unites different *aspects* and it has to be *known* – at least to a certain extent – by all members of a development team. It is based on different concepts of *abstraction* (architecture paradigm). It should have a clear syntax and semantics (not often formally defined); it is not a vague "conceptual picture". Its role should be commonly accepted, as it is the case for architectures in house building. The architecture is the center of the development results (here overall configuration, BIM for house building).

We find in architecture modeling *tight* and *loose coupling*: (i) for interfaces (tight) and their use (loose), (ii) for interface and body of a module, (iii) for the aggregated interface and the body architecture of a subsystem, (iv) in syntax rules and method patterns, (v) for locality or OO structures on one hand and their import on the other, (vi) for the methodology of one working area (as AR) and the transformation between working areas, (vii) for local patterns and for global patterns, (viii) for abstract architectures and corresponding details and annotations, (ix) for handling the stages of the architecture and the architecture sequence, (x) for the method rules for a specific class (embedded systems) and the general method repertoire for all systems. There is (xi) tighter coupling in the way to build a new system than in long-term mainte-nance, reuse, or family development.

Tight and loose is only one dimension. Other *methodological topics*, as modularity, handling similarity, etc. can be discussed similarly. We can also look globally: There is tighter coupling within the architectural configuration and looser coupling to the other parts of the overall configuration.

Integration 3: Integration within Architecture **Languages** *(Chs. 2, 5)*

The architecture *language is integrated*, as it contains different concepts, having been integrated: *Different forms* of *components* (fo, ft, ado, adt, subsystems), differ-ent forms of *relations* (locality, general layers, similarities and differences (OO)), different *granularities* (from parts of an interface to the complete architecture). We have a multi-paradigmatic architectural design language.

Furthermore, we have syntax rules and method rules (or different forms of patterns). Relations can be understood as abstract and concrete, ch. 5. There are diverse anno-tations for semantics, concurrency, and distribution. Different styles can be ex-pressed by the architectural language, such that they are abbreviations of situations in the standard language. Different *language elements* and how to *combine* them, should be clear, as also the *mutual relations* of artifacts in the overall configuration.

Integration 4: Architecture Modeling in **Development** Processes *(Chs. 3, 9, 8)*

There are (**i**) *different architectures* (a sequence of architectures) from abstract to those in detail, describing the final solution, see ch. 3. Their order depends on the structure class of the system (batch, interactive, embedded), the application domain (business admin, technical software, etc.), the underlying execution infrastructure (from one computer to services in internet), etc. In some cases, (**ii**) we start with an insufficient structure, which has to be reverse engineered and reengineered (mostly only done in the coarse) to have a good starting point (ch. 9). In some cases, (**iii**) we combine systems by an integration architecture, ch. 8. (ii) and (iii) are long-lasting maintenance/ evolution activities. In (iii), the architectures of the systems are starting points, which allow integration. We dealt with integration *dimensions*: different *ar-chitectures of a process and even long-lasting processes* and putting them together.

Continuation of above: (**iv**) In ch. 4, we discuss which *rules* we can find and apply in the development of embedded systems for adaptability. (**v**) In ch. 6, we introduce a *notation* for coupling processes, more general than the usual output-input. (**vi**) In ch. 7, we explain demarcations and integration of *reuse* approaches. (**vii**) Ch. 5 in-troduces integration of different patterns/ styles. (**viii**) The integration aspects of soft-ware development and corresponding tools were discussed carefully.

Integration 5: How to Find all **Associated Information** *(Chs 2, 10, 11-14)*

Within the *architectural configuration* we get quite different information: (i) *ab-stract architectures* and their details, from single components, their types, interfaces, and imports (necessary for implementing the body). We get further information as, (ii) annotations for semantics, (iii) for embedded systems' processes and synchronization, controlled start/ stop, and emergency handling. We see (iv) different patterns, as well as (v) how to realize abstract relations by kinds of communication mechanisms, and (vi) different transformations for improving efficiency.

In the overall configuration we also see (vii) *coarse* information on lifecycle level (the complete architectural configuration), (viii) *middle*-grained info (as the managerial configuration) strongly related to architectural units. Finally, we see *fine-grained* information (inside the architectural configuration), but also between their increments and other increments.

Finally, looking on the overall configurations and the transformations between the results of the different working areas, we see (ix) corresponding management information, (x) quality assurance information (xi) and documentation associated to items of the architecture. If the transformation is supported by suitable tools which have installed links, and we can follow these links to access the related information.

Integration 6: Long-lasting Projects and Integration, Tools (Chs. 6, 7. 8, 9)

Maintenance and evolution are long-lasting activities. They demand for integrating software architectures over a long time. In this time, we apply different forms of reverse and reengineering, and we apply them multiple times.

The same applies for *reuse*, especially for deep reuse. In this case, we do not only integrate over the time, but also over different reuse mechanisms, and over the degree of reuse and automatism. This only pays off in long-lasting projects. PIDs (ch. 6) allow to describe process interaction in elaborate cases, see ch. 7.

This even applies to integration *approaches*, as a priori of IPSEN and *a-posteriori* of IMPROVE, see chs. 8, 9. More ambitious is the a posteriori approach: *Wrappers* are used, for equalizing the logically different levels of interfaces and to prepare for further integration and extension. This is the *reengineering* part. *New functionality* is added, provided by integrator tools, bridging different working areas, see chs. 10, 11, 12, 14. The adaptive management system, able to react on dynamic changes in the development process, offers novel management functionality, see ch. 13. This all can be put together to form a new *integrated overall* tool support *environment*.

Integration 7: Classes and Families (Chs. 7, 8, 9)

There are different *global classes* of software systems as batch, interactive, or embedded systems. Each class shares internal similarities, even if they belong to different domains, see a batch system for BA and a compiler in system programming. The class can be seen as unification of all members.

More specific are families of systems, as compilers. The similarities here are strong. An even stricter family are compilers for a certain class of languages, as strongly typed languages with many context-sensitive rules, developed by deep reuse.

Much *weaker* are the *similarities* between systems which are transformed from others by maintenance/ or evolution. Changes can prevent the similarity or disrupt it. In maintenance in order to improve reuse, similarities may *grow*.

Development can be seen in a *timely difference and order*: new, maintenance, evolution, reuse and experience, families, deep reuse, see above. Again, architecture modelling is the center of the long-lasting process/ product results.

Intellectual Activity: Architecture *Modeling is for Humans* (all chapters)

Support for this *intellectual activity* is given by experience through methods how to develop the architecture indifferent stages and the role of architectures in the whole development process. The whole book contributes for that.

The *character* of software *architecture design* is technical and creative, but patterns play a certain role. The architecture is based on a specific abstraction: precise, sometimes formal, including dimensions as aesthetics, simplicity, understandability.

This is *rarely automatable*. In certain areas and domains, automation can be achieved by a demanding design process, ch. 7. Parametric design, patterns for the whole system, reuse design, algorithmic design, etc. play an important role, created by humans.

15.3 Open Problems, Chapter by Chapter

Ch. 1: *Standard* Model for *Architectures*, Connection to *Engineering, Tools*

There is no *standard model for software architectures*. Object-oriented architectures in BA applications and data flow architectures in embedded systems have little in common. Unifying different architectural notations/ styles by a component/relation-oriented approach or a classical module/ subsystems/ usability relations approach, are not used in industry. There is no standardization as for houses (ground, floor plans, views from different directions, refinements for installation, plumbing, ch.2).

Architectures have also a central role in *all engineering disciplines*. Again, the commonalities of architectures in electrical engineering and subdisciplines as layout plans, in mechanical engineering for machines/ factories, in process engineering for plants are not worked out. There is room for *bridging* dis*ciplines*.

In all the above domains, the architecture has a central role for the development process and even further, as pointed out for software systems in ch. 1. There are different opinions about architectures in various domains. Is there at least some agreement which *questions* the *architecture* of different engineering domains *should answer*, or which problems should be *solved* by using the architecture?

There is a *growing importance* for all engineering domains, namely the *software* part of *engineered systems*. Can this be the starting point of thinking in a deeper way?

In any of the above disciplines, there is room for *intelligent tools*, more than painting or writing. We need intelligent tools, which give in-depth syntactical and semantical support for the work in specific working areas, or integrating the different aspect- and domain-specific artifacts, and organizing a project.

Ch. 2: *Further Aspects of Architectures and Overall Configurations*

Further aspects and corresponding annotations are possible. (**i**) We could have discussed *efficiency transformations*. There is a more abstract and possible inefficient form of an architecture and there are possible ways to make it more efficient. Thus, we introduce different annotations by supplements or even transformation patterns.

We introduced several forms of further aspects/ additions, as semantics, concurrency, concrete use of connectors, and distribution. However, (**ii**) we did not explain, how to *organize* such *additions* and in *which order*. We only gave some rules, ch. 3. The order depends on the structure class, the application domain, the history of development in the company, etc. It has to be well thought-out.

Building Information Models collect and compose all artifacts belonging to the design and construction of buildings. A similar approach (**iii**) could be used for the design and realization of software systems and further documents around, as e.g. technical acceptance and validation, the contract, the protocols of sessions, etc. All this information is called the *product and process model*. There is *no accepted standard* available for this overall model today. Such a standard cannot be fixed, to allow differences of domains, cultures , methodologies, etc. A standard includes our overall configuration. A checklist for structure classes, application domains, would help.

Ch. 3: *Long Term and Similarities*

In ch. 3 we argued in a static manner looking on one system. However, there are *dimensions,* which have a longer range and imply architectural sequences:

(**i**) Discuss *maintenance/ extension*, by looking not only on one system, but also on the history of a system, from reverse engineering to integrating the system with others to extend the system. (**ii**) Regard a *family of systems*. Essential knowledge you do not get top-down, you get it bottom-up. Starting with one system, you recognize similarities within following systems until you end with a family development approach. (**iii**) The same is true for *reuse*, especially if you try to abandon shallow reuse (doing it as the last time) and to reach *deep reuse* (like generation of code instead of handcrafting the code).

In all these cases (i) to (iii), you have architectures in a long-term maintenance/ or family/ or reuse project. What is the *effect on the architectural sequences*? Can we find general *patterns* for changes in sequences?

Ch. 4: *Better Understanding of Reuse in Embedded Systems and of MDD*

Reuse in Embedded Systems is more difficult, due to the many *technical details*. Therefore, there is no unique and uniform structure class build plan describing how an embedded system looks like. We have different forms: (a) small systems on one control unit, (b) systems with a hardware of many and cheap CUs (automotive), (c) those with powerful and connected control hardware (aircrafts), (d) those for big chemical/ manufacture plants with layers in centralized or decentralized form.

How to describe these different forms? With global *patterns* for such *systems*, it would be simpler to decide what to take from a given system, if a system in the same/ similar domain is developed. At least, one could take parts of the solution (basic layer, important components, methodology for parts). *Reuse* would be *easier*.

To look on different systems through an abstract view makes it easier to *develop system families* or *product lines*, which may evolve over the time, or which may even be configured dynamically. Here, you have to detect similarities in a systematic way: Which differences are less important as coming up only in one member, which parts are essential and characterize the family. To develop one embedded system is rather complicated. Even more ambitious is to get a family of systems. The build plan for the family must contain the commonalities, and indicate the differences. Ideally, members are configured automatically.

A specific *problem for families* is in automotive. The turnaround time of a car is about 7 years. A producer has several models (each with many variants). So, the systems of different models are developed in some order, to avoid to overload developers. We call this order the big cycle. At the beginning of this big cycle, the company has to decide, what to *reuse from the model of the last big cycle*. The same holds for the earlier models within *the big cycle*. So, there are system families, which consist of smaller families: How to use *the knowledge* of the big cycle for the rest of the big cycle, and also for the next big cycle?

Model-driven Development (MDD) is an *ambitious* approach. In MDD we start with abstract *models* denoted in a suitable language and transform these models into software, ideally by code generation. This model can be a control loop Simulink model (cruise control), a Statechart model for opening/ closing a car, a spec for the communication of the car with others or the road.

In all these cases, the generator has to be written such that it automatically and always follows the methods to produce adaptable software. Or, the generated code is put into a framework for components which fulfills the hints. The *generation approach is suitable for partial solutions* (cruise control, locking, etc.). It has to be integrated into the realization process of the whole system, as the integration of all models in one overall model and then generating the code is not realistic. Neither the models, nor the corresponding tools for different models are integrated, nor the generation processes. There is a *gap* between the current *MDD state and* the *adaptability/ variability architectural approach*.

In our approach, in every step a *person* is involved. The designer, programmer, etc. follows hints, *makes architectural decisions,* achieves adaptability, and masters variability. This is simpler than an MDD approach, where the machinery is built such that decisions are made automatically by the generator.

Ch. 5: *Embedded Systems: Needed **Styles** and **Tools***

There are application domains where specific problems occur. In the development of *embedded systems*, we often find that solutions are *bound to technical* and *detailed items* of the technical target environment. We have discussed this, when we argued for first making abstractions. Especially in embedded systems, we find the task of changing given systems by reverse/ reengineering to make them understandable, or flexible and adaptable. The question is, how to *combine* such objectives and approaches with styles or patterns.

In *development processes* of software engineering but also of other engineering processes, there is a lack of *tools* which serve for the *integration* of the different working areas, for example from RE to AR, or AR and PO. Solutions are more in academic projects for software development, chemical engineering, or for architecture and civil engineering. Even more evident is that there are few tools for supporting the *approaches addressed* above (model-driven, product lines, generation, etc.). Also missing are tools for *integrating* these new approaches with the definition and application of *styles and patterns*.

Ch. 6: *PIDs Allow to Describe **Complex Interactions** of Processes*

PIDs describe *complex interactions* of processes, which are usually only discussed in an informal way. Only some of them are discussed in ch. 6,7 as the steps to get a multi-phase compiler by deep reuse. Many other coupling and influencing process interactions are possible, see the dynamics problems sketched in ch. 1 and 13.

We specialized in ch. 6 only on the process part of process modeling and ignored the product, the human actor, and the support part, all of them on abstract and detailed level. Research we carried out included these parts. PIDs can be used to reformulate and *extend* the *process* part of the literature. The chapter remains in the tradition of having a clear *focus* in process investigations.

We concentrated in our process research on middle-grained processes (and on coarse-grained processes). Furthermore, we concentrated on the product part (the outcome) of processes, by building tools to get the product of a process easier or of a better quality and, thereby, supporting the process as well. We did not regard *fine-grained processes* how a single developer is doing his work.

Ch. 7: *Long-term Changes, Deep Reuse, Classes and Families*

In ch. 7, we have sketched how reuse changes products and processes for software. This could also be done for other fields. The first is **(i)** *long-term maintenance*. Systems live 20 and more years and change dramatically. The systems' changes and its maintenance could be described in the same way as it was done for reuse. The same can be done **(ii)** for *system families/ lines*. They usually arise from single system development. We could describe the changes of the product and of the process in a suitable way. Both is missing.

We need more intelligence in software construction. Shallow reuse is dominating in industrial software development. This is acceptable *in an often changing* context: New applications come up, extensions of applications appear often, using new methods and tools happens frequently, starting new domains is daily practice. This hinders to think in the long term. Time is hectic – there is no time and money for sustainable development, and no corresponding understanding and insight at the management level of companies. If you develop software in a stable environment, (**iii**) think about careful development and *deep reuse*. That needs time, money, and excellent developers, but it is worth a *long-term investment*.

All of above (**iv**) works for *specific classes* of *software systems*. The more *specialized* and precise the class is, and the more you *know* about this class, the *deeper* are the results. In this way, deep reuse contributes to the knowledge of software classes, to deep understanding in a company, and to deep understanding in software subdomains, thereby *contributing* to (**v**) software engineering *knowledge acquisition*.

Ch. 8: *Long-term Steps, **Deep Understanding** of **Change** and **Gluing***

In ch. 8, we dealt with maintenance/ evolution, (re)use of existing systems, and their *integration*. This all can again be seen as *development in longer time*: What are the steps of maintenance and integration, and how do the results change in these steps.

The same is true for *families* of systems, which are found after trials and experience, looking for general parts, using similarity, and starting again on a more general level having the specifics in mind.

Again, we can go from single development to families/ lines, now under the aspect of *change* over time, from *incremental to radical*. Compared to the problems and solutions of single systems in this chapter, the questions and solutions of integration are more difficult. Are there results for this more general view of use and integration?

Ch. 9: *Practical Reverse and **Reengineering** in a **Wider Sense***

Two examples are discussed in ch. 9 of a practical approach to reverse and reengineering. Many *further examples* in different domains are possible for applying this moderate approach, which we named *reengineering* in the *coarse*.

The discussion deals with modernizing *one specific* system. We get a *new quality* of problems, if we regard a *series of systems* which share some similarity:
(a) Make a *family of systems* or a product *line* out of similar systems This means that inherent similarities and differences have to be found, worked out, and made explicit.
(b) The *complexity* of *systems* and their *similarity* w.r.t. structure and complexity should be clear. For both, software metrics could be applied to formalize reasoning.
(c) Extract *domain knowledge* from different programming in a domain.
(d) If, in a certain and specific context programs are developed, then reuse is usually applied. Deep reuse in the sense of ch. 7 is rarely found. *Reuse steps* might be regarded as specific reengineering modifications. Can the finding of deep reuse steps be supported? Can the reuse knowledge be extracted?

Ch. 10: *Process and **Model Transformations: Different Levels** and Long-Term*

We discussed different process models on lifecycle level from waterfall to agile. Furthermore, we explained that *processes*, *products*, and also *relations* exist on three *levels*, from lifecycle to fine-grained. This also applies to the *overall configurations*, and there to the transformations between models. The discussion was focused on regarding these topics when developing one system.

Again, all problem discussion gets more complicated, if we regard *long-term changes*, which demand for complex structural modifications. This is the case for long-term *maintenance/ integration*, which appears for some software systems within decades. This is also the case for changing a system by applying reuse, especially by *deep reuse* (ch. 7). Finally, this also happens, if we go from a system to the family of similar systems (*families* or product *lines*). How to structure these changes and to support them by tools is also widely unknown.

Ch. 11: *RE to AR and Wider Problems*

We argued that requirements can be transformed automatically to software architectures only in rare cases; rather, the transformation involves many design decisions that have to be performed by humans. An interactive transformation process is laborious and difficult to perform. There, more *guidance* is required in order to ease the transition from RE to AR. To this end, *domain-specific rules* have to be developed that reduce the number of design decisions, such that at least an initial software architecture may be derived from the requirements more easily. It should be noted that "syntactic" transformation rules for mapping language constructs are not sufficient. Rather, typical *patterns* and transformation *methods* need to be identified to make the transformation of requirements to architectures more manageable.

These considerations imply a more general approach to *reuse*, which usually focuses on the reuse of artifacts produced throughout the software lifecycle (requirements, architectures, program code, etc.). For the transition from requirements engineering to architectural design, an approach to the *reuse of transformations* needs to be developed. Thus, product reuse has to be complemented with process reuse.

Ch. 12: *AR and PS: Practical Use*

In ch. 12, we clarified the conceptual relation between architectural design and programming in the small: The software architecture serves as a blueprint for the implementation. Furthermore, we identified incremental forward engineering as the process that matches best this conceptual relation.

However, further work is required in *exploring* the *practical use* of this approach. To this end, the incremental forward engineering process needs to be applied and elaborated further in order to clarify how software architects and programmers should cooperate: How frequently should the architecture and the implementation be synchronized? To what extent (if any) may deviations of the implementation from the prescribed architecture be permitted? How can we ensure that programmers accept the software architecture as a useful aid in their work?

To apply the incremental forward engineering process successfully, powerful *tool support* is required. We need tools for both checking and enforcing conformance. These tools should operate incrementally, such that changes of the architecture may be propagated precisely to the implementation, without affecting code that is independent from changes. So far, incremental integration tools have been developed primarily as research tools that need to be developed further into industrial tools.

Ch. 13 *Project Organization and Architectures*

With respect to architecture-centered project organization, several issues have not been addressed by the management approach presented in ch. 13:

(a) *Long-term software maintenance.* Primarily, software development processes following an incremental forward engineering approach were considered. Long-term software maintenance of existing systems was not studied.

(b) *Long-term process evolution.* Software processes evolve with increasing experience gained in the respective domains. In order to obtain significant advances in software process performance, non-incremental process improvements may be required, as exemplified e.g. by compiler construction, which proceeded from systematically handwritten to generated code (*deep reuse*).

(c) *Software product lines.* Families of software systems managed in a software product line imply many additional challenges to be covered by the presented management approach. To this end, the software process needs to be decomposed into two parts: *domain engineering* (of the product line) and *application engineering* (of a specific product). The respective subprocesses need to be synchronized, providing for change propagation in both directions. Furthermore, an adequate representation of multi-variant artifacts needs to be designed. Finally, reverse engineering of multiple products (potentially created by clone-and-own) has to be supported.

Ch. 14: *Extended QA and DOC*

In ch. 3, we have seen that there is not only one architecture but a *series of architectures*, ranging from the abstract and static architecture (logical architecture) to that with distribution and efficiency (physical or target architecture). Intermediate steps are semantic annotations, concurrency, distribution, and technical concurrency. In ch. 4. on embedded systems, we found *further development tasks* as regulated start/stop of the system and emergency handling.

In the examples regarded on documentation and quality assurance, we mostly discussed static architectures and semantic annotations. We could have *regarded* the *other aspects* of architectures as well. That makes the examples more complicated. The arguments of the chapter are still valid.

What we learn is that the discussion of the *overall configuration*, as given in chs. 1 and 10, is still simple. Please think about the architectural configuration now also *regarding* the *different forms* of architectures and further tasks.

We concentrated on documentation (DOC) and quality assurance (QA) of architectures. The discussion could be *extended* to the technical *working areas* RE, PS, and to PO. Thus,, the other parts of the overall configuration from the RE to PS, and also the parts corresponding to PO, QA, DOC, *would have to be extended*. It could even be extended to the areas QA and DOC themselves, as even the *documentation* and also the *quality assurance* can be *documented* and *quality assured*. Furthermore, all the *transformations* between different working areas could be handled. This implies an extension of the results of this chapter to further areas and transformations between these areas. We expect only a quantitative and not a qualitative extension.

There are many QA and DOC approaches. For all of them we might ask for *specific* ways how to develop specific *documentation* or *quality assurance* methods, tools, or experiences. This is specifically important and *useful* for companies, working in such environments for a *long time*. As an example, please think of a company having been building aircrafts or telecom systems for 50 years, where more and more software is involved, and where specific rules, knowledge, and experience have to be applied, which have tremendously extended over the years.

15.4 Open Problems, across Chapters

Working out the **Similarity** to **Engineering** (all chapters of this book)

An *overall configuration* we find in *all engineering domains*: outside view for requirements, essential architectural view, from an abstract level (conceptual modeling) down to the level of describing the system with details. We concentrated on architecture modeling, regarding upwards the requirements and downwards the detail engineering. We specifically regarded the links from and to architectural units. The overall configuration corresponds to the BIM for buildings, it is our product information model for software.

The same applies to *processes* corresponding to working areas, *transformations* between working areas and their *results*, and the relations between processes and products. Processes, products and relations appear on *different levels*.

More research is necessary to study the *similarities* and *differences* of *design* and *development* in *different engineering domains* and to compare it w.r.t. what we can contribute from and learn for software engineering. Activities can collect advantages of different approaches to get profit. There are merits in the areas of production engineering, chemical process engineering, automation and control, and communication systems, which can push software engineering forward. Conversely, intelligent software construction can influence engineering. Especially, thinking in classes, families, long-term, etc. is useful for engineering.

Integration of different *methods*, *models*, and *tools* are still big topics for software development in any domain, e.g. for tools and embedded systems. The process has to be improved to better understand it, to make it precise, and to support novel techniques, as model-driven development and generation of code. Even more ambitious is it, if we do not regard a single system but a *family of systems*, or specific problems, see below. There is a moderate goal to learn from each other and improve to the big question "Is there a common design methodology across different disciplines?"

Adaptability *and* ***Flexibility*** *(Chs. 1,2,3,4 and following)*

In any kind of systems, batch, interactive, embedded or subfields thereof, according to domain, specific approach etc., *adaptability* and *flexibility* are *important*.

For batch, IO and intermediate data are important, for interactive systems IO device, window system, UIMS, style and taste, abstract interface what to get/ deliver but no details. For embedded systems, we try to get independent of deliverers, their specific interfaces, etc., see ch. 4. An important question is: Is there a list of *specific topics* for any *class of systems*, not only for structure classes as batch, but also specific subclasses thereof (like compilers, of specific forms)?

Adaptability and flexibility are not only important for the final product. They also apply for the *processes* to get them, for *methods* to be used, the specific *contexts* (company, department, etc.) where they are used. The WAM (ch. 10) is a generic base model, adaptable to different global process models. The overall configuration has invariant parts (as RE processes and products), which have specific instantiations, as shown in ch. 11. Furthermore, adaptability/ flexibility are not only important for new development. They are also important for *maintenance*, as correction, modification, extension. What are the essential answers?

Methods *and* ***Changes:*** *Rules, Patterns, Theory (Chs. 4, 6, 7, 13)*

For specific *method problems* in software development, as rules to develop and follow, patterns to extend and follow, styles to use, how to get forward with reuse, etc. there are papers, but no consistent body of *knowledge*. We miss a corresponding "theory". This theory is not easy to get, as we find a variety of different parameters and approaches. An example is ch. 6, where we have explained that process interaction needs a broader perspective. Another example is ch. 13 on project organization, where we show that dynamic problems (reorganization in a running project) are necessary, or ch. 7 that deep reuse is profitable in a specific domain.

Let us concentrate on reuse as example (for other topics we may argue similarly): We miss to have more intelligence in software construction. As stated above, the *simple reuse* forms (shallow reuse) are dominating in industrial software development. This is acceptable *in an often changing* context: Informatics is developing rapidly, extensions of applications appear often, using new methods and tools always happens, new application domains are daily practice, etc. This hinders to think in the long term. Often there is no time and money for sustainable development, and there is no corresponding understanding and insight at the management level.

Deep reuse pays off in stable contexts. We get magnitudes of profit, if there is time/ money/ the management is aware, we have intelligent people, see ch. 7.

Long-term Tasks *aside of New Development (Chs 7, 8, 9)*

Only a minor part of the workload in software industry is going into *new* development. The major part is maintenance, evolution, connection and integration of *existing* systems. Thereby reverse and reengineering plays a prominent role. Even in new development reuse is mostly concentrating on simple forms as do it as in the last round. In families of systems or in product lines a systematic treatment is often missing, as quick solution have priority.

Maintenance, evolution, reuse, integration, etc. come *in steps* and take a *long time*. Flexibility and adaptability should be regarded at the beginning and also at the end of each step. Also reuse in form of deep reuse is not achieved in one activity. The same is true for system families or product lines. We can argue: The corresponding awareness for such important problems is missing. The cross dependency of these problems is not worked out. All these goals have to do with changes, but there is *no consistent "theory" of changes*. The problems are integrated but the integration is not seen. This book concentrated on architecture, the mentioned problems deal with the complete development.

Everywhere Different **Views** *(Chs. 2, 3, 10, 11-14)*

In architectures we have *different views*, from abstract to concrete, from closed to distributed, from static to regarding other aspects (semantics, distribution, efficiency, etc.), see chs. 2 and 3. In this book, we concentrated on the architectural view. But there are also the requirements and code view and there are the views organization, quality and documentation, accompanying the technical work.

We have addressed the view problem on architectures and how to get the related information (annotations, links to other increments, etc.). All the above open and across chapter *problems* can be *extended* by looking on these *different views*. How do they interact, how can we make use of this interaction?

Transition, Update, *and* **Extension**: *A general Problem?* (Chs. 11 – 14)

In ch. 11 we discussed a *general problem*: After we have made the transformation from the RE spec to the architecture, the architecture could have been worked out. We have parts which are not related to the requirements. Afterwards, the RE spec is extended/ changed. We can make an incremental *forward* transformation and we can set those parts of the architecture as to be eventually changed, which are now not related to the new RE spec, either directly or indirectly. It seems that this situation can appear *in all situations* of chs. 11-14.

We can also find a corresponding *general situation* in the case of *backward transformations,* e.g. between architecture and code, if the architecture has been transformed to code, the code is changed, and then the architecture. Now, we look whether the code is related to the architecture. Or, it can happen between architecture and project organization, if the architecture is mapped to project organization, this project organization is further refined, and then the architecture is changed. The same happens between architecture and quality assurance or architecture and documentation.

We have developed tools for the specific transformations of chs. 11-14. The effort to get these tools is remarkable. Therefore, a further general question arises: Can we build *generic transformation tools*, forward or backward, which can be *instantiated* for a *specific situation*? That would dramatically save effort.

*Separation and **Integration** as **General Concepts** (see also section Messages)*

Above we have discussed that *separation* and *integration* appear nearly everywhere in this book. Also, we have discussed that this way of thinking can be applied to other *engineering* disciplines. The principles of separation and integration on process, product, resources, cooperation, groups of actors, *tools*, integration, etc. can even be *generalized* to quite different and complex other systems as political or social systems. It is a general way of handling complex structures/ processes/ organizations. What are the *results* of this *broad discussion*? Is there a *general form* of integration throughout different disciplines? Is there a general scheme with different *instantiations*?

*Suitable and **Useful Tools** (all chapters)*

Tools for software development belong to working areas (RE, AR, etc.), or to corresponding transformations (RE to AR). They can be further *classified* (as different test tools for quality assurance), and can be further *differentiated* according to domains, system classes, etc. These topics can share underlying characteristics and can be integrated (specific environments for working areas, integrated overall environments, general or specialized environments).

This is not a book on tools, but on *suitable behavior* of tools. *Tools* are *specific* (domain, structures, methods, rules, companies, habits, etc.). A huge question remains: How to *get* the specific *environments efficiently*?

Tool parametrization: How do the overall configuration, the process model, the product model, the transformation model from product to product, look like. There are two directions: Minor changes might be solved by adaptation of general tools. More specific tools we only get by a specific development. Thereby, the minimization of the development effort is the major problem.

*Tools for Specific **Long-term Topics**: Maintenance, Integration, Families, Styles*

There are *few tools* for supporting *approaches addressed* in this book, as long-term maintenance, long-term reuse, development of families or lines, model-driven and integration, etc. Also urgent are tools for *integrating* these approaches with the development and application of *styles and patterns*.

The *architecture* of a system comes in *different stages*, see ch. 3. This is even more evident for systems, which live for a long time (reengineering, maintenance and evolution, integration of systems) or series of systems for a long-term goal as e.g. families, product lines, classes of systems, systems with deep reuse. We hardly find tools for the stages of these long-term activities. Also *missing* are *tools* for efficiency improvements, tools for structure classes (batch, interactive, embedded) and subclasses thereof, and for knowledge acquisition and use.

Index

A

abstraction
  data or detail 28, 32, 44, 232
  functional 28, 35, 43, 232
  functional req. spec. 223, 225
activity diagram 237
activity in project organization 269
analysis class diagram 238
annotations
  for abstract use 38
  for concurrency 35
  for distribution 39, 59, 113
  for semantics 33
adaptability 69, 72
algebraic equations 33
AR, architecture modeling 1, 4, 8, 250
architectural configuration 10, 210
architecture
  abstract 53, 55, 59, 78
  and mastering changes 13
  blueprint for code 249
  conceptual 75
  data flow 101
  distributed 113
  event-based 108
  framework 146
  glue 174
  in one notation 46
  of houses 23, 26
  order 56
  physical 78
  pipelining a. 41
  rel. to project org. 283
  sequences 53, 55
  stages 51
  traces 15
architecture
  and documentation 290
  and project organization 15, 273
  and quality assurance 294
arch. language
  requirements for 65
  aspects, views 52
architecture standard model 19
automation pyramid 84

automotive 74, 81, 87, 91
  problems 75, 91

B

BIM 28
blackboard 116
bootstrapping 134, 152
brainstorming 223
broadcasting 110

C

C 255
changes in architecture 13
class diagram 240
classes of systems 32
CMM 141
coarse-grained relation 210
compiler, multiphase 31, 143, 155
completeness of mapping 259
components 27
  for data abstraction ado, adt 28
  functional fo, ft 28
concrete connectors 36
concurrency 33
configuration
  architecture c. 10, 211
  documentation c. 10, 210
  project organiz. c. 10, 210
  programming/ code c. 10, 210
  quality assurance c. 10, 210
  requirements c. 10, 210
conformance of mapping 258
connectors 27, 36
consistency 5, 27, 210, 215, 222
context-sens. syntax of AR lang. 27, 29
CORBA 113
CTR 226
control-feedback loop 269

D

design class diagram 240
design recovery 186, 190
development steps 215
development, model-driven 206